The Role of the Helping Professions in Treating the Victims and Perpetrators of Violence

The Role of the Helping Professions in Treating the Victims and Perpetrators of Violence

Morley D. Glicken, DSW

Dale K. Sechrest, D. Crim.

Boston ■ New York ■ San Francisco ■ Mexico City
Montreal ■ Toronto ■ London ■ Madrid ■ Munich ■ Paris
Hong Kong ■ Singapore ■ Tokyo ■ Cape Town ■ Sydney

Series Editor: *Patricia Quinlin*
Editorial Assistant: *Annemarie Kennedy*
Editorial-Production Administrator: *Joe Sweeney*
Editorial-Production Service: *Colophon*
Composition Buyer: *JoAnne Sweeney*
Cover Administrator: *Kristina Mose-Libon*
Text Composition: *Modern Graphics*

For related titles and support materials, visit our online catalog at www.ablongman.com.

Between the time Website information is gathered and then published, it is not unusual for some sites to have closed. Also, the transcription of URLs can result in unintended typographical errors. The publisher would appreciate notification were these errors occur so that they may be corrected in subsequent editions.

Library of Congress Cataloging-in-Publication Data

Glicken, Morely D.
    The role of the helping professions in treating the victims and perpetrators of violence/Morley D. Glicken and Dale Sechrest.
        p. cm.
    Included bibliographical references and index.
    ISBN 0-205-32686-2 (alk. paper)
    1. Victims of crimes—Services for—United States. 2. Violent offenders—Rehabilitation—Unites States. 3. Social work with criminals—United States. 4. Social work with juvenile delinquents—United States. 5. Violence—United States. 6. Violence—United States—Prevention. I. Sechrest, Dale K. II. Title.

HV6250.3.U5 G54 2002
362.88'0973—dc21
                                                                2002025361

10 9 8 7 6 5 4 3 2 1   07 06 05 04 03 02

We dedicate this book to the innocent victims of violence and to the men and women who have lost their lives in America's war on terrorism. May their memory be a strong motivation to eliminate violence with its terrible legacy of sorrow and despair.

CONTENTS

5 Violence to Children   104

6 Sexual Violence   131

PREFACE

Violence in the United States. How could anything so unexpected and troubling be a part of life in one of the world's most affluent and technologically advanced nations? Killings in schools, workplace violence, random violence, date rape, family violence, and now the awful reality of violence by terrorists. Life may never be the same in the Unites States and no longer can anyone be entirely safe from the impact of violence. For the helping professionals who indirectly or directly work with the short- and long-term impact of violence, it is an ever-increasing part of our job.

While FBI reports continue to suggest that violence in the United States is on the decline since the peak years of 1983 to 1993, when violence was at epidemic proportions, a recent report by the Eisenhower Commission (1999) included in Chapter 12 notes that while violence levels are at the same rates nationally as they were in 1969, violence in urban areas since 1969 has increased by 40 percent. In fact, 80 percent of all violent acts are committed in the urban areas of fifty major U.S. cities, resulting in a 120 percent increase of the fear of violence since 1969. The U.S. Surgeon General, in a 2001 report on youth violence (see Chapter 12) notes that confidential reports from youth regarding their own violent activities indicate no change since 1993 in the proportion of youth who have committed dangerous and possibly lethal acts of violence. Moreover, arrests for aggravated assault have declined only slightly, and in 1999 were nearly 70 [percent] higher than preepidemic years (1983–1993)" (p. 1). The Surgeon General goes on to report that for every youth arrested in any given year in the late 1990s, at least ten youth who were not arrested engaged in violent behavior that could have seriously harmed or killed another person. These data come from research studies in which youth report their own behavior (p. 1) and may be found in Chapter 12.

To make these data even more troubling, while funding for the building of new schools and universities to accommodate an increasing population have not kept pace with population increases—forcing students to go to year-round schools or to attend school in two or three shifts—the building of prisons in America has undergone a sevenfold increase since 1969.

Anyone who travels to the mental health facilities or the prisons in the United States knows that in almost every case history of violent behavior, one will find multiple episodes of severe childhood violence. It might be domestic violence observed by the child, or it might be rape, molestation, or the random violence that is so often experienced at an early age by a vast number of people across socioeconomic lines. Early life violence continues to serve as a reminder of the damage done to the body and soul of legions of people in this country and the enormous work we face in healing the victims and the perpetrators of violent crime.

This book is written by two academics who deal with violence by choice. One is a social worker and the other is in criminal justice. Both of us are concerned that our students know too little about violence. Someone, we have been saying for years, should write a book to help students and helping professionals understand the origins of violence and its social, economic, and emotional impact. The book should also provide ways to treat and prevent violence. We have been waiting for such a book to be published and finally, because we both teach clinically-oriented courses at our respective universities and departments, we decided that if a book wasn't going to be written, that we would write one. It would be a user-friendly book with numerous case studies, good research, and practical suggestions; a book that would help both students and professionals understand the responsibilities to effectively treat the innocent victims of violent crime and the perpetrators who create such dysfunction and chaos in our lives.

This is a book that integrates theory with practice. It is concerned with prevention, intervention, and treatment in the control and management of violent behavior. The book includes the latest research available coupled with the clinical experiences and case studies of helping professionals working in forensic facilities and agencies around the country. It is a book, we hope, that will serve as a reference for helping professionals who are suddenly faced with violence where it hadn't existed until recently: in U.S. schoolyards, in the parking lots of stores, and in the lunchrooms of the U.S. workplace. It is a book for the organizational and community workers among us who believe that changing the social context of life for people in the United States may actually reduce violence. People living in poverty face the potential for violent behavior in far greater numbers than the general population. Lowering the rates of violent crime for the poorest of the poor would be cause to exalt.

The format of the book is simple. The first three chapters deal with the facts about violence: how much, why, where, and the impact violence has on the lives of people. The second part of the book is written to help professionals in training and those already in practice understand the origins of violence and a range of helpful treatment approaches for a particular type of violent behavior. The third part of the book presents past efforts and future directions to cope with violence. We want to give equal time to victims and to perpetrators in this process because to ignore victims would be to ignore a terrible tragedy to the body and to the spirit. Without hope that perpetrators can change, we face ever-increasing numbers of new prisons and an endless line of perpetrators spending time in jail often without the possibility of receiving needed help. When perpetrators leave the U.S. prisons, we fear that their level of violence will only increase.

We will, in this book, be cognizant of cultural, racial, and ethnic factors and we will use real cases from real professionals who work with the victims and perpetrators of crime. We believe that a book on violence should offer help to both groups. If we can help perpetrators, than just maybe there will be fewer victims.

To help the reader, the chapters dealing with treatment include a number of cases with a final case presenting integrating questions about the case for the reader to answer. We think this type of exercise comes close to the actual work to be done in the helping agencies and facilities that employ professionals for work in forensic settings. The cases in this book are those that the authors know about through their professional involvement and contacts. Care has been taken to protect the identities of the individuals in the case studies. We also include extended lists of references, including some from the Internet and websites that offer the reader a rich combination of theoretical articles and research studies.

We wish to recognize the reviewers of this text who provided valuable feedback and suggestions: Pamela Higgins-Saulsberry, The University of Louisiana at Monroe; Lynn B. Cooper, California State University–Sacramento; and Michel Coconis, Grand Valley State University.

For the students and professionals who read this book, we offer thanks, and we wish you well in your work. Those of us who work with violence are a very small army and we need all the help and encouragement we can get.

ACKNOWLEDGMENTS

We would like to thank the many people who helped us make this book possible. First and foremost, we would like to thank Ms. Megan Dwyer, our wonderful student assistant at Central Michigan University, whose cheerful, positive presence belied the fact that she found all too many references we'd forgotten in the text and who kept us on the straight and narrow. Megan did a great deal of editing and is responsible for the massive number of references existing in some rational order. Julie Baker, my [Morley Glicken] administrative assistant in the social work program at Central Michigan University, helped in many ways to brighten our days when the going got tough. Graduate students from the California State University–San Bernardino MSW Program also helped by finding suitable and sometimes arcane literature sources for our book. Without them, we would not have been able to undertake such an ambitious project. Karen Hanson and Alyssa Pratt of Allyn & Bacon encouraged us and kept our spirits alive when we felt that we would never be able to complete the book. Patricia Quinlin and Annemarie Kennedy of Allyn & Bacon kept us going when we were near the home stretch.

Both of us had a conviction that violence was a terribly serious problem that seemed to be fading in importance as report after report said that it was decreasing in every geographic area of the nation. We lived in California in a high-crime area and felt that the reports were not only wrong and misleading, but that we had lost the resolve to deal with violence in a humane and rational way. Three strike laws and more prisons seemed a foolish and wasteful way for us to resolve serious problems with violence. We acknowledge the terrible tragedy of September 11, 2001 and hope that it will encourage a reappraisal of the factors that contribute to violent behavior. Perhaps that reappraisal will move us in the direction of prevention and treatment, a direction so lacking in our present approach to violence. We acknowledge the lives lost to violent crime and terrorism and hope that this book does a little to enlighten and persuade readers that violence can be prevented and, if not eliminated, substantially reduced.

We were asked by our publisher to complete the book in time for instructor use in fall 2002. Given the terrible time we were going through in the United States in fall 2001 with multiple terrorist attacks and an anthrax threat, we felt responsible to complete the book in record time. We have tried to be very careful in our scholarship and we have included hundreds of sources in the book to make our presentation of the material more compelling. We felt responsible to have the book completed in time for use by those of you who deal with violence in the real world. If in our haste to complete the book we inadvertently made some errors, we certainly apologize to you, the reader.

Morley D. Glicken
Dale K. Sechrest

The Role of the Helping Professions in Treating the Victims and Perpetrators of Violence

PART ONE

In Part I of the book, which includes Chapters 1, 2, and 3, we discuss the impact of violence on the lives of people. Chapter 1 is an overview of the reasons we have such high levels of violence in America, including concerns that America has a greater tolerance for violence and that the popular culture sensationalizes violence to such an extent that it has a numbing effect on people. Perhaps, as we grapple with the meaning of our lives in the context of international and domestic terrorism, this obsession with violence will become tempered. At the moment and through the last decade, however, America has saturated itself with violence in the mass media and in the popular culture. We also note in Chapter 1 that with a greater tolerance for violence, violent crimes in the past that would have been reported to the authorities are either not being reported or are not being responded to by the police. This is particularly true when these crimes occur in minority communities or affect people of color.

We are doubtful that violence has declined to the extent that FBI Reports note from 1994 to 2001. We believe that fear of violence data, and interviews with perpetrators who have not been caught but have admitted to committing violent crimes, support this belief. In Chapter 1, we also discuss the history of violent crime in America and note that it is not a new phenomenon. Nor has the debate over the most effective ways to deal with violent crime been resolved. After many years, Americans are still ambivalent about whether to treat or to punish perpetrators of violent crime. Although we have increasing numbers of treatment programs, they are generally a small part of the annual budget of the justice system in America. Nowhere is treatment less likely to be given than in the case of convicted felons in prison with substance abuse problems even though drugs and alcohol continue to be one of the primary catalysts of violent crimes.

In Chapter 2, we continue the discussion of the amount of violence in America by looking at the various reporting documents that seem to present contradictory information. We identify high-risk offenders and suggest ways of predicting the likelihood that they will commit violent acts based upon research evidence. We also discuss information related to the impact of drugs and alcohol on violent crime and the extent and types of violent behavior.

In Chapter 3, we discuss the enormous cost of violent crime to victims and to taxpayers who pay for the ever-increasing costs of a legal system incarcerating more and more people. These costs can be seen in the expense of running prisons that are more expensive to maintain than systems of higher education and seem incapable of reducing violent crime once perpetrators leave prison.

Part I of the book should be of particular interest to those who are trying to understand the overall issue of violence in America and the attempts we have made over the past twenty years to respond to increasing levels of violence. We are particularly concerned about youth violence because we believe that youth violence is the best indicator of violence in a society. If youth violence is high, we can expect violence rates to be high among the remainder of the population.

1 Reasons for Violence in America

Violence by individuals and groups has been a concern in America for many years. Several national and local commissions on crime and violence have convened, studied, and reported on the extent of violence in American society and offered proposed solutions. The first was the National Commission on Law Enforcement and Observance (the Wickersham Commission) of 1930. The National Advisory Commission on Civil Disorders (the Kerner Commission) was appointed after the urban riots of the 1960s and issued its report in 1968. The National Commission on the Causes and Prevention of Violence followed, which was chaired by Milton S. Eisenhower (see Graham & Gurr, 1969).

In addition to the national commissions, many studies have been done in an effort to understand and explain both collective and individual violence. Representatives of the mass media have participated in this process by attempting to summarize and interpret these reports for the public and propose solutions. For example, in 1969, in the midst of significant levels of urban violence, an editorial appeared in *Look* magazine discussing national concerns about increasing violence in America (Poppy, 1969). It was published in the wake of the assassinations of President John F. Kennedy, Senator Robert Kennedy, and Martin Luther King, Jr., and the related urban riots that were part of the civil rights movement. The editorial paraphrased the upcoming report of the Eisenhower Commission, which concluded that American society can and should control violence. However, citing the work of a group of professors at Stanford University, the concern of the editorial was not the destructive violence of urban riots or civil unrest, but focused on individual violence.

The editorial distinguished destructive violence from the level of aggressive behavior that is necessary for survival and human progress. After all, America was founded on a violent revolution. Also, military, law enforcement, and similar groups often are required to use violence in socially condoned ways. To meet the goals of reducing violence in America, the editorial recommended that American society stop sanctioning and admiring violence, control guns, cut the amount of violence depicted by the mass media, and teach about the processes of nonviolent change. These conclusions remain relevant thirty years later.

Destructive violent behavior is found in many settings, inclusive of violent criminal acts, domestic violence, youth gang violence, and violence in schools and in the workplace. Its incidence varies within social and cultural groups. Also of concern is the use of violence or deadly force by agents of government. An important question is how society is to respond to violent events: Through efforts at prevention or deterrence, or after the fact through measures to work with and help the perpetrators and victims of violent acts?

This book is concerned primarily with the destructive violent behavior of individuals, both adults and youth, who may act alone or with others. Violence is defined in many ways by various groups. Weiner, Zahn, and Sagi (1990) documented several elements of violence and proposed a suggested definition:

> A number of elements need to be considered when formulating a definition of violence: (1) the degree and type of injury; (2) the intent of the participant(s) to apply or to threaten to apply force; (3) the object of the attack (i.e., a person, property, or an animal); (4) the causes of and motivations and justifications for the behavior; (5) the numbers of persons involved in the incident; and (6) whether the harm is the result of behavior that is committed or omitted . . . a suggested definition . . . *is the threat, attempt, or use of physical force by one or more persons that results in physical or nonphysical harm to one or more other persons.* [emphasis in original]

The definition of violence adopted by the National Academy of Science (NAS) Panel on the Understanding and Control of Violent Behavior states that it is *behaviors by individuals that intentionally threaten, attempt, or inflict physical harm on others* (Reiss & Roth, 1993, p. 2). This definition is very close to that recommended by Weiner, Zahn, and Sagi, but provides the additional element of intent. With the victim's death as the most serious outcome, they comment on the diversity of underlying violent behaviors that cause death, noting that many types of violent behavior do not result in death. These fundamental definitions of violence do not attempt to define the various types of criminal acts involved, although they subsequently describe acts of violence that are usually encompassed by penal codes. Also, the NAS report pointed out that some violent behaviors are not counted as crimes, such as school fights, prison riots, and violence in the home. It did not attempt to analyze violence as part of social movements, state acts, or wars.

History of Violence

Violence of different types has been defined and examined in many ways, often in relation to the historical period of concern. Violent behavior in American society in the twentieth century appears to have moved from the collective forms found in labor strife and the civil rights movement to more individualized forms, such as mob warfare, urban gangs, and incidents of violent behavior that appear to be of a personal nature. The history of collective violence has been well documented in the work of the National Commission on the Causes and Prevention of Violence and its related reports. In a report for the commission by Graham and Gurr (1969), the causes of violence in the larger society are various, described as emanating from the "psychological residues of slavery," poverty, and competition among various ethnic groups for scarce resources. After documenting the barriers to conducting good research on violence, they note that definitions of violence are colored by the beliefs and cultural experience of members of a society. For example, when we as individuals agree to use necessary force or violence to reach a goal, we call it *protest*; when it is used by public officials, we call it *legitimate force*. Graham and Gurr narrowly define violence as "behavior designed to inflict physical injury to people or damage to property" (p. xiv), again capturing the notion of intent.

We are reminded that America was born out of strife and revolution, which was followed by a period of unregulated industrial growth wherein competing interests sometimes resorted to violent action, particularly the union violence of the industrial era. While our concerns are more specific to individual or group violence, rather than large-scale social protest resulting in violence, these individual acts cannot be fully separated from their deeper historical roots.

Individual acts of violence are the subject of other reports and studies that focus more specifically on the causes of violent behavior. A summary report that focused on understanding and controlling violence was published in 1993 by the National Research Council of the National Academy of Sciences (Reiss & Roth, 1993). The report drew upon three volumes of papers that were published separately, subsequent to review by the Panel on the Understanding and Control of Violent Behavior, the Committee on Law and Justice, the Commission on Behavioral and Social Sciences and Education, and the National Research Council. Topics ranged from patterns of violence in American society to its manifestation in substance users and in family members. The availability of firearms and methods of control were addressed in the context of public concerns about violence prevention.

Additional sources that focus on violent behavior include Brownstein (2000), Karmen (1990), and Weiner et al. (1990). These and other sources offer general descriptions (patterns) and specific examples of violence in American society, as well as proposed solutions. Generally, American society reacts to violence in three ways: by suppression, prevention and intervention, and treatment. Suppression is an attempt at both specific and general deterrence. It is manifested in laws designed to incapacitate violent offenders and send a message to potential perpetrators of violence that such behavior will not be tolerated. Tough laws and strong punishments are called for. An example of a suppression tactic can be found in the various "three strikes" laws passed by many states, which provide fixed, long sentences for two violent offenses, and, in California, a sentence of twenty-five years to life for a third felony offense of any kind (see Shichor & Sechrest, 1996). Recent studies indicate that these types of laws are often applied unevenly to similar types of offenders across jurisdictions, even in the same state (see Byer, 2000; Greenwood, 2000).

One approach that may deter or reduce the effects of criminal activity is the emerging area of "social defense," which attempts to prevent the criminal act from occurring by hardening targets, or, failing this, by reducing the damage done. A recent work by Zimring and Hawkins (1997) applies this philosophy to the field of lethal violence, primarily homicide and robbery. They first make the case that the crime problem in America is not that of ordinary crime; it is a problem of lethal violence. Using comparative data from primarily European countries, but including Japan and Australia, they document U.S. violent crime rates many times greater than other developing nations, while nonviolent crimes occur at about the same rates. For example, the U.S. homicide rate is 9.9 per 100,000, compared to countries such as England and Wales at 0.5, Japan at 0.6, France at 1.1, and Australia at 2.2. Even countries that are in the highest 25 percent crime rate category (U.S., New Zealand, Australia, Canada, and Netherlands), the U.S. has four times the highest homicide rate.

Zimring and Hawkins (1997) see lethal violence as an important issue due to people's concern for their own survival and the damaging effects of being a victim of violence. These concerns are different from those of property crimes, which can be managed through insurance claims and better protection of property. They note, however, that the three strikes laws in California targeted burglary (tripling the costs of the implementation of the law) just because people feared being injured in a residential burglary, even though most burglaries are of unoccupied dwellings. Their solution or "strategy of prevention" (p. 185) is a "loss prevention" approach based on policy tools that would reduce the number of deaths from lethal violence. They reject the idea that violence is a disease requiring public health agency attention. "Labeling lethal violence a disease is . . . neither necessary nor constructive. [It] is the undesirable outcome of a wide variety of socially determined causes. It is a symptom of dangerous dysfunction in some social relations; a disorder rather than a disease" (p. 188).

The loss prevention approach is described with an analogy to reducing traffic accident losses through multiple strategies, such as controlling drunk driving and using better technologies. California's approach attempts to provide strategies to reduce the volume of dangerous crimes and to insure that those that do occur are less destructive to their victims. Strategies include reducing the availability of guns, controlling the "propensity to attack" (p. 189), providing better lighting in possible high-risk areas for robbery, and instituting various governmental methods of controlling behavior, the details of which are not entirely clear. They suggest the use of an inductive approach that would carefully analyze the problem and determine priority areas for action. As examples, they suggest that gun availability, high rates of lethal violence among African Americans, and stranger-to-stranger violence might emerge as possible areas where new strategies might be developed based on this analysis. They might well add some of the suggestions mentioned in the *Look* magazine editorial regarding management of the American appetite for, and sometimes admiration of, violence in the mass media.

Prevention and intervention strategies are an attempt to help individuals who are potentially violent offenders before they become involved in this behavior. These might include programs for families such as "Parent Effectiveness Training," which allows parents to learn how to manage their children by using positive behavior modification techniques. Programs for parents involved in child abuse are also used. Intervention programs for problem youth in schools are being attempted in many areas of the country, and gang intervention strategies are also being tested and improved in many American communities.

Human Service Approaches

Our book is specific to the causation, treatment, and prevention of violence and the important role that human services play in managing all aspects of destructive, violent behavior in individuals. We suggest that it is an important to work with individuals who have been identified as either violent or potentially violent in their home, at work, in school, or in other pursuits. In doing so we should use the best human services approaches available, drawing on medicine, psychology, psychiatry, social work, and other disciplines and approaches that can help manage the behavior of these individuals. These approaches may include the use of medications, team approaches, youth intervention strategies, recreation programs, and the like. As Zimring and Hawkins suggest (1997), priorities must be established within governments regarding goals for prevention and intervention.

While we present the latest information on violent behavior from the research literature, we also provide a number of case studies from the field with implications for social work practice, which should serve to guide workers in the field involved in the treatment of violent and abusive perpetrators and their victims. Programs to treat the victims and perpetrators of violence, and the related training of professionals, requires useful information for workers to use in promoting effective treatment.

Methods for the effective treatment for both perpetrators and victims of violence will be presented in the context of the latest research on the causes and treatment of violence. Case studies are provided that describe the cause(s), preventive measures, and possible types of interventions or treatments for individuals using violence in a variety of settings, including the family, schools, the workplace, dating and interpersonal violence, and the random violent episodes that often describe life in urban America. Also of concern is the violence of serial killings and terrorism—violent acts that increasingly define life in America. As we make progress toward a greater understanding of violence and its prevention and control, it is necessary to explore both societal and individual factors.

Violent Crime Victimization

Due to concerns about the impact of violence on American society, there has been a proliferation of information made available on crimes of violence, including homicide, robbery, assault, and rape. These data are available through the Uniform Crime Reports of the Federal Bureau of Investigation, which have been compiled since 1929, and the Bureau of Justice Statistics of the Department of Justice, which oversees crime victimization surveys nationally. Additional data on deaths by homicide are found in public health records locally and nationally. These data are discussed more fully in Chapter 2.

In 1985 the Bureau of Justice Statistics (BJS), using interview data from the National Crime Victimization Survey (NCVS), developed a Crime Risk Index. They reported that each year about 3 percent (six million) of Americans were victims of violent crime. This was a conservative figure because it only included reports of rape, robbery, and assault, but not murder, manslaughter by drunk drivers, kidnapping, child abuse, or other types of violent crime not captured in crime survey interviews (Langan & Innes, 1985). Moreover, these victimizations were only for one year. Lifetime homicide estimates compiled with the help of the National Center for Health Statistics showed that an American had about a 1 in 10,000 chance of being murdered in a single year but a 1 in 133 chance in an entire lifetime (p. 1; see also Koppel, 1987).

Of all violent crime victims, most were victims of assault (2.5% of the population); more were males (4%) than females (2%), with females more likely to be raped and males more likely to be robbed or assaulted; more were African Americans (4%, or about 1 in 25) than whites (3%), although about the same proportions were victims in the 16 to 24 age group; and persons 16 to 24 were more likely to be victimized than other age groups. No relationship was found between family income and victimization for African Americans and whites. The proportion of the population victimized by violent crime was fairly constant between 1978 (2.94%) and 1982 (3.15%). Married persons were less likely to be victims of violent crime in 1982 than those never married, separated, or divorced (p. 4).

The National Crime Victimization Survey of the Bureau of Justice Statistics has provided self-reported data on crimes of all types since 1973 (Bureau of Justice Statistics, 1998; see Rand, Lynch, & Cantor, 1997). Violent crimes of all types (murder, rape, sexual assault, robbery, aggravated assault, and simple assault) have been declining since 1973, from a rate of 47.62 per 1,000 of the population age 12 and over in 1973 to 41.5 per 1,000 in 1996, peaking in 1981 at 52.17 per 1,000. The years from 1991 through 1994 saw increases to levels greater than 1973 (48.68, 47.85, 49, and 51.10, respectively). Rand et al. (1997) report declines since 1973 in rape, robbery, and aggravated assault, with simple assault showing an increase. During this same period most property crime rates declined. However, as Wilson (1994) has pointed out, and many local editorial pages confirm, falling crime statistics don't make us feel more secure. His main concern is the increase of juvenile homicide, which he sees as more frightening than adult homicides because of its irrationality. Blame falls to the restraints put on law enforcement, poor treatment and offender supervision programs, lack of drug testing, and our inability to determine what might effectively prevent juvenile homicide.

The FBI's Uniform Crime Reports (UCR) provides a measure only of crimes known to the police. Violent crimes are defined as murder and nonnegligent manslaughter, forcible rape, robbery, and aggravated assault. The UCR reports an increase of 40 percent in the violent crime rate per 100,000 inhabitants from 1975 to 1996 (206.7 to 288.6). Reports show rates that peaked in 1982, declined until the mid-1980s, and increased through 1996, when declines were again evident. The overall increase since the base year of 1971 to 1997 is 97.8 percent (175.8 to 273.6) (Bureau of Justice Statistics, 1999, p. 329, Table 4.2).

It appears that NCVS self-reported household victimizations underestimate violent crime and UCR rates may overestimate the extent of violent crime. The apparent increase in violent crimes reported to the police is based, perhaps in part, on better reporting procedures. Recent surges in violent crime are largely attributed to increasing numbers of youth offenders involved in gang and drug activity. Other important differences in these statistics will be addressed in Chapter 2.

Official reports of crime from the UCR and NCVS are reported in the mass media on a regular basis in order to keep the public advised of the problem. In recent times, official statistics from the UCR have shown reported crime rates dropping in all categories. In Los Angeles, California, for example, violent crimes were down in 1999 with the exception of homicide, which showed a 2.5 percent increase from 1998. Similar decreases were seen in crime nationally for 1998 to 1999, especially for murder, assault, robbery, and other serious offenses. However, murder rates leveled off or increased from previous years in several cities, as in Los Angeles (Lichtblau, 2000). Other cities with no decrease or an increase in murders included Long Beach, San Diego, Sacramento, San Francisco, New York City, Denver, Phoenix, and St. Louis.

The Bureau of Justice Statistics summarized these data for the period through 1998 (not including 1999), indicating that the nation's murder rate in 1998 fell to its lowest level in three decades (Fox & Zawitz, 2000, p. 1). The report notes, "Despite the encouraging improvement since 1993, the levels of gun homicides by juveniles and young adults are well above those of the mid-1980s" (p. 1). The report included the finding that the murder rate was 4.6 per 100,000 population in 1950 compared to 6.3 in 1998. Also, there have been declines in homicides against intimates (relatives, family members, dating partners) for all race and gender groups. However, African Americans were six times more likely to be homicide victims and seven times more likely than whites to commit homicides (p. 2). The number of infanticides, or murders of victims under age 5, grew roughly in proportion to the number of young children in the population, with most perpetrators being the parents (p. 3).

Concerning the perpetrators of violence, they report that "Few homicides involve multiple offenders and fewer involve multiple victims. The percentage of homicides involving multiple offenders increased dramatically in the late 1980s and early 1990s, increasing from 10 percent in 1976 to 17 percent in 1998" (p. 3). This appears to be an indicator of increased gang activity. Arguments are the most frequently cited circumstance surrounding a homicide.

The overall decrease in crime during the past eight years is attributed to the strong economy, stabilization of the illegal drug trade, stronger sentencing laws, improved police work, truces among street gangs, and an overall decrease in the number people in the age groups most likely to commit crimes. The fear, however, is that a turnaround will take place, especially in the incidence of violent crime. This may be brought about by the sharply increased numbers of 15- to 24-year-old persons in this decade, which is the group most likely to become involved in crime, especially violent types of crime (Lichtblau, 2000). While public officials stress prevention and intervention, no local reference is made in these reports to government or private initiatives to manage a possible upturn in violent crime, or toward efforts to improve the capability of the helping professions to work with individuals involved in these types of crimes.

Organizations such as the National Council on Crime and Delinquency (NCCD, 1997) provide a blueprint for reducing crime in American that is specific to the helping professions. They present both immediate reforms and long-term crime prevention strategies. While they document the general decline in violent crime, it is still seen as intolerably high, and further use of incarceration is not seen as a viable strategy to reduce crime significantly. Their particular focus is on youth and the reduction of violence in families, possibly through the implementation of special family violence courts and family violence prevention and counseling programs (p. 3). Long-term goals include the strengthening of families and children by reducing unplanned pregnancies, providing better health care, improving educational preparation, and reducing the incidence of child abuse and neglect (p. 5).

In the previously mentioned National Academy of Sciences report on understanding and preventing violence (Reiss & Roth, 1993), recommendations for "problem-solving initiatives" to control violence are made in several areas. These include the prevention of biological and psychosocial damage to children that may lead to violent behavior. They also recommend better controls on those commodities that are related to and/or promote violent behavior, such as firearms, alcohol, and psychoactive drugs. Among other recommendations is the implementation of a comprehensive initiative to reduce partner assault. These initiatives might well be some of those that should be examined in implementing the Zimring and Hawkins proposal.

Factors in Increasing Violence

The reasons for violence in America are as diverse as our culture. They include family problems, social isolation, community disorganization, institutional discrimination, economic and social inequality, the portrayal of violence in American culture in the media, and a greater tolerance for violence in society. Violence can be a symptom of various types of biological influences in individuals, whether genetic or neurological, inclusive of various types of brain dysfunctions and reactions brought about by substance abuse (see Reiss & Roth, 1993). Many of these factors are present in all crime, not just violent crime, and it is often difficult to determine those factors that contribute specifically to violent crime as opposed to other types of crime.

Drawing on the National Academy of Sciences (NAS) report they prepared, Reiss and Roth (1993) defined violence within the framework of aggressive behavior from infancy to adulthood. Children may learn that violent behavior "works" by observing their parents, their peers, or from media portrayals of the efficiency of violent solutions. No greater example of this can be found than in the *Godfather* films and the rash of organized crime films that followed. These stories portray individuals as successful when they use intimidation, bullying, fear, and outright violence to achieve their goals. Many Americans appear to find portrayals of these aggressive and violent solutions to their problems as instructive. Popular culture has indulged a growing fascination with violence by producing television shows and films in which violence and life-threatening situations are standard fare.

Nonetheless, Reiss and Roth (1993) draw on NAS reports to show that many factors contribute to violent results. These factors can have psychosocial, biomedical, and social origins. As they state, "Research strongly suggests that violence arises from *interactions among* individuals' psychosocial development, their neurological and hormonal differences, and social processes" (p. 102). They cite evidence from longitudinal studies indicating "children who show aggressive behavior at around age 8 are more likely than others to exhibit delinquent, criminal, or violent behavior in adolescence and adulthood" (p. 103).

Longitudinal studies by Widom (1999) and by McCord (1999) support the concern about aggressive behavior at an early age, especially its linkages to child abuse and neglect. McCord, whose study of families and child rearing spanned thirty years, found that parents' response to aggressive behavior in their sons was critical to later aggressive behavior (p. 169). These and similar studies will be discussed throughout this book.

A recent survey of self-reported delinquency, part of a longitudinal study of youth sponsored by the Office of Juvenile Justice and Delinquency Prevention, revealed several factors in the lives of these youth that may be helpful in looking at later violent behavior. They found that one in seven 12–year-olds, or 14 percent (18% of the males), had engaged in assaultive behaviors, with 7 percent (13% males) reporting carrying a handgun (Puzzanchera, 2000).

Recent statistics on juvenile offenders and victims found that the number of children abused, neglected, or endangered more than doubled from 1986 to 1993 (Snyder & Sickmund, 1999, p. 40). In 1993 there were almost 3 million "maltreated or endangered" children, up from 1.4 million in 1986. Abuse and neglect were classified as physical, sexual, or emotional. Most of these youth enter the child welfare system through child protective services. In 1997, 14.1 million juveniles lived in poverty, or one-fifth of all juveniles, which was 42 percent more than in 1978, but 10 percent fewer than in 1993 (p. 5).

Thornberry, Smith, Rivera, Huizina, and Stouthamer-Loeber (1999) report on the effects of family disruption and its effects on delinquency. Citing census data (Lugaila, 1998), they report that from 1970 to 1997, the proportion of American households that have children who live with both parents declined: 64 percent to 35 percent for African Americans, and 90 percent to 74 percent for whites. Their conclusions were that "Overall, the data reported here indicate a consistent relationship between a greater number of family transitions and a higher level of delinquency and drug abuse" (Thornberry et al., p. 4). They indicate that adolescents who experience family stress may be more likely to have difficulty managing anger and other negative emotions, although further research is needed.

Another factor is the relative isolation of some neighborhoods from their larger communities, especially when ghettos or barrios insulate youth and adults from outside influences. Poor schools and weak social institutions can lead to lack of achievement and motivation to do better. Economic and social discrimination, and poor employment prospects, can lead to participation in gangs and criminal activity, which may ultimately lead to violent crimes. The *1999 National Report Series* of the Office of Juvenile Justice and Delinquency Prevention (Bilchik, 1999, p. 1) describes minority involvement in the juvenile justice system:

> The most recent statistics available reveal significant racial and ethnic disparity in the confinement of juvenile offenders. In 1997, minorities made up one-third of the juvenile population nationwide but accounted for nearly two-thirds of the detained and committed population in secure juvenile facilities. For black juveniles, the disparities were most evident.

Juveniles ages 16 to 17 accounted for 48 percent of all juvenile arrests and 51 percent of the violent crimes. Black youth were 15 percent of the juvenile population in 1997 but accounted for 26 percent of all arrests and 44 percent of all juvenile arrests for violent offenses. Minorities accounted for 7 in 10 youth held in custody for a violent offense (p. 11). The report calls for an effort to provide "all youth with an equal opportunity to learn, thrive, and achieve at every stage of their lives" (p. 1). It provides self-reported delinquent and deviant behaviors of youth by race and ethnicity. These included carrying a handgun, belonging to a gang, and committing an assault.

A Violent Popular Culture

Are we a violent culture? Are we becoming more violent as a society? As the American population grows and becomes more diverse, violence has become a matter of great concern to individuals, communities, the criminal justice system, and various branches of government. In recent times, even with the statistics on violence showing decreases, isolated incidents of unexpected, uncontrolled violence appear almost nightly on the news.

No one appears willing to suggest that we may actually be a less violent society than we have been in the past with respect to individual, civil, or group violence. In fact, in his historical review of violence in America, which includes the Revolution, Civil War, the Indian wars, vigilante violence, agrarian and labor violence, racial/civil rights violence, and criminal violence, Brown (1969, p. 76) concluded that violence is part of an "unacknowledged (or underground) value structure" in America. Perhaps the greatest period of civil violence and unrest in the country came with the labor movements of the late nineteenth and early twentieth centuries. In their review of labor violence in America, Taft and Ross (1969, p. 281) note that this period, from about 1870 through about 1933, gave America the "bloodiest and most violent labor history of any industrial nation in the world." They say that labor violence has declined since the implementation of the National Industrial Recovery Act in 1933, and the subsequent creation of the National Labor Relations Board.

The concern of this book is for violence at the individual or group level, and there are few indications that it is declining historically. Reiss and Roth (1993) find that, in general, the United States is more violent than other societies, but not necessarily more violent than ever before. Using homicide rates, they conclude that homicides are high by historical standards, especially in certain cities. Certainly they are high for minorities.

Serious violent crime among juveniles follows an upward trend. Youthful violent crime increased 57.1 percent for juveniles under the age of eighteen in the 1980s (Bureau of Justice Statistics, 1992, 429). Snyder et al. (1996) report that the number of juvenile murder victims increased 82 percent between 1984 and 1994. Fox, Dean of the College of Criminal Justice at Northeastern University, in his report to the U.S. Attorney General on Youth Violence, *Trends in Juvenile Violence* (1997), stated that "There are actually two crime trends in America: one for the young, one for the mature, which are moving in opposite directions." Fox (1997) says that the recent surge in youth crime actually occurred while the population of teenagers was on the decline. But this demographic benefit is about to change. As a consequence of the "baby boomerang" (the offspring of the baby boomers), there are now 39 million children in this country who are under the age of ten, more young children than we've had for decades.

This trend is true for California. As Fox has found, recent population projections indicate that there will be a substantial increase in the percentage of juveniles in the general population during the next fifteen years, especially in California.

Growth of the number of children under five years old is a critical factor in future projections: 14.3 percent of California's population was under 5 in 1995 and 12.2 percent was aged 10 to 17, indicating a potential growth of those under 18 to 14.2 percent by 2005 and to 15 percent of the population by 2010. This projected population increase is expected to be even higher in those population groups that are over represented in the criminal and juvenile justice system (African Americans and Hispanics). For example, between 2000 and 2010 the following increases are expected: 6.2 percent whites, 13.9 percent African Americans, and 30 percent for Hispanics (U.S. Department of Commerce, 1995).

Schools have begun to experience this trend already. California schools have had a 7 percent increase in violent crime in schools, along with an 11 percent increase in drug and alcohol crimes for the 1998 to 1999 school year (Kerr, 2000). This represents an increase from 3.74 incidents per 1,000 students in the 1997 to 1998 school year to 4.02 in 1998 to 1999.

Magazines and tabloids thrive on stories of violence. "If it bleeds, it leads" is attributed to editors who know such copy will sell their product. Although they will argue that these incidents are important news and require reporting. For example, the headline "Boy kills first-grade classmate" shook the nation in March 2000. A 6-year-old boy shot and killed a girl the same age in front of their classmates in a small town in Michigan. Questions must be raised about where the child got the weapon, what his motivation was, and how similar incidents can be prevented in the future.

A 1994 cover of *Newsweek* magazine advertised a "Special Report on Murder: A Week in the Death of America." Much of the violence is attributed to drugs and gang behavior related to protecting their illegal drug sales. Thus, much of the violence was directed at individuals who were also operating outside the law, although innocent bystanders or misidentified individuals sometimes got in the way of these operations and became victims of violence. Most of the crimes described in the special report were drug-related or otherwise gratuitous acts of violence against strangers. The individuals committing these acts are probably not candidates who can be "treated" for their violent behavior, as one might work with a wife beater or child abuser. As such, they are generally beyond the scope of this book, although their victims are not.

With an increase of concern for the victims of crime, there have been studies of the criminal justice system's response to victim harm. Professionals of all educational backgrounds, from police to social workers, must learn how to best assist the victims of these encounters who suffer harm short of death. And, at some point, the perpetrators will have to deal with the act itself, as well as its consequences. Perhaps it is at this point, with these individuals, that the human services professions can intervene to provide assistance in preventing future violent behavior.

Reaction to crime is an indicator of the extent to which society is concerned with crime, especially violent crime. "Three strikes" laws have been passed around the country that specifically target violent offenders. Several pieces of federal legislation in the 1980s showed a concern for the victims of violent crime. The federal government and many states established victim assistance funds. The creation of an Office of Victims' Assistance within the Federal Department of Justice attempted to address the concerns of victims of all types of crimes, but specifically those of the victims of and witness to violent crime.

As will be documented further in this book, violence against women has become an increasingly important issue. Annually, women experience more than ten times as many incidents of family violence as men. In 1994 the Violence Against Women Act was passed, which stated that "[a]ll persons within the United States shall have the right to be free from crimes of violence motivated by gender" and established a private cause of action in federal court for violation of that right (42 U.S.C. 13981 [b]; (Goelman, Lehrman, & Valente, 1996, pp. 9–15).

Greater Tolerance for Violence

Crime, and crime committed by juveniles in particular, has become a major focus of public attention. Americans now view their world as an increasingly dangerous place to live, and the fear of violent adolescent criminal activity may be at an all-time high (Federal Register, 1994). Stories of drug abuse, sex crimes, and violence routinely dominate local news programs and all too often capture newspaper headlines. Almost nightly, television shows, such as *Cops* and *True Stories of the Highway Patrol,* take viewers into the front seat of a police car to witness firsthand the effects of a gang retaliatory "drive-by shooting" or the aftermath of a senseless "carjacking," where the victim placed the value of a material possession above his or her own life. In the comfort of their living rooms, Americans are presented with detailed recreations of heinous and brutal unsolved murders. These "virtual reality" crime shows leave the citizenry angry, afraid, and, almost inexplicably, entertained.

Is there a greater tolerance for violence in American society than in the past? Based on the passage of legislation aimed at controlling violent crimes, such as the various three strikes laws around the country and the Violence Against Women Act, it seems more likely that tolerance for violence has decreased, although Americans sometime appear hypocritical in this regard. For example, violence in the mass media, and especially on television, is enjoyed as entertainment in many homes. At another level, Americans appear unwilling to tolerate acts of violent crime, family violence (especially child abuse and neglect), and violence in their schools.

The media portrayal of youth crime has been accompanied by more arrests of youngsters for violent offenses. For example, the number of juveniles under the age of eighteen arrested for murder increased by 168 percent from 1984 to 1993 (Bureau of Justice Statistics, 1994). In California, juvenile arrests for murder increased by 125 percent from 1985 through 1993 (Legislative Analyst's Office, 1995). Arrests of at-risk juveniles (ages 10 through 17) for violent offenses increased 67.6 percent from 1984 through 1993 (Bureau of Justice Statistics, 1994), a period of time when the population increase of this entire age group was less than 4 percent (U.S. Department of Commerce, 1995). Writers who believe that youthful violence has increased attribute it to changing social forces (cf. Blumstein, 1995; Cox & Conrad, 1991; Dryfoos, 1990; Flowers, 1990; and Krisberg & Austin, 1993, among others). Life experiences for both the young and old are changing (Regoli & Hewitt, 1994). The economic environment is more difficult and competitive. Three decades ago, statistics indicate that the most likely poor person was a senior citizen; today it is a child (Regoli & Hewitt, 1994). The traditional socializing institutions of the community—families, schools, and churches—have been weakened (Currie, 1993).

Adding to this explosive societal mix has been the easy availability of dangerous drugs and guns. After a period of relative stability in the rates of violent crime committed by juvenile offenders, there was a major turning point starting in 1985 (Bureau of Justice Statistics, 1994). In a recent National Institute of Justice report on juvenile homicides, Blumstein (1995) reports a steady growth during the past ten years in the use of guns by juveniles ". . . leading to a doubling in the number of juvenile murders committed with guns" (p. 5). Blumstein attributes the sudden upsurge in juvenile violence to the increased drug trafficking of crack cocaine in the mid-1980s. To service that drug market, ". . . juveniles were recruited, they were armed with guns . . . guns that were diffused into the larger community of juveniles" (p. 6).

Rising recognition of youth violence has also focused attention on the handling of young offenders by the juvenile justice system. The advocates of "get tough" laws have dominated the political debate on youth crime. Terms such as *delinquency prevention, diversion,* and *aftercare* are not often heard in this changing political climate. The recent upsurge in violent juvenile crime only increased the pressure to handle more children in adult courts and youth offender correctional facilities, secure institutions that quite often resemble adult prisons. The fear that was generated by recent increases has resulted in the myth of the juvenile "super predator," which has been discredited in a recent analysis of the Office of Juvenile Justice and Delinquency Prevention. The administrator reported that juvenile crime is down and predictions about its resurgence are very difficult to make (Bilchik, 2000). The report concludes that arrest increases for violent crime in the late 1990s may have been largely the result of policy changes, most notably "an increase in law enforcement response to the crime of domestic violence . . . Juveniles are not immune to domestic violence arrests. Family problems . . . can now result in an assault arrest" (p. 4).

Policy choices, such as those driving domestic violence policy, are now being debated and will have far-reaching implications for future generations and for our communities. Growing concerns about adult and juvenile violent crime, high rates of recidivism, and escalating costs of confinement have fueled interest in bringing innovative ideas and programming to communities interested in managing violent crime for both adults and juveniles. What better area than that of domestic violence, or simply in working with disrupted families?

The use of innovative ideas and programs in this or any area of concern is not a matter of increased spending alone, however. Solutions involve an understanding of the causes of violent behavior and the creative use of existing resources to help manage the problem. This means providing better information and training to human services professionals, as well as to officials of the criminal justice community who often encounter violence in their work. It may require a greater degree of coordination between human services professionals and justice system professionals in order to arrive at solutions. The private sector must not be excluded from this process, since many of the helping professions operate in private agencies that see many individuals who can and should be helped in managing the frustrations of life that may yield to aggressive or violent actions.

REFERENCES

Bilchik, S. (1999). Minorities in the juvenile justice system. *1999 National Report Series.* Washington, DC: Office of Juvenile Justice and Delinquency Prevention, U.S. Department of Justice.

Bilchik, S. (2000). Challenging the myths. *1999 National Report Series, Juvenile Justice Bulletin.* Washington, DC: Office of Juvenile Justice and Delinquency Prevention, U.S. Department of Justice.

Blumstein, A. (1995). Violence by young people: Why the deadly nexus? *National Institute of Justice Journal, 229,* 2–9.

Brown, R. M. (1969). Historical patterns of violence in America. In H. D. Graham and T. R. Davis, (Eds.), *The history of violence in America.* New York: Bantam Books.

Brownstein, H. H. (2000). *The social reality of violence and violent crime.* Boston: Allyn and Bacon.

Bureau of Justice Statistics. (1992). *Sourcebook of criminal justice statistics: 1992.* Washington, DC: U.S. Department of Justice.

Bureau of Justice Statistics. (1994). *Sourcebook of criminal justice statistics: 1994.* Washington, DC: U.S. Department of Justice.

Bureau of Justice Statistics. (1998). *National Crime Victimization Survey, crime trends, 1973–1996.* Washington, DC: Bureau of Justice Statistics, U.S. Department of Justice.

Bureau of Justice Statistics (1999). *Sourcebook of criminal justice statistics—1998.* The Hindelang Criminal Justice Research Center, Office of Justice Programs (NCJ-176356). U.S. Department of Justice.

Byer, A. (2000). Three strikes sentencing: Administrative Office of the Courts, California, study. Paper presented at the Association for Criminal Justice Research (California), May 5, 2000.

Cox, S. M., & Conrad, J. J. (1991). *Juvenile justice: A guide to practice and theory* (3rd ed.). New York: McGraw–Hill.

Currie, E. (1993). *Reckoning: Drugs, the cities, and the American future.* New York: Hill and Wang.

Dryfoos, J. G. (1990). *Adolescents at risk.* New York: Oxford University Press.

Federal Bureau of Investigation (1992). *Uniform crime reports.* Washington, DC: U.S. Department of Justice.

Federal Register: Part II. (1994). Washington, DC: U.S. Government Printing Office.

Flowers, R. B. (1990). *The adolescent criminal: An examination of today's juvenile offender.* Jefferson, NC: McFarland Press.

Fox, J. A. (1997). *Trends in juvenile homicide: Report to the U.S. Attorney General.* Retrieved 4–9–02 from the World Wide Web: <www.ojp.usdoj.gov/bjs/abstract/tjvfox.htm>.

Fox, J. A., & Zawitz, M. W. (2000, March). *Homicide trends in the United States. Crime Data Brief.* Washington, DC: Bureau of Justice Statistics, U.S. Department of Justice.

Goelman, D. M., Lehrman, F. L., Valente, R. L. (1996). *The impact of domestic violence on your legal practice.* Washington, DC: American Bar Association Commission on Domestic Violence.

Graham, H. D., & Gurr, T. R. (1969). *Violence in America: Historical and comparative perspectives.* Washington, DC: U.S. Government Printing Office.

Greenwood, P. (2000). Three strikes sentencing: Rand Corporation study. Paper presented at the Association for Criminal Justice Research (California), May 5, 2000.

Karmen, A. (1990). *Crimes and victims.* Belmont, CA: Wadsworth.

Kerr, J. (2000, March 1). Violent crime rises, state reports. *San Bernardino County Sun,* p. A6.

Koppel, H. (1987, March). *Lifetime likelihood of victimization. Technical Report.* Washington, DC: Bureau of Justice Statistics, U.S. Department of Justice.

Krisberg, B., & Austin, J. F. (1993). *Reinventing juvenile justice.* Newbury Park, CA: Sage.

Lait, M. (1999, December 24). Violent crimes, except homicide, decrease in L.A. *L.A. Times,* p. B1.

Langan, P. A., & Innes, C. A. (1985, May). *The risk of violent crime. Special Report.* Washington, DC: Bureau of Justice Statistics, U.S. Department of Justice.

Legislative Analyst's Office. (1995). *Juvenile crime: Outlook for California.* Sacramento, CA: Legislative Analyst's Office.

Lichtblau, E. (2000, May 8). U.S. crime falls 8th year in a row, setting record. *L. A. Times,* p. A1.

Lugaila, T. (1998). Marital status and living arrangements: March 1998 (Update). *U.S. Census Bureau Current Population Survey Report,* pp. 20–514. Washington, DC: U.S. Government Printing Office.

McCord, J. (1999). Family relationships, juvenile delinquency, and adult criminality. In F. R. Scarpitti and A. L. Nielson (Eds.), *Crime and criminals: Contemporary and classic readings* (pp. 167–176). Los Angeles: Roxbury.

National Council on Crime and Delinquency. (1997). *Reducing crime in America.* San Francisco, CA: National Council on Crime and Delinquency.

Poppy, J. (1969). Violence: We can end it. *Look, 33*(12), 21–23.

Puzzanchera, Charles. (2000, February). *Self-reported delinquency by 12–year-olds, 1997.* Washington, DC: Office of Juvenile Justice and Delinquency Prevention, U.S. Department of Justice.

Rand, M. R., Lynch, J. P., & Cantor, D. (1997). *Criminal victimization, 1973–95.* Washington, DC: Bureau of Justice Statistics, U.S. Department of Justice.

Regoli, R. M., & Hewitt, J. D. (1994). *Delinquency in society: A child centered approach* (2nd ed.). New York: McGraw-Hill.

Reiss Jr., A. J., & Roth, J. A. (Eds.). (1993). *Understanding and preventing violence.* Washington, DC: National Academy Press.

Scarpitti, F. R., & Nielsen, A. L. (Eds.) (1999). *Crime and criminals: Contemporary and classic readings in criminology.* Los Angeles: Roxbury.

Shichor, D., & Sechrest, D. K. (1996). *Three strikes and you're out: Vengeance as public policy.* Newbury Park, CA: Sage.

Snyder, H. N., & Sickmund, M. (1999). *Juvenile offenders and victims: 1999 national report.* Washington, DC: Office of Juvenile Justice and Delinquency Prevention, U.S. Department of Justice.

Snyder, H. N., Sickmund, M., & Poe-Yamagata, E. (1996). *Juvenile offenders and victims: 1996 update on violence.* Summary. Washington, DC: Office of Juvenile Justice and Delinquency Prevention, U.S. Department of Justice.

Taft, P., & Ross, P. (1969). American labor violence: Its causes, character, and outcome. In H. D. Graham and T. R. Davis (Eds.), *The history of violence in America.* New York: Bantam Books.

Thornberry, T. P., Smith, C. A., Rivera, C., Huizina, D., & Stouthamer-Loeber, M. (1999, September). *Family disruption and delinquency.* Washington, DC: Office of Juvenile Justice and Delinquency Prevention, U.S. Department of Justice.

U.S. Department of Commerce. (1995). *Statistical abstracts of the United States, 1995.* Washington, DC: U.S. Government Printing Office.

U.S. Department of Justice. (1994). Violence Against Women Act of 1994. Retrieved 4–9–02 from the World Wide Web: <http://www.ojp.usdoj.gov/vawo/laws/vawa/vawa.htm>.

Weiner, N. A., Zahn, M. A., & Sagi, R. J. (1990). *Violence: Patterns, causes, public policy.* San Diego, CA: Harcourt Brace Jovanovich.

Wilson, J. Q. (1994, September 25). Why falling crime statistics don't make us feel more secure. *L.A. Times.*

Widom, C. S. (1999). The cycle of violence. In F. R. Scarpitti and A.L. Nielson (Eds.), *Crime and criminals: Contemporary and classic readings* (pp. 332–334). Los Angeles: Roxbury.

Zimring, F. E., & Hawkins, G. (1997). *Crime is not the problem: Lethal violence in America.* New York: Oxford University.

2 Extent of Violence in America

Historical Trends

Chapter 1 discussed the history of violence in America. Here we focus more on historical trends. As Currie (1990) points out, it is often very difficult to know what crime trends mean, largely because the patterns change over time, especially with respect to age-specific rates. Citing the work of the 1969 National Commission on the Causes and Prevention of Violence (Eisenhower Commission) and President Reagan's White House Conference on Violent Crime (circa 1984), Currie noted the frustration often found in governmental efforts to track and manage violent crime.

In a recent symposium, on the thirtieth anniversary of the President Lyndon Johnson's crime commission (Robinson, 1997), Fagan provided an analysis of crime patterns over this thirty-year period, noting the stability of definitions, trends, and explanations of crime over this time (Fagan, 1997, p. 17). Trends in crime and violence were summarized for the years 1967–1997, and included a section on the changing nature of offenders, victims, and types of crime. Variations in the explanations of crime, criminality, and violence were examined and the future speculated upon.

Fagan begins his analysis with a discussion of homicide, which he refers to as the bellwether of violent crime (p. 18). He provides data on the cyclical pattern, covering a sixty-year period beginning in the 1930s (prohibition era). The homicide rate in 1933 was relatively high (about 9.8 per 100,000 population), slowly decreasing to a low in 1960 (5.1), followed by increasing rates that reached a new high in 1980 (10.2). With the shortening period of the cycle, there was a dip in the mid-1980s (7.6 in 1984), and another high in 1991 (9.8), followed by a decline through 2000. As reported by the Bureau of Justice Statistics, with the largest cities leading the way, the nation's murder rate in 1998 was the lowest in three decades (Fox & Zawitz, 2000). During this period, however, homicide victims and offenders have been getting younger and the victims are more likely to be strangers and nonintimates than in the past. Certain groups, such as African Americans, are more likely to be homicide victims.

Fagan's (1997) analysis of assault and robbery, or street crimes, showed a peak in 1982 followed by a plateau from 1985 onward. Crime victim surveys verify the stability of assault rates, but police reporting of assault has shown increases, probably due to reporting practices that upgraded simple assaults to more serious ones. However, while assault rates may have remained somewhat stable, the percentage of incidents involving serious injury has grown, especially among younger victims and offenders (p. 20). As suggested by Zimring and Hawkins (1997), there is a trend toward an increase in the severity of violence, but perhaps not its prevalence (Fagan, 1997, p. 20).

Fagan examines the victimization of women, which has been the subject of much interest in recent years, culminating in 1994 with the Violence Against Women Act, and evoking National Academy of Sciences panels on the subject in 1995 and 1996. The acts of violence against women include sexual assault (since reclassified separately from rape), violence between intimates, and marital rape. He cites an increase in reported forcible rapes from 9.6 per 100,000 people in 1960 to 42.8 in 1992, although self-report surveys showed a far lower incidence, actually documenting a decline in rates since 1981 (the peak year from 1973 to 1992) (pp. 21, 40). Consistent with Currie's concern about the meaning of crime statistics, these discrepancies are difficult to explain. Fagan sees the crime victimization surveys as more reliable since they are not as much influenced by changes in reporting or organizational practices.

Knowledge about intimate partner violence, or domestic violence, has increased over the past thirty years, partially in response to increasing concerns about child abuse and feminist activism (Fagan, 1997). Successful litigation has forced law enforcement to begin dealing with this problem, and many experiments have been done to determine the best approaches, as discussed in Chapter 4. Shelters and crisis intervention programs have been created to deal with the aftermath of this violence. Fagan indicates that statistics in this area are very poor, but that the two most comprehensive national surveys reported stable rates of intimate partner violence from 1975 to 1985, with approximately 12 percent of both women and men reporting victimization at least once in the past year by a spouse, ex-spouse or partner (p. 22). Marital rape showed a pattern of change similar to that of domestic violence, although rates of forced sex vary from 1.3 percent to as high as 50 percent, depending on the source of the survey.

Fagan concludes by stating that the story of American crime since the Commission's report is a story of violence (1997, p. 24). Reported violence has increased from two crimes per 100 citizens in 1960 to more than 5 crimes per 100 citizens in 1980 (p. 24). This violence ranges from everyday violence, such as youth and domestic violence, to the increased use of weapons that produce lethal results. These increases have affected the political landscape. As noted elsewhere in this book, the use and sale of illegal drugs and the participation of gangs in this trade is an important trend in examining violent crime. Drugs and alcohol are cited as correlating to violent crime with remarkable consistency over time. Finally, the mass media is cited as a complicating factor in explaining increases in violent behavior, especially among youth. While direct effects are hard to document, certain media portrayals of attitudes of toughness and control may contribute to increased aggressiveness and violent outcomes.

Trends in juvenile crime are not encouraging. While overall violent crime decreased between 1985 and 1994, the number of juvenile arrests for serious crimes increased (Bishop, 1997; Gramckow & Tompkins, 1999). During this period, juvenile courts experienced disproportionate increases in cases involving violent offenses and weapons (Gramckow & Tompkins, 1999):

> Cases involving crimes against persons were up 93 percent; Violent Crime Index offenses (a subset of person offenses) were up 98 percent, and weapons law violations were up 156 percent. (Snyder, Sickmund, and Poe-Yamagata, 1996)

Currie (1993) attributes much of the increases to the weakening of traditional socializing institutions of the community—the family, the schools, and the churches. However, as pointed out by Fagan, social conditions have changed. Schools have had to increasingly deal with problems of misbehavior in the classroom. Also, the easy availability of dangerous drugs and guns has changed the juvenile justice landscape. After the period of relative stability in the rates of violent crime committed by juvenile offenders, the growth in juvenile violence beginning in 1985 was accompanied by a steady growth, from 1985 to 1995, in the use of guns by juveniles ". . . leading to a doubling in the number of juvenile murders committed with guns" (Blumstein, 1995, p. 5). Blumstein attributes the sudden upsurge in juvenile violence to the increased drug trafficking of crack cocaine in the mid-1980s. To service that drug market, ". . . juveniles were recruited, they were armed with guns . . . guns that were diffused into the larger community of juveniles" (p. 6).

While increases of both adult and juvenile violent crime are cyclical, an overall upward trend is evident for the past thirty years. There is evidence that the intensity of these crimes and their potential for serious injury or death to victims has increased. Also, because violent crimes appear more likely to involve strangers than in the past, citizens feel violent crime is out of their control. These random events occur in schools, at work, and in public places of assembly. Currie (1993) poses the question of what society is to do about this problem, or who should take responsibility. Is it a local, state, or a national problem? Who is responsible for prevention efforts? Do solutions go beyond the criminal justice system to the various social agencies that deal with these individuals?

Recent Trends in Violent Crime Rates

Data on crime rates are provided from two sources within the U.S. Department of Justice: the Uniform Crime Reports (UCR), which have been published by the FBI since 1929, and the newer National Crime Victimization Survey (NCVS) of the U.S. Department of Justice Bureau of Justice Statistics, which has conducted surveys of victims since 1973. These data are reported separately by their respective agencies. Data for homicides are available from the U.S. Department of Health Center for Disease Prevention and Control (CDPC), which is very similar to the UCR homicide rates. The many sources of criminal justice data are discussed by

Schmalleger (1999), who also documents the criticisms of each reporting system, for example, that the UCR underreports crime and the NCVS overreports it.

In addition to these sources, there are international data on crime that are increasingly being used to compare crime rates in the United States, based on UCR and NCVS data, with rates in other countries. A recent comparison of transnational patterns has been provided by Zimring and Hawkins (1997) in which they indicate that crime is not the factor that sets America apart from other nations, it is the prevalence of lethal violence, especially a "preference for crimes of personal force and the willingness and ability to use guns . . ." in property crimes (p. 2).

Violent Crime

Our major concern is the extent of violent crime in the United States. Criminal victimization studies of the NCVS reported approximately 31 million violent and property victimizations for Americans age 12 or older in 1998 (Rennison, 1999). Unfortunately, the NCVS does not report homicides and must rely on UCR data for comparative purposes. The NCVS found 8.1 million violent crimes (rape or sexual assault, robbery, aggravated assault, and simple assault) in 1998, compared to 22.9 million property crimes (burglary, motor vehicle theft, and household theft), and about 3 million personal thefts (pocket picking and purse snatching). For the 1997 to 1998 year, violent crime dropped 7.1 percent, although decreases for income groups between $7,500 and $24,999 per year were smallest (and rates actually increased for the $25,000 to $34,000 income group).

The NCVS reports a downward trend in crime since 1973, when there were approximately 44 million reported victimizations of all types. From 1993 to 1998 reported crimes of violence decreased from 49.9 to 36.6 per 1,000 persons age 12 and older, a 26.7 percent decrease. Rape and sexual assault were down 40 percent.

Juvenile Crime

Juvenile crime rates will be discussed extensively in Chapter 7. Crime and violent acts by juveniles are a serious societal problem. At times it escalates, as it did through the mid-1990s, and then it declines. Although only 20 percent of violent crimes are attributed to juveniles, they have become noticeably more involved in violent acts in the 1990s. Youth violence is often seen as a problem of youth gangs, which accounted for sharp increases in the late 1990s, although recent random acts of school violence across the country have heightened concern about violence by juveniles in all segments of society. The increased availability of firearms has led to the escalation of physical confrontations, with results ranging from minor injuries to the use of lethal weapons and death. Between 1984 and 1993, the number of juveniles arrested for murder increased 168 percent, and weapons violations rose 126 percent (Fraser, 1996).

Howell (1995) and others reported that juvenile violent crime arrests increased 47 percent from 1988 to 1992, and that juvenile arrests increased for specific offenses, such as 51 percent for murder, 17 percent for rape, 50 percent for robbery, and 49 percent for aggravated assault (Howell, 1995, p. 2). While these rates have decreased since the mid-1990s, they are still 49 percent higher than in 1988, and experts predict that youth violence may get worse in the next 10 years because the population of juveniles is projected to increase by 22 percent over that period (Fraser, 1996).

It is difficult to predict juvenile violence and crime trends. Part of the problem is the way studies are conducted. Studies may define violence or crime differently, which may confound comparisons between study findings. Different data collection methods, with variations in the wording of survey questions, may make it difficult to interpret and compare research findings. Methods for the aggregation of survey data and methods of combining crime categories often make it difficult to understand the prevalence of certain types of juvenile crime or violence. Juvenile crime and violence studies are often only applicable to the period of time for which data were gathered. Aside from considering potential definition, data collection, and other testing problems, it is important to be careful when drawing conclusions or making predictions about juvenile crime or violence trends when evidence is weak or not relevant.

Predicting the Offenders

It is difficult to predict who will become part of the violent juvenile population (Bilchik, 1999). Reasons for this vary. The major reason is that many serious and violent juveniles [SVJ] are never arrested and the majority have only one officially recorded violent crime, which makes prediction difficult because it is usually based on past offenses. It is important to remember, however, that studies of chronic youthful offending demonstrate that a small proportion of juveniles account for the bulk of serious and violent juvenile delinquency (Wolfgang, Figlio & Sellin, 1972). It is often difficult to identify the small percentage of youth who commit many of the serious and violent crimes. More needs to be done within the field of criminal justice to try and identify those who are part of the small group of youth that commit many of the worst types of crimes or engage in the most serious forms of illegal behavior. If identified, intervention and/or prevention resources should be better targeted at these criminal or violence prone juveniles in order to improve life outcomes or reduce recidivism.

A recent publication by the Office of Juvenile Justice and Delinquency Prevention (Hawkins, Herrenkohl, Farrington, et al., 2000) presents various predictors of youth violence based on an analysis of sixty-six longitudinal studies. Studies were chosen that examined nonincarcerated youth in their own communities who were not chosen for having committed prior criminal or violent offenses. The study measured various acts of interpersonal violence, excluding suicidal behavior, and focused on specific indicators of violent behavior with individuals as the unit of analysis. Five domains of predictors were identified: *individual factors* (including medical, physical, and psychological); *family factors* (parental criminality, child maltreatment, poor family management practices, poor bonding, parental substance use and violence, mobility, parent-child separation); *school factors* (academic failure, low bonding to school, truancy and dropout, frequent school transitions, high delinquency rate); *peer-related factors* (delinquent siblings, peers, and gang membership); and *community and neighborhood factors* (poverty, community disorganization, drug and firearm availability, adult criminals, and exposure to violence and racial prejudice).

The best predictors of violent or serious delinquency are presented. They varied by age group, with a juvenile offense at ages 6 to 11 as the strongest predictor of subsequent violent or serious delinquency, *even if the offense did not involve violence,* and substance abuse among the best predictors of future violence for children ages 11 to 16 (Hawkins et al., p. 6).

For 12- to 14-year-olds, the two strongest predictors were the "lack of social ties and involvement with antisocial peers . . . [these] are rather weak [predictors] for the 6 [to] 11 age group" (Hawkins et al., p. 6). Second- and third-rank predictors were relatively fixed personal characteristics, such as gender (male), family socioeconomic status, and antisocial parents. The 12 to 14 year old group had a heavier representation of behavioral predictors of subsequent violence (general offenses, aggression, and school performance) (p. 6). Interestingly, broken homes and abusive parents were among the poorest predictors of subsequent violence for both age groups. Having antisocial peers is a better predictor for the 12 to 14 group but weak for the 6 to 11 group.

Most studies, including this one, conclude that the larger number of risk factors to which the child is exposed, the greater the probability of engaging in violent behavior. However, Hawkins et al. (2000) suggest that interventions must target those areas that are malleable, such as substance abuse and antisocial (negative) peers as opposed to attempts to change socioeconomic status or antisocial parents: This suggests that disrupting early patterns of antisocial behavior and negative peer support is a promising strategy for the prevention of violence and serious delinquency (p. 6). Of all the factors discussed, academic performance and behavioral problems at school appeared to be an area of difficulty that could be addressed through the use of available resources.

High-Risk Juveniles

The correctional field has compiled a dismal record in its effort to reduce the recidivism rate of juvenile offenders released from secure correctional confinement. This recidivism appears to occur sooner for juveniles than for their adult counterparts and disproportionately within a subgroup of institutionalized juvenile offenders who have established a long record of criminal misconduct and other dysfunctional behavior such as substance abuse. This subpopulation has been identified and tracked repeatedly over the past thirty years starting with the youth cohort studies by Wolfgang et al. (1972), and more recently by Altschuler and Armstrong (1991), Armstrong (1991); Dickinson (1981); Elliott, Huizinga, & Ageton (1985); Greenwood and Zimring (1985); and Haggerty (1989), among others.

These studies have a common thread in that all reveal a persistent pattern of intense and serious delinquent activity by a small percentage of individuals. Not surprisingly, substantial numbers of this high-risk group are plagued by a multitude of problems. They have not only engaged in frequent criminal acts against persons and property, but also experience a variety of emotional and interpersonal problems, a great many accompanied by physical and mental problems associated with continued abusive behavior related to illegal drugs and/or alcohol.

The need to identify and respond appropriately to this category of youthful offender has, in turn, led to a major rethinking of how the juvenile justice system should be structured and operated, both in terms of philosophy and practice. Among researchers and practitioners alike, this realization carries with it a sense of urgency to develop and implement specially-designed intensive programs, the goals of which include the closely supervised reentry of this subpopulation back into the host community, accompanied by sufficient service and support to ensure a reasonable level of community protection and public safety.

Recent Reductions in Youth Violence and Crime

More recent sources indicate that youth violence and crime have gone down. Snyder (1999) indicates that the increase in violence and crime by juveniles began during the late 1980s and peaked in 1994 (p. 1). According to the Federal Bureau of Investigation (FBI), crime index offenses, such as murder, forcible rape, robbery, and aggravated assault declined for juveniles during the four years from 1994 to 1998 (Snyder, 1999, pp. 1–11). Snyder and Sickmund (1999) indicate that serious violence by juveniles dropped 33 percent between 1993 and 1997 (p. 62). While juvenile arrests for violent crimes were reduced by 19 percent during this period, the number of juvenile violent crime index arrests in 1998 was still 15 percent above the 1989 level (pp. 1–4). When comparing the 1988 juvenile arrest rate for violent crime with the rate in 1997, Bilchik (1999) indicates that the 1997 rate "was still 49 percent higher than in 1988" (p. 15). According to Snyder (1999) juveniles in 1988 were involved in 12 percent of murder arrests, 14 percent of aggravated assault arrests, 35 percent of burglary arrests, 27 percent of robbery arrests, and 24 percent of weapons arrests (p. 11). Therefore, crime and violence committed by juveniles in the United States continues to be a serious problem (Bilchik, 1999, p. 15). Some improvements have been made in recent years. In contrast to many sources from the late 1980s and early 1990s, at least juvenile violence and crime is not spiraling out of control at this time, as predicted earlier.

Youth Delinquency and Crime

A substantial amount of youth misbehavior results in minor violations against accepted societal norms, values, and practices. To describe the characteristics and prevalence of such misbehavior, Emler and Reicher (1995) suggest that "delinquent action is rarely creative, frequently self-destructive, mostly mundane, and still a minority pastime among adolescents as a whole" (p. 2). Of those juveniles that are arrested for any reason, "the vast majority . . . are arrested for property crimes and other less serious offenses—not crimes of violence" (Howell, 1995, p. 2). With respect to violent delinquent behavior, Dohrn (1997) relies on Snyder and Sickmund (1999) to confirm that "less than one-half of 1 percent of all juveniles in the United States were arrested for violent offenses . . . [and that] only 5 percent of youth ages 10–17 were arrested for anything, and of that 5 percent, only 9 percent were arrested for a violent crime" (p. 3). In Abraham Blumberg's *Law and Order: The Scales of Justice,* Lemert (1973), with the following, clarifies the nature of typical youth delinquency in relation to life processes and changes:

> [thus] most youths outgrow their so-called predelinquency and their law flouting; they put away childish things as they become established in society by a job, marriage, further education, or by the slow growth of wisdom. (p. 222)

This statement, made almost thirty years ago, still applies to many youth who have become involved with the criminal justice system. However, it is suggested that the combination of gangs, guns, illegal drugs, and the illegal drug trade may be working to extend this period of predelinquency into adult criminal behavior for more youth than in the past. These youth must be the subject of improved efforts at prevention and intervention.

Undocumented Juvenile Delinquency

A significant amount of juvenile delinquency and crime goes undocumented. Dryfoos (1990) points out that official statistics underrepresent the prevalence of juvenile crime and violence in society (pp. 30–31). Even though the U.S. Department of Justice attempts to keep track of the number of cases that end up in juvenile court, not very many of the juvenile arrests turn into cases that can be documented for official statistical purposes (Dryfoos, 1990). Few of the juveniles that are even arrested are actually taken into custody (Dryfoos, 1990). Even though FBI arrest statistics represent the number of juveniles arrested for particular crimes, the statistics do not accurately account for the total number of crimes committed by young people (Snyder, 1999). The FBI data underrepresent the level of youth crime because police departments may report to the FBI that a crime is cleared when a person is arrested and turned over for prosecution, but clearance by arrest does not signify that a person is guilty, does not imply that a person will be convicted, does not indicate that only one youth was involved in the offense, and it does not designate that only one offense was committed (Snyder, 1999).

Youth Crime Statistics Problems in Criminal Justice

The problem with official statistics generated by the police and sent to the FBI is that some data may be inaccurate, some could not be reported, some could be based upon different crime definitions, and some could be missing because police only report the crimes that they know about (Snyder, 1999). With less serious juvenile crime or delinquency, often no official record is made because such youth misbehavior is perceived to be not serious enough for police to report. As early as 1966, Kvaraceus (1973) suggested a reason why some serious delinquency goes unreported; he suggested that "a kind of screening which tends to shelter or protect the offender against becoming a court statistic often takes place in the average community; this accounts for the so-called hidden delinquency which is never recorded but which, nevertheless, is very real" (p. 33).

The levels of both secondary youth deviance and misbehavior and primary crime and violence are more widespread in society than many current official sources would lead one to believe. Yet, most youth illegal behavior is not severe, and most arrests do not involve serious crimes or violence. Most youth misbehavior only violates conventional societal norms and values, and it generally does not impact society in any extremely dangerous way. In terms of percents of all juveniles, not many juveniles are even arrested. Studies indicate that a small group of youth commits a majority of the most serious types of offenses. With certain forms of serious or primary juvenile crime and violence there have been significant rate reductions in the United States in recent years. But juvenile crime and violence is still a problem that requires effective public attention and response because it continues to produce a variety of negative consequences for individuals, society, and within the school context. This can be found in individual acts of school violence around the country, in periodic outbursts of gang violence often related to drug wars, and crimes such as carjacking.

Carjacking

Carjacking has increasingly become a problem in the United States. It is defined as a completed or attempted theft in which a motor vehicle is taken by force or threat of force (Klaus, 1999, p. 1). Using National Crime Victimization Survey (NCVS) data, the Bureau of Justice Statistics (Klaus, 1999) reported an annual average of 48,787 carjackings per year between 1992 and 1996, a rate of 2.5 per 10,000 persons. About half were completed, and 7 of 10 *completed* carjackings involved firearms (72%), compared to 2 of 10 for attempts; although, most completions and attempts did not result in injury as 83 percent involved some kind of weapon.

Only incidents in which offenders were strangers to the victim were included in these figures. While deaths related to carjackings were not reported in the NCVS, the Uniform Crime Reports (UCR) showed about 27 homicides by strangers, each year, involving automobile theft.

The victims of carjackings, in general, were the categories of people typically found to be most vulnerable to violent crime, overall: men, African Americans and Hispanics, unmarried persons in urban areas, and people under the age of 50. About one-third (38%) of the victims offered no resistance; 19 percent confronted the offender, and about a third used nonconfrontational methods, such as running away or calling for help. Data were not sufficient to indicate the success of these methods. About 17 percent of the victims were injured, 4 percent seriously.

Just under half (45%) of carjackings were committed by a lone offender. Only 3 percent of carjackings involved both male and female perpetrators, while the remaining 97 percent were by male offenders only. Fifty-eight percent of perpetrators were African American, 19 percent white, and the remainder other or more than one race. About half were committed by offenders between the ages of 21 and 29, and 12 percent by those 18 to 20. Completed carjackings were more likely to occur in daylight (64%) as opposed to night (42%). Most occurred within five miles of the victim's home, and the property was recovered about 70 percent of the time, in whole or part. These reports give no indication of the motives of carjackers (Klaus 1999; Rand, 1994).

Carjackers are the same young, minority males who are involved in much of the violent crime being reported. UCR data indicate that in 1997 youth age 16 to 21 made up 8.4 percent of the U.S. population, yet accounted for 23.6 percent of all arrests, and persons age 22 to 29 made up 10.8 percent of the population and accounted for 23 percent of all arrests. Thirty to 39 year olds made up 16.2 percent of the population and accounted for 24.5 percent of all arrests. The highest arrest to population ratio is in the 16 to 21 age group followed by the 22 to 29 age group.

The number of carjackings appears to be on the increase. A 1994 report based on National Crime Victimization Survey data (Rand, 1994) found an average of 35,000 attempted and completed carjackings between 1987 and 1992, which were successful 52 percent of the time. This is an increase in average rates of about 39 percent over the 1982–1986 report. The 1994 report (Rand, 1994) provides the risk of carjacking as compared to risks of other life events per 1,000 adults per year: 31 per 1,000 for violent victimization, 25 for assault, 22 for injury in motor vehicle accident, 1 for rape, .2 for motor vehicle accident death, and .2 for carjacking.

Drugs and Crime

Research indicates that there is a connection between drug use and crime. What is not clear is whether crime leads to drug use, or if drug use leads to crime (Inciardi, 1984). Drug and alcohol use has had a persistent impact on crime. Two-thirds of violent crime offenders self-reported that they or their victims had used alcohol or drugs when the crime occurred (Califano, 1997). According to Joseph Califano Jr., president of the National Center on Addiction and Substance Abuse at Columbia

University, criminals commit six times as many homicides, four times as many assaults, and almost one and a half times as many robberies under the influence of drugs as they do in order to get money to buy drugs (p. 46). Gerald Lynch, President of John Jay College of Criminal Justice of City University of New York, and Roberta Blotner, director of the City of New York's substance abuse programs, 80 percent of violent crime involves the use of alcohol and drugs (Lynch & Blotner, 1993). Specifically, cocaine has the tendency to elicit violent behavior because of the changes that take place in the neurotransmitter systems in the brain (p. 47).

According to researcher Barry Spunt (Inciardi, 1984), at the National Development and Research Institutes in New York City, people become violent when they use drugs. In addition, chronic cocaine users often experience *cocaine psychosis*, during which they experience hallucinations and often believe that the police and their family members are plotting against them. This causes then to incorrectly view innocent actions by other people as threats to them, and can lead to a violent response which they believe is self-defense against their imagined enemies.

Spunt and colleagues found that of 269 murderers incarcerated in state prisons, 45 percent of them were under the influence of drugs when they killed their victims. Although many people argue that marijuana is harmless, Spunt found that of those murderers who considered themselves to be high when they killed, 31 percent of them reported that the homicide and marijuana were related (Inciardi & Saum, 1996).

While it is widely reported in the media that drug-induced violence is common, the pharmacological, economic, and systemic effects of drug use are the three major ways that drug use affects crime (Mocan & Corman, 1998; Musto, 1987). These three factors can be described as drug abuse–related crime, economically motivated drug crime, and drug market–related crime.

The use of drugs has an obvious and well-known pharmacological affect on criminality, because the drug-induced state may cause the individual user to be more violent (Mocan & Corman, 1998). According to the Drug Use Forecasting (DUF) program initiated in 1987 by the National Institute of Justice, which tested arrestees who were booked for drug use in twenty-three major cities across the nation, 50 percent or more of those who were booked on other criminal charges also tested positive for illegal drugs. Cocaine was the most commonly found drug, followed by marijuana and opiates, and the lowest rate of offending in this study was among those who had not used drugs or alcohol within the past year. Crime involvement appeared to be a function of drug use, and in particular, getting drunk monthly and using marijuana and cocaine within the past year were significantly related to criminal behavior. Cocaine use was the strongest predictor of being booked for a violent or property crime (National Institute of Justice [NIJ], 1991 in Harrison & Gfroerer, 1992).

Clearly, when addressing issues surrounding violent behavior of individuals, drug and alcohol use are critical factors. They appear to be precursors to various types of crime, often in support of an illegal drug habit, and they may lead directly to violent behavior.

Female Crime

Since the 1970s there has been growing interest in female criminality and female offenders. This interest is due to a large degree to the changes in female roles in modern societies, at least partly as an outcome of the feminist movement, and partly as result of the official crime rate among females increasing faster than among males. These developments are reflected also in a large number of professional publications dealing with various aspects of women and crime (e.g., Adler, 1975; Campbell, 1983; Daly & Chesney-Lind, 1988; Morris, 1987; Simon, 1975; Simon & Landis, 1991; Weisheit & Mahan, 1988).

This by no means indicates that there were no earlier works dealing with female criminality (see, for example, Lombroso, 1898; Pollak, 1950), but more systematic study of this subject began only in the last twenty-five years. Most of the research in this topic centered on criminal behavior connected with female social roles, a role being a "set of behavior patterns expected of a person occupying a specific social position" (Hirsch, 1981). Crimes traditionally characteristic of women are shoplifting, infanticide, and prostitution. As an outcome of growing female participation in the labor force, there was also an increase in white-collar offenses among women. In terms of violent crimes, research in female criminality centered on domestic violence and murder, which is often a result of long-term physical abuse (battered wife syndrome; see Kurz, 1993). There was relatively little attention being paid to female offenders involved in other types of violent crimes.

Women constitute more than 50 percent of the total population, less than 20 percent of arrestees, and less than 12 percent of serious violent crimes (Maguire, Pastore, & Flanigan, 1993). Correspondingly, the large majority of criminological research was focused on male criminals and their criminal behavior. This is especially the case when violent criminal behavior is concerned. While there were some pioneering works in this area, systematic empirical research was a rarity until the 1970s.

It is well known that males commit the great majority of violent offenses. According to official statistics, which may be somewhat inaccurate for various reasons, between 88 to 90 percent of the arrestees for violent offenses are males, and about 10 to 12 percent are females (Maguire et al., 1993; Simon and Landis, 1991). Citing Uniform Crime Reports data, Weiner et al. (1990) notes that in the face of increases for robbery and aggravated assault by males and females in the past decade there were greater increases for females than males for robbery. While the percentage of female violent offenders is low, in absolute numbers they are between 50,000 to 55,000 annually.

One of the more comprehensive studies was conducted by the National Commission on the Causes and Prevention of Violence. In the staff report, Ward, Jackson, and Ward (1969) published a chapter, "Crimes of Violence by Women," based on their research conducted at the California Institution for Women. They reviewed these inmates' personal background and offense patterns. Among other things, they found that minority women are overrepresented, that a larger percent of violent offenders had lower scores on their IQ tests than other offenders, and that many had substance abuse problems.

These authors state in their conclusions that "one of the interesting aspects of crimes of violence and burglary by women is that these actions seem to directly contradict the role women in our society are supposed to play" (Ward et al., 1969 p. 906). Since that time there have been major changes in the role of women in the United States and many other Western societies.

The focus of this research is to learn more about violent female offenders and to see what the differences between them are and other female offenders. However, there are problems in conducting such research. Simon and Landis (1991) documented some of the problems of studying and explaining female violent crime:

> A major difficulty in integrating studies of women and violent crime stems from the absence of gender as a major analytic variable in contemporary theoretical approaches.

These authors (Simon & Landis, 1991, p. 108) continue:

> Criminological theories offer scant explanations for the long-observed disparity in the proportions of men and women who are arrested for violent and nonviolent crimes. Consequently, these theories have not guided research on female criminal behavior.

In studying the violent behavior of women, or of any subpopulation, two of the major areas of concern are biological and sociological.

Biological Explanations

Biological explanations have their roots in Lombroso's claim that women engaged in crime are more *masculine* than those who do not commit crimes (Lombroso, 1898). Some theorize that higher levels of male sex hormones in females may influence their aggressive behavior. In a recent article Fishbein (1992, pp. 116–117) suggests that:

> just as male aggression is influenced by hormonal and other biological factors, an as yet unidentified subgroup of females may also be particularly susceptible to aggression or behavioral disruptions related to neurobiological conditions experienced pre- or post-natally.

Biological conditions may increase the likelihood of aggression in the face of environmental adversity. She concludes that ". . . diagnostic studies of women with arrest histories or self-reported criminal activities may distinguish aggressive female offenders from those who are nonaggressive on the basis of biomedical and social factors" (Fishbein, 1992, pp. 117–118).

Sociological Explanations

The sociological approach focuses on women's liberation, opportunity theories, and on subcultural explanations. Women's liberation and opportunity explanations argue that female crime rates will increase as women achieve greater equality with men. The liberation perspective emphasizes the social psychological changes in female self-definition and self-concept (Simon & Landis, 1991) as a result of changes in the above-mentioned social roles; these will alter social expectations and will lead to an assertive behavior pattern that may include a certain amount of violence. Similarly, the opportunity perspective projects that women who are increasingly freed from home-based activities will have more opportunities for criminal (especially property) activities. This development, it is believed, will provide women with more economic independence and concomitantly their behavior will be more independent from the previously proscribed norms of female roles.

There are several works following the subcultural perspective that deal with violent behavior among females. Several of them are based on research conducted in the United Kingdom. Carlen (1988) found certain correlates of female criminality, including violent crimes. These correlates included growing up in poverty, being in the state's care as a juvenile, abusing drugs, and questing for excitement. Some of these were found to be related to lower-class male delinquency in the United States (see Miller, 1958).

Other British research shows that there is a substantial extent of aggressive behavior among lower-class teenage girls. It was found that the roles females played in the youth culture were far from being marginal. Schoolgirls agreed that it is justifiable to use physical violence to defend one's sexual reputation. Older girls gave different reasons for fights. The justifications often involved the violation of a territory or a direct challenge by staring or laughing. Among the older girls there was a degree of enthusiasm for fighting. Some of them felt that it relieved them from depression. Campbell (1983), in her research of 16-year-old girls from working-class areas in the United Kingdom, found that they were involved in many fights, often in the school. A considerable number of them were started because of insulting remarks made about their sexual reputation. Among other reasons for fights, jealousy was mentioned as well. Self-respect and social status were very important for these juveniles. Usually the fights were among individuals and not groups, as is the case for boys. Sometimes the girls got into gang fights supporting their male friends. One of the conclusions of these studies was that working-class girls, similar to boys from the same class, held that standing up for one's self is an important value. Wolfgang and Ferracuti (1967) in their well-known book, *The Subculture of Violence*, based mainly on the U.S. experience, suggests that in certain lower-class neighborhoods violent behavior is an accepted way to deal with other people. Females, who grow up in their social environment, will also use violent and aggressive behavior in conflict situations.

The information gleaned from official statistics and the professional literature about violence in women, while growing, is still limited at best and is based largely on research with women in prisons. Recent studies by Baskin & Sommers (Baskin & Sommers, 1993) involved interviews with women involved in street crime to look at various correlates of such behavior. Baskin and Sommers (1993) interviewed eighty-five women from community and prison settings to gather "life event histories." In another of their studies, thirty women in various offender and drug treatment programs were interviewed regarding the termination of their criminal careers. They found that social factors, such as neighborhood environment and the degree of attachment to conventional institutions, were important determinants of behavior in these women. This finding has particular theoretical relevance with respect to current social control theory, an area that is largely unexplored or openly rejected for women (Daly & Chesney-Lind, 1988). Baskin and Sommers (1993, p. 577) say that their findings "as well as their interpretation, are suggestive and require further validation with a more geographically diverse and larger sample." In any case, their findings appear to support an integrated theoretical perspective in which several social theories converge and combine with individual and situational factors to create violent criminal behavior.

The study of females who commit crimes against persons, aside from the human interest that pertains, has important policy implications on the penological, managerial, and even the legislative levels. In the current reality of increasing crime rates, growing fear of crime, and concerns with allocation of financial resources in a stagnant economy, it is important to establish reliable information on which rational, pragmatic, and successful public policy decisions can be made in the spirit of the new trend of reinventing government (Osborne & Gaebler, 1992).

Female crimes range from homicide to ATM robberies. Issues that arise include making a determination of the major antecedents of violent behavior, or person-to-person crimes, in these women; the relationship between violent crime by women and the age of onset of violent behavior (Baskin & Sommers, 1993); and the causes of spousal abuse/battering (Reiss & Roth, 1993). Related concerns involve the role of men in bringing women into the violent act, both as a defensive measure (e.g., sexual assault, spousal abuse, child abuse) and as part of ongoing criminal activity (e.g., ATM robberies) (Reiss & Roth, 1993, Weisheit & Mahan, 1988). Another major concern is the relationship of these women's children to the violent act—that is, was the violent act the result of efforts to protect their children?

An earlier self-report survey of all women in the San Bernardino County, California jails by one of the authors included 426 incarcerated women using a precoded form that the women completed under supervision of a correctional officer; 368 (86.4%) of these surveys were usable for analysis. One in ten of the San Bernardino females (37, or 10.1%) were incarcerated for crimes against persons, which is lower than the California or national proportions. These inmates were lower in crimes against property and higher in the area of arrests for drug violations.

The San Bernardino County females differed ethnically from state and national jail female populations in being more likely to be Caucasian (47.8% versus

38% and 36.3% respectively), about as likely to be Hispanic as the California population, and less likely to be African American than the state or national populations. The 37 crimes against persons offenders were more likely to African American (37.8%); property offenders, Caucasian (48.4%). The finding for African American women is consistent with the findings of Ward et al. (1969). Ages for San Bernardino jail females ranged from 18 to 62, with the majority (55.4%) between the ages of 26 and 35. Three quarters of this population were under the age of 36. The mean age for San Bernardino females was 31.3 years.

San Bernardino County had 37 women in jail classified as having committed crimes against persons. This survey showed that women involved in violent behavior were less educated, younger, more likely not to be married, having fewer prior arrests and misdemeanor arrests, and less likely to have used illegal drugs, although their use is still high.

Less than half of the incarcerated females (44.5%) made it through the twelfth grade, with one in four (25.3%) having graduated from high school or having received a GED certificate. About one in four (25.5%) was currently married, less than half (46.7%) never married. Prior to their latest incarceration in county jail, 92.6 percent had at least one prior arrest, and 46.3 percent had five or more prior arrests. Fifty-four percent reported at least one or more prior felony arrest; 72.6 percent report one or more misdemeanor arrest. More than half (57.3%) are currently on parole or probation. Of the 368 participants surveyed, 2.2 months was the mean average of time spent at the facility under the current incarceration, with 2.5 months as the average time remaining at the facility until release.

More than three-fourths of the San Bernardino sample were either unemployed (46.5%) or listed marginal, semi-skilled employment (33.4%) as a means of support. As previously stated, approximately 80 percent of all female inmates incarcerated in federal, state, or county facilities have a problem with substance abuse. Therefore, it is not surprising that an overwhelming majority of the subjects in this survey, 85.9 percent, admit to a previous problem with drugs and/or alcohol (compared to a national average of 82% for incarcerated women). Seven in ten (72.6%) admit to a current use and/or abuse of illegal drugs and/or alcohol (versus 55.1% nationally). Illegal drugs were the overwhelming substance of choice (71.3%), followed by marijuana (8%), and alcohol (6.7%); approximately four subjects in ten (37.8%) admitted to previous multiple substance abuse, with one in five (21.2%) admitted to current multiple abuse.

Issues of dependency, victimization, and manner of jail involvement (length and type of interface with the criminal justice system) are categories that tend to distinguish women from men in this setting. But most noteworthy is the way in which children affect the lives of these women over time. Three out of four San Bernardino females surveyed for this report have children (78.8%), compared to a national average of 73.8 percent, although they may not possess physical or legal custody. Program participants (with children) have, on average, two children, and approximately 9 percent of the participants were pregnant at the time of the survey. Eighty-six percent of those with children (208 of 241) report they have custody and have placed their children with family members while incarcerated (compared to a national average of 71%). Thirty-three report their children have been removed and are currently with a foster family or Child Protective Services.

Thus, children were an important issue for these women. Child care (and custody) remains an issue until the child becomes an independent adult. The quality of this issue is significant as it could involve fetal alcohol syndrome (FAS), so-called crack babies, as well as parenting skills. It can have implications for the management of these women in the future. Children may serve as a positive motivation to get clean and sober or as a negative motivation to leave a treatment facility too early.

This survey, combined with national data, shows that women involved in violent behavior were less educated, younger, more likely not to be married, had fewer prior arrests and misdemeanor arrests, and less likely to have used illegal drugs, although their use is still high. These women suffer from issues of dependency, victimization, and the fact of their incarceration (length and type of interface with the criminal justice system). Many have suffered from neglect in their own childhoods and are quite often victims in abusive adult relationships, which are categories that tend to distinguish women from men in this setting.

Extent and Types of Violent Behavior

As concluded by Zimring and Hawkins (1997), crime is not the factor that sets America apart from other nations; it is the existence of lethal violence, especially a preference for crimes of "personal force and the willingness and ability to use guns . . ." in property crimes (p. 2). Criminal victimization studies of the NCVS reported approximately 31 million violent and property victimizations for Americans age 12 or older in 1998. Although violent crimes of all types (murder, rape, sexual assault, robbery, aggravated assault, and simple assault) have been declining since 1973, peaking in 1981, the years from 1991 through 1994 saw increases to levels greater than 1973.

Juvenile crime, and violent juvenile crime in particular, is a serious societal problem, as discussed more fully in Chapter 7. At times it escalates, as it did through the mid-1990s, and then it declines. Although only 20 percent of violent crimes are attributed to juveniles, they have become noticeably more involved in violent acts over the last ten years. Youth violence is often seen as a problem of youth gangs, which accounted for sharp increases in the late 1990s, although recent random acts of school violence across the country have heightened concern about very young juveniles and their involvement in seemingly random acts of violence.

While trends are difficult to document, the coming increase in the youthful population of the United States may lead to increases in juvenile crime and violence, and to an increased concern over overt acts of violence by adults, such as workplace violence. These increases are driven by factors in our society that may be biological, psychological, or social in origin. Based on these factors and the deleterious outcomes of violent acts, it is possible to take action working with individuals, especially youth who have become involved in violent criminal behavior.

The role of drugs, both legal and illegal, is a significant factor in violent behavior. Reports of 45 percent of violent offenders being under the influence of drugs when they killed their victims strongly suggest that a first concern should be the drug background of individuals involved in violent acts. Even marijuana, which many people see as harmless, has been found to be a factor in murder; almost one-third of the murderers studied by Inciardi and Saum (1996) considered themselves to be high when they killed, often citing marijuana use as a contributing factor. As noted by Fagan (1997), serious crime and violence have taken their toll on America, from youthful fighting and assaults and domestic violence to the increased use of weapons that produce lethal results. Violent crime rates rose from 2 crimes per 100 citizens to more than 5 crimes per 100 citizens from 1960 to 1980 (Fagan, 1997, p. 24), an unacceptable increase that must be addressed in American society.

REFERENCES

Adler, F. (1975). *Sisters in crime: The rise of the new female criminal.* New York: McGraw-Hill.

Altschuler, D. M., & Armstrong, T. L. (1991). Intensive interventions with high-risk youths. In T. L. Armstrong (Ed.), *Intensive interventions with high-risk youths: Promising approaches in juvenile probation and parole* (pp. 45–85). New York: Criminal Justice Press.

Armstrong, T. L. (Ed.). (1991). *Intensive interventions with high-risk youths: Promising approaches in juvenile probation and parole.* New York: Criminal Justice Press.

Baskin, D. R., & Sommers, I. (1993). Females' initiation into violent street crime. *Justice Quarterly* 10(4), 559–581.

Bilchik, S. (1999). Minorities in the juvenile justice system. *1999 National Report Series.* Washington, DC: Office of Juvenile Justice and Delinquency Prevention, U.S. Department of Justice.

Bishop, D. R. (1997). Juvenile record-handling and practices of the Federal Bureau of Investigation. Paper presented at the Conference on Juvenile Justice Records: Appropriate Criminal and Noncriminal Justice Uses. Washington, DC: Office of Justice Programs, Bureau of Justice Statistics.

Blumstein, A. (1995). Violence by young people: Why the deadly nexus? *National Institute of Justice Journal, 229,* 2–9.

Califano, J. (1997). Legalization of narcotics: Myths and reality. *U.S.A. Today Magazine, 125*(2622), p. 46.

Campbell, A. (1983). Female aggression. In P. Marsh and A. Campbell (Eds.), *Aggression and violence.* New York: St. Martin's Press.

Carlen, P. (1988). *Women, crime and poverty.* Philadelphia, PA: Open University Press.

Currie, E. (1990). Violence is increasing. In H. Rohr (Ed.), *Violence in America* (pp. 17–23). New York: Greenhaven Press.

Currie, E. (1993). *Reckoning: Drugs, the cities, and the American future.* New York: Hill and Wang.

Daly, K., & Chesney-Lind, M. (1988). Feminism and criminology. *Justice Quarterly* 5(4), 101–145.

Dickinson, K. (1981). Supported work for ex-addicts: An exploration of endogenous tastes. *Journal of Human Resources* 16(4), 551–587.

Dohrn, B. (1997). Youth violence: False fears and hard truths. *Educational Leadership, 55*(2), 45–47.

Dryfoos, J. G. (1990). *Adolescents at risk.* New York: Oxford University Press.

Elliott, D. S., & Huizinga, D. (1984). *The relationship between delinquent behavior and ADM problems.* Denver, CO: Behavioral Research Institute.

Elliott, D. S., Huizinga, D., & Ageton, S. S. (1985). *Explaining delinquency and drug use.* Newbury Park, CA: Sage.

Emler, N., & Reicher, S. (1995). *Adolescence and delinquency.* Cambridge, MA: Blackwell.

Fagan, J. (1997). Continuity and change in American crime: Lessons from three decades. In *Symposium of the 30th Anniversary of the President's Commission on Law Enforcement and the Administration of Justice*, June 19–21, 1997, pp. 16–47. Washington, DC: Office of Justice Programs, U.S. Department of Justice.

Fishbein, D. H. (1992). The psychobiology of female aggression. *Criminal Justice and Behavior 19*(2), 99–126.

Fox, J. A., & Zawitz, M. W. (2000). *Homicide trends in the United States: 1988 update.* Washington, DC: Office of Justice Programs, Bureau of Justice Statistics, U.S. Department of Justice.

Fraser, M. W. (1996). Addressive behavior in childhood and early adolescence: An ecological-developmental perspective on youth violence. *Social Work, 41*(4), 347–357.

Gramckow, H. P., & Tompkins, E. (1999). Enabling prosecutors to address drug, gang, and youth violence. *Bulletin,* Juvenile Accountability Incentive Block Grant Programs. Washington, DC: Office of Juvenile Justice and Delinquency Prevention, U.S. Department of Justice.

Greenwood, P. W., & Zimring, F. E. (1985). *One more chance: The pursuit of promising intervention strategies for chronic juvenile offenders.* Santa Monica, CA: The Rand Corporation.

Haggerty, K. P. (1989). Delinquents and drug use: A model program for community reintegration. *Adolesence, 24*(94), 439–456.

Harrison, L., & Gfroerer, J. (1992). The intersection of drug use and criminal behavior: Results from the National Household Survey on Drugs. *Crime and Delinquency 38*(4), 422–444.

Hawkins, J. D., Herrenkohl, T. I., Farrington, D. P., Brewer, D., Catalano, R. F., Harachi, T. W., & Cothern, L. (2000). *Predictors of youth violence.* Bureau of Justice Statistics Juvenile Justice Bulletin. Washington, DC: Office of Juvenile Justice and Delinquency Prevention, U.S. Department of Justice.

Hirsch, M. F. (1981). *Women and violence.* New York: Van Nostrand Reinhold.

Howell, J. C. (Ed.). (1995). *Guide for implementing the comprehensive strategy for serious, violent, and chronic juvenile offenders.* Washington DC: Office of Juvenile Justice and Delinquency Prevention, U.S. Department of Justice.

Inciardi, J. (1984). *The war on drugs.* Mountain View, CA: Mayfield.

Inciardi, J., & Saum, C. (1996). Legalization madness. *The Public Interest 123*, 72–83.

Klaus, P. (1999, March). *Carjackings in the United States.* Special Report. Washington, DC: Bureau of Justice Statistics, U.S. Department of Justice.

Kvaraceus, W. C. (1973). *Anxious youth: Dynamics of delinquency.* Columbus, OH: Charles E. Merrill.

Kurz, D. (1993). Physical assaults by husbands: A major social problem. In R. J. Gelles and D. R. Loseke (Eds.), *Current controversies on family violence.* Newbury Park, CA: Sage.

Lemert, E. M. (1973). Juvenile justice: questions and realities. In A. Blumberg (Ed.), *Law and order: The scales of justice* (2nd ed.) (pp. 219–303). New Brunswick, NJ: Transaction Books.

Lombroso, C. (1898). *The female offender.* New York: D. Appleton.

Lynch, G., & Blotner, R. (1993). Legalizing drugs is not the solution. *America 168*(5), 7.

Maguire, K., Pastore, A. L., & Flanigan, T. J. (1993). *Sourcebook of criminal justice statistics, 1992.* Washington, DC: Bureau of Justice Statistics, U. S. Department of Justice.

Marsh, P., & Paton, R. (1986). Gender, social class and conceptual schemes of aggression. In A. Campbell and J. Gibbs (Eds.), *Violent transactions.* London: Basil Blackwell.

Miller, W. B. (1958). Lower class culture as a generating milieu of gang delinquency. *Journal of Social Issues, 14*, 5–19.

Mocan, H., & Corman, H. (1998). An economic analysis of drug use issues and crime. *Journal of Drug Use and Crime 28*(3), 613–640.

Morris, A. (1987). *Women, crime and criminal justice.* London: Basil Blackwell.

Musto, D. (1987). *The American disease: Origins of narcotics control.* New York: Oxford University Press.

Osborne, D., & Gaebler, T. (1992). *Reinventing government.* New York: Penguin.

Pollack, O. (1950). *The criminality of women.* Philadelphia, PA: University of Pennsylvania Press.

Rand, M. R. (1994, March). *Carjackings.* Crime Data Brief. Washington, DC: Bureau of Justice Statistics, U.S. Department of Justice.

Reiss, A. J., & Roth, J. A. (Eds.). (1993). *Understanding and preventing violence.* Washington, DC: National Academy Press.

Rennison, C. M. (1999, July). *Criminal victimization in 1998, changes 1997–98 with trends 1993–1998.* National Crime Victimization Survey. Washington, DC: Bureau of Justice Statistics, U.S. Department of Justice.

Robinson, L. (1997). *Symposium of the 30th Anniversary of the President's Commission on Law Enforcement and the Administration of Justice,* June 19–21, 1997. Washington, DC: Office of Justice Programs, U.S. Department of Justice.

Schmalleger, F. (1999). *Criminology today.* Upper Saddle River, NJ: Prentice-Hall.

Simon, R. J. (1975). *Women and crime.* Lexington, MA: Lexington Books.

Simon, R. J., & Landis, J. (1991). *The crimes women commit, the punishments they receive.* Lexington, MA: Lexington Books.

Snyder, H. N. (1999). Juvenile arrests 1998. Bulletin. Washington, DC: Office of Justice Programs, Office of Juvenile Justice and Delinquency Prevention, U.S. Department of Justice.

Snyder H. N., & Sickmund, M. (1999). *Juvenile offenders and victims: 1999 national report.* Washington, DC: Office of Juvenile Justice and Delinquency Prevention, U.S. Department of Justice.

Snyder, H., Sickmund, M., & Poe-Yamagata, E. (1996). *Juvenile offenders and victims: 1996 update on violence.* Summary. Washington, DC: Office of Juvenile Justice and Delinquency Prevention, U.S. Department of Justice.

Ward, D., Jackson, M., & Ward, R. E. (1969). Crimes of violence by women. In D. J. Mulvihill and M. M. Tumin (co-directors), *A Staff Report to the National Commission on the Causes and Prevention of Violence.* Washington, DC: U.S. Government Printing Office.

Weiner, N. A., Zahn, M. A., & Sagi, R. (1990). *Violence: Patterns, causes and public policy.* Orlando, FL: Harcourt Brace Jovanovich.

Weisheit, R., & Mahan S. (1988). *Women, crime and criminal justice.* Cincinnati, OH: Anderson.

Wolfgang, M. E., & Ferracuti, F. (1967). *The subculture of violence.* London: Social Science Paperbacks.

Wolfgang, M. E., Figlio, R. M., & Sellin, T. (1972). *Delinquency in a birth cohort.* Chicago, IL: University of Chicago Press.

Zimring, F. E., & Hawkins, G. (1997). *Crime is not the problem: Lethal violence in America.* New York: Oxford University Press.

3 The Social and Economic Cost of Violence

The economic and social costs of crime, and violent crime in particular, have become an increasing concern to American society. The most costly aspect of violent crime is often related to the injuries, long-term disabilities, and deaths of victims. Economic costs are often measured in direct terms, or actual costs to victims, although social, or nonmonetary, costs are equally important. Direct costs include the actual dollar losses to victims, loss of future income, costs of health care, law enforcement, courts, and corrections systems, various types of social agencies that work to assist victims, and even those agencies that work to assist the families of offenders. Social costs are more difficult to determine.

Many techniques are used to estimate the losses suffered by victims of violence. These include actual monetary costs and nonmonetary costs, such as the pain and suffering inflicted on individuals as a result of violent acts, or the loss of quality of life as a result of injury or while living in fear of violence, or the long-term effects of child abuse. Often the groups most affected are those with the greatest potential exposure to violence, such as individuals who live in high-crime communities. The often-ignored aspect of the cost picture is the issue of prevention, which is an attempt to intercede with individuals who might become violent, or have experienced a violent episode and need help to prevent future occurrences. Prevention is the primary concern of this book.

We feel that the bulk of the prevention effort belongs with the helping professions. As discussed by Moore, Prothrow-Stith, Guyer, and Spivak (1997), interventions are critical in reducing risk factors, which is an extension of the public health approach to controlling infectious diseases. Interventions include violence prevention measures that "(1) operate prior to the incident of violence . . . (2) those that affect the violent encounter as it develops . . . and (3) measures that operate to minimize the damage associated with violence . . ." (p. 187).

In this chapter the cost of violence to society and to individuals, including both victims and perpetrators, will be discussed prior to addressing some of the techniques that may be used to prevent and control violence in individuals. Our primary concern is not just to provide estimates of costs and losses due to violence, but also to specify methods and techniques that can help reduce any real or potential costs to individuals and society. It is important in this context, as pointed out by Warr (1994), to be aware of the distinction between the direct and indirect experience of individuals with violence, because the proportion of individuals who actually experience violence in America is rather small. In this sense, it is also necessary to understand and measure how much of the cost of violence is associated with efforts by people to prepare for or avoid violence in their lives. These are the *indirect victims* of violence who act out of fear of violence due to their overexposure to it, which occurs largely through the media.

Warr (1994) points out that news media coverage of violent crime constitutes a larger share of the daily news than other types of crime. For instance, quoting Graber (1980), Warr points out that stories of individual crimes in the *Chicago Tribune* "received nearly three times as much attention as the presidency or the Congress or the state of the economy" (p. 29), and Skogan and Maxfield (1981) found similar emphasis on crime reporting in three major daily newspapers. This type of reporting has implications for the types of individuals seen as violent in American society with the major implication being that a disportionate number of violent males are young, unemployed black men. In fact, "An estimated 11% of black males in their twenties and early thirties were in prison or jail in 1999 . . . 12.3% of black non-Hispanic males age 25 to 29 were in prison or jail, compared to 4.2% of Hispanic males and about 1.5% of white males in the same age group" (Beck, 2001, p. 10). Collins (1983) attributes this disparity to the frustration of African American men in the U.S. that results in street violence, a topic that will be discussed in greater detail in the sections addressing treatment.

The cost of violence has an intangible dimension, which includes losses that "do not have a market value and cannot be bought or sold" (Miller, Cohen, & Weirsema, 1996). As shown in the accompanying table, this is essentially lost "quality of life," which is the most uncertain area of costs. It is also the area of largest costs. These costs include long-term disability, fear of crime, and reduced activity (shopping, etc.), which may have economic consequences, but not necessarily. Intangible costs are especially high in communities directly affected by high levels of crime and violence. Warr (1994) cited several surveys indicating respondent's fear of violence, noting that fear reported by individuals is based on their perceptions of violence being both serious *and* likely. This chapter will address direct and indirect monetary and nonmonetary costs as well as newer problem-solving approaches that have gained some support from criminal justice professionals and the public.

Monetary Costs

Much of the literature on the costs of crime and violence is found in the victimization literature under topics such as reducing victim harm and intentional injuries. This literature was developed out of the concern for victims of crime that emerged in the 1980s, as found, for example, in the renaming of the National Crime Survey to the National Crime *Victimization* Survey in 1990. Three reports will be summarized here. The first is a special report in 1984 that discussed the "economic cost of crime to victims" (Shenk & Klaus, 1984), which states that questions of cost are not simple to answer. The second special report (Harlow, 1989) is more specific to violence because it focuses on injuries resulting from rape, robbery, or assault. The BJS report by Harlow was the basis for much of the data reported by Cohen, Miller, and Rossman (1994), as presented below. Finally, Klaus (1994) provides an update of direct costs in 1992.

The economic cost paper (Shenk & Klaus, 1984) will be summarized first because it raises questions about how these costs are best calculated, and considers what legitimate expenses can be considered costs. For example, to what extent are prevention measures, such as private security costs and security hardware, even watchdogs, considered the costs of crime, much less the anxiety experienced by victims and nonvictims? Out of these reports, a *cost matrix* has been developed by the authors that encompasses types of costs (monetary and nonmonetary), although the preferred terms now seem to be tangible and intangible costs (Miller et al., 1996), and costs to victims, direct and indirect. All of these types of costs must be considered in discussing the impact of violence on individuals and society. (See Table 3.1.)

The data relied upon by the BJS for their reports were collected through the National Crime (Victimization) Survey that began in 1973. This survey interviewed individuals in 49,000 households (99,000 individuals), at six-month intervals over a two-year period, about being victimized. Only certain categories of crime are identified for questions regarding costs, including actual theft losses, property damage, and medical expenses resulting from crimes. Statisticians warn that the survey only captures a small portion of total economic cost of crime, and that physical injuries are often associated with violent crime, while economic loss is associated with property crime; however, they stress that economic loss is a factor in both types of crimes.

Limited calculations are used in the report. These include total cost per victim, percentage of victims who have costs in different ranges, and aggregate total economic loss, which is used in various crime and victim categories to reflect the magnitude of loss. As they caution:

Table 3.1   Cost Matrix

Type of Cost	Cost to Victim (Society)	
	Direct	Indirect
Monetary or Tangible	Actual dollar costs to victims (medical, etc.); economic loss	Insurance premiums; protective measures; shared societal costs (prisons, social agencies)
Nonmonetary or Intangible	Injury, disability; long-term aggravation of preexisting condition	Fear of crime; reduced activity; unseen losses to local businesses

The number of victims in each category affects these figures. For example, total losses for personal and household property crimes are much higher than for violent crimes, since about 85% of all crime is property crime. Also, the ratio of crimes that involve economic loss to crimes with no loss is much higher for property crimes than for violent crimes. (Shenk & Klaus, 1984, p. 2)

BJS statisticians emphasize the importance of determining economic loss in terms of *direct* and *indirect* costs, the latter being those costs *shared by everyone in society* (e.g., criminal justice system costs, higher insurance premiums). The BJS report focuses on direct costs to victims, or those incidents where costs are readily quantifiable, such as actual medical expenses, as opposed to those that are not readily quantifiable, such as feelings of fear and anxiety. And, they also include the "dimensions" of material and psychic costs, which are seen to overlap. Thus, the BJS report assesses "direct economic or material costs of NCS-measured crimes that victims are able to quantify in dollar terms" (p. 2), although questions are asked about costs recovered through insurance or other types of recovery and are presented in the report.

The total crime costs to individuals, not to the entire system, in 1981 dollars, including personal and household crimes, went from $5.6 billion in 1975 to $10.9 billion in 1981 (see Figure 3.1). This constituted a increase of 94 percent in six

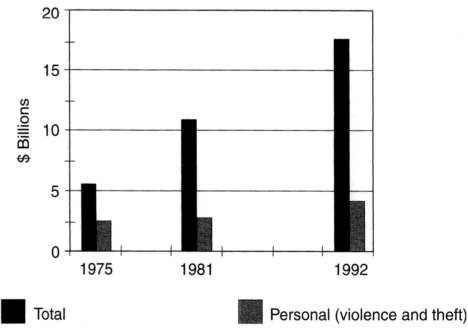

FIGURE 3.1 Cost of Crime in Billions (U.S.) for 1975, 1981, and 1992

years. It rose another 61 percent by 1992 to $17.6 billion (Klaus, 1994; Shenk & Klaus, 1984). For personal crimes, which included violence and theft, the total cost in 1981 dollars was $2.8 billion, increasing from $2.6 billion in 1975 and reaching $4.1 billion in 1992. Violent crimes include rape, robbery, and assault, and constituted 5.9 percent of total losses reported in 1975, 5.7 percent in 1981, and 7.7 percent in 1992.

Most crimes do not involve victim contact: "More than 93% of the 1981 aggregate loss from crime ($10.2 billion out of $10.9 billion) occurred as a result of crimes in which there was no victim-offender contact, [that is] burglary, household larceny, motor vehicle theft, and personal larceny without contact" (Klaus, 1994, p. 3). Of the three violent crimes, robbery provided the largest total economic loss (in 1981 constant dollars), although the loss per incident was greatest for rape. More current actual costs are provided by Miller et al. (1996) and Klaus (1994), and are discussed below.

Medical expenses contributed relatively little to overall economic costs. BJS statisticians broke costs down into medical, property damage, and actual property and theft losses. In 1981, for example, just 2 percent of the total of $10.9 billion cost of crime was derived from medical expenses, with about 65 percent of that the result of assault, 31 percent from robbery, and 4 percent from rape (1984, p. 4): "The median medical expense for victims of crimes of violence as a whole was $120; however, 25% of victims of violent crime spent $375 or more on medical bills" (1984, p. 4). For 1992, Klaus (1994, p. 2) found that for crimes of violence involving injuries, 65 percent involved costs of $250 or more.

Economic loss tends to differ between race/ethnic groups. The median economic loss for black victims of personal crimes was significantly higher than for white victims: $58 versus $43 in 1981 dollars; although for the subcategory of violent crimes, the median economic loss was $97 for blacks and $75 for whites. Differences for household crimes, while favoring whites, were not statistically significant (Shenk & Klaus, 1984, p. 6).

Consistent with the notion that the media drives perception of crime, the report concludes, "It may be surprising that the median economic losses to victims of many types of crimes are relatively low. However, the types of crimes portrayed by the media that involved staggering losses become newsworthy precisely because they are so unusual" (p. 6). Low economic costs, however, do not necessarily mitigate the victim's feelings of safety and security in relation to any type of crime. Since people vary in their responses to crime, the relatively small economic loss for a particular victimization may not reflect the degree of personal loss experienced by that individual.

Injuries from Violent Crime

The BJS special report on injuries from crimes (Harlow, 1989) is far more specific to violent offenses, but does not include specific cost estimates. Nonetheless, the figures provide an indication of the extent of harm caused by violent victimizations. She reports that 63 million persons in the U.S. were victims of rape, robbery, or assault between 1979 and 1986, with 17.7 million experiencing injury during the crime. There was an average of 2.2 million injuries to victims per year, with one million receiving medical care and half a million getting emergency room or hospital treatment. About 82,000 persons were hospitalized for at least one night as a result of injuries from violent crime and remained an average of nine days. Based on National Crime Victimization Survey data:

> About 1 in 6 of these injured victims survived serious injuries: gunshot or knife wounds, broken bones, teeth knocked out, loss of consciousness, internal injuries, or unspecified injuries requiring a hospital stay of at least 2 days . . . An estimated 28 percent . . . were injured during the crime; over 13 percent had an injury serious enough to require some medical attention; for 7 percent the injury was serious enough to require hospital care; and for 1 percent a hospital stay was necessary. (p. 1)

The injury *rate* per 1,000 persons age 12 or older has remained about the same from the inception of the crime survey in 1973 to 1986. Over this same period the violent crime rate dropped 11 percent, which means that a higher proportion of crime victims were injured over time. Gunshot wounds accounted for an estimated 1 percent of these injuries, 3 percent were knife wounds, and 6 percent broken bones or teeth. "Rates of injury for violent crime were highest for males, blacks, persons age 19 to 24, persons who were separated or divorced, those earning less than $10,000 per year, and residents of central cities" (Harlow, 1989, p. 1). Klaus (1994, p. 2) found that in 1992 dollars, about 69 percent of the victims who were injured had health insurance or were eligible for public medical services: 70 percent of all whites and 66 percent of all blacks.

According to Harlow (1989), black or elderly crime victims more likely to require overnight hospitalization. Also, injuries caused by crime accounted for more than 700,000 days of hospitalization annually, which she notes is about 30 percent of the hospital days for traffic injuries and just over 1 percent of those for heart disease (p. 1). The report found that 14 percent of all persons fatally injured in 1985 were the victims of homicide and legal intervention. These findings represent significant costs for individuals injured in violent crimes.

Monetary and Nonmonetary Cost Analysis

The report of the National Research Council of the National Academy of Sciences by Cohen, Miller, and Rossman (1994) documents actual costs of violent behavior, inclusive of economic and noneconomic (or intangible) costs. First, however, they provide a theoretical framework to evaluate the consequences and costs of violent behavior, and provide a review and update of existing estimates of the cost of victimization. The focus is on the traditional violent crimes of homicide, robbery, assault, and rape, essentially for victims over age 12, using primarily NCVS data.

Their concern is with comparing aggregate crime costs with other social ills in terms of the establishment of public priorities requiring action. We need to know the potential costs and benefits that can be realized by taking action to reduce crime as opposed to addressing other social problems, such as highway deaths. This is a position not unlike that of Zimring and Hawkins (1997), who are concerned about the intensity of violence crime more than its prevalence.

Cohen et al. (1994) seek solutions that are cost effective. They begin with a discussion of benefit-cost analysis, and the attempts to produce savings in offender management with varied approaches, such as electronic monitoring, intensive probation supervision, and shock incarceration. Also included are preventive police patrols and domestic violence arrest programs. Were it written today, they would also evaluate community policing programs and the results of "three strikes" determinate sentencing laws that have proliferated around the country, which require longer sentences for second- and third-time serious or violent offenders. Their concern is that accurate estimates of costs and potential savings are necessary in order to make adequate comparisons of the success of these programs.

Cohen et al. (1994) differentiate four types of costs:

(1) Those caused directly by violence (i.e., external costs imposed by the offender); (2) those costs society incurs in its attempt to deter or prevent future incidents (through deterrence, incapacitation, or rehabilitation of offenders as well as preventive measures taken by potential victims); and (3) those costs incurred by the offender (such as the opportunity cost of an offender's time while either engaging in the offense or being punished) . . . To this . . . we add (at least conceptually) a fourth—the cost of society's desire to punish socially unacceptable behavior. (p. 72–73)

The fourth concern overlaps with the deterrence objective (number 2), as when the rapist is sent to jail to meet the goals of prevention (deterrence) and retribution. They appear to agree with the conclusion reached by Waldfogel (1989), that for certain types of offenders the costs of incarceration do not achieve a cost benefit, but it is done simply for retribution. That is, the incarceration "pays for itself" through deterrence and incapacitation for some offenders, but not for others. However, two later studies support the cost effectiveness of prisons in reducing crime, as reported by Zimring and Hawkins (1997). The first, by Levitt (1996), found that a 10 percent increase in the prison population can lead to between a 3 to 4 percent decline in crime rates; a similar study by Marvell and Moody (1994) found similar results, although considered a less sophisticated study.

Cohen et al. (1994) distinguish between monetary, or out-of-pocket (direct) expenses, and nonmonetary costs, or the pain and suffering or loss of quality of life that defy quantification. Nonmonetary costs are often referred to as social costs. They then present the concepts of *willingness to pay* (WTP), which is the amount people are willing to pay for avoidance of injury, and *willingness to accept* (WTA), which is the amount required to convince a person to accept an injury or death. The WTP is the *ransom value,* or maximum amount a person will pay to avoid an injury, and the WTA the *price* of enduring the injury, or minimum amount they will accept to voluntarily endure the injury (p. 74). The essential difference between the two concepts is who pays.

Cohen et al. (1994) discuss the direct costs of the criminal justice system for both society and the offender, seeing the loss of freedom by the offender as a nonmonetary cost. However, the possibility that the incarceration experience might enhance future criminal activity can be considered a potential monetary cost to society. Cohen et al. (1994) see additional actual costs in the use of extra deterrence expenses, inclusive of law enforcement and the courts. Probably no better example of this has been in the use of the courts to process and incarcerate drug offenders who are potentially not dangerous to society.

Actual Costs

The Cohen et al. (1994) report provides actual costs for the areas of medical treatment, including mental health care, and for nonmedical, or monetary loss to victims. Most of these data are for 1987 and are drawn from sources similar to those described above. They note that a conversion to 1994 dollars would require an increase of about 25 to 30 percent in the figures given (p. 141). Some examples follow, which are based largely upon self-reported crime victimization survey data, with appropriate cautions.

Average medical costs *per murdered victim* were $5,370 for 20,100 (all) murders in 1987 (Cohen et al., 1994, p. 91), although the total estimated cost per victim was $2,212,000 (p. 143), which is inclusive of five major categories of costs: direct victim losses (medical and mental health care, monetary losses), emergency response (victim services, police, emergency transport), victim productivity, program administration costs (insurance claims, legal costs, costs of pain, suffering and quality of life), and risk of death. Just 36 percent of all robbery victims (383,000 of 1,068,500) were injured, at an average medical cost of $344 each (p. 91). (All murdered victims qualified as injured.) However, averaged across *all* victims (injured or not) the figure dropped to $124 for robbery, $376 for rape, and $153 for assault. It is made clear that these costs do not encompass long-term effects of crimes such as rape, nor do they include aggravation of preexisting injuries or medical conditions.

Mental health costs are cast in the established category of post-traumatic stress disorder (PTSD), an event that lies outside the range of common experiences, such as a mugging, assault, military combat, natural disaster, or accident. Estimates of the proportion of *traumatic neurosis* caused by rape and robbery are given (p. 95). Total 1987 cost of psychological injury, per victim, for rape is given as $5,250, with mental health costs of $3,886 coupled with a productivity loss of $1,364. Similar analyses are provided for robbery, with costs which are less than one-fourth of those for rape, and assault, with costs one-tenth of that for rape.

Since figures for psychological injury were not available, Cohen et. al. (1994) used jury award data.

Nonmedical monetary losses in the form of cash and property were provided by Cohen et al. (1994), with the realization that long-term or ancillary losses, such as the consequences of an unpaid mortgage or loss of a job, are difficult to quantify. Robbery showed the highest average rate of property loss at $335, over all victims (1987 figures).

Cohen et al. (1994) then discuss costs that are more indirect in that they involve the creation and maintenance of victim service organizations. There are more than 2,000 such organizations around the country. They provide counseling, financial assistance, and shelters for battered women and their children. A 1988 estimate indicates that $200 million annually is provided to 1,489 programs, based on $34.4 million in Federal Victims of Crime Act (VOCA) matching funds, which make up about 26 percent of all funds expended (p. 102). Costs would be higher if volunteer services were included. Victim compensation programs operating in 41 states reported eligible compensation during 1987 at $101,563,900, with average compensation per victim of murder at $765, rape $36, and assault $12 (no estimate available for robbery; Cohen et al., 1994, p. 104).

About 85 percent of the estimated costs are nonmonetary losses. The report provides the *average* total cost per victimization, which ranged from $16,500 for assault to $2,212,000 for murder. In a subsequent study Miller, Cohen, and Weirsema (1996) found that this cost per victimization for murder had risen to $2,940,000 by 1990: $1,030,000 tangible and $1,910,000 intangible costs. For rape, the total cost had risen to $86,500 by 1990 ($5,100 in tangible and $81,400 in intangible costs).

Total Aggregate Costs of Violence

The total aggregate costs of violent behavior attributed directly to victims in the U.S. in 1994 (Cohen et al., 1994, Table 26) came to $109.8 billion in 1987 dollars, which would be about $137 billion in 1994 dollars (25% increase). An additional, perhaps modest, 20 percent increase through the year 2000 would make the annual cost of crime to victims about $159.21 billion. For comparison purposes, the total education expenditures in 1987 were $374.1 billion, and $458 billion in 1993 (U.S. Department of Commerce, 1996, p. 156, Table 235). As shown below, Miller et al. (1996) provide a much larger estimate of $450 billion in tangible and intangible costs, based on 1993 dollars. This estimate includes the intangible cost of pain and suffering by the victim.

These costs from the 1994 (Cohen et al.) study do not include the cost of society's response to violent behavior, which they divide also into average cost per victim and aggregate costs. Categories used (Cohen et al., Table 25, p. 144) include the costs of precautionary measures and fear, criminal justice-related costs, and losses in incarcerated offender productivity. A summary of estimated costs for violent behavior (1987) found averages ranging from $5,600 for robbery and for aggravated assault to $10,900 for rape, and $103,800 for murder (p. 144). Aggregate costs for rape, robbery, and assault (Table 26) were $109.8 billion.

In a later study, Miller, Cohen, and Weirsema present a "Comprehensive List of Costs and Consequences of Crime" (1996, p. 11). Also, the "monetized losses per crime victimization or per crime victim (in 1993 dollars)" are provided (p. 17). They found that the cost per crime victimization for robbery with risk of death had risen to $13,000 by 1993. For assault or attempted assault, Miller et al. (1996) found that the cost per victimization with risk of death had risen to $19,000 by 1993. The estimated percent distributions of personal and household victimizations resulting in economic loss are reported for 1992 from the victimization surveys. Of a total of 13,371,440 victimizations, 1,548,680 were crimes of violence. About half of these reported a direct economic loss, with 12.7 percent reporting $500 or more in losses.

With about three-fourths of the criminal justice system budget allocated to violent crime, Cohen et al. (1994) suggest "a good proportion of the cost of sanctions in the United States is associated with punishment of violent offenders. This is consistent with the fact that about 55 percent of all prison inmates are serving time for violent offenses" (p. 147). In 1991, 46.6 percent of all state inmates were sentenced for violent offenses (47.4% of males, 32.1% of females); 17.3 % of all federal inmates were violent offenders (18.1% of males, 7.7% of females) (Harlow, 1994, p. 3), rising to 20.6 percent by 1996 (Maguire & Pastore, 1999). Jail populations consisted of 26.3 percent violent offenders in 1996 (21.8% convicted; 36.6% unconvicted; 27.6% males, 14.9% females), up from 22.5 percent in 1989 (Harlow, 1998). Criminal justice system direct and indirect expenditures for 1994 were $107,929 billion; $19 million federal and $88.9 million state and local (Maguire & Pastore, 1999, p. 2), which is three times the 1982 expenditure of $35.8 billion.

Miller and Cohen, with Weirsema (Miller, Cohen, & Weirsema, 1996), much of whose work is cited above (with Rossman), summarized and updated their work in presenting a new look at victim costs and consequences in 1994 dollars. They state that personal crimes "cost $105 billion annually in medical costs, lost earning, and public program costs related to victim assistance . . . [but] they ignore pain, suffering, and lost quality of life . . . an estimated $450 billion annually" (p. 1) based on 1993 dollars; $426 billion of this total results from violent crime (including drunk driving and arson). These figures exceed 1987 estimates, which appear to be based more specifically on aggregate costs to victims. The authors provide some yardsticks for comparing costs: violent crime causes 3 percent of medical spending and 14 percent of injury-related medical spending; wage losses from violent crime are one percent of American earnings; 10 to 20 percent of mental health care expenditures are attributable to violent crime, much of it for child abuse victims. They state "Personal crime reduces the average American's quality of life by 1.8 percent. Violence alone causes a 1.7 [percent] loss" (Miller et al., 1996), and they consider these estimates conservative.

More importantly, Miller et al. (1996) indicate that the pain, suffering, and lost quality of life caused by a crime such as rape far outweigh the estimated costs of burglary or larceny. Rape estimates for this report were based on 1992 data from the National Women's Study. Using adjustments to these data (Kilpatrick, Resnick, Saunders, & Best, 1994) and NCVS data, it is estimated that between 834,000 and 1.1 million rape and sexual assault victimizations occurred in 1992 with a total cost estimate of $87 million (p. 5). Similar estimates were done for assaults, domestic violence, etc. Preliminary findings for violence against children are significant. Miller et al. (1996), using National Crime Victimization Survey (NCVS) data, state that "Out-of-pocket costs for child victims are estimated to be more than 20 percent of all out-of-pocket crime victim costs, and more than 35 percent of all costs (including pain, suffering, and lost quality of life)" (p. 2).

A comparison of victim costs from five studies (Miller et al., 1996, Table 9, p. 24) shows that comparable estimates are generally made for various types of crime, in terms of both costs per victimization and aggregate costs. The most obvious cost differences by year of data collection are for assault, which are greatest across the studies; "fatal crimes" estimates most consistent.

Unfortunately, many figures that express costs for violent crime, as well as other types of crime, do not provide these data in current dollars for comparative purposes. The studies cited here attempt to correct for this problem. Also, data showing increases are rarely given on a per capita basis, that is, rate. For example, U.S. Department of Justice data indicate that government expenditures for criminal justice nationally have increased from 1982 to 1992 by 65 percent, with corrections (jails, prisons, probation and parole) leading the way. This increase is apparently due to rising crime rates, enhanced law enforcement, and tougher sentencing (Weiss, 1998, p. 126). During this period, the U.S. population increased 10 percent. The number of individuals arrested for murder and robbery who were convicted rose also; 17 percent for murder and 7 percent for robbery, although drug convictions also rose 13 percent (Weiss, 1998, p. 127). Costs appear to be increasing at a much greater rate than population figures might suggest.

Nonmonetary costs have been discussed above, and can include both individual and societal costs. Cohen et al. (1994) sometimes mix the categories of monetary and nonmonetary costs, while BJS reports focus strictly on economic losses to victims. Temporary or permanent inability to do housework, lost schoolwork, pain and suffering, family support costs (during recuperation, etc.) might be considered nonmonetary. However, the costs of death, inclusive of the funeral and the loss of lifetime wages can be calculated. There are also long-term consequences of violent behavior to persons who are not directly victimized. These effects can include increased fear generated by victimization that leads to reduction in social activity with others.

Beyond actual expenditures for the criminal justice system, agents of the system may develop a so-called siege mentality in reacting to various types of crime, which can be very costly in the use of resources that could better be devoted to positive social activity. These factors represent the costs of crime in monetary terms and in terms of less tangible losses to victims and to society.

The Cost of Diversion of Resources from More Socially Useful Functions

Perhaps the most dramatic recent example of the problem of diversion of resources to criminal justice from other social needs is the advent of "truth in sentencing" and "three strikes and you're out" laws across the United States. These laws, which began being implemented in the late 1980s, are targeted at toughening prison terms for repeat serious or violent offenders. Three strikes laws have been implemented in some form in at least twenty-four states and the Federal government since 1993 (see Austin, Clark, Hardyman, & Henry, 1999 for a complete listing of states with these laws). While laws vary, some allowing only two strikes, the laws generally reduce judicial discretion by mandating severe prison sentences based upon the types of crimes committed.

Initial comparisons by the RAND Corporation put expenditures for implementing the California three strikes law at very close to the cost of operating the system of higher education. The prison system had 9 percent of the General Fund Appropriations as compared to 12 percent for higher education. They found that "Higher education's share of the budget has already fallen from 17 [percent] to 12 [percent] in the past 25 years . . . [and] To support implementation of the law, total spending for higher education and other services would have to fall by more than 40 [percent] over the next 8 years" (Greenwood, Rydell, Abrahamse, Caulkins, Chiesa, Model, & Klein, 1999, p. 85).

In an analysis of the three strikes laws nationally for the five-year period through 1998, a report of the Campaign for an Effective Crime Policy (Dickey & Hollenhorst, 1998) saw a limited impact for most states and the federal government. However, they specify great economic costs in implementing the California law, which included increased preconviction jail time and case processing, often based on appeals, increased prison construction, and the long-term costs of increased prison time, including substantial geriatric costs yet to be determined.

Violence can be costly in many ways. Fully five years before the senseless shootings at Columbine High School in Colorado in 1999, an apparent unease about violent crime existed throughout the state, which changed people's behavior (Evans, 1994). This uneasiness endured in the face of declines in overall violent crime: a decline in homicides from 1980 to 1992 of 6.06 percent, rape down 37.93 percent, robbery down 23.75 percent, assault down 26.2 percent (Evans, 1994). It is the *nature* of the violence that had people upset. It appeared more random, putting everyone at risk. Citizens questioned the effectiveness of their prevention systems, and lamented the economic loss from crime. The 1992 total economic loss due to violent crime in Denver was estimated at $873.02 million. Over $1 billion were spent in Colorado in 1994 on police protection, prisons, and the legal system. Other estimated losses were: to victims, $2.41 million; hospitalization, $6.5 million, and police and corrections, $978 million; child abuse, $76.1 million.

The primary concern of Colorado citizens, according to Evans, was the effects of crime on the business climate, as well as losses to workers and their productivity. Money allotted to security guards could be better spent elsewhere. Then-Governor Romer said the effects of increasing violence were not limited by locale or social strata, and lamented the fact that "When children aren't safe on the sidewalks in front of their houses it affects all of us, including our business atmosphere" (p. 22). The Columbine school massacre occurred in April 1999. Romer became the new Superintendent of Schools for Los Angeles County in June 2000.

Reductions in violent crime in society are necessary to stop the diversion of resources from education and other positive functions of government, as well as improving the overall quality of life for Americans. Beyond the tangible and intangible costs of violent behavior, the maintenance of individuals convicted of violent offenses is an intolerable cost. The best approaches are prevention and intervention, about which we are concerned.

Victimization of the Elderly

Of all the groups affected by violence in society at the intangible level, the elderly, or people age 65 or older, are probably most affected. This is the case even though they are the least likely to be victimized. Bureau of Justice Statistics reports for the 1992 to 1994 period found persons 50 or older are 7 percent of the serious violent crime victims, compared to 49 percent of age 12 to 24 and 44 percent of age 25 to 49. Persons age 18 to 21 were in the most likely to be victims of serious violent crime, with African Americans experiencing 72 victimizations per 1,000 compared to 50 for Hispanics and 46 for whites.

Despite their smaller number of victimizations, fear of crime among the elderly is viewed as an important social issue in the United States. National magazines and local newspapers periodically remind us that the elderly are vulnerable and victimized in our society. The extent of this victimization is well documented (Clemente and Kleiman, 1976; Covey & Menard, 1988; Warr, 1994; Whitaker, 1987; Yin, 1982). The elderly are more vulnerable to crime because their attackers can more easily manipulate, dominate, and control them than they could a younger person. Also, the impact of crime is more severe for them. Elderly persons may suffer from declining health, may be living alone, and may lack social support systems. Often crimes against the elderly are crimes of opportunity that, in many cases, could be reduced or prevented by appropriate programs in the community. An understanding of the problems and fears of the elderly are of particular relevance for the planning, design, and implementation of crime prevention programs for them.

In 1987, one of the authors participated the analysis of a survey of the elderly regarding their fear of crime, their concerns about personal safety in the community, and the implications of this fear for their personal health and well-being (Sechrest & Siddharthan, 1992). Findings, which are reported below, are quite consistent with other research on the vulnerability of the elderly to crime, especially violent crime, and their fears, real or imagined, about their vulnerability. As several reports show, the elderly experience less violent and property crime than younger persons, on a rate basis, yet their fears remain high. Yet, probably due to the fact that there is less likelihood of financial and/or physical health recovery than for younger persons, aside from the nonmonetary costs of their real or potential victimization.

While victimization of the elderly is a problem, its occurrence is relatively less than for other age groups, although often more serious (Whitaker, 1987). National Crime Victimization Survey data on elderly victims between 1980 and 1985 indicated that the elderly are proportionately less likely than younger persons to be victims of crime. Whitaker (1987) found that persons under 25 years of age, for example, were about four times more likely to be victims of robbery than the elderly population. NCVS data have confirmed this finding: "Persons between ages 12 and 15 and between 16 and 19 had higher rates of violent crime victimization than those 25 or older . . . Persons age 12 [to] 19 had a violent crime victimization rate 20 times higher than those age 65 or older" (Ringel, 1997). Also, for persons between 25 and 49 years of age the incidence of robbery and assault were two and eight times, respectively, more probable than for a corresponding group of the elderly.

For the six years from 1992 through 1997, the elderly made up 15 percent of the population age 12 or older, but accounted for 7 percent of measured crimes (Klaus, 2000, p. 1). In California, "The number of reported homicides committed against senior citizens declined 46.5 [percent] from 226 in 1988 to 121 in 1998 . . . From 1997 to 1998 the homicide rate per 100,000 declined 16.7 percent for the entire population, from 7.8 to 6.5. The senior citizen homicide rate per 100,000 declined 13.3 [percent] from 3.0 in 1997 to 2.6 in 1998" (Lockyear, 2000, p. 10). Similar declines occurred for crimes such as robbery, although aggravated assaults increased 9.7 percent from 1988 to 1998 (p. 16).

Because the incidence of crime against the elderly is lower than other age groups, public concern has shifted from the actual extent of crimes against the elderly to an examination of their exaggerated fear of crime, especially as other victim groups have achieved a priority, such as drunk driving and random violence victims. Senior citizens perceive more serious consequences in terms of monetary damage and mental anguish. In fact, the elderly are often victims of more serious crimes than younger persons. Whitaker (1987) found that elderly victims of violent crimes were more likely to be confronted by offenders armed with guns than younger victims (16% versus 12%); the offenders were more often total strangers (62% versus 47%); and, these crimes were likely to occur at or near the homes of the elderly.

Most important, the elderly were less likely than younger victims to attempt to protect themselves during a crime incident (52% versus 72%), and, as noted by Alston (1986), crimes against them were more likely to be completed than just attempted. Whitaker (1987), however, found no differences between persons 65 and older and younger persons in the proportion being attacked or injured, or for the amount of loss sustained. Alston (1986) reported similar findings, concluding that theft-related crimes dominated victimization of the elderly.

Clemente and Kleiman (1976, p. 207) found that while actual rates of crime against the elderly were lower, fear of crime among the elderly was "real and pervasive." Lindquist and Duke (1982) explained this paradox as a function of the risk of victimization experienced by the elderly. This fear is sometimes referred to as "vicarious victimization," a fear not based on anything that has happened to the individual but one that has been created by publicity about a few crimes (Lent & Harpold, 1988). Warr (1994), citing the low incidence of risk among females and the elderly who fear crime the most, refers to the "paradox of fear" (p. 12). Taylor and Hale (1986, p. 156) define this phenomenon as the "indirect victimization perspective," wherein criminal events send out "shock waves" throughout community social networks that amplify feelings of fear. These fears, real or imagined, lead to isolation and erosion in the quality of the lives of older persons. They may lead to mental or physical stress sufficient to concern families, health and social agencies, and others concerned about the elderly.

Alston (1986) found that for minor crimes "victimization has few long-lasting psychological or behavioral consequences," but for personal crimes the result is more damaging. Being a victim of crime is a stressful event. Coakley and Woodford-Williams (1979) document cases where being a victim of a crime has affected physical and mental well-being. They found that even petty theft could set in motion a sequence of events involving extreme agitation, restlessness, and deterioration of health, immobility, and sometimes confinement to bed.

Vulnerability and Fear

Vulnerability, the potential for serious consequences, and loss of control are key variables in explaining fear of crime by women and low-income nonwhites at any age, and these fears are exaggerated for the elderly (Alston, 1986). Other determinants of fear of crime are a sense of powerlessness, alienation, and low self-esteem. The impact of actual victimization is greater because it confirms these feelings of vulnerability and powerlessness. Alston (1986), however, indicates that the connection between powerlessness and more pronounced reactions to victimization, while plausible, has not been adequately tested, and that elderly persons with greater financial resources may be less fearful. She notes that there are many dimensions to power. For example, the loss of physical power may serve to heighten the fear of crime, and the greater financial resources necessary to change one's physical environment to more secure conditions may serve to enhance feelings of personal safety.

Yin (1980) addressed three dimensions of fear of crime, assuming that several characteristics influence fear of crime in the elderly. These were the demographic characteristics of elderly "fearful" individuals, the social determinants of fear, and the psychological determinants of fear. Demographic characteristics were age, gender, income, and residential locale, which included living alone, ability to get around, contact with neighbors, and actual prior victimization experience. Social determinants included living arrangements, community contact (i.e., social support), and prior victimizations. Psychological determinants were essentially perceptions of the seriousness of crime and the chances of being victimized. Yin (1980) was concerned that researchers might err in using only estimates of the probability of being victimized as the "implicit" cause of fear of crime in the elderly. Fear is based on other factors, such as possible injury from crime and the ability to recuperate from it and/or related economic loss. Thus, three factors—the probability of victimization, the seriousness of injury, and recuperative ability—were seen as critical to a full analysis of the problem. Warr and Stafford (1983; see also Warr, 1994) found that both perceived risk and perceived seriousness of victimization were necessary elements in developing a fear of crime.

Regardless of the source of the fear of crime, or its reality, the critical concern is how this fear affects the overall well-being of all members of the community, especially the elderly. The sense of well-being is sometimes expressed as a measure of morale or satisfaction gained from living in a particular neighborhood. Yin (1982) asked elderly subjects questions relating to feelings of safety in their respective neighborhoods, followed by more general questions about problems and worries in their lives, controlling for neighborhood satisfaction, morale, and involuntary isolation. He found that fear of crime itself was not as important as other factors in the lives of the elderly, particularly social support. Morale was seen as strongly related to feelings of safety in a neighborhood.

In summary, a fear of crime can be generated by actual crimes in the community or elsewhere, which are usually reported by the media. This fear can be exacerbated by actual victimization and/or feelings of vulnerability. Fear, real or imagined, may be mediated by the ability to cope with it in some way, often simply by having greater economic resources. These factors represent the linkages between crime and fear. Eventually, fear affects the individual, as suggested by Yin (1980), both with respect to lifestyle and overall well-being. Actual victimization serves to heighten these fears for personal safety and feeds into the causal loop that creates additional fear in the community. The concern is how this real or imagined fear affects the overall well-being of the elderly. It includes a consideration of the relationship between fear of crime and the individual's physical and mental health.

A Study of Crime against the Elderly

A Florida study looked at how a sample of 1,448 elderly individuals who expressed a fear of crime were affected mentally and physically. Is expressing a fear of crime related to the mental or physical health or general well-being of the elderly? The behavioral model used in the study considered fear of crime as part of more general concerns for overall well-being of the elderly, which include the need for personal safety. Feelings of well-being in the elderly are, in turn, dependent on a set of socioeconomic, attitudinal, and physical and mental health variables. While fear of crime was seen as related to several factors beyond just the probability of victimization, being a victim of any type of crime in the last year was thought to be a principal indicator of reduced feelings of personal safety and subsequent physical and mental deterioration, (i.e., a reduced sense of well-being). Standardized logistic regression models were constructed to determine the effect of these variables on the elderly population-at-risk regarding their feelings of personal safety; essentially, vulnerability may precede and exacerbate feelings that crime is a problem. Findings suggested that efforts to manage fear of crime in the elderly should focus on mental health and physical problems generally rather than simply those related to crime victimization.

Socioeconomic variables that were examined included gender, race, immigrant status, and income. Residential variables included whether subjects were living alone and whether they could get around the neighborhood (i.e., their mobility as an indicator of feelings of security in the neighborhood.) Of the psychological determinants evaluated, the feeling of being safe alone in the neighborhood was used. Physical and mental health variables included providing self-reported physical health and mental health ratings to the interviewers, indicating feelings of being relaxed or tension-free, having a bright future outlook, whether loneliness was a problem, and feeling like crying or feeling depressed. Respondents provided a rating of their general satisfaction with life and any indications of generally feeling fearful.

Subjects' assessments of their physical and mental well-being were used in the analysis of the effects of fear of crime and actual victimization. Thus, it could be ascertained whether an individual who is fearful of crime reported that his or her physical or mental health was affected. Subsequent to the regression analysis to determine those variables that contribute to fear of crime, fear of crime was correlated with physical and mental health variables to determine the significance of the relationship between them and fear. Standardized logistic regression models were constructed to determine the effect of socioeconomic characteristics and attitudes of the elderly population at risk on their perception of crime as a problem (cf. McFadden, 1973). In our case, given a set of independent characteristics of the population of concern, this would involve predicting the probability that any demographic or attitudinal variable used would influence the fear of crime.

Data for the study were obtained by a telephone survey of 1,448 elderly citizens, aged 60 or over by the Center for Aging, Florida International University, with the cooperation of the United Way of Dade County. The phone survey used a two-stage random digit dialing sample design, yielding a random sample of the noninstitutionalized population 60 and over. The sample was stratified with respect to geographic considerations within the county to capture the effect of racial and ethnic characteristics of different neighborhoods. Initial contacts screened out businesses, institutions, and nonoperating numbers. If more than one person in a household was over 60, the actual person to be interviewed was randomly selected from this group. It was estimated that 6.9 percent of the older population did not have telephones and, therefore, could not be included in the sample. Native-born Americans (n=746) constituted a little more than half of the survey population. Slightly less than half of the respondents (n=702) claimed to have as their place of birth a country other than the United States. Of these, 470 gave Cuba as their country of birth. For purposes of analysis, the 702 individuals who claimed a country other than the United States represented the immigrant sub-population.

The survey instrument was designed to assess the problems and needs of the elderly population of Dade County, Florida. The majority of survey items were previously used and validated from studies in Detroit, Michigan, the so-called little Havana area of Miami, and other national needs assessment studies. A total of 297 questions were asked of each respondent in extensive telephone interviews lasting an average of forty minutes. Topics included demography, social status, fear of crime, health-related issues, discrimination, social needs, and behavior. Questions were asked in the same way by each interviewer and the sequence of questions was fixed and identical for each completed interview. Ongoing auditing, supervision, and quality assurance checks contributed to the accuracy of these data.

Logistic regression analysis determined that the variables significantly related to crime as a problem for this elderly sample were being female, having a higher income, a lack of mobility in the community (mobility), being a victim of crime in the last year. Feeling safe alone in the neighborhood was most significantly related to a lower fear of crime. Race, ethnicity, immigrant status, and living alone do not appear to predict a fear of crime, which was not expected based on comparable findings from other research (Ragan, 1977; Whitaker, 1987). In their discussion of crime against elderly immigrant Jews in the crime-ridden Strawberry Mansion section of Philadelphia, Dussich and Eichman (1976) note that residents were more often "single and widowed . . . foreign born, and had a much lower income (p. 96). They either choose or are trapped in environments where they pay low rent or own their homes and cannot afford to move (p. 96). Due to their location in the community they suffer deprivations in health care, neighborhood mobility, leisure time activity, peer interaction, morale, and housing satisfaction. Dussich and Eichman (1976) suggest a "differential vulnerability" hypothesis with respect to the inability of the elderly to escape from crime-ridden environments. That is, they are primarily vulnerable when they leave their isolation in these communities.

Using chi-square tests, mental and physical health variables were compared separately with fear of crime in the past year. Findings indicate that elderly individuals who reported no fear of crime were more relaxed, had a more positive view of the future, and reported better physical health with fewer reporting health problems. They rated their mental health better and were less likely to report "feeling fearful" generally. These findings are consistent with the view that fear of crime is only one dimension of a poor sense of well-being overall.

Conclusions and Implications

Based on a survey conducted in Florida in 1987, elderly persons who report fewer mental and physical health problems also report fewer problems with crime. Deterioration in mental and physical health does not necessarily appear to be the result of being a victim of a crime, as suggested by Coakley and Woodford-Williams (1979). In this study there is a strong level of association between variables related to mental health and fear of crime. Fear of crime appears more likely to be the product of feelings of depression rather than the result of actual crimes committed against these individuals. This is not to say, however, that victims of crime do not show signs of mental and physical deterioration. It does suggest that those who do show such deterioration probably have been depressed or physically limited prior to their victimization.

Conclusions do not provide support for Alston's (1986) finding that personal crimes result in longer-lasting psychological and behavioral consequences. The consequences of being a victim of crime appear to be more closely related to one's mental and physical health prior to victimization. Contrary to the conclusions of Clemente and Kleiman (1976), it may be the case that the "isolation and erosion" in the quality of these individual's lives began to occur prior to, or are occurring concurrent with, an increased fear of crime. These are the conditions that lead to vulnerability and loss of control that are consistent with Alston's (1986) analysis of fear of crime in the elderly. Concern must shift to individual factors that condition the fear of crime rather than with crime itself.

Findings are consistent with Yin's (1980) thesis that perceptions of the seriousness of crime and the chances of being victimized are important psychological determinants of fear. Elderly people who perceive themselves as vulnerable appear to be so in many areas of life. These "vulnerables" are less likely to feel safe alone in the neighborhood. They are less able to get around the community, and they appear unable to find companionship or "solidarity" within their neighborhood sufficient to overcome their fears.

What can be done to deal with fear of crime among the elderly or any group of citizens who live in fear of crime? Clearly, the reduction of crime is the ideal. However, if the fear is perceived but not necessarily real, the primary target is a reduction in that fear. But how should this be accomplished? One approach might be the organization of the elderly into groups (by blocks or areas) to discuss actual criminal activity in the community. This could help dispel rumors, and perhaps could provide support to those who have been victimized. If, however, fear of crime feeds primarily on predisposing mental and physical problems, as suggested by these data, such a plan can only be a first step. It is imperative that social agencies and health care professionals, especially mental health professionals, be alerted to the need go beyond simply educating the elderly. They must identify also the "vulnerable elderly" and arrange special assistance for them.

For the "vulnerable elderly," social, police, and mental health agency professionals should first deal with the depression and anxiety that often accompany many problems, including a fear of crime. Being an actual victim of crime, of course, could only confirm their fears and exacerbate the original symptoms for these individuals. In any case, efforts to improve general mental or physical functioning may assist the elderly also in coping with other problems that beset them, be they real or imagined. This suggests that just organizing all elderly citizens into groups to discuss crime problems may not be as important as assisting them in all areas of their lives, and that some may require more attention than others to overcome their fears.

Prison Costs

A major cost of crime is the cost of incarceration in prison, jail, and mental institutions, which is included in the cost estimates cited above. The political climate surrounding increases in violent crime in America, and in many other industrial societies, became more conservative since the 1980s. This development had an impact also on penal philosophy and practice, with a strong emphasis on effectively controlling a so-called dangerous population and the effective management of the criminal justice system. These developments were reflected in the get tough attitude toward crime, the declaration of war on drugs, the legislation of increasingly severe penalties culminating in more mandatory prison terms, and various three-strikes statutes, which are of questionable effectiveness (see Dickey & Hollenhorst, 1998).

As a result of changing policy, prison and jail populations have grown rapidly. For example, the U.S. prison and jail population (state and federal) grew from 1,148,702 at the end of 1990 to 1,931,859 by midyear 2000, a 68.2 percent increase (Beck & Karberg, 2001), with concomitant increases in correctional costs at all levels of government (Maguire & Pastore, 1999, Table 12 p. 3; U.S. Department of Justice, 1998). States spent about $22 billion on prisons in fiscal year 1996 (Stephan, 1999).

California, once a progressive state in correctional programs, serves as an example of the costs involved in the use of prisons. California now leads the nation with over 164,000 prison inmates, up from a population of 23,000 in 1970, a six-fold increase. More offenders are getting prison sentences, and for longer periods of time. Nationally, "Seventy-five percent of state inmates and 60 percent of federal inmates in 1997 reported that they had served prior sentences" (Stana, 2000, p. 4). New *truth in sentencing* laws were put in place in many states in the late 1980s in response to fear about crime. These laws, which generally preceded *three strikes and you're out* laws, are designed ensure that offenders, especially violent offenders, serve a larger proportion of their sentences (see Austin & Irwin, 2001). A BJS report states that "Prisoners released in 1996 served on average 30 months in prison and jail or 44 [percent] of their sentence . . . [and] Nearly 7 in 10 state prison admissions in 1997 were in states requiring offenders to serve at least 85 [percent] of their sentence" (Ditton & Wilson, 1999, p. 1). A major reason for the increase in prison populations in the United States has been the increased length of sentences for offenders.

Data for selected years from 1880 to 1972 to 1973 indicate that inmates who committed crimes against other persons (homicide, assault, rape, and robbery) went from 23.3 percent of all inmates in 1880 to 39.1 percent in 1972 to 1973, a progressive increase. Federal Bureau of Justice Statistics (BJS) comparisons found that 57.9 percent of all inmates in 1979 were convicted of a violent offense, although this proportion rises about 10 percent when either the current or past violent offenses are also used (Innes, 1988, p. 2). In 1997, 47 percent of all state inmates and 15 percent of federal inmates were in prison for violent offenses (Stana, 2000, p. 4), which is a decrease from 1979. A 1995 report on violent offenders in state prison documents the numbers of violent offenders in prison for each state (Beck & Greenfeld, 1995), noting that the average time served for all violent offenses is 46 percent of the sentence received, ranging from 47 percent for murder to 41 percent for robbery (p. 2). One-third (33.4%) of the 105,790 juveniles in public or private detention in 1997 were there for violent offenses, 1.8 percent for murder, 8.9 percent for robbery, and 9 percent for aggravated assault (Maguire & Pastore, 1999).

One reason for the increases in prison and jail populations is the increase in prison and jail construction over the past twenty years, which has been documented by Austin and Irwin (2001). They report BJS figures that indicate "Between 1990 and 1998, the bed capacity of the country's prison system increased by approximately 350,000 beds from 580,362 to 933,478" (p. 93). The costs of new construction are documented by the American Correctional Association (Gondles, 2000) for fiscal 1998, which were $2.1 billion in new construction projects, $841 million in major renovation, and $1.2 billion in maintenance, repair, and so on (p. 5). There were 155 major new projects under way with 47,293 new beds planned. For juvenile corrections, comparable expenditures are $350 million in new construction, $76.4 million in major renovation, and $35.3 million in maintenance, repair, and so on. There were 66 major new projects under way with 1,370 new beds planned.

Prison Costs in California

During the decade of 1980–1989, California spent $3.2 billion to house 86,000 inmates in space designed for 50,458. In 1998, with an annual budget of $3.7 billion, a staff of 41,161, and 33 prisons, California has 75,079 beds to hold 144,897 prisoners, 93 percent over design capacity (CDC Facts, 1998). California prison construction has been nothing short of incredible, claiming the largest prison building program in the United States at a cost of $5.7 billion. A new institution in California can cost from $90 to $230 million and provide 700 to 1,200 jobs, with an additional 350 to 600 new jobs generated in the community. The annual payroll will be about $20 to $35 million, and $2 million per year will be purchased in local goods and services. A 1989 survey of all correctional systems found California with the highest reported costs for new construction at $1.29 billion for 15,030 beds, a cost of $84,000 per bed.

The 1993 to 1994 state budget provided $200 million more for the California Department of Corrections (CDC) than 1992 to 1993. The CDC operating budget is approaching three billion dollars per year. California's Blue Ribbon Commission on Inmate Population Management (Trask, 1990) estimated that an additional $5.22 billion would be needed by 1994 to meet current jail, prison, and youth facility needs. This is in addition to the $3 billion already spent in the 1980s. During the years of increasing inmate populations concerns with planning, research, staff training, and inmate programs of all types have been pushed aside to create and operate more prisons. Security has been the major concern, and at great cost.

California is spending from its general fund at twice the rate of health, education, and human services agencies—largely to provide prison beds. As noted earlier, the RAND study of projected costs for the three strikes laws in California found that higher education's share of the general fund fell from 17 percent to 12 percent in the 25 years before the law (Greenwood et al., 1999). The Justice Policy Institute found that [in California] "from 1984 [to] 1992 spending per $1,000 of personal income increased less than 1 [percent] for higher education while the increase for prisons was 47%"(Carter, 1998, p. 15). The Legislative Analyst's Office (1993, p. 7) noted that "Spending for corrections increased, on average, about 15 percent annually while total state spending increased about 7 percent per year over the past decade." Austin and Irwin (2001) found similar comparisons for New York State where "since 1988, spending for New York's public universities has dropped by 29 percent, while funding for prisons has increased by 76 percent" (p. 222), an overall decline in real dollars for education as compared to prisons.

Have these expenditures and related programs been successful in reducing crime and improving the public safety? Austin and Irwin (2001) argue that this has not happened. There is talk of "new approaches" in many quarters to a problem that appears to be out of hand—that is, we have too many people in prison and it is costing too much. Can we ensure the public safety at less cost, perhaps so we can invest scarce dollars in areas of potential prevention? The California Blue Ribbon Commission found its criminal justice system out of balance with respect to the broad range of activities needed for an effective system. They called for more prevention programs, the greater use intermediate sanctions (fines, restitution, house arrest, etc.) for certain nonviolent, noncareer offenders, including less serious juvenile offenders, and a greater concern for community programs. However, probably due to the punitive climate of the times, no mention was made of working with violent offenders in or outside institutions.

The Commission's report concluded that *the relationship between public safety, recidivism, and drug abuse is undeniable and significant.* Drug and alcohol abuse was found to be a major contributor to the increase in parole violators and new commitments to the CDC, the California Youth Authority (prison), and local corrections. However, CDC has very few drug and alcohol treatment programs in its prisons or available to parolees that would intervene with this major contributor to criminality. There is little legislative action nor are there adequate resources for the corrections system to do anything significant with substance abusers while they are confined.

The Commission said that model substance abuse programs should include treatment in the early stages of the inmate's incarceration; a multifaceted continuum of care; treatment provided over a long period of time that would increase in intensity; and, inmate involvement in prerelease programming.

If programs are put in place, what real evidence is there that they will work? The best hope may simply be that they are less expensive than prisons at more than $22,000 per prisoner per year. Alternatives and prevention programs, to the extent they can be used with aggressive or violent individuals, must be properly funded and adequately monitored and evaluated for effectiveness. Community residential programs can cost half this figure per year per bed and nonresidential programs much less. Illegal substance abuse is the leading reason for parole failure. Substance abusers must be kept in treatment longer because, upon departure from institutions, relapse occurs within a year for about two-thirds of these individuals. Additional cycles of treatment, relapse, and treatment are associated with slow improvements toward rehabilitation. Drug treatment programs are too few, and many are too poorly funded to be effective in the public or private sector.

Categories of Violent Acts and the Helping Strategies for Victims and Perpetrators: The Danger of Panaceas

Various quick solutions to the problems of aggressive behavior and violent crime have been proposed. Many of these are grouped under the rubric of shock programs designed to bring the individual back to a law-abiding life by a short and intense taste of punishment. These include Scared Straight, an intense exposure to prison life by inmates in prisons, and prison boot camps designed to teach respect for authority and proper values. Other less severe methods include the use of house arrest, weekend sentences, electronic monitoring, intensive probation, or parole supervision (see Gottfredson, 1999). Apparent frustration with these so-called solutions has given way to punishments designed with long, fixed prison sentences, such as truth in sentencing and three strikes laws. Americans want a magic bullet—a social Salk vaccine—aimed at a solution for our hemorrhaging crime problem. This is the American way. Americans want solutions to problems that are fast and effective, like the Gulf War, but not untidy ones like the assault on the Branch Davidian compound in Waco, Texas on April 19, 1993 by the Federal Bureau of Alcohol, Tobacco, and Firearms, where more than eighty individuals died. Unfortunately, crime, and especially violent crime, is a difficult target for immediate reform, although newer approaches are being tried in law enforcement and in the treatment of violent perpetrators using public health approaches (see Roth & Moore, 1995).

Panacea-type solutions such as boot camps for young offenders rarely work well. They do not and often cannot address deeply entrenched problems that actually require well-planned, long-term approaches. Regardless of what has been seen in the media, there is not one iota of evidence that these programs work for the offenders who need to be reached. Yet these tired old purgatives linger on. In fact, just before the television version of Scared Straight was aired in late 1978, the New Jersey Department of Corrections evaluated the program and did not find such astounding success rates. Scared Straight only *seemed* to be effective in changing behavior. Also, staff recommended that the Lifer's Group at Rahway Prison discontinue their use of threatening and intimidating tactics and the use of false or exaggerated information, and that less serious juveniles be screened out of participation. Later investigation found that the seventeen volunteers for Scared Straight were not hard-core juveniles, as characterized. In the 1987 ten-year televised follow-up, only nine of the seventeen were interviewed; two were criminals, one in prison.

In 1977, Dr. James Finkenauer of Rutgers University did an intensive evaluation of the Rahway Scared Straight program, following accepted social science research procedures. Using a standardized delinquency prediction scale, only 8 percent of the juveniles in the program had a high probability of delinquent behavior; 20 percent had a medium probability, and the rest (over 70%) a low probability. Up to 60 percent of all the youth who participated had never been in a correctional institution or had contact with the law. In comparisons between Scared Straight participants and nonparticipants, there were no significant differences in attitudes toward the law or justice, toward police, or toward punishment. Comparisons of juvenile court records showed that the participants committed more offenses and more serious offenses after the program than nonparticipants.

So, if we can't scare them out of crime, we'll drill it out of them! Georgia, Florida, Louisiana, and Mississippi tried the boot camp prisons, and a later program in California for young offenders was not successful. Not unlike Scared Straight, emphasis is on the use of fear and intimidation to transform young offenders into confident, upstanding citizens, using a program of about ninety days of grueling paramilitary spit and polish. Note, however, that boot camp graduates with a G.E.D. diploma won't be accepted by the military. High success rates for boot camp graduates are claimed, with no evidence of how these people were selected or what the dropout rate might be. These programs may be successful for some types of inmates, although they must be properly evaluated, and abuses can occur. In the 1960s several drug rehabilitation programs found that confrontation or haircut-type approaches, were damaging to some individuals. Most evaluations of shock programs, whether jail, prison, or probation, have shown that gains are most often short-term unless follow-up is available. Sometimes even more hostility toward the system is engendered. Current evaluations of boot camp approaches are not encouraging.

Both Scared Straight and the boot camp programs appeared to be right, based on what many people understand to be how punishment works. But organizations such as the American Correctional Association note, "This deeply-rooted social problem [of juvenile delinquency] cannot be eradicated by exposing juveniles to threats of force, intimidation, verbal abuse, or other practices that are meant to shock youths out of delinquent-prone behavior." Most experts agree that without the help of the family, and without addressing social problems emanating from poor schools, unemployment, poverty, and racial discrimination, there is little likelihood that the scare or the drill will last for any length of time. The inmates doing life sentences at Rahway know this and tried to develop a follow-up program for the kids they contacted. Real long-term effects will be achieved only if the youth involved can get help from individuals and organizations committed to long-term programs of assistance, including the utilization of legitimate alternatives to crime and violence in American society.

Prisons and jails are seen by the general public as easy solutions to social problems, and many violent offenders reside in them who need to be there. Indeed, the punishment through prisons approach has been tried in recent times. What has been done in California and in the nation for the past dozen years has been dubbed "the great conservative experiment." According to a federal criminal justice official, they "met the challenge of the 1980s" by imprisoning four times the adult offenders as in the mid-1960s, and also doubling juvenile incarceration rates. The United States now leads the world in rates of incarceration per 100,000 citizens. All across the country the social engineers tinkered with the figures on our criminal justice system to determine if prisons, and later alternative sanctions, could decrease crime through the use of punishment. They (and we) look at the numbers and debate whether prisons work in relation to crime reductions. There is some evidence that the incarceration strategy, coupled with other factors, has been a factor in the reductions in crime and violence we have experienced in recent times, although some researchers dispute this conclusion.

Convincing arguments can be made that prisons are not as effective a response as we may hope. Austin and Irwin (2001) could find little support for the argument that more incarceration yields declining crime; the relationship is not a clear one. They also found that the public is not convinced that prisons are the answer for nonviolent offenders, although prisons themselves have become more violent places for all inmates. They lament America's "imprisonment binge," noting that the cost of a projected 260,000 new prison beds (nationwide) would be nearly $30 billion (p. 241). Nonetheless, many Americans believe these tougher approaches are the best answer to the problems of crime and violence. We want less crime and violence.

Many questions are raised: Are our streets and homes really safer than they were in 1980, which was the benchmark year for change in the criminal justice system? How do drug arrests affect crime, especially violent crime, and prison and jail populations? Crime rates are down nationally and in California, but have shown periodic fluctuations that make us uneasy, especially in violent crimes and for different age groups. Snyder et al. (1996) report that the number of juveniles murdered increased 82 percent between 1984 and 1994, and Fox (1996, p. 2) found that the homicide rate among 18 to 24 year olds increased 61 percent between 1985 and 1994, from 15.7 to 25.3 per 100,000. James Alan Fox, Dean of the College of Criminal Justice at Northeastern University, in his report to the U.S. Attorney General on Youth Violence, *Trends in Juvenile Violence* (1996, p. 1), stated that "there are actually two crime trends in America, one for the young, one for the mature, which are moving in opposite directions." He continues:

The recent surge in youth crime actually occurred while the population of teenagers was on the decline. But this demographic benefit is about to change. As a consequence of the "baby boomerang" (the offspring of the baby boomers), there are now 39 million children in this country who are under the age of ten, more young children than we've had for decades.

More recently, Fox (1997) reports that recent population projections indicate a substantial increase in the percentage of juveniles in the general population in the next ten years, particularly African Americans and Hispanics (p. 1).

As the population in the United States ages and the youth population grows, which it appears to be doing, the problem of fear of crime may be exacerbated in society. As shown in Figure 3.1, population figures for 1995 foresee a minority youth cohort within the next five to ten years that may, in fact, begin to drive violent crime rates higher. In documenting homicide trends for the Bureau of Justice Statistics, Fox and Zawitz (2000) note "Despite the encouraging improvements since 1993, levels of youth homicide remain well above those of the early and mid-1980s" (p. 2). In order to reduce violent crime, it will be necessary to address the needs of this youthful cohort. As Hawkins, Herrenkohl, Farrington, Brewer, Catalano, Harachi, and Cothern (2000) indicate, "The best predictors of violent or serious delinquency differ according to age group. A juvenile offense at ages 6 [to]11 is the strongest predictor of subsequent violent or serious delinquency" (p. 6), and it is the second strongest predictor for 12 to 14 year olds.

Prison populations are up, and they are driven by drug arrests, even though drug arrest rates (per 100,000 population at risk) have shown an overall decrease of 13.6 percent since 1986 for adults and 43 percent for juveniles. Adult felony new admissions to the California Department of Corrections (CDC) for drug offenses has more than doubled, increasing 127 percent from 1986 to 1991 (to 12,459). Drug offenders now make up 24.5 percent of the prison population, a 194 percent increase since the end of 1986. The vast majority of prisoners have experienced serious drug or alcohol problems, and few mechanisms exist for treating these problems. CDC's five formal substance abuse treatment programs reach less than 4 percent of the total CDC population (CDC Facts, 1998).

In fact, imprisonment alone does not appear to reduce crime. Other efforts must continue. A good example is the effort to reduce drunk driving traffic fatalities through the passage of stricter laws, especially for youthful drivers. Fatalities have gone down. However, evidence shows that movements, such as Mothers Against Drunk Drivers (MADD), have had an equally strong impact on this problem.

There are no easy, quick, miracle cures. It is doubtful that the problems found in prison populations can be managed without the help of families, and without addressing social problems emanating from poor schools, unemployment, poverty, and racial discrimination. Experts agree that young people require well-rounded, community-based programs that will assist them in growth at home, in school, and in finding and financing education and training for jobs. Shock and scare programs, prison boot camps, fixed sentence lengths, intermedi-

ate sanctions, intensive supervision, decriminalization of drugs, and other so-
called instant solutions for individuals who have resorted to crime will not have
a long-term deterrent effect if these people cannot get satisfaction through legitimate alternatives in society. Solutions must address deeply rooted social and economic problems. While these solutions are not necessarily inexpensive, they can
be less expensive than prisons and the long-term benefits can be far greater.

The need for reforms must not become a partisan political issue, although
the methods to be used should be debated. Neither liberal nor conservative approaches appear to yield ideal solutions. Perhaps there is a middle ground that
will satisfy all concerned—what is referred to in California as a balanced approach. No one would disagree that dangerous, violent offenders should be incarcerated, especially when they show that their behavior will not change. Scarce
prison space should always be available for these individuals. But what about the
others?

It appears that there has been a failure of organizations and leadership in
addressing these problems both in California and nationally. We do not have
the leadership necessary to reform the organizations that cannot deal with the
problem at its sources. Past approaches to social problems have been only
partially successful or not successful at all because resources have not reached
those affected in a way that has allowed for the maximum positive impact on
them.

One reason these programs have not been successful, or reached their respective potentials, may be because problems are attacked by single social agencies. Thus, only part of complex, multifaceted social problems are addressed.
Limited resources are further diluted in attempting to deal with just one aspect
of these problems. Overlap and waste of resources is found.

There are approaches to a solution. First, we must understand the panacea
phenomenon that is based on short-term policies emanating from proposed single-agency solutions. We must determine how single-agency solutions can be
overcome through multiagency approaches to social problems. We must explore
ways to develop a balance between social policy, research, and practical experience that will serve the interests of society in managing social problems.

Violent crime is costly to society in many ways. Tangible, direct costs to victims
and the intangible costs of pain and suffering coupled with the larger societal
costs of managing violent crime can amount to $450 billion annually for American
society. These costs are too high, and they use resources that should be devoted to
more positive societal goals, including education, youth programs, and needed
social services.

Solutions to violent crime range from strict law enforcement approaches
to efforts to protect citizens, such as the elderly, from violent crime through
prevention, intervention, and efforts at treatment of offenders. Law enforcement
professionals, such as former Sheriff Block of Los Angeles, understand the importance of intervening with violent gangs, helping individuals who may resort
to violence to manage a personal problem, or working with violent or poten-

tially violent offenders of all types. Certainly, social agencies must play a greater role in working with potentially violent or troubled individuals, as well as with victims.

According to Roth and Moore (1995), two movements have emerged as problem-solving approaches to violent crime. Both have gained in public prominence:

> The first is the adoption or revival of policing styles that are variously called *community policing, problem-oriented policing,* or *fixing "hot spots" of violence.* The second movement is called *treatment of violence as a public health problem* . . . [while] both movements . . . emphasize somewhat different priorities and tactics, the problem-solving elements of modern policing and public health complement each other in many ways. (p. 1)

The law enforcement approach is not the subject of this book, although such innovations are important and rapidly developing as efforts to work with troubled individuals in communities. The public health component of working with victims has been suggested, especially in relation to crimes against the elderly. The primary concern of this book is the management of individuals involved in violent behavior within a human services context.

REFERENCES

Alston, L. T. (1986). *Crime and older Americans.* Springfield, IL: Charles C. Thomas.

Austin, J., & Irwin, J. (2001). *It's about time: America's imprisonment binge* (3rd ed). Belmont, CA: Wadsworth.

Austin, J., Clark, J., Hardyman, P., & Henry, A. (1999). The impact of "three strikes and you're out." *Punishment & Society, 1*(2), 131–162.

Beck, A. J., & Greenfeld, L. A. (1995). Violent offenders in state prison: Sentence and time served. *Bureau of Justice Statistics Selected Findings.* Washington, DC: Office of Justice Programs, U.S. Department of Justice.

Beck, A. J., & Karberg, J. C. (2001, March). Prison and jail inmates at midyear 2000. *Bureau of Justice Statistics Bulletin.* Washington, DC: Office of Justice Programs, U.S. Department of Justice.

Carter, B. (1998, November). *"Three strikes": Five years later. Public policy reports.* Washington, DC: Campaign for an Effective Crime Policy.

Clemente, F., & Kleiman, M. B. (1976). Fear of crime among the aged. *Gerontologist, 16*(3), 207–210.

Coakley, D., & Woodford-Williams, E. (1979, November 17). Effects of burglary and vandalism on the health of old people. *The Lancet,* 1066–1067.

Cohen, M. A., Miller, T. R., & Rossman, S. B. (1994). The costs and consequences of violent behavior in the United States. In A. J. Reiss and J. A. Roth (Eds.), *Understanding and preventing violence: Consequences and control* (Vol. 4). Washington, DC: National Academy Press.

Collins, W. (1983, Summer). Black men fighting for their manhood. *Jericho, 32*(5), 8.

Covey, H. C., & Menard, S. (1988). Trends in elderly criminal victimization from 1973 to 1984. *Research on Aging, 10,* 329–341.

CDC Facts. (1998). *About the department.* [Online]. California Department of Corrections, Communications Office. Available: *www.cdc.state.ca.us/cdcfacts.htm.*

Dickey, W. J., & Hollenhorst, P. S. (1998). Three strikes: Five years later. *Public policy reports.* Washington, DC: Campaign for an Effective Crime Policy.

Ditton, P., & Wilson, D. J. (1999). Truth in sentencing in state prisons. *Bureau of Justice Statistics Special Report.* Washington, DC: Office of Justice Programs, U.S. Department of Justice.

Dussich, J. P., & Eichman, C. J. (1976). The elderly victim: Vulnerability to the criminal act. In J. Goldsmith and S. Goldsmith, (Eds.), *Crime and the elderly: Challenge and response.* Lexington, MA: D.C. Heath.

Evans, C. (1994, June). *Colorado Business, 21*(6), 10.

Fox, J. A. (1996). *Trends in juvenile violence.* Washington, DC: Bureau of Justice Statistics, U.S. Department of Justice.

Fox, J. A. (1997, March). *Trends in juvenile homicide.* An update of the March, 1996 Report to the U.S. Attorney General on Current and Future Rates of Juvenile Violence. Washington, DC: Bureau of Justice Statistics, U.S. Department of Justice.

Fox, J. A., & Zawitz, M. W. (2000). *Homicide trends in the United States: 1988 update.* Washington, DC: Office of Justice Programs, Bureau of Justice Statistics, U.S. Department of Justice.

Gondles, J. A. (2000). *Vital statistics in corrections.* Lanham, MD: American Correctional Association.

Gottfredson, D. M. (1999). *Exploring criminal justice: An introduction.* Los Angeles, CA: Roxbury.

Graber, D. A. (1980). *Crime news and the public.* New York: Praeger.

Greenwood, P., Rydell, C. P., Abrahamse, A. F., Caulkins, J. P., Chiesa, J., Model, K., & Klein, S. P. (1999). Implementing the law. In D. Shichor and D. K. Sechrest, *Three strikes and you're out: Vengeance as public policy.* Thousand Oaks, CA: Sage.

Greenwood, P., Rydell, C. P., Abrahamse, A. F., Caulkins, J. F., Chiesa, J., Model, K. E., & Klein, S. P. (1999). Estimated benefits and costs of California's new mandatory sentencing law. In D. Shichor and D. K. Sechrest, *Three strikes and you're out: Vengeance as public policy.* Thousand Oaks, CA: Sage.

Harlow, C. W. (1989). *Injuries from crime.* Washington, DC: Bureau of Justice Statistics, U.S. Department of Justice.

Harlow, C. W. (1994). *Comparing federal and state prison inmates 1991.* Washington, DC: Bureau of Justice Statistics, U.S. Department of Justice.

Harlow, C. W. (1998, April). *Profile of jail inmates 1996.* Washington, DC: Bureau of Justice Statistics, U.S. Department of Justice.

Hawkins, J. D., Herrenkohl, T. I., Farrington, D. P., Brewer, D., Catalano, R. F., Harachi, T. W., & Cothern, L. (2000). Predictors of youth violence. *Bureau of Justice Statistics Juvenile Justice Bulletin.* Washington, DC: Office of Juvenile Justice and Delinquency Prevention, U.S. Department of Justice.

Innes, C. A. (1988, January) *Profile of state prison inmates, 1986.* Washington, DC: Bureau of Justice Statistics, U.S. Department of Justice.

Kilpatrick, D. G., Resnick, H. S., Saunders, B. E., & Best, C. L. (1994). Survey research on violence against women: Measuring violent assaults against women. Paper presented at the 46th annual meeting of the American Society of Criminology, Miami, FL.

Klaus, P. A. (1994). The costs of crime to victims. *Bureau of Justice Statistics Crime Data Brief.* Washington, DC: Office of Justice Programs, U.S. Department of Justice.

Klaus, P. A. (2000, January). *Crimes against persons age 65 or older, 1992–1997.* Washington, DC: Office of Justice Programs, Bureau of Justice Statistics, U.S. Department of Justice.

LaGrange, R. L., & Ferraro, K. F. (1987). The elderly's fear of crime: A critical examination of the research. *Research on Aging, 9,* 372–391.

Legislative Analyst's Office [California]. (1993). *Proposition 184—The 'Three Strikes and You're Out" Law.* Sacramento, CA.

Lent, C. J., & Harpold, J. A. (1988). Violent crime against the aging. *FBI Law Enforcement Bulletin, 57,* 11–19.

Levitt, S. D. (1996). The effect of prison population size on crime rates: Evidence from prison overcrowding litigation. *Quarterly Journal of Economics 3*(2), 319–351.

Lindquist, J. H., & Duke, J. M. (1982). The elderly victim at risk. *Criminology, 20,* 115–126.

Lockyear, B. (2000, January). *Report on violent crimes committed against senior citizens in California, 1998.* Sacramento, CA: Criminal Justice Statistics Center, California Department of Justice.

Maguire, K., & Pastore, A. L. (Eds). (1999). *Sourcebook of criminal justice.* Washington, DC: Bureau of Justice Statistics, U.S. Department of Justice.

Marvell, T., & Moody, C. E., Jr. (1994). Prison population growth and crime reduction. *Journal of Quantitative Criminology, 10*(2): 109–140.

McFadden, D. (1973). Conditional logit analysis of qualitative choice behavior. In P. Zarembka (Ed.), *Frontiers in economics.* New York: Academic Press.

Miller, T. R., Cohen, M. A., & Weirsema, B. (1996). *Victim costs and consequences: A new look.* Washington, DC: National Institute of Justice.

Moore, M. H., Prothrow-Stith, D., Guyer, B., & Spivak, H. (1997). Violence and intentional injuries: Criminal justice and public health perspectives on an urgent national problem. In C. A Perkins (Ed.), Age patterns of victims of serious violent crime, *Bureau of Justice Statistics Special Report.* Washington, DC: Office of Justice Programs, U.S. Department of Justice.

Reiss, A. J., & Roth, J. A. (Eds.) 1994. *Understanding and preventing violence, volume 4: Consequences and control.* Washington, DC: National Academy Press.

Ragan, P. K. (1977). Crimes against the elderly: Findings from interviews with blacks, Mexican Americans, and whites. In M. A. Y. Rifai (Ed.), *Justice and older Americans.* Lexington, MA: D.C. Heath.

Ringel, C. (1997). Criminal victimization 1996: changes 1995–96 with trends 1993–96. *Bureau of Justice Statistics National Crime Victimization Survey.* Washington, DC: Office of Justice Programs, U.S. Department of Justice.

Roth, J. A., & Moore, M. H. (1995, October). Reducing violent crimes and intentional injuries. *National Institute of Justice Research in Action.* Washington, DC: Office of Justice Programs, U.S. Department of Justice.

Sechrest, D. K., & Siddharthan, K. (1992, August). Health implications of the fear of crime among elderly populations. Unpublished paper using data available from Milan Dluhy and the Southeast Center on Aging, Florida International University.

Shenk, F. J., & Klaus, P. A. (1984, April). The economic cost of crime to victims. *Bureau of Justice Statistics Special Report.* Washington, DC: Office of Justice Programs, U.S. Department of Justice.

Skogan, W. G., & Maxfield, M. G. (1981). *Coping with crime: Individual and neighborhood reactions.* Beverly Hills, CA: Sage.

Snyder, H. N., & Sickmund, M. (1995). *Juvenile offenders and victims: A focus on violence.* Washington, DC: Office of Juvenile Justice and Delinquency Prevention, U.S. Department of Justice.

Snyder, H. N., Sickmund, M., & Poe-Yamagata, E. (1996). *Juvenile offenders and victims: 1996 update on violence.* Washington, DC: Office of Juvenile Justice and Delinquency Prevention, National Center for Juvenile Justice, U.S. Department of Justice.

Stana, R. M. (2000, May). *State and federal prisoners: Profile of inmate characteristics in 1991 and 1997.* Washington, DC: U.S. General Accounting Office.

Stephan, J. J. (1999). *State prison expenditures, 1996.* Washington, DC: Office of Justice Programs, Bureau of Justice Statistics, U.S. Department of Justice.

Taylor, R. B., & Hale, M. (1986). Testing alternative models of fear of crime. *Journal of Criminal Law and Criminology, 77,* 151–189.

Trask II, G. C. (1990). *Blue ribbon commission on inmate population management: Final report, January 1990.* Sacramento, CA: Prison Industry Authority.

U.S. Department of Commerce. (1996). *Statistical abstract of the United States, 1994.* Washington, DC: U.S. Government Printing Office.

Waldfogel, J. (1989). Does the criminal justice system "pay for itself" through deterrence and incapacitation? Working paper, Stanford University.

Warr, M. (1994). Public perceptions and reactions to violent offending and victimization. In A. J. Reiss and J. A. Roth (Eds.), *Understanding and preventing violence, volume 4: Consequences and control*. Washington, DC: National Academy Press.

Warr, M., & Stafford, M. (1983). Fear of victimization: A look at the proximate causes. *Social Forces, 61,* 1033–1043.

Weiss, J. C. (1998). *Crime and justice atlas*. Washington, DC: Justice Research and Statistics Association.

Whitaker, C. J. (1987). Elderly victims. *Special Report*. Washington, DC: Bureau of Justice Statistics.

Yin, P. (1980). Fear of crime among the elderly. *Social Problems, 27,* 492–504.

Yin, P. (1982). Fear of crime as a problem for the elderly. *Social Problems, 30,* 240–245.

Zimring, F. E., & Hawkins, G. (1997). *Crime is not the problem: Lethal violence in America*. New York: Oxford University Press.

PART TWO

Part II of the book deals with violence in actual life situations. Chapters 4, 5, and 6 are about personal violence: in the home, to children, and to intimates and non-intimates in the form of sexual violence. All three chapters have actual case studies and extensive case analysis and include the impact of violence on victims as well as information about perpetrators. All of the case studies include issues related to treatment. While these cases are all real, significant changes have been made in the names and locations of the events to protect confidential information.

As we will note in Chapter 4 on domestic violence, the impact of domestic violence often affects children who observe violence at home. Children in violent homes frequently become victims or perpetrators of violence in their own relationships. Most studies of domestic violence show that men are the primary perpetrators. We agree with this but are concerned about growing indications that women are becoming perpetrators of domestic violence and that their involvement is more than just retaliatory violence in defense of being hurt by the male perpetrator. Nonetheless, domestic violence is a serious problem and the men and women of America are doing harm to themselves and to their children, harm that often reaches the level of serious assaults and homicide.

In Chapter 5, we discuss the issue of child abuse, an increasingly serious problem that affects all ethnicities, socioeconomic groups, and genders. The hitting, neglect, and sexual assault on children is epidemic in America and is, in no small way, a catalyst for later crimes of violence by victims. Graphic case studies of violence to children are presented in this chapter.

Chapter 6 discusses sexual violence, a problem of enormous and profound ramifications to victims in America who include children and adults in ever increasing numbers. Rape has long-term repercussions for victims and represents among the most intrusive and troubling violent crimes in America. As we will note, many of the victims of sexual violence are young women on the university campuses of America who experience date-rape during binge drinking bouts. Children are particularly at risk of molestation and the data since the early 1970s, when child rape was felt to be a very uncommon event, now show us that child molestation has always been and continues to be a very underreported and serious offense affecting far too many American children. Sadly, most sexual abuse of children occurs in their own homes with the molestation done by family members. Very graphic case studies are also provided throughout the chapter.

Chapter 7 discusses juvenile violence and includes discussion of gang-related violence, violence in schools, and the general problem experienced in

America of serious concern for violence among those who are not yet adults. A number of studies are reviewed showing the effectiveness of programs to reduce violence among youth. Case studies are also included that show the ever increasingly serious impact of juvenile crime on victims and the difficulties experienced in treating juvenile offenders.

Chapter 8 is about workplace violence, a problem that grows in severity as the workplace becomes increasingly more dangerous. Organizations that were once considered violence free, including universities, now experience rapes, assaults, and homicides in seriously increasing numbers. This chapter presents data on workplace violence and a number of troubling case studies. Workplace violence is particularly dangerous to mental health and child-care workers who often work with the victims and perpetrators of violent behavior.

Chapter 9 discusses the most feared type of violence: the random violence that increasingly defines the way Americans live their lives. Random violence includes muggings, carjackings, unprovoked assaults, and now, terrorism. It is unpredictable, sudden, and difficult to defend against. Case studies are presented in this chapter along with data reporting the amount of random violence as well as the success rates of programs to decrease random violence.

Chapter 10 is an overview of treatment approaches useful in work with perpetrators of violence. We are in our infancy in terms of developing ways of treating violence and preventing the cycle of violent behavior that defines violent perpetrators. This chapter includes a number of case studies and examples that describe the way treatment approaches might be applied in real-life situations.

4 Family Violence Involving Adults

For a long time now, the men and women of America have been engaged in a war that we politely call domestic violence. It is an homogenized term for the punching, the kicking, and the disfigurement of the body and soul of legions of men, women, and children in America. While domestic violence is thought to be violence between two adults, in reality it is violence to the entire family. Children watch adults in violent interactions and whether or not the violence affects them physically, it has a predictable psychological impact that is almost as serious as physical violence.

Many states define domestic violence as any act of violence that results in a physical impact including bruising, scaring, and damage to the functioning of the body. It may include slapping, kicking, or using a foreign object or weapon to cause bodily harm. In states such as California where the violence described in the O. J. Simpson trial between Simpson and his murdered ex-wife advanced our understanding of the psychological and physical harm caused by perpetrators, domestic violence is now considered a felony punishable by more than a year in jail.

The Amount of Domestic Violence

The data related to the actual amounts of domestic violence are clouded by methodological differences among researchers. As Elena Neuman (1995) notes, many researchers confuse domestic violence (violence between loved ones) with general violence. The result is that the absolute amount of domestic violence has become confused. As an example, the Surgeon General in 1992 estimated that the number of women experiencing physical abuse in a domestic environment ranged between 2 and 4 million a year. However, a 1993 telephone survey of 2,500 women by Louis Harris for the Commonwealth Fund (Neuman, 1995, p. 69) found that 2 percent had been "kicked, bit, or hit with a fist or some other object." According to Harris, this would amount to an overall rate of violence to women of 1.8 million acts of domestic violence per year.

Neuman (1995) goes on to note that to come up with the larger numbers of 2 to 4 million cases of domestic violence, the survey would have had to add women to the report who experience less violent acts such as pushing, shoving, grabbing, or throwing something at a partner, acts which are aggressive but are often, unfortunately, associated with men and women in relationships over the normal course of their lives. Using this definition of domestic violence, almost all of us may, at one point or another, be guilty of having committed acts defined as domestic violence.

To further confuse the picture, the data fail to include violence by women to men, or violence between same-sex partners. Rates of violence among lesbian women have been estimated at almost 60 percent as compared to rates of violence of 27 to 33 percent between heterosexual couples (Neuman, 1995). Rates of violence to men by women, always felt to be low, are now beginning to show levels almost as high as those of men abusing women. Straus and Gelles (1996) in a National Family Violence Survey from 1975 to 1985 found that women initiated violent acts at rates similar to that of men. In a later article, Straus and Walsh (1997) maintain that female to male violence in relationships parallels that of male to female violence but when under reporting by men is included, it may actually be higher. Police reports, which rely on the actual number of people arrested for domestic violence, note a significant increase in female to male violence but at rates that are still lower than arrests made for male to female violence. The Los Angeles Police Department in 1995 (1997) noted a 14.3 percent arrest rate for women accused of abuse to an intimate adult, a 100 percent increase over arrests for women in 1987. Neuman (1995) reports on a 1992 national survey and comparing it to the National Family Violence Surveys for the preceding seventeen-year period, noted that the rate of severe wife assault by husbands had decreased by 47 percent over the prior seventeen years while minor assaults by wives to husbands had actually increased. And to add to the confusion, these numbers only cover reported cases of violence, always an area of disagreement among researchers. While clearly there are unreported episodes of domestic violence, how many cases of domestic violence actually go unreported? No one can say for certain.

Even with the awareness that domestic violence is underreported, Pagelow (1984) notes that 12,000,000 married women have been or are currently being physically abused by their husbands, a figure representing one-third of all married women in America. One-third of all pregnant women report physical abuse by men. In a number of studies, one-third to one-half of all women seeking therapy for help with emotional problems as adults have been abused by men, many before the age of eighteen (Bagley, 1990; Hale, Duckworth, Zimostrad, & Scott, 1988).

Schuerger and Reigle (1988) note that in a national sample of married women, 30 percent of all married women in the United States experience physical abuse at some point in their marriage (Straus, 1978). Furthermore, five million American wives have been abused, chronically and severely, by their husbands (Straus, 1978).

Jones (in Neuman [1995]) reports that an average of four women a day are killed by men who batter. In a random study of 3,676 medical records of women admitted to the Yale/New Haven Hospital emergency room between 1978 and 1983, Stark and Flitcraft found a rate of domestic violence of 18.7 percent (Neuman, 1995), leading the authors to conclude "that battering is the single most common cause of injury for which women seek medical attention" (Neuman, 1995, p. 71). This position is also held by Jones (in Neuman, 1995) who believes that domestic violence is the single largest cause of violence to women in America. Dewhurst, Moore, and Alfano (1992) report that sexual and physical assaults are identified as the two major crimes by men against women in our society. Victimization rates for both types of offenses have been estimated at between 10 and 30 percent of all women.

The U. S. Department of Justice (1998) reports that in 1996, female victims of intimate violence experienced an estimated 840,000 rapes, sexual assaults, robberies, aggravated assaults, and simple assaults at the hands of intimates, down from 1.1 million in 1993. Three out of four of the victims of murder by intimates (1,800) were women. In the same year (1996), one in ten women victims of domestic violence sought medical treatment for injuries sustained at the hands of perpetrators. In 40 percent of the cases of violence among adult intimates, children were residing at home during episodes of violence. The report goes on to note that in 1996, 150,000 men were victims of intimate violence, a figure that has remained fairly constant since 1992.

Dutton, in the *Los Angeles Times* (1994), reports that in national surveys, 72 percent of all men surveyed are not violent in their homes and that the remaining 28 percent use violence occasionally to frequently. Of those who do use violence, Dutton (1994) notes that 55 percent are stifled men who have poor impulse control and do not know how to control anger, while 20 percent of those surveyed are "prone to intensive anger in intimate relationships. A quarter of the remaining abusers are so entrenched in their violent behavior that they are considered untreatable."

It is generally assumed that men are far more likely to be violent in domestic situations. The reality is that physical abuse of men by women is roughly as common as physical abuse of women by men. Straus and Gelles (1986), in a national survey of severe violence, show that there is more abuse of husbands by women than abuse of women by husbands. The 1985 data suggest that the rate of husband abuse is 4.4 per 100 couples as compared to 3.0 for abuse of wives for the same number of couples. Steinmetz and Lucca (1988) believe that the entire issue of abuse of men by women has been ignored in the literature. The authors note that not only don't men report abuse because of concerns with stigmatization, but that they frequently use their own and not public resources to receive help. Consequently, data available to researchers seldom show very high rates of husband abuse.

Regarding the data on homicide involving intimates, Steinmetz and Lucca write that:

> Data on homicide between spouses suggest that almost an equal number of wives kill their husbands as husbands kill their wives. Thus it appears that men and women might have an equal potential for violent marital interaction; initiate similar acts of violence; and when differences of physical strength are equalized by weapons commit similar amounts of spousal homicide. (p. 241)

The Dynamics of Abuse

Adult abusers appear to have shared characteristics. For example, many abusers have been physically abused themselves by parents, caretakers, or other family members. Roy (1982) indicates that, although abusive men are not distinguished by a history of criminal arrests, over 80 percent of the men who abuse women have witnessed or experienced abuse as children. Waldo (1987) notes that battering is often a family pattern that is transmitted from one generation to the next. Kalmuss (1984) reports that a disproportionate number of men who engage in physical aggression against their partners learn their behavior as a direct result of witnessing abuse between their parents. Often men who are prone to the use of violence in their relationships with women have a generalized belief in the use of violence as a way of controlling others. These men are frequently unable to separate seductive from friendly behavior, or hostile from assertive behavior. The aggressive, hostile, emotionally labile men who lack empathy are likely to physically and emotionally abuse both women and children (Kalmuss, 1984).

Wiederholt (1992) found that abusive men are likely to batter when they have minor doubts about the way in which their partner's view the competency and integrity of the abusive male. This loss of trust leads to a breakdown of the mechanisms that control impulsive violence and result in "emotionally chaotic behavior" which is, according to the author, similar to a presuicidal state.

A great deal of abusive behavior comes in the midst of substance abuse. Substances not only give abusers the courage to abuse, but they permit the release of repressed rage. For victims of abuse, abusers may appear irrational in their outbursts. However, the abuser is often in touch with his or her own abuse under the influence of alcohol or drugs. This may not be a conscious memory as much as a reminder of feelings of powerlessness and rage. Hotaling and Sugarman (1984) note that alcohol use can be viewed as a disinhibitor of controls against the use of violence that leads to higher levels of conflict. The authors believe that either the increased marital conflict brought on by the use of violence or the loss of inhibitions caused by the use of substances can substantially increase the probability of violent behavior.

Abusers often need to control the adults and children around them. The need to have others comply with their wishes is a way of preventing unfaithfulness and deceit. Abusers often see failure to comply with increasingly confusing expectations as sure signs of deceit. Frequently, they test adult partners and children by making expectations so unclear that failure is almost always likely to result. Waldo (1987) reports that abusive men imitate their father's abusive behavior as a way of exerting authority and control over family members.

Peterson (1980) suggests that husband to wife violence results from past exposure to violent role models and is reinforced by a lack of legal punishment for abusive and violent behavior. This reinforcement process is further solidified by the way in which the abuser's gender role model provided the child with positive messages regarding the appropriateness of abuse to adult partners, parents, and siblings. The desired impact of abuse is the *emotional surrendering* of the adult partner in the abuser's life to his or her violent and abusive behavior.

Abusers socialize those whom they abuse. Children of abusive parents often abuse others or move into abusive relationships where they are the victims of abuse. These patterns, while dysfunctional, are normal to victims. Often abusers who encourage grown children to use abuse with their own spouses and children reinforce the cycle of abuse. Generations of violence may be perpetuated by a single angry man or woman with poor skills at containing rage.

Dodge and Richard (1986) report that aggressive children have a greater tendency to see "malevolent intent from ambiguous aggressive acts than nonaggressive children. As a consequence, aggressive children are more likely to retaliate against the perceived aggressor." This finding suggests that children who experience early abuse develop an attribution toward violent behavior and that abusive role models are likely to encourage the use of violence, including violence in the family, from a very early age.

Many writers note the tendency of abusers to feel remorse after an episode of abuse. The term *honeymoon period* is used to define the remorseful period in which the abuser becomes warm, loving, and tender. Abuse victims describe this period as the time in which their lives are the happiest. Like other reinforcers, the victim is addicted to these moments and may put up with continued abuse because it may result in a short period in which the relationship is at its best.

Giles-Sims (1983) believes that violence may be rewarding to the abuser because it often results in "pleasing changes" in the spouse's behavior. However, having temporally satisfied their esteem needs through violence, the abuser may become guilt-ridden and afraid that he or she will lose the relationship because of their violent behavior. In this moment of sorrow and anxiety, the abuser tries to win his spouse's heart back by being overly solicitous and intimate. In the honeymoon period, Waldo (1987) suggests that abusers experience a heightened sense of intimacy which acts to help negate the violence. These sets of emotional reactions serve to reinforce the cycle of violence.

Waldo (1987) notes that the honeymoon period is perceived of as a period of fragility where the abuser is less willing to be assertive about personal needs than they were before the abusive incident. However, when the same relationship problems reoccur, they are more powerfully felt because they touch on old wounds. Eventually, the reservoir of anger again breaks out in violent incidents, completing the cycle and starting it over again. Although the violence is repetitive, it is likely to become more frequent and severe because it takes stronger abuse to get the same effect from the spouse. Consequently, the abuser's level of anger increases. The fundamental problems in the relationship, which are set aside during the honeymoon period, remain unchanged. Because of the onset of the honeymoon period, many victims are unwilling to press charges against their abuser believing that *this* time the honeymoon period will last indefinitely.

Adams (1988) reports that intrapsychic problems often lead to violent behavior in male and female abusers. The list of potential problems include poor impulse control, low frustration tolerance, fear of intimacy, fear of abandonment, dependency, and underlying depression. Adams also believes that the abuser is emotionally fragile and is overwhelmed by feelings of uncertainty and confusion. In this respect, abusers feel as if *they* have been victimized and that their abusive behavior may be justified by what was done to them.

Scher and Stevens (1985) report that violence to women and children is rooted in cultural and historical folkways and mores, which define men as caretakers who are necessarily tough and aggressive. This view of abusive behavior is explained by a society that trains men to be winners at any cost. The role given to men to be winners often interferes with intimacy and trust in relationships and causes men to act aggressively toward those who might be potential competitors. Anxiety related to the need to always be a winner may result in violent acts.

In the case of abused women, the abuser has often systematically reduced the abused woman's ability to feel independent and to seek autonomous work and relationships. Often, the abuser has significant financial and emotional power that permits continued abusive behavior. Many women who experience long-term abuse are so emotionally dependent that autonomous living is all but impossible. Glicken (1995) found that abusers look to friends, family, and those they choose as people of wisdom to reinforce their use of abusive behavior. People of wisdom are the parent substitutes whom abusers choose as their primary source for advice, information, and guidance. Because the people of wisdom chosen as friends of abusers often have abusive patterns, the abuser not only finds their abuse reinforced, but they may also be chided for not being abusive enough. In truth, abusers may believe that their abusive behavior is far too mild.

Glicken (1995) also found that abusers are frequently insensitive to the pain they inflict. When one asks them about an abusive episode, they frequently understate the harm done. They deny hearing bones break or believe that the victim is the responsible one since they should not have been sitting the way they were when they were struck. Or the abuser will argue that the victim should have seen that the abuser was angry and removed themselves from the situation. Many abusive men, in particular, believe that victims like to be abused and, therefore, the abusive man is only fulfilling the wishes of the victim.

Multiple pregnancies often serve the male abuser's wish to keep women from being attractive to other men (Glicken, 1995; Pagelow, 1984). The abuser may encourage weight gain in women as a further way of keeping women unattractive. Multiple pregnancies may serve to reinforce the abusive man's sense of his masculinity. This attempt to negate the attractiveness of a wife or girlfriend is further assured by the abuser's infidelity. Many abusers report that they have affairs as preemptive strikes to guarantee their emotional safety when wives or girlfriends "inevitably" become unfaithful. This belief in the inevitability of infidelity is true even when women are so emotionally and physically scared that they no longer have the emotional strength to seek out other men. The more the woman becomes unattractive, the more the abusive man ridicules her looks to further negate her as someone who might seek other men or cause the abusive man psychological harm.

Glicken (1995), in surveys of treatment programs offering mandated services to abusive men in lieu of jail time, found that treatment staffs often believe that abusive men have extreme difficulty using language to convey emotions, desires, and expectations and that abusive men distrust language. For them, words are signs of weakness. When they *do* use language to convey feelings, the experience makes them feel oddly effeminate and unmasculine. Men, they believe, use action and not words to convey desires. Not surprisingly, these men use violence in other arenas of their life, including work. However, to a surprising degree, abusive men may be seen as mild-mannered away from home, reverting to abuse and tyranny only in the safety of their homes.

It should be noted that many professionals believe that women who abuse men see the abuse as either retaliatory or preemptive to diminish the abuse the victim knows is coming. The lack of information on female to male abuse is interesting. At a time when research shows an increase in female to male domestic violence, there is limited research to suggest the emotional or social state of women who abuse and we are left, primarily, with research on male abusers, research that may not be applicable to female abusers.

A final theory of abuse suggests that male abusers are quite dependent on the very people they abuse. As Dutton reports (1994), "They come in believing that women have power. They sense that they do not have control. When they act out is when they feel helpless and powerless."

Case Study of an Abuser

Rosalie Myron is a twenty-six-year-old Caucasian woman attending a master's degree program in counseling psychology. She is married to Louis, a twenty-eight-year-old Hispanic police officer. Rosalie attended a workshop one of the authors gave on domestic violence in which wife to husband battering was discussed. She related the following story:

> I never thought of myself as an abuser until I took this class, but I often hit and kick my husband. In the morning when the alarm goes off and my husband has to go to work, he has a hard time waking up. Sometimes I kick him or punch him to wake up. I've doused him with cold water. He's so even-tempered, he hardly ever gets mad at me. I go into violent tantrums at the drop of a hat. Everything he does makes me angry.
>
> I never had violence in my home and I know my mother would have never tolerated my dad being violent with her. I don't know where my violence comes from. Just out of frustration, I've kicked my husband in the privates. He's a very large man and I know he could hurt me if he wanted to but the more angry I get, the more gentle and understanding he seems to be. It drives me crazy that he's so nice to me when I treat him so badly. I go into rages sometimes when he comes home. I don't have any idea why. I'm under a lot of pressure going to school and

working. It's like I feel it's his fault I'm under so much stress and that he should pay for it. But he never told me to go to school and work at the same time. It's just something I wanted to do.

By everything I've learned in this class, I know I'm abusive. I sometimes wonder if a day will come when he won't put up with it anymore, but the more abusive I get, the more gentle and calm he seems to me. It makes me furious and I think if he'd hit me or put his foot down that I'd stop. I don't know why I'm being this way and it worries me that at some point he'll leave. I'm full of suspicions that he's seeing somebody although I have absolutely no proof of it. I think he must be sick of my behavior and that other women must look better to him than me.

I'm going to go for help. Something inside of me is making me angry and taking it out on him. I don't know what it is and maybe help is what I need right now.

Discussion of the Case

Like many abusers, Rosalie isn't in touch with her anger. She believes that her husband must be the reason for her anger and takes it out on him, but a rational look at the situation makes her realize that the anger comes from within. But why? She has no history of abuse in her family and she has a mother who clearly would not have permitted her husband to be abusive. In Rosalie's case, it would appear that she is channeling the reason for her stress and anxiety to her husband. And because he doesn't seem to put an end to her abusive behavior, Rosalie feels more and more prompted to be angry at him. One might guess that the relationship has elements of dependency in which Louis has framed the relationship by being the strong partner who will take care of his spouse in any situation. But now that Rosalie is under great emotional stress because of decisions she's made to go to school and to work, stress she can't handle anymore, Louis isn't helping her, and she feels that he is responsible, in some way, for the pain she feels. By being abusive, she is telling him that she hurts and that she wants help. But rather than doing something proactive to stop the abuse, Louis, like all too many victims who are codependent, is acting to enable Rosalie to continue her abuse. One can only predict more of the same until the abuse becomes too serious for even Louis to ignore. The prognosis for the marriage seems poor at this point without some help for both the abuser and the abused.

Predicting Potential for Abuse

Hotaling and Sugarman (1984) reviewed the literature on the risk markers in predicting abuse. These markers indicated six characteristics of male abusers, five characteristics of the women whom they victimize, and eight characteristics of the marital relationships in which violence to women and children were most likely to occur.

Characteristics of the abusive men themselves revealed the following: lower self-esteem than nonbatterers, lower levels of income and lower occupational status, a higher probability of abusing alcohol, more likelihood than nonabusers of having been abused as children and to seeing parental violence while growing up. Battered women were also likely to have lower levels of self-esteem, to have more traditional sex-role expectations, to use drugs more often, to have been abused by parents when they were children, and to have seen more parental abuse while growing up. The marital relationships in violence-prone families were marked by conflict and maladjustment, higher levels of educational and religious incompatibility, lower family incomes, higher levels of verbal abuse, and the increased likelihood that separation or divorce would occur in the marriage.

Schuerger and Reigle (1988) explored the personality markers of violent men and found the following: most of the men studied had DSM-III diagnosis of explosive disorders (312.34, 312.39). More than 60 percent of the men were chemically dependent, mainly on alcohol. Twenty-four percent of the sample were more severely disturbed and could be diagnosed as schizoid, schizophrenic, or borderline personalities. Twenty-five percent of the men studied had depressive disorders. Interestingly, aside from violence toward women and children, about 25 percent of the abusive men studied had no discernable or significant disorders. Although it is often difficult to distinguish violent from nonviolent men on tests such as the 16PF, the authors note that abusive men often tend to be more withdrawn, compulsive, rigidly tough-minded, and anxious than nonviolent men. While a significant number of the men in the sample were substance abusers, the authors note that resolving the substance abuse often does not lead to a lessening of violence.

Wolf-Smith and LaRossa (1992) report that abusive men tend to continue the use of excuses and apologies as an aftermath to episodes of violence but that, as time progresses, the excuses are more frequently characterized as ones which blame the victims for the abuse. Consequently, as a predictor of violence, the more disassociated the man becomes from the reason for the violence (his internalized anger) the more likely the violence is to increase in severity.

Dewhurst, Moore, and Alfano (1992) suggest, in their research on abusive men, that men in their studies were more hostile to women than nonabusers. Often the abuse was coupled with alcohol use and "situational intolerance and general frustration coupled with a thinking pattern that tends toward pessimism, suspicion, and catastrophizing, particularly about their partners" (p. 44).

Bernard and Bernard (1984) believe that because of a lack of ego strength, abusive men choose spouses upon whom they can focus their dependency needs. Abusive men are highly dependent, in the authors' opinion, because they are incapable of developing other sources of emotional intimacy and validation. Consequently, the abusive man has difficulty seeing his spouse as a separate person with her own individual needs and thoughts. Furthermore, the abusive man expects his wife to understand all of his thoughts and feelings without hesitation. When the spouse is unable to anticipate and satisfy the man's needs and desires, Waldo (1987) reports that the man becomes outraged and resorts to violence.

According to Waldo (1987), the abuser has low self-esteem, which makes him highly vulnerable to criticism. The abuser then becomes overly reactive when he feels threatened. In time, he may become hypervigilant to threats to the relationship and his behavior toward women may become increasingly defined by jealousy and lack of trust.

In summarizing the risk markers for violent behavior to women and children, it should be noted that the demographic data that suggest violence is more likely to occur in lower socioeconomic families is marred by the reality that men with higher levels of income and status are more likely to be able to hide their abuse and to keep it from being reported. In general, however, the data would suggest that abusive men have problems in controlling anger and tend to have explosive tempers. They are also highly likely to have been abused as children and to have witnessed parental abuse when they were growing up. Abusive men are more likely to marry women who have been abused and to maintain their abuse as part of the expectations of marriage. Not surprisingly, abusive relationships are marked by severe conflicts, verbal abuse, and separations that often end with apologies and short honeymoon periods before the cycle of violence begins again.

The Impact of Abuse on Victims

There are considerable data to show that domestic violence has a particularly negative physical and emotional impact on the adult victim and children in the home.

There is a very high probability that children who watch domestic abuse, or are themselves victims of abuse, will abuse their children and spouses. Dodge, Bates, and Petit (1990) offer evidence that the experience of physical abuse in early childhood is a risk marker for the development of aggressive behavior patterns. The authors report a threefold increase in the risk to be abusive in children who have witnessed abuse in their families and a significant increase in the way in which these children incorrectly view the hostile intent of others. Van Hasselt, Morrison, Bellack, and Hessen (1992) note that the literature is "replete with descriptions of the severely damaging impact of family on the social and physical functioning of their victims" (p. 3).

National crime data collected by the U. S. Department of Justice (March 1998) indicate that violence to women by intimates (husbands, siblings, parents, boyfriends, etc.) is the primary reason women are injured in America. The report goes on to note the following:

- Half of the female victims of violence reported an injury of some type after an incident of adult abuse by an intimate. (p. 17)
- Twenty percent of those reporting an incident of abuse by an intimate sought medical assistance. (p. 17)
- In 1994, a quarter million hospital visits were made to treat violence done by an intimate.

Van Hasselt et al. (1992) report that battering is the major source of injuries to women, accounting for more injuries than "auto accidents, muggings, and rapes combined" (p. 301). Stark et al. (1981), in studying the medical records of women randomly selected and presenting injuries at the emergency room, report that 40 percent of these women said that the injury was done by an intimate. Van Hasselt notes that 20 percent of the abused population evidence mental health problems with more than a third carrying a diagnosis of depression or another situational disorder while one in ten suffer psychotic episodes. Stark (1985) reports that 25 percent of the women using psychiatric emergency services have a history of abuse. Stark and Flitcraft (1985) studied the suicide attempts of abused women and found that suicide attempts after an initial suicide try were 4.8 times higher for abused women attempting suicide than for nonabused women. A Texas study (Teske & Parker, 1983) found that 28 percent of a population of abused women were beaten while they were pregnant and that abused pregnant women were "significantly" more likely to suffer miscarriages or abortions.

Treating Abusive Behavior: The Perpetrator

A review of the literature on abusive men suggests a wide range of interventions with a number of borrowed treatment approaches and theories to drive the interventions. As Eisikovits and Edelson (1989) note, "It can still be said that the intervention literature is often atheoretical or it has borrowed its theoretical grounding from other areas" (p. 407).

The following review of the literature summarizes the primary approaches to modifying or eliminating abusive behavior by using the models of treatment most often mentioned in the literature.

1. Individual Treatment

Eisikovits and Edelson (1989) note two studies using individual treatment approaches. Both studies used a behavioral-cognitive approach and were concerned with changing obsessive thought patterns which might result in abusive behavior. This approach also tried to help abusive men communicate more objectively. The two studies, while suggesting a reduction in violent thoughts and abusive communication patterns, were not successful in reducing violent behavior. Neither came from a theoretical framework specific to abusive men but were derivative in nature, assuming that helping men understand patterns of abuse would lead to change.

The problem with individual treatment may be the lack of reinforcers related to individual treatment. Individual treatment suffers, to some degree, from the limited numbers of people involved in working to motivate behavioral change in the abuser. Group techniques do not have this problem because the abuser must face other abusers, week after week, who understand the abuser's reluctance to change. While individual treatment may be more pleasurable for the client, there is concern that it lacks the motivating power of group techniques and is, therefore, unlikely to work with abusive men regardless of the theoretical approach used.

2. Work with Couples

On the face of it, work with couples offers promise in treating abusive behavior. A desire to maintain relationships and family life would seem to be highly motivating. Additionally, couples work offers an opportunity to resolve abusive patterns, which may require the spouse to respond differently to situations and interactions that often result in abuse. Finally, couples work offers the spouse an opportunity to work on those elements of their behavior that allow the abuser to continue the abuse.

While couples therapy may offer hope, most writers suggest that couples work is inappropriate when: a) the victim's safety is in jeopardy; b) there is severe and frequent abuse; c) substance abuse exists; d) mental illness is present; and e) one of the partners rejects treatment. For the reader familiar with abusive marriages, many of these conditions exist in most abusive marriages and would, unfortunately, limit couples work to the most healthy couples, a small group at best.

Still, there is some promise in this approach when the data are reviewed. Most of the couples work noted in the literature use a communications approach consistent with conjoint therapy supplemented by cognitive-behavioral approaches geared to identifying and changing certain behaviors. Lindquist, Telch, and Taylor (1983) reported that half the couples receiving couples treatment experienced one episode of male violence within six weeks while all the couples studied had experienced violent male behavior within six months.

However, Harris (1986) reports that in thirty couples worked with by the authors, 65 percent reported no new episodes of violence, while 73 percent viewed their relationships as successful. Others commenting on the research note that the authors are unclear as to how data were collected and that the term *successful* was never specifically defined as an absence of violence.

Other reports that present positive feedback on couples work are problematic in terms of research procedures used. Nedig, Friedman, and Collins (1985) report positive changes on measures of Locus of Control and Social Adjustment Scales in most of the hundred couples worked with. The authors, however, provide no compelling evidence that the couples are violence free or if the measures used would suggest a relationship between reduced violence and higher test scores. Descher, McNeil, and Moore (1986) report that changes in the number of violent episodes in a sample of couples produced no evidence of significant improvement.

Clearly, methodological problems plague all researchers who lack primary ways of evaluating change. Whenever one is limited to self-reporting by clients, there is difficulty in fully believing the results. Such is the case with the research on couples work. There are numerous reasons for couples to not accurately report abuse including legal ramifications and a desire to maintain a relationship pattern, even if it is deeply troubled. Clinicians often note that clients experience inertia in changing old forms of behavior. They explain reluctance to change as the clients' fear that new patterns of behavior may result in more unhappiness than old, predictable patterns.

Additionally, couples work suffers from the lack of a unified theoretical framework. As any clinician knows who has worked with troubled couples, the work is difficult. Many couples have such high-internalized levels of anger at one another that sessions often become exercises in anger management. It is difficult to work with two very different perceptions of reality that may be complicated by differential levels of personal power, different degrees of intelligence, different abilities to use language creatively, and levels of commitment to maintain a relationship that may be severely strained by financial dependence and realistic family needs. In this context, women are often the hard workers in couples work while abusive men are often much less willing to change. Consequently, what appears theoretically sound becomes very difficult to apply in reality.

3. Behavioral Marital Therapy

A form of treatment called behavioral marital therapy (BMT) may reduce domestic violence among alcoholics for up to two years following treatment according to O'Farrell, Van Hutton, and Murphy (1999). BMT focuses on lowering use of alcohol through a combination of marital work with couples and alcohol rehabilitation. Significant in this approach is that lowered rates of alcoholism also brought about lowered rates of domestic violence.

4. Men's Groups

Over fifty recently published articles on the use of groups with abusive men describe a series of theoretical approaches in the context of group treatment. In these groups, the approach to treatment may vary but the purpose of the group is to modify and eliminate violent behavior. The theoretical approaches used derive from the theories of abuse described earlier in the paper. Consequently, goals of men's groups include:

a) Attempts to provide "moral training" so that abusive men may be sensitized to the harm their abuse causes. Moral training is also called *victim awareness* in the literature as well as moral development. It attempts to reduce violence by reeducating men through an awareness of the harm they do;

b) Jealousy training to reduce the violence which may stem from intense jealousy and the need to dominate and control women and children. This goal uses the group process to provide feedback on those behaviors that underlie patterns of violence and abuse;

c) More traditional attempts to develop a systematic approach to the everyday interaction of variables in the client's life that may create conditions that result in violence.

The techniques of intervention in men's groups are largely those of all group treatment. Size and composition are as variable as the therapists doing the work. There are arguments for groups as large as twenty and as small as five. Some writers argue for male-female therapy teams while others suggest only male leaders. Some writers urge homogeneity while others suggest heterogeneity in composition. Some writers argue for highly structured groups while others suggest groups that force members to develop their own style of leadership and structure. What does seem consistent in the newer articles on male groups is the use of certain techniques that appear to show promise. In a study of treatment approaches used in diversion projects in California (Glicken, 1995) those techniques are:

1. Self-assessment techniques including the use of logs and diaries that help the male abuser analyze a series of events and behaviors that may have ended in violence.
2. Helping abusers develop plans to deal with volatile situations which are likely to result in violence. Some writes call these plans *safety plans*.
3. Helping the client understand the cycle of violence, the legal ramifications of violence, and the underlying reasons for violence. This approach is also called a *reeducation approach* in the literature.
4. Providing nonviolent skills to help in conflict resolution. These skills may include teaching clients to remove themselves from stressful situations and are called *creative timeouts*. Also useful are the following techniques: helping the client develop language to express feelings and opinions about situations which may lead to violence, helping change rigid role expectations of others, and relaxation techniques to help remove stress from the client's life.
5. Techniques that encourage clients to examine early life situations that may underlie and explain abusive behavior, consciousness raising, as well as confronting group members when they try and manipulate others or deny the use of violence.
6. Analyzing material presented on video that shows abusive situations. This approach attempts to teach abusers the way abuse develops and the strategies abusers might use to avoid violent confrontations. This may be done in conjunction with such cognitive-behavioral tools as the power wheel (Anderson), which provides the abuser with a definition of the underlying reasons for episodes of abuse followed by suggested ways of changing that behavior to something more positive.

Reports on outcomes from group approaches are very promising, although they suffer from many of the concerns raised in the preceding outcome studies. Feazell, Mayers, and Deschner (1984) surveyed ninety men's treatment programs in North America and found that 66 to 75 percent of the men had ceased their violent behavior one year after treatment had ended. Tollman, Beeman, and Mendoza (1987) sampled 149 men who participated in a unique program providing joint group treatment to men and women during a woman's stay in a shelter for abused and battered women and children. Of the men who participated in at least 1 session with their spouses, just over half (53%) of the men were nonviolent in follow-up at intervals of up to four years posttreatment. A number of other studies employing differing approaches to evaluating success of treatment (Dutton, 1994) notes successful resolution in violent behavior in more than half of the group members who underwent group treatment. This is a decidedly promising set of findings and should encourage continued research into the use of group techniques.

While the group approaches are promising, the outcome studies reviewed are marred by many of the criticisms noted in the individual and couples research evaluated. Most of the findings are generated through self-report and fail to include other sources validating the abuser's perception of his behavior. Since men who batter are notorious under-evaluators of their violent behavior, another criticism is that the research suffers from skewed notions of what constitutes evidence of violence. While it would be helpful to report those specific interventions that lead to change, the literature is nonspecific in its report of what does and does not work. What we do find in the reports of group treatment effectiveness is a notion of group treatment working without any recognition of the elements or techniques that are most likely to be helpful. Finally, group treatment is always a questionable approach because of contagion. In a given group, one may have very destructive members who negatively influence other members by reinforcing those dysfunctional attitudes and beliefs that may lead to additional violence. Sometimes group therapists are unaware that this is happening because it may take place outside of the group experience. Group approaches to the treatment of male abuse seem little more effective in reducing treatment attrition than other forms of treatment. Treatment attrition stills hovers at the 50 percent mark regardless of the treatment approach used.

5. Crisis Intervention

Ewing's (1978; 1990) work on crisis intervention as a form of brief psychotherapy might help frame the general approach treatment staff might use with adult perpetrators of domestic violence. Ewing summarized the general principles of crisis intervention as:

1. readily available and brief or time-limited;
2. dealing not only with the individual in crisis but also his or her significant family and social network;
3. addressing a broad, rather than a narrowly-defined, range of critical human problems;
4. focusing on present-time or current problems;
5. dealing not only with the current problem and symptom relief, but also assisting the client in developing new coping skills;
6. reality-oriented and reality-focused;

7. requiring the worker to assume nontraditional therapist role-responsibilities (e. g., directive, active, advocating, pragmatic, etc.); and
8. serving a preparatory function for possible future mental health treatment. (1990, pp. 281–284)

Ewing goes on to outline the basic stages of crisis intervention as:

1. quickly delineating the problem focus;
2. rapid assessment and evaluation of the client and the crisis situation;
3. contracting for a mutually-agreeable crisis intervention treatment plan;
4. entering into the actual collaborative work of crisis intervention;
5. agreeing to explicit time-limits, and preparing for termination as soon as treatment begins; and
6. doing a follow-up contact after formal termination of treatment (1990, p. 284).

He notes that while these stages may seem to be sequential, they do not follow a simple linear progression in an actual crisis intervention.

Ewing's definition of crisis work suggests that work with abusers might logically include issues other than the abusive behavior, a criticism of most group treatment that focuses almost solely on abuse. The assumption in this is that abusers have a variety of problems and dealing with all of them in a short term but very directive way may have more of an impact than just dealing with the abuse.

Reasons Treatment May Not Work with Some Perpetrators

Growing numbers of writers note that men resist the treatment experience and that even when it is court-mandated, abusers drop out in numbers that make its use highly problematic. This section reviews the reasons for resistance to treatment.

Therapy as Incompatible with Male Roles

Robertson and Fitzgerald (1990) found that men with traditional masculine attitudes were less willing to seek professional help. Furthermore, men with highly masculine attitudes were resistant to descriptions of therapy that implied the use of insight techniques or promised to help men relive early life experiences. The authors found that descriptions of therapy which suggested that it was a class, a seminar, or workshop were much more likely to result in men attending. They hypothesize that male socialization makes it very difficult for men to admit problems, seek help, and then follow through on the help when it is framed in a way which forces self-awareness or insight. Men are more likely to stay in treatment when the service offered is supportive, reinforcing, instructional (with advice-giving), and nonconfrontational.

O'Neil (1981) suggests a number of propositions about what he calls the "masculine mystique" that are in conflict with notions of what a good client would be like. Robertson and Fitzgerald (1990) note the elements of O'Neil's propositions come from the belief that men are taught to be dominant and competitive as a way of showing masculinity. Vulnerabilities, feelings, and emotions may be signs of femininity and men try to avoid those feelings. Seeking help for problems related to relationship issues "show signs of weakness, vulnerability, and potential incompetence" (p. 240).

Mistreatment of Men by Therapists

Robertson and Fitzgerald (1990) considered another reason men do poorly in therapy: mistreatment by therapists. In their research, the authors found that men who deviate from predetermined roles such as work and caregiving were viewed more negatively by therapists than men who maintained those predetermined roles. Furthermore, the authors found that many therapists view a man's desire to work a problem out by himself as resistance to treatment or a lack of motivation. Many of the elements of O'Neil's (1981) masculine mystique were, in fact, seen as negatives by therapists in the study. The authors note "psychotherapy may be as unprepared to deal effectively with such men (men who do not conform to traditional role expectations) as it was with nontraditional women a generation ago."

Female Models of Treatment

Glicken (1991) notes that most clients in treatment have been women and that most therapists learn to do treatment by working with women. The techniques that work with women vary considerably from those that may be useful for men. Robertson and Fitzgerald (1990), among others, note that the core ingredients for successful treatment are often more descriptive of female clients in treatment than of men. Those characteristics include:

a. a sense of awareness, something men are often socialized not to have since they are encouraged to hide their feelings;
b. the need to admit that one has a problem, something men are socialized not to do since men are taught to compete on their own and not to admit that they have problems that are irresolvable without help;
c. the willingness to disclose vulnerabilities, something most men are taught to hide so that they might maintain a competitive edge;
d. the ability to explore one's problems with another person, something men have been taught not to do, having been socialized, instead, to resolve problems alone and not to trust others.

Fear of the Loss of Autonomy and Independence

Many writers believe that abusive men have strong needs to maintain autonomy and that trust and dependence on others are very problematic conditions for these men. Treatment, as an immediate condition, requires the client to trust the therapist and to permit that person to guide the client toward new behaviors. These requirements are extremely aversive for many abusive men. They have trusted others in the past (e.g., their parents) and the results have often been pain and emotional abuse. Abusive men take advice only from those who meet their highly ritualized notions of men who have wisdom. In other words, men who provide direction and advice that is consistent with what the abusive man wants to hear. Therapy, for many of these men, is a condition similar to falling in love with someone who will deceive you. Consequently, abusive men resist therapy much as they resist any experience that may be emotionally difficult to control.

Abusive men often enter treatment with an absolute promise to themselves that therapy will not affect them. This need to maintain control and not to trust others results in predictable ploys to manipulate the therapy. Techniques to negate the process may include outwardly agreeing with the therapist while disagreeing internally, arguing with the therapist by using the most logical arguments possible, framing the therapist as someone who dislikes men or dislikes this man (a ploy that keeps the therapist from dealing with the real problem), poor attendance, coming to sessions drunk or late, and, finally, dropping out of treatment when it begins to create discomfort. Data from a number of studies indicate dropout rates for abusive men in therapy are more than 50 percent.

Jouard and Landsman (1969) believe the stage of development related to intimacy versus shame is often unresolved in abusive men because of the significant conflicts in abusive families that leave victims confused over self-worth and dignity. Many abused children in adulthood are unable, or unwilling, to disclose their private personas since that would require them to disclose the distorted notions they may incorrectly have of their role in creating the abuse they experienced as children. As a consequence, they grow into adulthood emotionally disconnected from significant experiences in their lives and become socially isolated. Not surprisingly, men often come to psychotherapy to try and cope with the dysfunctional consequence of isolation and the inability to understand repetitive behaviors that are frequently troublesome. Symptoms in psychotherapy related to unresolved guilt include: silence and nondisclosure, intellectualization and hypermasculine identification, dependency, identification with aggressors, and difficulty connecting current behavior with early life experiences.

Reasons for Treatment Attrition

In therapy, the ultimate rejection of the process is to stop attending sessions. Attrition for batterers is more than 50 percent in most studies conducted in North America. While some researchers have looked at demographic reasons for attrition (DeMaris, 1989), others have focused on the degree of masculinization of subjects believing that the more highly internalized the masculine role, the less likely subjects are to stay in treatment. DeMaris (1989) found that demographic issues that correlated with attrition and noncompliance include: employment status, use of substances, arrest records, age, income, desire to reduce violent behavior, age of the partner, and the timing or reason for the abuse. The author found that these demographic explanations explained attrition at a level only 12 percent above chance. In other words, it is difficult to find precise reasons for attrition when one looks at the mass of abusers in treatment.

Other theories suffer from similar problems in that an abuser's reasons for staying in treatment may be less therapeutic than legal. In diversion projects, abusers stay in treatment or go to jail. It may be most useful to study the reasons abusers stay in treatment and then correlate those reasons with evidence of reduction in violent behavior. In this way, we might develop profiles of abusers in treatment who stay in treatment and have successful resolution of the problem. Similarly, we don't know if those who drop out of treatment have reductions in violent behavior that are much different from those who complete treatment.

Ethnicity and Treatment

As might be expected from the limited amount of material on the treatment of abusive men, the literature on the treatment of abusive men of color is very limited. The reasons for this are not easy to discern. However, the few articles we found relating to abusive African American and Latino men do provide some explanation.

Issues of African American Men Who Are Abusive

Williams (1992) notes the "sparse" literature on the treatment of abusing African American men and suggests that workers should be sensitized to black culture before working with black male batterers. He also provides some guidelines for effective practice with black men who batter. They include:

Confronting Negative and Acknowledging Positive Behaviors This guideline suggests that black males who batter should be recognized for their many strengths and that, while the battering needs to be confronted, the therapist must remember that the client is doing well in many aspects of his life and that the positive behaviors must be considered when confronting the negative behaviors.

The Influence of Labels Williams notes that African American men want to see themselves as "partners in treatment" and resent labels that suggest pathology since labels send up signals to black men who have had to deal with labels that subtly or overtly suggest racism.

Addressing Sexism and Racism   Williams notes that black men are particularly sensitive to sexist notions that berate or bash men and that they are likely to increase violence. Workers must be particularly careful not to generalize male behavior and they must be aware that black men are very sensitive to racist notions that may include negative attitudes toward black men.

Cultural Congruence   Williams suggests that workers need to value the black experience to be effective with black male clients. If black workers are available, they should be used. If not, other workers need to approach black men with respect, concern, and awareness of the many factors that create tensions in the lives of black men that may not be true of other men.

Working with the Black Community   Williams suggests that as important as treatment might be, that it is equally important to work with black institutions, including the church and the family unit, to prevent and treat abuse. Black institutions are particularly powerful in the lives of black males and they can be used effectively to deal with domestic violence.

In a more generalized article on therapy with black males, Franklin (1992) acknowledges that black men have very low participation rates in therapy. He believes that the reasons for low participation rates are explained by a belief among some black men that therapy indicates weakness. He also notes that therapy is not a traditionally black way of resolving problems. Franklin also suggests that trust is often difficult for black males since relationships with wives and girlfriends are often based on the woman's perception of the man as a provider. When men are not providers, or when they experience personal difficulty, black men believe that their spouses are likely to dismiss them as men of value. According to Franklin, while black men may seem to be intimately involved in treatment, particularly group treatment where concern and interaction with others is so important, "doubts and inadequacies of the inner self are tightly guarded secrets. African American men are not likely to share personal vulnerabilities" (p. 351).

Elsewhere Franklin notes, "Masking true feelings or thoughts and being guarded has unique consequences for both African American men and women. Learning to trust is difficult to achieve in a climate of racism. Seeing a therapist is perceived as an abdication of a man's fundamental right and ability to solve his own problems" (p. 352).

Franklin notes that all therapy must recognize the invisible factor of racism. This provides messages from childhood that black males "lack value and worth and deny black males full access to life's amenities and opportunities" (p. 353). Franklin believes that the African American man's sense of invisibility "damages self-esteem by constant messages that he is unacceptable and of little worth." Franklin goes on to note that in order to deal with the indignities of racism, African American men may "devise strategies including immobilization, chronic indignation, acquiescence, depression, suicide or homicide, anger, and/or internalized rage" (p. 353).

To deal with these complex issues, Franklin suggests that therapists must go slowly with African American male clients allowing them to gradually develop trust. He also notes that therapists must keep in mind the need to frame the client in a positive way by approaching him with respect and positive reinforcement. Insights should be approached gently and should not appear magical or outrageous, but should convey "knowledge, understanding, and empathy, all of which will strengthen the client's sense of trust in the therapists humanity and competence" (p. 354).

Issues of Latino Men Who Are Abusive

One common factor in the abuse of women by Latino men is machismo. In machismo, men supposedly distrust women and believe that they are generally unfaithful and deceptive. To prove their dominance over women, men mistreat women while being unfaithful themselves. Machismo often suggests deeply hostile feelings toward women that show themselves in the need to dominate, humiliate, and negate spouses. Girlfriends or lovers may be treated superbly during courtship, but once courtship is over, men may become unfeeling, distant, and abusive, particularly if the woman complains. These men more often seek the company of men than the company of women.

However, Baca Zinn (1888) notes that this traditional view of male roles in the Latino culture also includes such exaggerated masculine behaviors as dominance, aggressiveness, physical prowess, and other highly stereotypic masculine behaviors that, "May be characteristic of most men in the lower ranges of the socioeconomic ladder" (Chafetz, 1979). In this same vein, Goff says that:

> We ought not to assume that machismo automatically means abuse . . . Machismo is a way of providing men who have very little social esteem with self-importance and self-worth. (1994)

Glicken (1995) interviewed a number of men in the Mexican state of Morelos who were undergoing voluntary treatment for abusive behavior during the summer of 1994. Most of these men were planning to move to the United States so their feedback is relevant to immigrant Latinos who abuse in North America. Summarizing the data gathered, the following information was found:

1. Abusive Mexican men, like their U. S. counterparts, do not view their behavior as abusive. They find men in the States to be overly feminized and cannot comprehend how families work without a strong, and sometimes quick to discipline, male. They think that they are doing a good job as husbands and fathers given the extreme problems they must contend with including unemployment and, when they are employed, very low wages. They think that their abusive behavior stems from drinking problems and

not from psychological origins. Drinking is a way of escaping the difficulties of life, in their view and, as such, is an integral part of Mexican life.

2. Most of the abusive men think of themselves as hardworking with little support or regard from family. A few, however, were decidedly of the opinion that they were not worthwhile people who had wives and children who were too good for them. A few, as in the United States, were clearly personality disordered and thought their problem with abuse was a joke. "Someone else's problem," as one man said, "not mine."

3. Most of the men held low regard for treatment. "Change my wife. Make her a nicer person," was often a typical statement. "Give me work and I'll be nicer to the wife and children," was another frequent statement. The notion of prior behavior influencing present behavior was not well accepted by these men although, interestingly enough, many of the men interviewed reported extreme abuse to them, their siblings, and their mothers by their fathers or by other adult males in the family when they were young.

4. Most of the men interviewed had a very poor opinion of women, reinforcing the findings related to non-Latino men in the United States. Frequent statements were made to support the notion that these men are extremely jealous and had very weak core self-concepts. It was not unusual for them to blame their abusive behavior on the women and children in their lives who, as one man said, "You cannot ever trust. Women are the slaves of their vanity," one articulate man told me in Spanish. "If a man shows that he's interested in your woman, she'll go running after him. A good man does not have a chance. If a woman wants to be unfaithful, there is nothing a man can do except make her realize that she will be punished."

As with couples and families in the states, Mexican women and families often collude to protect the abusive man. The social and economic fallout of a divorce or a separation in Mexico is devastating and women and children protect abusive men to avoid the calamity of single life.

Only a few of the men could articulate their feelings and perceptions clearly. Most of the men had limited language skills.

In a different vein, Carlson (1990) describes a scale developed for evaluating Latino males involved in violent crime, including physical abuse to women and children. His findings suggest that Latino batterers might score high on scales related to chemical abuse, emotional disturbance, antisocial tendencies, and self-depreciation. Several of the scales appear particularly sensitive to evaluating the degree of danger related to abusive behavior. They include the following:

Emotional disturbance, which is the degree to which the perpetrator has disturbances in thought and affect. It is particularly sensitive in detecting perceptual problems, anxiety, and moodiness. High scores on this scale indicate that perpetrators have problems dealing with reality because they cannot organize the world around them.

Antisocial tendencies, or the level of hostile animosity toward the world and those around them. High scores on this scale suggest that perpetrators are cynical about others and interpret the behavior of others as self-serving and manipulative.

Self-depreciation, or the tendency to devalue self. These perpetrators act to cover up feelings of low self-worth and depression.

All the characteristics noted are associated with men who abuse women and children and might help diagnostically to determine the degree of danger inherent in those 15 percent to 30 percent percent of men who, charged in abuse cases, go on to do more severe abuse of women and children.

Case Study of a Perpetrator in Treatment

Dale Jordan is a twenty-six-year-old Caucasian male who beat his girlfriend after a party in which he thought she was flirting with another man. Dale has a history of abusive behavior. This is his second sentence for abuse. The first sentence required community service but no therapy. He is now expected to attend up to a year of treatment under state law. If he hasn't progressed, the therapist can recommend more therapy or that he be remanded back to court for jail sentencing.

Dale attends a group that uses a cognitive-behavioral approach. The group uses a concept known as the power wheel to show group members how they believe their victims should be, as opposed to a more healthy way of seeing spouses and girlfriends. There is a great deal of processing and self-disclosure with homework assignments in which the group member is expected to practice a new behavior whenever they feel they might be abusive. Dale has been asked to practice a frequently-used technique called a *timeout.* Whenever Dale hears his voice getting louder or if his hands begin to raise to a point of peril where he might hit, he is asked by the group to remove himself from the situation and cool off. He is also asked to freeze-frame the situation that made him angry (to see it as it actually happened) and to develop strategies for dealing with the situation that do not involve verbal of physical abuse.

After six months of nonproductive therapy, Dale finally took a timeout from an argument with his girlfriend and used the time to develop a healthier strategy. He was able to resolve the situation without battering her or being verbally abusive. He told the group, "I didn't believe in any of this crap until I finally tried it and I could see that it works. I suggest that you guys try it sometime. I'm sick of myself beating my girlfriend up when you can talk things through instead."

Discussion of the Case

Batterers often don't get it in therapy right away. Some never get it all but many therapists report a moment in time when the discussion in the group starts to reach the abuser. At that moment in time, the client begins to see connections between how they function in relationships and ways to improve their functioning without being abusive. This realization does not always stick, however, and expect clients to lose ground from time to time or to substitute physical abuse with stinging and hurtful verbal abuse. Most treatment workers will tell you that physical and verbal abuse coexist among batterers, and victims report that verbal abuse can be more painful than the physical abuse.

Treating the Victims of Adult Violence

Social Institutions

In this approach to abuse, the perpetrator is dealt with by legal institutions and the victim is provided services. Examples of this approach would include early response by the police, mandatory prosecution of the abuser even if the victim does not file charges, and mandatory arrest when the police are called in domestic violence and see probable cause to arrest. Most of the studies of institutional change techniques with abusive men have been done with the police. Consequently, this discussion will center on that unit of intervention.

When police are involved in violent domestic calls, the normal procedure is to use mediation to diffuse the situation and to seldom press charges against the male abuser. Services to help the couple are recommended and the police leave when the situation calms itself. If the abuse continues and the courts became involved, the effort remains one of diversion from the legal system to treatment facilities where the goal is to modify/eliminate the abusive behavior.

In the early 1980s, Lerman (1984) began to argue for a set of policies that required a more specific role for the police and the courts in intervening in abuse cases. She recommended the following:

1. A policy for prosecutors not to drop domestic violence charges once they were filed.
2. Providing advocacy services for victims.
3. Charging perpetrators whether they were related to victims or not.
4. Releasing perpetrators only if restraining orders were issued.
5. Taking the victim's desires into consideration when sentencing the perpetrator.

Additional attempts to modify the legal consequences of abuse have been developed in many cities, including Duluth, where advocates are provided to victims to:

1. Provide battered women and children with legal information and assistance.
2. Educate and evaluate judges, police officers, and prosecutors.
3. Advocate for conviction as well as mandated treatment of perpetrators.

4. Monitor perpetrators to make certain that the conditions of sentencing are completed.

The outcome data on these approaches are at best confusing. Some studies (Mulvey & Repucci, 1981) suggest that training police in crisis work with domestic violence cases results in better ratings by citizens who found that police were more helpful than police not trained in crisis work. Others, including Driscoll, Meyer, and Schanie (1973) and Mulvey and Repucci (1981), found no difference in the way citizens rated the trained and untrained police.

Sherman and Berk (1984) in the Minneapolis study found that arrests of perpetrators reduced the likelihood of continued violence by half as compared to mediation by the police or asking the abuser to leave the home for eight hours. In the Duluth domestic violence study (1983), when arrests were made by the police on their own volition as opposed to citizen request, more arrests were made, the number of dismissed cases were reduced, victims were more satisfied, and victims were less likely to experience violence in follow-up studies.

Unfortunately, when these data were examined by other researchers in follow-up studies, it was determined that 15 percent of the men with violent histories of abuse were more likely to continue their abuse when arrested and dealt with by the legal system than were men with less violent histories of abuse (Fagan et al., 1983). Fagan et al. (1983) found that mediation and victim assistance by the police tended to be as effective as police arrest. Unfortunately, abusers who reoffended after their victims were helped by the police or community sources committed more severe offenses than men who were arrested but were not provided additional services.

Other studies following prosecutors of abuse and the court systems found little consistency in the way cases were handled. The decision to prosecute and the sentences handed out were done primarily by chance. Several small studies found little consistency in the long-term safety of victims of battering when the legal system worked well as opposed to when it was less likely to be sensitive to safety issues. Completely lost in these studies is the issue of abusive men recycling themselves back into new family situations where their battering is likely to continue. One other finding of note is that restraining orders which disallow contact with battered victims are seldom enforced by the police with regularity. Consequently, women who are most at risk of continued violence are much more likely to be stalked, verbally abused, physically abused, or murdered when restraining orders are not enforced by the legal system.

What these conflicting studies seem to suggest are:

1. A strong response by the police and the courts is helpful to victims when the male perpetrators are less dangerous. When perpetrators are more violent, the probability of violence continuing increases.
2. Legal and community sanctions against perpetrators are inconsistent in most communities.
3. There is no consistent evidence that early intervention by the police and the courts increase the short- and long-term safety of the victim, although there

is reason to believe that, with consistency and a strong community resolve, that this is more likely to be the case.

4. Studies of institutional protection of victims do not consider what happens to the male perpetrators of domestic violence and whether, as many suspect, they cycle their violence onto other women when relationships end with current wives/girlfriends.

5. It is troubling to note the lack of data on the use of institutions other than the police and the courts to reduce violence. As Eisikovits and Edelson (1989) note, "Outside of a few studies in the criminal justice system, it remains unclear what actions are taken by the various actors, professions, or organizations that react to domestic violence and what influence, if any, these actions have on ending violence" (p. 406).

Cultural Values and Beliefs

As one might suspect, given the widespread nature of battering in our society, there are always prevailing attitudes among a number of people that violence is the fault of women and children, or that it serves as a positive control mechanism for keeping dysfunctional families together. While one hears these ideas at social gatherings and they clearly continue to plague us as a society, there is no data in the literature to indicate strategies to change such attitudes. Clearly, the women's movement and our increased concern for children has helped to dramatize the deeply disturbed nature of such attitudes, but whether they have served to decrease violence is difficult to say given the absence of any critical research in the literature.

Protecting Women and Children

The shelter movement addresses the issue of removing women and children from unsafe environments. Wolf-Smith and LaRossa (1992) looked at the impact of removing at-risk victims from the home and, consequently, from the abuser. They found that the shelter experience did not decrease the violent man's tendency to blame women and children for their own violent behavior. What shelters were able to do was to decrease the woman's willingness to honor the male's perception of the abusive behavior. Shelters and the treatment provided in the shelters were able to change the cycle of abuse by helping women to not accept apologies and excuses in lieu of modification and elimination of abusive behavior.

It is clear that much more work needs to be done on the theory and technique of modifying and reducing violent behavior in male batterers. That we have little to help us understand ways of changing violent male behavior is not surprising. Men, in general, have been understudied in the social sciences. In a number of literature reviews on issues related to men in the social work journals, findings suggest a painfully small number of articles on men between the years 1970 and 1991, years that saw the increase in gang violence and a new recognition of the harmful effects of domestic violence. Obviously, more research needs to be done and a more systematic approach to developing and testing models of treatment with violent men needs to be developed.

What we do know at present would suggest that the most promising deterrents to violence are swift and sure responses by the legal system, including protection of the safety of victims and sure and just prosecution. That this is often not the case for victims of male abuse is shameful. Group approaches to male violence also seem the most promising way of therapeutically dealing with violent men, although we have little way of knowing why. Perhaps groups are more successful because they permit other abusive men who wish to change their behavior to act as "men of wisdom" for new abusers. One just can't be sure. Nor can we be sure about small group theory issues to direct group treatment. Size, composition, length of treatment, leadership styles, and so on, are all issues that need to be studied in much more detail.

Case Study of a Victim of Adult Family Violence with Integrating Questions

Rebecca Bartlow is a thirty-six-year-old Caucasian woman with three children who has been married to Oscar for fourteen years. Rebecca reports that their marriage was initially very good with Oscar showing a great deal of love and concern for Rebecca in the early years of the marriage. With her pregnancy and the subsequent birth of her child, Oscar became increasingly jealous of the time she was spending with the child and was offended that Rebecca did not always want to be intimate with him even though she was tired and suffering from postpartum depression. The first incident of actual physical abuse came when the baby was three months old. Upon being told that she was just too tired to be intimate, Oscar hit Rebecca repeatedly with his fists, sending her to the emergency room with a hospital stay of three days as a result of a concussion and deep cuts on her face.

Oscar was very apologetic after the attack and was the perfect father and husband for the next several months. The incidences of abuse began to increase, however, and they would have a familiar pattern. When Rebecca would have to spend extra time with their child, Oscar would begin to make disparaging statements about Rebecca's mothering skills, calling her lazy and stupid. He would sometime punch her in the arm or stomach at these times. The abuse was almost weekly. With the birth of their second child, Oscar's abuse became almost daily and has continued at that rate with their third child. Rebecca has suffered a broken collarbone, repeated black eyes, cuts and bruises to the face, a dislocated shoulder, and a total assault on her self-esteem. She feels incapable of leaving Oscar and doesn't think she has any capacity to be self-supportive. Oscar, she thinks, would kill her if she left. He has told her that many times.

After an assault that sent Rebecca to the emergency room, an advocate for battered women from a local abuse center helped Rebecca and the children move to a shelter. There, she was protected from Oscar and given a safe place to live for up to six months. She also received counseling services from the staff whose purpose was to help empower Rebecca so that she could make rational decisions regarding the abuse and determine whether she wanted to stay in an abusive situation. On the staff's advice, Rebecca reported Oscar's abuse to the police. He was tried and sent to mandatory treatment in lieu of a year of jail time. Oscar goes for treatment only occasionally and when he does, he is often drunk and belligerent. He has tried to break into the shelter and demands that he see Rebecca and the children. The children are frightened of Oscar and have nightmares that he will harm them. They urge their mother not to return to their father. All three children are receiving schooling in the shelter and psychological treatment. They are responding well to living in a safe environment.

Oscar agreed to meet with a counselor in a neutral place so that he and Rebecca could talk about their relationship. The counselor brought a police officer along. This proved to be a good idea since Oscar tried to assault both the counselor and Rebecca. He was remanded to jail and is currently serving a one-year sentence.

Rebecca comes from a home where violence to her mother and to the children was common. She often witnessed her mother being beaten by her father in drunken rages. He sometimes transferred his rage to the children. On occasion, when her father was very drunk, he would also sexually molest her. This went on from age 8 to 12. A concerned aunt took Rebecca from the home and she finished high school and community college before meeting Oscar and marrying. She was attracted to Oscar immediately. He seemed gentle and loving and very passive and he didn't drink. She later found out that Oscar was physically and sexually abused as a child by his father. They thought the bond of abuse would make them a better couple and told one another that on the first sign of abuse, they would seek help. When the abuse happened, however, they failed to seek help and made multiple excuses to the emergency room personnel for the problems. They were also careful to choose different hospitals or to use assumed names and pay by cash for hospital care.

Rebecca's self-esteem is very low. She feels worthless and is frequently depressed and lethargic. She may also, according to the treatment staff, have suffered brain damage from her multiple beatings. The treatment staff is focusing on helping Rebecca understand the danger of being married to someone who has also suffered abuse in his childhood. The unconscious rage in people who have been abused and the tendency to play roles they have been taught as children make the union of abused adults very likely to end in abuse. Rebecca can see this but fears that if she leaves Oscar that she will cycle into another abusive relationship. It is something she should worry about since it happens often after women receive help in shelters.

The staff is helping her recognize the difference between abusive and nonabusive men and the qualities she should look for in a man who will not be abusive. They are also working with her to help her see connections between her abusive experiences as a child and her choice of an abusive partner. People who have been abused as children often feel an easy bond with others who have also been abused. In a crazy sort of way, abuse can sometimes be seen as a loving act.

In a group Rebecca attends at the shelter, a social worker spoke about the fact that abusive behavior in relationships are even seen as loving experiences in the mass media. She played some songs where either the abused or the abuser excused and explained away abuse by calling it an act of love. The women in the group are all aware of this belief having heard it from their husbands and families on many occasions. The social worker said that many people still believe that if they are abused by a spouse, they (the victim) must be responsible. The women have all heard that statement too, all too many times.

As her six-month period is coming to a close, Rebecca has found an apartment to live in close to school for the children. She is currently on aid to families with dependent children (AFDC) and has been accepted in a retraining program that will allow her to get her benefits and enroll at a local college to finish her degree. She originally wanted to be a nurse and is going to pursue a degree in nursing. The children, who were withdrawn and frightened, are blossoming and doing well in school. She has had no contact with Oscar but through some friends of Oscar, she has been told that he intends to find her, kill her, and take the children. She doesn't take the threat seriously and has a restraining order. She is also taking self-defense courses and has bought a gun. "If he comes by for a chat, he'll be talking to Smith and Wesson," she told her counselor as she was leaving the shelter. The counselor cautioned her against such an act but Rebecca is very much in touch with her anger at Oscar. She thinks it would be self-defense and that nobody would care if Oscar was killed, least of all her.

Integrating Questions

1. Rebecca made a fairly quick recovery. Do you think this is normal for women experiencing long-term physical and emotional abuse? What might be the more normal outcome of treatment?
2. Do you think the pattern of abused people usually bonding with abusers is so strong that Rebecca will begin to date abusive men? More specifically, do you think she may begin to see Oscar again when he leaves jail?
3. Do you think that the anger both partners have for one another might result in violence? Might Oscar hurt or kill Rebecca or might she do the same to Oscar?
4. Many people who have been abused as children are neither abusive nor do they have relationships with abusers. What reasons can you give for this?
5. It seems inherently wrong that Rebecca and the children, who are the victims, must leave their home and go to a shelter while the perpetrator stays in the home. What might be done to change this situation?

REFERENCES

Adams, D. (1988). Counseling men who batter: A profeminist analysis of five treatment models. In K. Yllo and M. Bograd (Eds.), *Feminist perspectives on wife abuse* (pp. 176–199). Newbury Park, CA: Sage.

Baca Zinn, M. (1988). Gender and ethnic identity among Chicanos. *Frontiers, (2)*, 18–24.

Bagley, C. (1990). Development of a measure of unwanted sexual contact in childhood, for use in community mental health surveys. *Psychological Reports, 66*, 401–402.

Bernard, J. L., & Bernard, M. L. (1984). The abusive male seeking treatment: Jekyll and Hyde. *Family Relations, 33,* 543–547.

Brannon, R. C. (1976). No sissy stuff: The stigma of anything vaguely feminine. In D. David and R. Brannon (Eds.), *The forty-nine percent majority.* New York: Addison-Wesley.

Brooks, M. (1994, July 17). Interview in Cuernavaca, Morelos, Mexico.

Carlson, K. A. (1990). A personality test for Spanish-literate offenders: The Psicologico Texto. *Journal of Offender Rehabilitation, 16.*

Chafetz, J. (1979). *Masculine, feminine or human.* Ithaca, IL: Peacock.

DeMaris, A. (1989, March). Attrition in batterers counseling: The role of social and demographic factors. *Social Service Review, 63.*

Deschner, J. P., McNeil, J. S., & Moore, M. G. (1986). A treatment model for batterers. *Social Casework, 67* (5).

Dewhurst, A. M, Moore, R. J., & Alfano, D. P. (1992). Aggression against women by men: Sexual and spousal assault. *Journal of Offender Rehabilitation, 18.*

Dodge, K. A., Bates, J. E., & Petit, G. S. (1990). Mechanisms in the cycle of violence. *Science, 28.*

Dodge, K. A., & Richard, B. A. (1986). Peer perceptions, aggression and peer relations. In Pryor and Day (Eds.), *The development of social cognition* (pp. 35–58). New York: Springler-Verlag.

Driscoll, J. M., Meyer, R. G., & Shanie, C. F. (1973). Training police in family crisis intervention. *Journal of Applied Behavioral Science, 9.*

Duluth Domestic Abuse Intervention Project. (1983). *Hamline Law Review, 6,* 247–275.

Dutton, L. (1994, August 11). Domestic violence. *Los Angeles Times.*

Dutton, D. G., & Edelson, J. L. (1986). The outcome for court mandated treatment for wife assault: A quasi-experimental evaluation. *Violence and Victims, 1,* 86, (163–175).

Eisikovits, Z. C., & Edelson, J. L. (1989, September). Intervening with men who batter: A critical review of the literature. *Social Service Review, 63.*

Ewing, C. P. (1978). *Crisis intervention as psychotherapy.* New York: Oxford University Press.

Ewing, C. P. (1990). Crisis intervention as brief psychotherapy. In R. A. Wells and V. J. Giannetti (Eds.), *Handbook of brief psychotherapies* (pp. 277–294). New York: Plenum.

Fagan, J. A., Steward, D. K., & Hansen, K. V. (1983). Violent men or violent husbands: Background factors and situational correlates. In R. J. Finkelhor, G. T. Gelles, M. A. Hotaling, and M. A. Straus (Eds.), *The dark side of families* (pp. 49–67). Beverly Hills, CA: Sage.

Farrell, W. (1974). *The liberated man.* New York: Random House.

Feazell, C. S., Mayers, R. S, & Deschner, J. (1984). Services for men who batter: Implications for programs and policies. *Family Relations, 33,* 217–223.

Franklin, A. J. (1992). Therapy with African American men. *Families in Society, 73.*

Giles-Sims, J. (1983). *Wife battering: A systems theory.* New York: Guilford.

Glicken, M. (1991, October). Resolving male problems in therapy. Washington, DC: Social Work Board of Clinical Examiners Annual Meeting.

Glicken, M. (1995, October). Resolving male problems in therapy. Presented at Clinical Examiners annual meeting, Washington, DC.

Goff, C. (1994, July 23). Interview in Cuernavaca, Morelos, Mexico.

Greenfeld, et al. (1998, March). *Violence by intimates: Analysis of data on crimes by current or former spouses, boyfriends, and girlfriends.* Washington, DC: U. S. Department of Justice.

Hale, G., Duckworth, L. Zimostrad, N., & Scott, D. (1988). Abusive partners: MMPI profiles of male batterers. *Journal of Mental Health Counseling, 10,* 214–224.

Harris, J. (1986). Counseling violent couples using Walker's model. *Psychotherapy, 23.*

Hotaling, G. T., & Sugarman, D. B. (1984). An identification of risk factors. In Bowen et al. (Eds.), *Phase 1 feasibility study, domestic violence surveillance system feasibility study: Identification of outcomes and risk factors.* Rockville, MD: Westat.

Jouard, S., & Landsman, M. (1969). Cognition and the "didactic effect" in men's self-disclosing behavior. *Merrill-Palmer Quarterly, 6,* 176–184.

Kalmuss, D. (1984). The intergenerational transmission of marital aggression. *Journal of Marriage and the Family, 46,* 11–19.

Lerman, L. (1984). A model state act: Remedies for domestic abuse. *Harvard Journal on Legislation, 21.*

Linquist, C. U., & Telch, C. F. (1984). Violent versus nonviolent couples: A comparison of patterns. *Psychotherapy, 21*(2).

Linquist, C. U., Telch, C. F., & Taylor, J. (1983). Evaluation of conjugal violence treatment programs: A pilot study. *Behavioral Counseling and Community Intervention, 3.*

Longress, J., & Bailey, R. (1979, January). Men's issues and sexism: A journal review. *Social Work,* 26–32.

Los Angeles Police Department Data. (1997, January). The Family Bulletin.

Mirande, A. (1977). The Chicano family: A reanalysis of conflicting views. *Journal of Marriage and the Family, 39,* 747–756.

Mulvey, E. P., & Repucci, M. D. (1981). Police crisis intervention training: An empirical investigation. *American Journal of Community Psychology, 9.*

Nedig, P. H., Friedman, D. H., & Collins, B. S. (1985). Domestic conflict containment: A spousal abuse treatment program. *Social Casework, 66.*

Neuman, E. (1995, Winter). Trouble with domestic violence. *Media Critic, 2*(1), 67–73.

O'Farrell, T. J., Van Hutton, V., & Murphy, C. M. (1999). Domestic violence before and after alcoholism treatment: A two-year longitudinal study. *Journal of Studies on Alcohol, 60,* 317–321.

O'Neil, J. M. (1981). Patterns of gender role conflict: Sexism and fear of femininity in men's lives. *Personnel and Guidance Journal, 60.*

Osherson, S., & Krugman, S. (1990). Men, shame and psychotherapy. *Psychotherapy, 27.*

Pagelow, M. D. (1984). *Family violence.* New York: Praeger.

Peterson, R. (1980). Social class, social learning and wife abuse. *Social Service Review, 54,* 390–406.

Pirog-Good, M. A., & Stets, J. (1986). Programs for abusers: Who drops out and what can be done. *Response, 9* (2).

Robertson, J., & Fitzgerald, L. (1990). The mistreatment of men: Effects of client gender role and life style on diagnosis and attrition on pathology. *Journal of Counseling Psychology, 37*(1), 3–9.

Rosenbaum, A. (1986). Group treatment for abusive men: Process and outcome. *Psychotherapy, 23*(4).

Roy, M. (Ed). (1982). *The abusive partner: An analysis of domestic battering.* New York: Van Nostrand Reinhold.

Salgado, N. (1994, July 22). Personal interview, Mexico City, Mexico.

Scher, E., & Stevens, M. (1985). Men and violence. *Journal of Counseling and Development, 65.*

Schuerger, J. M., & Reigle, N. (1988). Personality and biographic data that characterize men who abuse their wives. *Journal of Clinical Psychology, 44*(1).

Sherman, L. W., & Berk, R. A. (1984). The specific deterrent effects of arrest for domestic assault. *American Sociological Review, 49,* 261–272.

Snyder, R. (1994, July 19). Interview in Cuernavaca, Morelos, Mexico.

Sonkin, D., Martin, D., & Walker, L. (1985). *The male batterer: A treatment approach.* New York: Springer.

Stark, E. (1985). The battering syndrome: Social knowledge, social therapy and the abuse of women. Unpublished Dissertation. SUNY-Binghampton.

Stark, E., & Flitcraft, A. (1985). Woman-battering, child abuse, and social heredity. In N. Johnson (Ed.), *Marital violence* (pp. 147– 171). London: Routledge and Kegan Paul.

Stark, E., Flitcraft, A., Zuckerman, D., Grey, A., Robinson, J., Frazier, W. (1981). *Wife abuse in the medical setting: An introduction for health personnel.* Monograph #7. Washington, DC.: Office of Domestic Violence.

Steinmetz, S. K., & Lucca, J. S. (1988). Husband battering. In V. B. Van Hasselt et al. (Eds.), *Handbook of family violence.* New York: Plenum.

Straus, M. A. (1978). Sexual inequality, cultural norms, and wife beating. *Victimology: An International Journal, 1,* 54–70.

Straus, M. A., & Gelles, R. J. (1986). Societal change and change in family violence from 1975 to 1985 as revealed by national surveys. *Journal of Marriage and the Family, 48,* 465–479.

Straus, M. A., & Walsh, M. R. (1997). *Women, men and gender.* New Haven: Yale Univ. Press.

Taylor, J. W. (1984). Structured conjoint therapy for spouse abuse cases. *Social Casework, 65.*

Teske, R. H. C., & Parker, M. L. (1983). *Spouse abuse in Texas.* Huntsville, TX: Criminal Justice Center, Sam Houston State University.

Tiller, P. (1967). Parental role division and the child's personality. In E. Dahlstrom (Ed.), *Changing roles of men and women.* Boston: Beacon.

Tollman, R. M., Beeman, S., & Mendoza, C. (1987, July). The effectiveness of a shelter sponsored program for men who batter: Preliminary results. Paper presented at the Third National Conference on Family Violence Research, University of New Hampshire, Durham, NH: U.S. Department of Justice Statistics. (1998, March).

Van Hasselt, V. B., Marrison, R. L, Bellack, A. S., & Hessen, M. (1992). *Handbook of family violence.* New York: Plenum.

Waldo, M. (1987). Also victims: Understanding and treating men arrested for spousal abuse. *Journal of Counselling and Development, 65.*

Widon, C. S. (1989). Does violence beget violence? A critical evaluation of the literature. *Psychology Bulletin, 106,* 3–28.

Wiederholt, I. C. (1992). The psychodynamics of sex offenses and implications for treatment. *The Haworth Press, 18,* 19–24.

Williams, O. J. (1992). Ethnically sensitive practices to enhance treatment participation of African American men who batter. *Families in Society, 73.*

Wolf-Smith, J. H., & LaRossa, L. (1992). After he hits her. *Family Relations, 41.*

5 Violence to Children

In 1991, the United States Advisory Board on Child Abuse and Neglect released a report indicating that more than 2.5 million American children suffered from abuse and neglect. By 1995, the number had risen to 3,111,000 (Juvenile Crime Bulletin, 1997, p. 2). The same publication indicted an increase of 49 percent in reported cases between 1985 and 1995 (1997, p. 2). It is uncertain whether this trend reflects an actual increase in the number of children being mistreated, an increase in public awareness, an increase in the number of people willing to report child abuse, or a combination of all three. As high as these numbers are, there are reasons to believe that these figures represent a fraction of the actual incidence of child abuse and neglect. Surveys consistently show that a large proportion of suspected child maltreatment cases remain unreported (U.S. Advisory Board on Child Abuse & Neglect, 1991).

Sedlak (1997) notes that there were 2.1 million reports of abused and neglected children in a 1986 study by the AAPC. The average abused child was 7.2 years old, ranging from a mean of "5.5 years of age for physical abuse to 9.2 years of age for sexual abuse" (p. 153). Fifty-four percent of the victims were male children who had been physically abused. Male children also accounted for 23 percent of all sexual abuse cases (p. 153), suggesting a much higher figure for male victims of sexual abuse than had previously been thought. In the National Family Violence Survey conducted by Straus and Gelles (1990), it was estimated that 110 out of every 1000 children in the general population experienced severe violence by their parents and that 23 in 1000 experienced very severe or life-threatening violence. Severe violence was defined as kicking, biting, punching, hitting, beating up, threatening with a weapon, or using a knife or gun (Sedlak, p. 178). Very severe violence resulted in serious bodily damage to a child. Since lower-income families were more likely to have abuse reported by an outside party than were more affluent families, it was estimated by Straus and Gelles (1990) that inclusion of potential abuse by more affluent families could raise the actual amount of abuse by 50 percent.

The U.S. Department of Justice (2000) reported that more than 1000 children died as a result of maltreatment in 1996. Three out of four of these victims were children under the age of 4. Of the 3 million victims of child abuse and neglect, 55 percent were white, 28 percent were black, 12 percent were Latino, and 5 percent were of other races. Nineteen percent of the victims were age 2 or younger while 52 percent of the victims were age 7 or younger. About 16 percent of the victims of substantiated abuse or neglect were removed from their homes (U.S. Department of Justice, 2000).

While the number of homicides committed in America is at its lowest point since 1971, the number of children murdered remains high. In 1997, the National Center for Health Statistics listed homicide as the fourth leading cause of death for children age 1 to 4, the third leading cause of death for children age 5 to 14, and the second leading cause of death for persons age 14 to 24. In 1997, six juveniles were murdered each day (U.S. Department of Justice, 2000).

When the home situation becomes extremely dysfunctional and abusive, children often run away. A 1988 study by Finkelhor, Hoatling, and Sedlak (2000) indicates that about 133,000 children run away from home each year and while away, stay in insecure and unfamiliar places. The same study reports that almost 60,000 children were thrown out of their homes. Almost 140,000 abused and neglected children were reported missing to the police. One hundred and sixty-three thousand children were abducted by one parent in an attempt to permanently conceal the whereabouts of the child from the other parent (U.S. Department of Justice, 2000). These additional data suggest that the impact of abuse and neglect often leads to children being abandoned or running away to other unsafe environments where they experience additional harm.

In 1991, the California Department of Social Services received 571,214 reports of *suspected* child abuse. Of these suspected cases, 32.3 percent were for physical abuse, 28.5 percent were for general neglect, 17.9 percent were for sexual abuse, 9.7 percent were for caretaker absence, 7.2 percent for were related to severe neglect, 4 percent for emotional abuse, and .4 percent for exploitation (California Department of Justice, 1993).

The U.S. Department of Justice maintains a Child Abuse Central Index that is a record of those cases *investigated* by child protective agencies in America. The cases investigated nationally by child protective agencies and reported to the Child Abuse Central Index increased from 25,500 in 1981 to over 54,000 in 1991 (U.S. Advisory Board on Child Abuse and Neglect, 1991, p. 3).

The available data from multiple sources indicate that much of the reported abuse and neglect is committed against children under the age of four. The probability that child abuse and neglect is a leading cause of childhood deaths seems to be generally accepted. However, official statistics identify causes of death from abuse and neglect mainly in medical terms and a child whose death is officially recorded as pneumonia may, in fact, have contracted the illness as a result of being poorly clothed, fed, bedded, or medically neglected. Many child abuse experts feel that abuse or neglect could be the underlying reason for death in many cases where the cause is attributed to medical reasons.

Although child abuse is frequently reported against young children, the problem of adolescent abuse is often underestimated. Unfortunately, child protective services frequently bypass adolescents because they are considered to be less at risk than younger children, and because adolescents are thought to have more options than younger children. However, many of the child prostitutes or the children involved in alcohol and drug abuse are victims of physical or sexual abuse and neglect at home. Adolescents may have more options than younger children, but they are not necessarily positive options. Adolescent abuse remains a serious problem that deserves attention and action.

Sedlak (1997), in her study of the factors that influence the multiple forms of child abuse and neglect, reports that family income is a strong factor. She notes that "compared to children whose families had incomes of $30,000 a year or more, children from families with incomes below $15,000 per year were found to have:

1. Twenty-one times greater risk of physical abuse.
2. More than 24 times the risk of sexual abuse.
3. Between 20 and 162 times the risk of physical neglect (depending on the children's other characteristics).
4. More than 13 times greater risk of emotional maltreatment.
5. Sixteen times greater risk of multiple maltreatment, and
6. Between 78 and 97 times greater risk of educational neglect (in Geffner, 1997, p. 171)."

Gathering accurate information and statistics is recognized as a problem at most levels of government. Efforts, however, are being made to develop systems that will more accurately reflect the scope and degree of child abuse and neglect. The number of suspected child abuse cases reported and investigated in America has steadily risen over the years as a result of better laws and increased attention paid to the problem by professionals and by the public.

Definitions of Abuse and Neglect

Each state can develop definitions of child abuse and neglect by the agencies charged with protecting children at the local level. However, most states use the following federal guidelines developed by the Office of Child Development in the Department of Health and Human Services (Feller, 1992).

An abused or neglected child is a child whose physical or mental health or welfare is harmed or threatened by the acts or omissions of his parent or other people responsible for his welfare. Harm to a child's health or welfare can occur when the parent or other person responsible for his or her welfare:

- Inflicts, or allows to be inflicted, upon the child, physical or mental injury, including injuries sustained as a result of excessive corporal punishment; or
- Commits or allows to be committed, against the child, a sexual offense, as defined by state law; or
- Fails to supply the child with adequate food, clothing, shelter, education (as defined by state law), or health care, though financially able to do so or offered financial or other reasonable means to do so. *Adequate health care*

includes any medical or nonmedical remedial health care permitted or authorized under state law; or

■ Abandons the child; or
■ Fails to provide the child with adequate supervision, or guardianship requiring the intervention of child protective services.

Sexual abuse might be defined as a sexual assault on, or the sexual exploitation of, a minor. Sexual abuse includes a wide range of behaviors consisting of many acts over a long period of time or a single incident. Victims of sexual abuse range in age from less than one year through adolescence. Sexual assault includes: rape, incest, sodomy, oral copulation, penetration of genital or anal opening by a foreign object, and child molestation. It also includes lewd or lascivious conduct with a child under the age of 14 and applies to any lewd touching if done with the intent of gratifying the sexual desires of either the person involved or the child. Sexual exploitation includes conduct or activities related to pornography depicting minors, and promoting prostitution by minors.

Clarifying Definitions of Abuse and Neglect for Child Protective Workers

In determining when child abuse and neglect exist, child protective agency workers frequently use the following federal and state mandated guidelines (Feller, 1992; DePanfilis and Salus, 1992; Brokenburr, 1994):

1. *The Age of the Child*   State laws provide upper age limits of children protected by reporting laws; however, it is important to recognize that abuse and neglect can have more harmful effects on younger children. If a parent has slapped an infant and believes that slapping and shaking a child is an appropriate discipline, the infant could be in danger where an older child might not be.
2. *The Location of the Injury*   Physical injuries to the face and head are more likely to cause severe or permanent damage than on other parts of the body. Accidental injuries will commonly leave bruises on the shins, knees, elbows, and forehead. The bruises will not have any uniform pattern if they are accidentally caused. Injuries inflicted on purpose will often have some patterns to them and may, for example, appear on both buttocks, both sides of the neck, and both hands or both ears (Kessler & Hyden, 1991).
3. *The Use of an Object*   Objects such as coat hangers, sandals, straps, belts, kitchen utensils, electric cords, pipes, or fists are more likely to cause serious injuries than an open-handed spanking. Often, the instrument used can be recognized by the shape of the injuries they inflict. Electrical cords will often leave a long loop-shaped bruise. Teeth marks are easily recognized in bite injuries (Kessler & Hyden, 1991).

4. *When Corporal Punishment Becomes Physical Abuse*   Parents will often try to excuse physical damage to their child by saying that the child deserved the punishment because they misbehaved. Sometimes punishment doesn't leave marks, but it is still abusive. An example might be when a child is locked in a closet or chained in the yard.

5. *Examples of Physical Neglect*   Neglect can be defined as a failure to provide proper care including insufficient food, clothing, shelter, hygiene, medical attention, and supervision. One form of neglect can be medical. If a child is ill and the parents fail to use medical options available to them, the worker might need a court order to ensure that the child gets immediate care. Shelter that is unheated in the winter or insect infested would be another reason for the worker to intervene. Malnutrition and failure to thrive are clear grounds for intervention. Inadequate clothing for the season or clothing that isn't washed would also require intervention. When money is used for drugs or alcohol by the parents and the children are deprived of basic needs this would be considered neglect in most states and could result in a loss of custody of the children.

6. *Educational Neglect*   Poor school attendance is another form of parental neglect that would be considered a reason for intervention by child protective services. The child may be missing school because of poor health or a parent may require an older child to stay home and care for younger siblings. Often, children may not be attending school because of chaos, domestic violence, child abuse, or other forms of crisis in the home.

7. *Insufficient Supervision*   There are many aspects to consider when determining that a lack of parental supervision constitutes neglect. The ages of the children, the time of day or night they may be left unsupervised, and the length of time they were alone are all important factors. Whether the parents have left a phone number and food for the children are also considerations. Abandonment of children is an extreme form of neglect. "Throwaways" are a term used for children whose parents "kick" them out of the home or move away, leaving the children to fend for themselves.

8. *Moral Neglect*   Children who are allowed or encouraged to steal or prostitute themselves suffer from moral neglect. Sometimes parents will use children to make pornography. Runaways are often the victims of moral neglect and physical neglect and abuse.

9. *Emotional Abuse and Neglect*   Emotional abuse is parental behavior that causes psychological harm to the child. Threats to lock the child up, have them arrested by the police, or send them away, frighten and intimidate children. When a parent or caretaker fails to provide adequate love and caring or intellectual stimulation, the child may suffer from emotional neglect. Children who are emotionally abused demonstrate developmental lags, withdrawal, or problems with intimacy that make it difficult for them to bond with others.

10. *Sexual Abuse*   When a parent or a caretaker commits or allows any sexual act to be committed on a child, it is considered sexual abuse. Sexual abuse

occurs most often within a family. The sexual activity between a family member and child is called incest and the most common form of incest is father-daughter sexual abuse. Another form of sexual abuse is sexual contact between the child and a nonrelative known to the child. This form of sexual abuse is considered sexual assault. Sexual assault also includes sexual activity initiated by a stranger. Sexual assault and incest are very traumatic to the child since force or threats are often used. Incest is also very damaging to the victim because the person responsible is usually in a position that would normally suggest trust and the belief that the molester should protect rather than exploit the child. There is no question of degree or definition in the case of sexual abuse. Any sexual activity between a child and an adult or someone significantly further along in their physical and emotional development is considered sexual abuse.

The Impact of Child Physical Abuse and Neglect: General Indicators

Hamarman and Bernet (2000) suggest the following indicators of post-traumatic stress disorder in child victims of abuse who have been traumatized: high levels of anxiety with panic attacks, aggressive behavior, substance abuse problems, hypervigilance, nightmares, social isolation and withdrawal, headaches and other somatic complaints, play that recreates the abuse, repetitive play, poor academic performance, and rebelliousness at home.

There are considerable data to show that child abuse has a particularly negative impact on children and that it may continue on into adulthood. That impact, both physical and emotional, may include a very high probability that children who witness domestic abuse or are themselves victims of abuse, will abuse their own children and spouses. Dodge, Bates, and Petit (1990) offer evidence that the experience of physical abuse in early childhood is a risk marker for the development of aggressive behavior patterns. The authors report a threefold increase in the risk to become abusive in children who have witnessed abuse in their families and a significant increase in the way in which these children incorrectly view the hostile intent of others. Children who have been abused suffer from an inability to solve personal problems (Dodge et al., 1990). Widom (1989) notes that individuals who have been identified by juvenile courts as abuse victims as children are 42 percent more likely than controls to continue the cycle of violence by committing violent acts as adults.

Glicken (1995) notes that victims of physical abuse are far more likely to enter into relationships with people who have themselves been abused, or who will abuse them. This tendency to form relationships with partners who have also been abused almost always assures the continuation of violence in relationships. Physical abuse of adults and children frequently moves into sexual abuse, particularly when substances are used and impulse control is at its lowest.

This change in the focus of the abuse from adults to children may be explained by the perpetrators' increasing rage at situations that unconsciously remind him or her of early life abuse. Abusive men and women may experience sadistic joy in abusing animals or in taking treasured personal items from others in the home. Abuse may also include destruction of property, delight in ridiculing, and special pleasure in making others feel as helpless and as powerless as the abuser felt as a child when they were being abused (Glicken, 1995).

There is considerable evidence that child abuse is one of the leading causes of death and disfigurement of children in America. However, because men are stronger physically, the damage done to children by men is often greater than that done by women and, consequently, children battered by men may have more serious physical problems. Those problems may include loss of sight, brain damage, severe disfigurement, particularly when hot fluids have been used or battering is repeated in the same physical area, loss of the use of limbs, paralysis, and deafness (ears and eyes are special targets of abusers) (Glicken, 1995; Kessler & Hyden, 1991).

The emotional harm to children who have witnessed domestic violence or who have, themselves, been victims of abuse include severe life-long depression, rages that translate into panic and anxiety disorders, substance abuse, underemployment or difficulty working, sexual disorders, low self-esteem, prostitution (85% of the prostitutes who have been interviewed report having been physically and/or sexually abused as children) (Utah Public Television, 1991), and continued rage reactions and difficulty in controlling anger. Children who have been physically abused are very likely to physically harm other children, as well (Utah Public Television, 1991).

Case Study of a Perpetrator of Child Physical Abuse

Edgar Johnson is a thirty-six-year-old Caucasian father of four who has systematically abused each of his children from birth. He has burned the feet and legs of his infant children with scalding bath water, broken bones, broken jaws, and, on at least two occasions, caused minimal organic brain damage to his children, Andy, 9, and Sam, 5. Edgar has been protected by his family and friends. It is only recently that a schoolteacher noticed bruising on Andy's face and after a lengthy discussion with Andy, found out that his father had battered him. As a mandated reporter, the teacher contacted child protective services and made a report. The agency did nothing at first, but several weeks later, when Andy reported that he'd had a concussion from being hit in the head by a rock his father held, the teacher bypassed the child protective agency and called the district attorney's office who immediately investigated the charge.

It was discovered that all of the children had, at one time or the other, been taken to emergency rooms around the metropolitan area for various traumas. Edgar is very convincing and sympathetic and hospital staff generally believe the stories he concocts. A favorite story he tells hospital staffs is that he's a single father who is overwhelmed by the responsibilities of raising a large family after the death of his wife while giving birth to his youngest child.

Edgar has a personality disorder and gets a great deal of pleasure out of the pain he inflicts on his children. He probably has a secondary diagnosis of sadistic personality. Edgar was severely beaten as a child and believes that the pain he inflicts on his children is payback for the pain inflicted on him. He doesn't beat his wife and only beats his children since they are the primary source of his rage. He told the police that he never beat them as badly as he was beaten and showed them scars on his body from repeated whippings with rods which he received from his father beginning at age five and ending at age eighteen when he left home to join the military.

When the extent and duration of the abuse was discovered, Edgar was found guilty of child abuse and was jailed for five years. The children were sent for foster care. The mother was accused of neglect for not stopping the abuse and, because of her passivity in not helping the children, was deemed an unfit mother. The children all suffer from various emotional problems including fear of the dark, regressed personality development, sleeping problems, social immaturity, and rage reactions when they don't get their way. All the children are presently being seen for medical and emotional treatment. Edgar is receiving anger management training and intensive psychotherapy for his rage. His prison therapist says that he is making headway but isn't certain that Edgar will ever be a fit parent or that children will be safe in his care.

Discussion of the Case

Like many victims of child abuse, Edgar is filled with rage at what was done to him by his father. He believes that beating his children will make them as strong as he is. He hopes that they will beat their children. Other than child abuse, Oscar argues that he's been a good citizen. He has worked, paid taxes, and fed and clothed his family. It never dawned on him that the children would suffer any ill effects from his abuse. He believed that, like him, they would turn out to be just fine. "Beatings toughen the spirit," he likes to tell his jailhouse cronies.

Unfortunately, Edgar's rampage of long-term child abuse isn't unusual. It isn't only families that protect abusers, but the institutions and the mandated reporters who work in those institutions often collude to protect child abusers from punishment and treatment. Only a fraction of the adults reported for child abuse ever get investigated and of those who do get investigated, only a fraction of those are prosecuted. (California Department of Justice, 1993). Of the reports of child abuse in California, only 7 percent are fully investigated. Of the fully investigated reports, punishment of the parents, other than loss of parental rights, is very rare.

Edgar's chances at rehabilitation might improve with the length of treatment. He may stay away from children and lead a fairly quiet life. The important issue is whether the rage inside, which Edgar doesn't really understand, will go away as treatment progresses. Anger management may not be enough to make this happen. Some insight-oriented work to help Edgar see connections between what was done to him, the development of his anger, the pleasure he gets in seeing his children in pain, as well as an awareness of what triggers his violent need to torture his children, will be necessary for Edgar to progress. One would always like to be optimistic, but without ongoing treatment and supervision after Edgar leaves jail, the possibility is all too great that he will find, or form, another family and that his rage will continue on in violence to children.

Sexual Abuse

Sexual abuse of a child may surface through a broad range of physical, behavioral, and social symptoms. Some of these symptoms, taken separately, may not be symptomatic of sexual abuse. They are listed below as a guide and should be examined in the context of other behavior(s) or situational factors. These indicators come from the State of California Ofice of Criminal Justice Planning in a 1987 report (State of California office of Criminal Justice Planning, 1987), and interviews with child protective service workers.

A child may report sexual activities to a friend, classmate, teacher, friend's mother, or other trusted adult. The disclosure may be direct or indirect ("I know someone . . ."; "What would do you do if . . . ?"; "I heard something about somebody . . ."). It is not uncommon for the disclosure of chronic or acute sexual abuse to be delayed. Or the child may wear torn, stained, or bloody underclothing that are discovered at school or at a friend's home. The child may have an injury/disease (vaginal trauma, sexually transmitted disease) that is unusual for a specific age group and can only be contracted by sexual activity. This may have happened before and knowledge of the child's medical history is very important (Brokenburr, 1994; DePanfilis & Salus, 1992). These injuries or diseases are often inconsistent with medical evaluations when parents or caretakers try to give explanations.

Another indicator of child sexual abuse is pregnancy. Pregnancy of a minor, regardless of her age, may not constitute reasonable suspicion of sexual abuse since it may be the result of consensual sex between minors close in age. This activity might be considered a reason for prosecution of statutory rape although consensual sex between minors is less frequently prosecuted in most states. However, when the pregnancy is the result of force, coercion, or when there is a significant age difference between the minor and her partner, it may suggest sexual abuse and it must be reported.

Behavioral Indicators of Sexual Abuse in Younger Children

Some specific behavioral indicators in younger children who have been sexually abused include the following (Kessler & Hyden, 1991; DePanfilis & Salus, 1992): age-inappropriate understanding of sexual terms and inappropriate, unusual, seductive, or aggressive sexual behavior with peers and adults; obsessive curiosity about sexual matters or sexual areas of the body in self and others; repeated concerns about homosexuality (particularly in boys who have been molested by a male perpetrator); fear of the child's parents or caretakers and fear of going home; eating disorders (overeating, eating too little, and aversion to certain foods); school problems or rapid changes in school performance including attitudes in class, friendships, involvement in activities and grades; false maturity or age-inappropriate behaviors including bed wetting and thumb sucking; sleep problems including nightmares, fear of falling asleep, troubled sleep patterns, or sleeping very long hours; enuresis (bed wetting), which may be a defense against the perpetrator molesting the child at night; important behavioral changes that seem new and abrupt; an inability to concentrate and withdrawal from activities and friends; and a preoccupation with death.

The guilt and shame of the child victim and the frequent involvement of parents, stepparents, friends, or other persons caring for the child make it very difficult for children to report sexual abuse. Despite these problems, as public awareness develops and as children are taught more about sexual abuse in school, reports of sexual abuse made to child protective agencies continue to increase.

Often a child who does seek help is accused of fabricating the story since people often cannot believe that a respected member of the community is capable of sexual abuse (Everson & Boat, 1989). Because it is the word of the child against that of an adult, the child may give in to pressure from parents or caretakers and take back the accusation of sexual abuse. This happens because the child may feel guilty and frightened about reporting the abuser or the possibility of breaking up the family and, consequently, might withdraw the complaint. This process often leads many child protective workers and law enforcement officers to be skeptical about a child's complaint of sexual abuse, particularly in children who appear manipulative or who have had numerous disagreements with parents. Recanting an accusation of sexual abuse may leave the child feeling helpless and guilty about causing so much trouble for the family. Without third-party confirmation or someone else reporting the abuse, the child often feels forced to keep the abuse secret. To ensure that the abuse is kept secret, the abuser may use shame, fear, and physical threats with the child. If the abuser is a parent, the child may worry that reporting the parent will result in foster care and that the abusing parent may be sent to jail. These and other concerns are often repeatedly told to the victim by the perpetrator until the child victim is more concerned about the results of reporting the abuse than the actual abuse itself.

Physical and Behavioral Problems in Older Children and Adolescents Who Have Been Sexually Abused

The following behavioral problems might be related to older children and adolescents who have been sexually abused: poor hygiene or excessive bathing; poor relations with friends and peers; poor interpersonal skills; isolation, loneliness, withdrawn behavior, and depression; acting out; running away; and aggressive, antisocial, or delinquent behavior. Children who have been sexually abused often have school problems that might include frequent absences, behavioral problems in the classroom, falling asleep in class, and drawings or stories by the child that suggest severe emotional distress. School-related problems might include a rapid decline in academic performance, an unwillingness to undress and shower in public for gym classes, or an unwillingness to be involved in activities requiring close physical contact with others. Adolescent prostitution or sexual acting out may also suggest sexual abuse. Children who have been sexually abused are often afraid of coming to school because they fear that the family may be broken up because the abuse has become known. The child may worry that he or she will then be alone in the world. Care must be taken not to assume sexual abuse because any of the symptoms listed here are observed in the child's behavior. Any of these symptoms may be indicative of other problems unrelated to sexual abuse (Brokenburr, 1994; Kessler & Hyden, 1991).

Children who have been sexually abused may also be seductive or sexual with others, or they feel great discomfort with intimate contact. They may have gifts given to them by the abuser that reinforce the agreement to keep the abuse secret. When asked where the gift came from, the child may have no logical answer. Children who have been sexually abused may also suffer from depression and chronic fatigue. Suicide attempts, even by very young children, are not uncommon in sexual abuse cases. One of the new areas of interest in the understanding of depression in children under the age of six is our tendency to confuse a suicide attempt with an accident. Children who run out into the street or who drink poisonous liquids but know better and have never exhibited a tendency to use bad judgment, may be very depressed and suicidal. Further symptoms related to child sexual abuse might include drug and alcohol use at a very early age, fire setting, frequent bouts of crying, anorexia and other eating disorders, and chronic unhappiness. Care must be taken to collect sufficient data before making a diagnosis of child sexual abuse (Brokenburr, 1994; Kessler & Hyden, 1991).

The following physical symptoms of sexual abuse may be found in younger children as well as older children and adolescents: physical trauma or irritations to the anal or genital area (pain, itching, swelling, bruising, bleeding, lacerations, especially if unexplained or inconsistent); difficulty in walking or sitting because of genital or anal pain; psychosomatic symptoms (stomachaches, headaches); sexually transmitted diseases; and pain upon urination or defecation (Brokenburr, 1994; Kessler & Hyden, 1991).

Incest and Intrafamilial Abuse

The legal definition of incest is sexual activity between persons who are blood-related. Intrafamilial sexual activity refers to sexual contact between family members not related by blood (stepparents, boyfriends, etc.). In most reported cases, the father or another man acting as the parent is the initiator, with girls as the most frequent victims. Sedlak (1997) writes,

The child's sex was significantly related to the risk of sexual abuse. However, after taking other important predictors into account, the child's sex was also related to risk in two other important categories (i.e., physical neglect and multiple maltreatment). In all cases, females were more at risk than males . . . and most at risk between ages 15–17. (in Brown and Brown, 1997 p. 168)

Boys are also victims of incest much more often than was previously believed. As Sedlak notes, boys may be more at risk of multiple forms of abuse at a younger age than girls (p. 168). There is reason to believe that the younger the age of onset of sexual abuse, the more harmful and long lasting the impact of the abuse tends to be. The number of children abused by women, usually mothers, has been underestimated and may be as high as 30 percent of all incest cases (Utah Public Television, 1991). Boys seldom report molestation by women.

The mother may purposely try to stay removed from a problem of sexual abuse. Sometimes this is out of insecurity because of the potential loss of her mate and the economic security he provides. Often, however, she may also have been a victim of child sexual abuse and may be unable to challenge her spouse or partner's authority. Some mothers actually know that their children are being sexually abused but respond with anger when the child informs her of the abuse, citing the negative impact it might have on the family if the child makes the accusation public. When a parent has been told that a child is being abused, or if she is suspicious of abuse, failure to stop or report the abuse may result in charges of child neglect and endangerment. Often, abused children never tell anyone until they are adults when symptoms related to the impact of sexual abuse begins to surface.

Repressed Memory Syndrome

In many victims of child sexual abuse, symptoms related to the abuse may carry forward into adulthood and may be very serious and require treatment. Symptoms related to child sexual abuse are particularly serious in adult victims who have been unable to confide in others about the abuse and have carried the secret with them for much of their life. Common adult symptoms of child sexual abuse include depression with suicidal attempts, anxiety with panic attacks, sleep and eating disorders, generalized poor health and psychosomatic problems, drug and alcohol abuse, repeatedly failed relationships and multiple marriages by an early age, sexual acting out, aversion to sexual contact, and intractable intimacy problems.

Because a number of therapists in the late 1980s and early 1990s treating clients with many of the above symptoms began to suspect child sexual abuse, even when their clients denied that it had taken place, a movement began to develop that advanced the notion that child sexual abuse had taken place but that the memory of the abuse had been repressed. The concept of *repressed memory* of the abuse suggested that the abuse was so highly traumatic that the child repressed the memory of the abuse even though it may have occurred repeatedly over a very long period of time.

To support the belief that many adults seeking treatment for nonspecific emotional problems, which didn't seem to improve with time or with multiple therapists, had been sexually abused as children, a number of people in the helping professions began to look at the post-traumatic stress disorder literature, particularly the reports of traumatic events that occurred during wartime and in workplace accidents (Glicken, 1986). In these two situations, repression, or memory loss of the event was not uncommon and therapists began to suspect child sexual abuse in their clients in ever-increasing numbers. Denials of abuse by parents were frequent and, in time, the idea of repressed memory began to decline in popularity as a reason for many of the symptoms noted in adult victims of child sexual abuse. In fact, a number of critics of the repressed memory controversy believed that therapists had encouraged false memories of events that had never taken place. They pointed to the multiple reasons for serious adult problems and that sexual abuse is such a powerful event in a child's life, that the child would be unlikely to repress the memory of the event.

Still, for a number of troubled adults in our society, child sexual abuse remains the reason for many serious emotional problems. While we may never know the absolute reason for many of the problems that plague adults throughout their lives, it seems reasonable to believe that incest and other forms of child sexual abuse may be an important reason for continued difficulty. One maxim of therapy is that when a client goes to a number of therapists and fails to improve, that the underlying reasons for the problems are serious and often difficult to ascertain. Denial and repression are powerful mechanisms and many adults have repressed other painful nonsexual memories and events from their past in order to function reasonably well. In time, the weight of these repressed events tends to have a negative impact, particularly when the adult is experiencing other forms of stress in their lives. While it is wise not to jump to conclusions regarding the cause of long-term adult unhappiness, it is also wise not to discount the possibility of sexual abuse in childhood. The trained and objective therapist always tries to collect information about a client's past in a way that doesn't permit the therapist to influence that information. However, the process of remaining objective is complex, and even very good therapists may see child sexual abuse as a cause of an adult's emotional problems when that may not be the case.

On the other side of the controversy are the therapists who point out that we should be studying the lives of adults who have been sexually abused as children but live reasonably normal, well-functioning, and productive lives. These "resilient" people can tell us a great deal about the way people who have been abused successfully deal with the trauma. Some workers in the field believe that resilient abuse victims experience a combination of positive factors that might include very good coping skills, supportive families, a network of friends, spiritual and religious convictions, early intervention related to the abuse, and exceptional problem solving skills. These notions remain to be tested and we clearly need to do a great deal more research on the long-term and pervasive impact of child sexual abuse on adult victims. It stands to reason that most people, however resilient they may be, will suffer some ill effects of abuse and that the symptoms may be subtle and hidden. It is difficult to think that abuse victims will not experience intimacy problems, or that relationships may not suffer as a result of the abuse.

Case Study of Repressed Memory Syndrome

Mary Kay is a twenty-eight-year-old Caucasian female who has just ended her fourth marriage in a bitter and angry divorce. She was married at age 16 for the first time and has been unable to sustain a marriage for more than a year. She says that all four of her husbands were physically and emotionally abusive and that all had drug or alcohol problems. Mary Kay admits that she has regularly used alcohol and drugs since she was 12. She has been in drug treatment three times since the age of 16, but she continues to abuse substances and feels unable to stop.

Mary Kay is a very unhappy woman. She suffers from depression with anxiety and panic attacks. She uses drugs and alcohol to help her sleep, but is often unable to sleep for more than an hour or two at a time and usually wakes up in the midst of a panic attack. She has difficulty keeping jobs and is frequently absent or late because of her drug and alcohol addictions. She has been fired several times for using drugs on the job. Mary Kay has been in therapy almost continually since she was 16, but feels as unhappy now as she did then. She has used prescribed anti-depressants and anti-anxiety medications but doesn't feel they help and prefers street drugs. She has attempted suicide on four occasions, usually by drug overdose, and frequently has mood swings that are severe and sometimes violent. On more than a few occasions, Mary Kay has been the perpetrator of spousal abuse.

Mary Kay's most recent therapist, noting the long history of emotional problems and substance abuse, began to suspect that Mary Kay had been sexually abused as a child. Mary Kay steadfastly denied the abuse and said that her parents were wonderful people. Both of her siblings have done well in life and have no known emotional problems. In the course of a regressions session in which Mary Kay was urged to recall upsetting dreams, Mary Kay described a reoccurring dream of a man chasing and then overpowering her. The dream is so frightening that she has frequently wet the bed. She is embarrassed by the adult bedwetting. She also has problems with intimacy and finds sex repulsive, a primary reason for the failure of her marriages. Some of her memories of adolescence include being fondled and touched on her genitalia and breasts by an unknown person. She admits that she can not remember much of her adolescence because of drug and alcohol abuse. If something *did* happen, she told her therapist, it's possible that it happened while she was using drugs.

As the regression therapy continued, Mary Kay began to have vivid memories of being sexually abused by her father, her brother, and her grandfather. The memories were very clear and she and the therapist began to suspect that she had suffered childhood sexual abuse. Mary Kay confronted her father who strongly denied that anything of the sort had ever happened, as did her brother. She is so certain of the sexual abuse that she has stopped having contact with either her brother or father and filed sexual molestation charges against them with the police. The charges were dropped because of a lack of evidence and because the county attorney felt that Mary Kay's story wasn't credible. The damage to her family, however, has been significant since the charges were made publicly.

Mary Kay is involved in a variety of recovery groups for the victims of childhood sexual abuse. She is a passionate advocate for early intervention by the courts and thinks that children are ignored and are all too frequently injured as a result. She has made no progress in her current therapy, however, and still suffers from debilitating bouts of depression, anxiety, and drug abuse. She is still a profoundly unhappy woman.

Discussion of the Case   It sounds as if Mary Kay has been abused. However, the denial of the abuse by her father and brother, and the county attorney's decision to drop the case because he didn't find the story credible, are indications that the abuse may not have happened. It is also entirely possible that the regression therapy may have encouraged false memory syndrome. By asking the client to remember something that didn't happen, the therapist might have helped Mary Kay tap into memories of sexual violence that are unrelated to her family. The sexual violence may have happened outside of her family, or it may be related to a movie or story from early childhood. The feelings of being molested are certainly real enough and the reoccurring dream sounds frightening and genuine.

Is it possible that Mary Kay has suffered minimal organic brain syndrome because of the abuse of substances? Might there be some biochemical changes caused by her long history of substance abuse? Could Mary Kay have borderline personality disorder? Consider the description of this diagnostic category in the Diagnostic Manual of Mental Disorders (1994) of the American Psychiatric Association (p. 654):

> A pervasive pattern of instability of interpersonal relationships, self-image, and affects, and marked impulsivity beginning by early adulthood and present in a variety of contexts with five or more of the following. (There are 9 areas. Five that seem to describe the client are noted here.)
>
> 1. A pattern of unattainable and intense interpersonal relationships . . .
> 2. Impulsivity in at least two areas that are self-damaging (sex and substance abuse are two of five areas noted).
> 3. Chronic feelings of emptiness.
> 4. Recurrent suicidal behavior, gestures or self-mutilation . . .
> 5. Intense mood swings.

Does this sound like Mary Kay? Perhaps it does. In borderline personality disorder, these symptoms generally begin at an early age. Treatment is usually ineffective with clients having a history of repeatedly failed therapy. To determine the correct diagnosis, we would need to do a more complete social history and include information from family members as well as medical information (Elliott & Briere, 1995).

It appears possible that Mary Kay had an abusive experience in her life. The reoccurring dream is a telltale sign of abuse. It also sounds as if the childhood drug abuse was an attempt to self-medicate, an all too frequent behavior in children who are being molested. Might it be possible that she was molested, but not by a family member? Or might the molestation have occurred when Mary Kay was using drugs? It would be important to find out if the reoccurring dream began before her use of drugs. Finally, could she have experienced abuse at such an early age that she has no specific memory of the abuse and her regression therapy, while inaccurate in suggesting that her family was involved, accurately discovered that abuse had taken place? We need more information before we can answer any of these questions, although it has been suggested that borderline personality disorder has, as one of the suspected causes, infantile childhood sexual abuse.

Regression therapy has been roundly criticized lately. Having clients regress is a surefire way of getting them to remember events that may never have happened. Still, in an attempt to help troubled adults who may have been abused as children, it's understandable that we would use many techniques to try and help our deeply troubled and unhappy adult clients who may, just may, have actually experienced abuse but have repressed the memory because it is too painful.

The Perpetrators of Incest

Brown and Brown (1997) report that incest has been attributed to many factors including, "dysfunctional relationships, chemical abuse, sexual problems, and social isolation" (p. 336). They go on to note that men commit incestuous acts because they:

> . . . find sexual contact with a child emotionally gratifying, because they are capable of being sexually aroused by a child, because they are unable to receive sexual stimulation and emotional gratification from adults, and because they are not deterred by the social convention and the inhibitors against having sexual relations with a child. (p. 337)

Brown and Brown go on to note further characteristics of men who sexually abuse children. These men often have poor impulse control, have low feelings of self-worth, have poor tolerance for frustration, and seek quick gratification for their sexual needs (p. 337). Furthermore, incest perpetrators are often described as angry individuals who do not learn from prior experience, have addictive personalities, experience low levels of guilt for their behavior, and tend to lie and be manipulative. Brown and Brown suggest that they share three deviant attributes:

> They tend to believe in the concept of male sexual entitlement, perceive children as sexually attractive and motivated to experience sex, and minimize harm caused by

their sexual abuse . . . [These characteristics] could prevent offenders from developing appropriate self-controls when presented with opportunities to offend. (1997, p. 337)

Extrafamilial Sexual Abuse

Children who are abused by someone outside of their family often know their abuser. They may meet them at school, youth programs, churches, in their neighborhood, or during other recreational activities. People who molest children fall into all age categories, including preteens and the elderly. Although there are several classifications of child molesters, a pedophile presents the greater danger to children because a pedophile's main sexual interest is a child (Brokenburr, 1994).

Pedophiles tend to be liked by children and often work in professions or volunteer organizations that allow them easy access to children and the trust and respect of children and their parents. Pedophiles believe that sex with children is appropriate and even beneficial to the child. Pedophiles often lure children into sexual relationships with love, rewards, promises, and gifts. Most cases of extrafamilial sexual abuse involve a perpetrator known to the child. However, cases of abuse by strangers do occur. Typically, in these cases, the stranger will entice the child ("Will you help me find my puppy?"), convince the child that his or her parent requested the stranger to pick up the child, or simply abduct the child (Brokenburr, 1994).

Case Study of a Female Child Victim of Sexual Abuse

Joan is a ten-year-old Caucasian girl who was molested by a stranger on the way home from school. The molestation included oral sex and intercourse with ejaculation. Joan was taken to a hospital emergency room by a police officer who was called to the scene by children who later found Joan naked in some bushes in a park near the school. Joan was highly agitated and was unable to give a description of the perpetrator. She was immediately taken to a local emergency room where staff who were trained to work with sexual abuse victims examined Joan for signs of rape, sexually transmitted diseases, and pregnancy. A rape kit was used upon initial examination. The kit included the equipment to place hair, semen samples, and other physical evidence into an evidence box witnessed by an officer of the law. The rape kit has proven very useful in treating the physical aspects of rape and in providing DNA and other physical evidence against rapists.

Joan remained in the hospital for three days in a special unit for sexually abused children. She was given intensive crisis intervention and treated for damage to her vaginal area and cuts and bruises on her body. Test results indicated that she was HIV negative but that she had been given syphilis by the perpetrator. Successful treatment with antibiotics was begun immediately in the hospital for the syphilis. She will be retested for HIV since tests done soon after intercourse are not always accurate.

During her stay in the hospital, Joan received emergency crisis counseling. The focus of the treatment was on helping her understand that the molestation wasn't her fault and that there was nothing she could have done to prevent it. The parents were told not to emphasize the molestation or to treat her differently because of the rape. Joan continued on in treatment after she left the hospital. During the first few weeks after the attack, Joan had eating problems, was often depressed and tearful, and appeared very withdrawn to her parents. She returned to school and while she was the object of some very mean-spirited ridicule and kidding, with some of the boys saying that she enjoyed the experience, Joan has begun to return to her old self. She is doing well again in school and her mood swings have subsided.

The counselor seeing her has been warm and supportive, allowing Joan to talk freely about any subject she wants to discuss. The counselor has also made certain that friends accompany Joan when she goes anywhere since she still has fearful moments. Hoping that she might benefit from a group experience, the counselor referred Joan to a self-help group for girls in her age group who have been molested. Joan feels that she is lucky to have survived her experience as well as she did since many of the girls in the group seem very dysfunctional because of long-term and aggressive sexual abuse by family members. The girls have formed a bond with one another and Joan continues going to the group because she feels that she can help some of the more troubled children. She used to fantasize about marriage and to play games about love and romance with her girlfriends, but she has stopped doing this. Love and romance seem unreachable to her now and she would rather focus on her schoolwork and on thinking about a career that will make her enough money to live without the help of a man. She thinks the physical things that were done to her were "disgusting" and doesn't think she'll ever be able to do them again, even with a man she loves.

Discussion of the Case

Joan has had a serious trauma. Like most traumas, time, good parenting, and counseling may help heal some of the damage done. No one knows for certain if she will ever be able to enjoy sexual intimacy or to trust a man in a loving relationship. Even one significant trauma such as the one that Joan had can have a lifelong negative impact. She may be someone who is very successful in her career but much less successful in relationships. She may suffer periodic and unexplained episodes of depression alternating with anxiety and panic attacks. These symptoms are often present as an aftermath of both child molestation and rape. Or she may come out of the experience, as some resilient children do, fairly unscathed. Continued treatment is certainly in order as is help to the parents to not subtly treat her as if she's fragile. Finally, work with the children in the school is very important. Considerable harm is done to children like Joan when classmates make fun of them, ostracize them for what happened, or spread rumors.

We are still at a beginning stage in knowing what the most effective treatment approaches may be for children who have been sexually molested. Increasingly, the notion of early intervention with atheoretical and nonresearch-oriented approaches raises questions regarding treatment effectiveness. There are some researchers who wonder if early intervention may even cause harm since it focuses attention on what happened to the child and can't help but make the child think that there is something wrong with them. Tyndall (1997) suggests that the treatment goals for child sexual and incest survivors are: "Ameliorate the presenting symptoms; develop a realistic and factual understanding of the abusive experience; ventilation of feelings associated with the abuse; develop healthy physical, psychological, and interpersonal boundaries; increase self-esteem; learn about healthy sexuality; and prevent perpetration of sexual acting out" (p. 281). These seem like good goals, but the issues of when to intervene, when not to intervene, and to what extent one should intervene, still seem to be the key issues in the treatment of sexual abuse of children. Lacking convincing evidence of treatment effectiveness, we think that the worker must be careful to ensure that the intervention is not overly intrusive and that it does not perpetuate a sense of differentness in the victim. This is an admittedly difficult task but one that may be made with more ease if the child has a strong family network who continue to treat the child as they have in the past: with support, respect, dignity, understanding, patience, and encouragement to do well in life.

Treatment Approaches for the Victims of Sexual Abuse

According to Biere (1992), any incestuous contact in a family setting is a very disturbing experience that can often have a lasting effect on children and for the generation of children whose lives are affected by the abuse the child has experienced. Appropriate treatment and careful case management can often lead to successful outcomes and frequently end the multigenerational cycle of abuse. (Brokenburr, 1994; DePanfilis & Salus, 1992).

In the initial stage of intervention when awareness of the molestation is made public, the child should be seen medically to determine if any physical harm has been done (Kessler & Hyden, 1991). Medical treatment should begin immediately and appropriate evidence gathering should take place to use in future testimony against the offender. Psychological testing and an in-depth psychosocial history should be taken to evaluate emotional trauma and to determine short- and long-term treatment goals. Crisis intervention services to the child might include supportive intervention and consistent feedback that the molestation was not the child's fault and that the child should recognize that only very troubled people molest children. Fear of guilt or reprisal by the offender or family members needs to be addressed and the child needs to know that his or her safety is the ultimate concern of everyone providing treatment services. In the case of incest, the perpetrator needs to be physically removed from the child's home and contact should be stopped until the court determines that supervised contact might be resumed.

DePanfilis and Salus, in their work for the National Center on Child Abuse and Neglect (1992), a federal center that is part of U.S. Department of Health and Human Services, describe the treatment needs of children and their families. Treatment, they believe, is complex. Since the origins of abuse lie in a multiple number of reasons, many of them existing over a long period of time, the authors believe that "interventions need to address as many of the contributing factors [of abuse] as possible" (p. 61). They go on to say:

> Early research in child abuse and neglect treatment effectiveness suggests that successful treatment with maltreating families requires a comprehensive package that addresses both the intrapersonal and concrete needs of all family members. . . . Recent research found that a broad range of therapeutic and other services for child sexual abuse exist including individual and group treatment, dyad treatment, family therapy, peer support groups, marital therapy, alcohol and drug counseling, client advocacy, parents aides, education and crisis intervention. (pp. 61–62)

DePanfilis and Salus (1992) suggest that issues to be addressed in the family include the past history of abuse; family attitudes toward violence; problem solving patterns; anger and impulse control issues; definitions of acceptable sexuality; stress management; substance abuse; patterns of abuse in families that may be historical and cross several or more generations; impulse control and judgment problems within families; conflicts with authority by perpetrators at work and in the community; manipulative and self-indulgent behavior; acting out behavior with patterns of anti-social activities related to sexual and a nonsexual behavior; demanding, controlling, and domineering behavior; a lack of the ability to trust; and reduced degrees of intimacy (pp. 63–64).

Case Study of a Sexual Perpetrator

James Carleton is a thirty-one-year-old Caucasian male pedophile. James is currently serving a five-year sentence for molesting a six-year-old boy. James told his counselor that he's molested over a hundred children, both boys and girls. He says that he likes the feel of young bodies and that it doesn't matter to him if the child is male or female. James is an "opportunistic" pedophile who takes advantage of children by the use of favors including money and presents. He doesn't hang around school yards or involve himself in activities that might require him to undergo close scrutiny of his life. He works at menial jobs and moves around the country a great deal. He never stays in the same community after molesting a child and believes that this is the reason he hadn't been caught up to this point.

James was caught in a police sting that lured pedophiles into motels with the promise of child victims as sexual partners. A close check of his background determined that he had outstanding warrants for child abuse. James accepted a plea bargain of eight to ten years in prison. He has served only a year and thinks he'll be out in six months.

James isn't repentant about his crimes. He believes that the children he molests get "a kind of love from me that they don't get from their parents." James says that the children he molests are street kids who will gladly have sex with him and enjoy his company. He says he'll refrain from molesting when he gets out but the treatment staff believes that James is a "robust" molester with an anti-social personality. They believe he will continue molesting at the first chance he gets.

James says that he has always been sexually stimulated by children. In fact, he molested his younger brother before his parents stopped it. He finds children over 10 unappealing and is mostly stimulated by children under the age of 6. He has gone for treatment twice but neither time helped him stop molesting very young children. He thinks it's cruel for society to try and take away this "gift" that God has given him to bring pleasure to unloved children and he says that while he will stop molesting children, he will continue to believe that God has graced him with the knowledge that he can bring love and comfort to unloved and lonely children.

Discussion of the Case

James is a fixed pedophile without sufficient moral development to make him stop his molestations. It is also likely that he has a personality disorder of the anti-social variety. Many pedophiles feel remorse and guilt over their attraction to children and see the behavior as wrong. James not only thinks it's right to molest children, but he sees value to the children he molests and even believes that he is providing love to unloved children. This denial of the harm he is doing to children is always a very poor sign that a diversion project or mandated treatment in prison will have a positive impact on James' sexual behavior. The probability is that James will continue to molest because he thinks it's the right thing to do. The threat of prison may not change the behavior and age, which sometimes reduces a pedophile's probability of molesting, is not likely to have an appreciable impact on James.

This is not to say that fixed pedophilia is untreatable or that pedophiles can't control their sexual impulses. The key ingredient for this to take place seems to be the degree of moral development in the pedophile. The more he or she may feel that it is wrong to molest children, and the more they experience remorse over sexual thoughts and acts that include children, the more likely it is that treatment will help pedophiles control their impulses (Brown & Brown, 1997). When thinking of the difficulty of changing the pedophile's sexual behavior, think of how difficult it might be for a fixed heterosexual or a fixed homosexual to change their behavior. As in many issues pertaining to sexual acting out, we are at a very early stage in our knowledge and use of effective treatment approaches.

Treatment of Sexual Predators

There is a considerable disagreement over the effectiveness of treatment approaches with child sexual molesters. Owen and Williams (1989) report that a year after treatment, 18 percent of the incest perpetrators had been convicted of a felony offense, although the authors were unclear about whether the conviction related to an additional episode of child sexual molestation or to broken rules of probation. Freeman-Longo and Wall (1986) note that in a treatment program for chronic sex offenders, of the men who completed all the phases of the program, less than 10 percent had reoffended. Hanson, Steffy, and Gauthier (1993) report that incest perpetrators were more likely to show positive results following treatment than nonrelated child molesters. Lang, Pugh, and Langevin (1988) note that nonrelated child molesters are much more resistant to treatment than incest perpetrators. Holmes (1991), in a study of reoffending by sexual predators treated at the Oregon State Hospital, found the recidivism rate for treated offenders over a six year period to be 10 to 14 percent.

Abel, Becker, Murphy, and Flanagan (1981) found that heterosexual incest perpetrators report an average of 2.1 victims while heterosexual nonincestuous pedophiles report an average of 62.4 victims. While a number of traditional treatment approaches have been used with pedophiles (individual treatment, group treatment, family treatment, twelve-step programs, empathy training), recidivism rates of 15 to 20 percent a year have been reported as fairly typical (Brown & Brown, 1997). Quincy (1977), as reported by Brown and Brown (1997), cites a number of factors related to recidivism in the treatment of pedophilia and believes that the following are most likely to interfere with effective treatment:

> Behaviors exhibited in childhood including experiences of brutality, bed-wetting, fire starting, cruelty to animals and delinquent acts between 8 and 13. Relapse predictors for adult life include: escalation of seriousness of the offenses over time, b) interrelated criminality with sex offenses, c) sustained sexual excitement prior to the offense, d) lack of concern for the victim, e) bizarre fantasies with minor offenses, f) explosive outbursts, g) the absence of psychosis, the absence of alcohol consumption related to the offense, i) low intelligence, j) lack of warmth and, k) the lack of social skills. (Brown & Brown, 1997, p. 349)

It should be noted that many of the studies of recidivism fail to follow the perpetrator for any length of time after a conviction and subsequent treatment, and that the accuracy of all data related to child sexual predators suffers from a lack of long-term follow-up.

Marshall (1996), as reported by Brown and Brown (1997), has developed a treatment program for sexual molesters of children that is based upon several factors in the perpetrator's history including: "criminal history, level of substance abuse, employment history, and pretreatment phallometric results" (p. 350). In this approach, offenders are assigned a level of risk ranging from 1 to 5. Treatment is tailored to each level of risk and may include "intensive outpatient therapy, inpatient treatment, and extensive postrelease supervision" (Brown & Brown, 1997, p. 350).

Prevention of Child Abuse and Neglect

The civil rights and safety of children must become a national priority. We need to find a way to provide early screening and rapid and appropriate intervention on behalf of our youngest and least vocal citizens. Since many writers and researchers feel that a relationship exists between unwanted children and child abuse, sex education and readily available contraception should be offered to adolescents in high school. Many believe that the right to choose abortion should also be protected. Parenting training and relationship training might also be offered through sex education classes.

The cost of protecting children cannot be higher than the high cost of health care and maintenance for the hundreds of thousands of abused children who suffer severe brain damage and spinal cord injuries each year. The emotional problems and learning difficulties experienced by children scarred by sexual abuse and incest are incredibly costly. All too frequently, the abused child pays the ultimate price with their life before the problems are recognized and intervention can be initiated.

Case Study of a Victim of Child Abuse with Integrating Questions

Gary is a nine-year-old African American youth who was repeatedly physically abused by his mother's boyfriends over a two-year period. During that time, Gary was slapped, kicked, beaten to the point of unconsciousness, and was forced to ingest hallucinogenic drugs. Gary has had teeth knocked out of his mouth and had fourteen stitches on his cheek when his mother's boyfriend cut him with a knife while the boyfriend was using hallucinogenic drugs and speed. His mother refused to stop the abuse, telling Gary that her boyfriend was her last chance to have a decent relationship with a man. "He's a good man when he isn't high," she says. "He's got a drug problem and you have to be loving and helpful when somebody has that kind of trouble. That's what I am." Gary's father abandoned him when Gary was one year old. Gary has no memory of him and is very angry with the father for leaving the family.

Gary has been seen in treatment for six months now. He resides in a foster home and feels safe but unhappy to be away from his mother. The mother has been deemed unfit to retain custody of her child but is allowed visitation under supervision. In treatment, Gary is seen individually and in group treatment. The individual therapy has focused on Gary's anger at the boyfriend, but more specifically, it has focused on *his* anger and *his* feelings of confusion at his mother's lack of willingness to stop the abuse. "Why wouldn't she stop that man from hurting me?" Gary asks the therapist repeatedly. "She used to watch me get beat up by that fool. It's not right for a mother to let that happen to her son. We were happy before he came to the house. All he is is a fool and mean bastard."

Gary is progressing nicely in his treatment and is doing well, both in the foster home and at school. He is a mild-mannered child and is liked by everyone. The therapist reports that he has used cognitive-behavioral work with Gary that focuses on how Gary can understand the situation that lead to the abuse as well as his mother's behavior. The individual therapy also helps him see logical solutions to his feelings of anger at his mother. "She was pretty lonely," he says. "I guess she has a right to a man, even if he is an ass. . . ."

The therapist feels that Gary will be all right and that he is resilient enough to cope with the violence done to him. The therapist wrote in his report to the supervising child welfare agency: "Gary is an amazingly resilient child. He has deep religious beliefs and goes to church quite often. He makes friends easily, is well-liked in his school, and gets along well with the foster family that adores him. My only concern is that the mother still sees the boyfriend, is unwilling to come for therapy, and just doesn't seem to care if she regains custody of her son. My concern is that Gary will begin to resent the situation and that when it's clear that he will not be able to return to his mother's house, he will begin to resent her for the mother's preference for her boyfriend. At that time, Gary may present himself as a behavioral problem. Currently, however, Gary is optimistic that they will be reunited and believes that his mom will continue to be the good mother he has always known. He believes that this current episode is temporary and that mom will stop seeing the boyfriend. My contacts with mother suggest that he is wrong in this view and that time will tell if he is able to handle rejection if his mother continues her relationship. The boyfriend is charged with child abuse and the case goes to trial shortly. The mother refuses to testify against the boyfriend. Gary is being urged to decline testifying as well. At this point, it is unknown whether Gary will testify against the boyfriend. He feels that to do so may lessen his chances of returning to his mother's care."

Currently, Gary is in both individual and group treatment. The group treatment is with a group of boys roughly Gary's age who have all been physically abused by family members or boyfriends or girlfriends of parents. The group focuses on helping the members discuss their feelings about the perpetrators and on trying to understand the abuse in a way that doesn't blame the victims. It is very common for abused children to blame themselves for the maltreatment. Gary reports that the children in the group have been very abused. Compared to them, he feels lucky. Many of them have been abused by a parent which makes their abuse worse in Gary's mind. "My mom never hit me," he says, "it was that boyfriend of hers who did this to me. She should have protected me, but love is pretty crazy and sometimes you don't think real clear. My mom loves me more than anybody and that makes it better, I think."

Integrating Questions

1. Do you believe Gary when he says that his abuse wasn't as tough on him as the abuse experienced by other group therapy members? Might not the reluctance of his mother to interfere with the abuse by the boyfriend be construed as collusion in the abuse between mom and the boyfriend?

2. Gary's explanation of why the mother allowed the abuse to continue (she was lonely and in love) has a ring of familiarity to it. Do you believe that this is mom's explanation for her behavior and do you think that a more mature Gary would accept the reason so easily?

3. Gary wasn't abused until he was seven. Do you think the fact that he had a loving life up to that point makes the abuse easier or more difficult for Gary to deal with?

4. Children almost never report their abuse to the authorities, but school personnel or friends should have been aware of the abuse and should have tried to stop it. Do you think that being African American made the authorities less willing to either care about or report Gary's abuse?

5. The therapist's report suggests that Gary is resilient. What does that mean and how well will it protect Gary from the emotional damage done to him over a two-year period?

There are no easy remedies for the problem of child abuse and neglect. Despite treatment efforts and more awareness of the impact of child abuse, much more must be done to correct this serious national problem. Prevention is one way to combat all forms of child abuse and neglect, and new programs must concentrate on prevention. The target population for prevention efforts includes schools, families, professionals, and communities.

Far more research needs to be done in developing effective approaches to child intervention when abuse and neglect have been committed. We still know too little about effective interventions and we may be using incorrect approaches and services that ultimately cause harm.

REFERENCES

Abel, G., Becker, J., Murphy, W., and Flanagan, D. 1981. Identifying dangerous child molesters. In R. Stuart (Ed.), *Violent behavior: Social learning approaches to prediction, management and treatment* (pp. 116–137). New York: Brunner/Mazel.

Biere, J. (1992). *Child abuse trauma: Theory and treatment of the lasting effects.* Newbury Park, CA: Sage.

Borgman, R., Edmunds, M., & MacDicken, R. (1979). *Crisis intervention: A manual for child protective workers.* Washington, DC: Department of Health, Education, and Welfare.

Briere, J., & Runtz, M. (1989). University males' interest in children: Predicting potential indices of pedophilia in a nonforensic sample. *Child Abuse and Neglect, 13,* 65–75.

Brokenburr, D. (1994). Personal interview.

Bross, D., Krugman, R., Lenherr, M., Rosenberg, D., & Schmitt, B. (1988). *The new child protection team handbook.* New York: Garland.

Brown, J., & Brown, G. (1997). Characteristics and treatment of incest offenders. A review. *Journal of Aggression, Maltreatment and Trauma, 1*(1), 335–354.

California Department of Justice. (1993). *Child abuse prevention handbook.* Sacramento, CA: California Department of Justice.

Daro, D. (1988). *Confronting child abuse.* New York: The Free Press.

DePanfilis, D., & Salus, M. (1992). *Child protective services: A guide for caseworkers.* McLean, VA: The Circle.

Diagnostic and statistical manual of mental disorders. (4th ed.). (1994). Washington, DC: American Psychiatric Association.

Dodge, K. A., Bates, J. E., & Petit, G. S. (1990). Mechanisms in the cycle of violence. *Science, 28.*

Ebeling, N., & Hill, D. (1975). *Child abuse: Intervention and treatment.* Acton, MA: Publishing Sciences Group.

Elliott D. M., & Briere, J. (1995). Post-traumatic stress associated with delayed recall of sexual abuse. A general population study. *Journal of Traumatic Stress, 8*(4), 629–647.

Everson, M. D., & Boat, B. (1989). False allegations of sexual abuse by children and adolescents. *American Academy of Child and Adolescent Psychiatry, 28,* 230–235.

Faller, K. (1981). *Social work with abused and neglected children.* New York: The Free Press.

Feller, J. (1992). *Working with the courts in child protection.* McLean, VA: The Circle.

Finkelhor, D., Hotaling, G. T., & Sedlak, A. (2000). *Missing, abducted, runaway and throwaway children in America. First report: Numbers and characteristics.* National Incident Report, 1988. Reported in 1999 National Report Series: Juvenile Justice Crime Bulletin, May 2000, NCJ-180753.

Freeman-Longo, R., & Wall, R. V. (1986, March 20). Changing a lifetime of sexual crimes. *Psychology Today,* 58–64.

Geffner, R. (1997). Family violence: Current issues, interventions, and research. *Journal of Aggression, Maltreatment and Trauma, 1*(1–26).

Gilgun, J., & Connor, T. (1989, May). How perpetrators view child sexual abuse. *Social Work,* 249–251.

Gilliland, B., & James, R. (1993). *Crisis intervention strategies.* Pacific Grove, CA: Brooks/Cole.

Glicken, M. (1986, September/October). The after-shock of on-the-job accidents. *EAP Digest.*

Glicken, M. (1995). Understanding and treating male abusive behavior. Unpublished Monograph.

Hamarman, S., & Bernet, W. (2000, July). Evaluating and reporting emotional abuse in children: Parent-based focus aids in clinical decision making. *Journal of American Academy of Child and Adolescent Psychiatry, 39*(6). *www.findarticle.com/cf_dls/m2250/7_39?637872621/p6/article.jhtm.*

Hanson, R. R., Steffy, R. A., & Gauthier. (1993). Long-term recidivism child molesters. *Journal of Consulting and Clinical Psychology, 61,* 646–652.

Holmes, M. (1987). *Protective services for abused and neglected children and their families.* Washington, DC: Department of Health, Education, and Welfare.

Holmes, R. M. (1991). *Sex Crimes.* Newbury Park, CA: Sage Creek Press.

Johnson, L., & Schwartz, C. (1991). *Social welfare.* Needham Heights, MA: Simon and Schuster.

Juvenile Crime Bulletin. (1997, May). 1999 National Report Series NCJ-180753.

Kessler, D. B., & Hyden, P. (1991). Physical, sexual and emotional abuse of children. *Clinical Symposia, 43*(1).

Knight, C. (1990, May). Use of support groups with adult female survivors of sexual abuse. *Social Work,* 202–208.

Lang, R. A., Pugh, G. M., & Langevin, R. (1988). Treatment of incest and pedophilic offenders: A pilot study. *Behavioral Science and the Law, 6,* 239–255.

Lanyan, R. I. (1989). Theory and treatment in child molestation. *Journal of Consulting and Clinical Psychology, 54*(2), 176–182.

Lie, G. Y., & Inman, A. (1991, September). The use of anatomical dolls as assessment and evidentiary tools. *Social Work, 36*(5), 396–399.

Marshall, W. L. (1996). Assessment, treatment and theorizing about sexual offenders. *Criminal Justice and Behavior, 231*(1), 162–199.

Mason, M. A. (1992, January). Social workers as expert witnesses in child sexual abuse cases. *Social Work, 37*(1), 30–34.

Mason, M. A. (1991, September). The McMartin case revisited: The conflict between social work and criminal justice. *Social Work, 36*(5), 391–395.

Mulvey, E. P., & Repucci, M. D. (1981). Police crisis intervention training: An empirical investigation. *American Journal of Community Psychology, 9.*

National Center on Child Abuse and Neglect. (1979). *Caregivers of young children: Preventing and responding to child maltreatment.* The User Manual Series. National Center on Child Abuse and Neglect.

Owen, G., & Williams, J. (1989). *Incest offenders after treatment: A follow-up study from the transitional offenders program at Lino Lakes correctional facility.* St. Paul, MN: Wilder Foundation.

Quincy, V. L. (1977). The assessment and treatment of child molestors: A review. *Canadian Psychological Review, 18,* 204–220.

Sedlak, A. (1997). Risk factors for the occurrence of child abuse and neglect. In J. Brown and G. Brown (Eds.), *Journal of Aggression, Maltreatment and Trauma 1*(1), 149–181.

State of California Office of Criminal Justice Planning. (1987). *State medical protocol for examination, treatment, and collection of evidence from sexual assault victims.* Sacramento, CA: State of California Office of Criminal Justice Planning.

Stein, T. (1981). *Social work practice in child welfare.* Englewood Cliffs, NJ: Prentice Hall.

Straus, M. A., & Gelles, R. J. (1990). *Physical violence in American families: Risk factors and adaptations to violence in families.* New Brunswick, NJ: Transaction.

Strean, H. (1988, September/October). Effects of childhood sexual abuse on the psychosocial functioning of adults. *Social Work,* 465–467.

Tower, C. (1989). *Understanding child abuse and neglect.* Boston: Allyn and Bacon.

Tyndall, C. (1997). Current treatment strategies for sexually abused children. *Journal of Aggression, Maltreatment and Trauma, 1*(1), 291.

U.S. Advisory Board on Child Abuse and Neglect. (1991, September 15). *Creating caring communities: Blueprints for an effective federal policy on child abuse and neglect. Second Report.* Washington, DC: Administration for Children and Families, U.S. Department of Health and Human Services.

U.S. Department of Health, Education, and Welfare. (1977). *Child abuse and neglect programs: Practice and theory.* Washington, DC: U.S. Government Printing Office.

U.S. Department of Health and Human Services. (1988). *Study of the national incidence and prevalence of child abuse and neglect: 1988.* Washington, DC: U.S. Department of Health and Human Services Publication, Office of Human Development Services.

U.S. Department of Justice. (2000, May). National report series publication. NCJ-180753. Washington, DC: U.S. Government Printing Office.

Utah Public Television. (1991, July). *Scared Silent.*

Van Hasselt, V. B., Morrison, R. L., Bellack, A. S., & Hersen, M. (1988). *Handbook of family violence.* New York: Plenum.

Widom, C. S. (1989). Does violence beget violence? A critical evaluation of the literature. *Psychology Bulletin, 106,* 3–28.

6 Sexual Violence

This chapter deals with sex-related violence including rape, physical assaults, threats, and harassment involving sexual issues between intimates, dating violence, as well as all sexual activity that occurs against a person's will. Under the subheading of dating violence, we are including violence between people involved in relationships who do not live together as a couple or as a family. Dating violence, one of the most common and seldom reported forms of sexual violence, includes all attempts by the perpetrator to have sexual relations with unwilling victims with whom they may have some level of physical or emotional intimacy. Consequently, sexual violence, as covered in this chapter, includes any behavior that is unwanted. Given the reports by many women, sexual violence tends to be epidemic in American society.

Sexual Violence Data

For the year 1995, the U.S. Census Department (1998) estimated that during a woman's lifetime, there is a 17.6 percent possibility of being raped (a 14.8% completion rate and a 2.8% attempt rate). However, when other aspects of violence including physical assaults are added to the rape data, American women have a startling 55 percent probability of being raped or assaulted sometime during their lifetime. Men have an even greater probability of some form of physical violence. Sixty-seven percent of all men face the probability of being victims of some form of violence sometime during their lives (U.S. Census Department, 1998).

However, not everyone accepts the data reported by the Census Department. The Bureau of Justice 1989 National Crime Victimization Survey (NCVS), which includes crimes not reported to the police as well as those that are reported, finds that about 8 percent of women in America will be victimized by rape in their lifetimes (1994). The usual acceptable finding for sexual abuse of women, however, is 25–33 percent. Dunn (1994) notes that two separate feminist researchers, Diana Russell and Mary P. Koss, did studies that found very high rates of rape. Dunn writes that "their surveys are fraught with scientific flaws. Russell and Koss have included everything from consensual sex to obscene phone calls in their figures on rape and sexual abuse" (p. 26). Such practices, Dunn notes, "inflate the statistics grotesquely" (p. 26).

Reporting on the work of Mark Warr, a fear researcher whose recent work on overstressing crime is the primary focus of Dunn's article, Dunn notes that:

> I asked his opinion about the numbers [of rapes]. "I am very much on the low end," he said. "Which is to say that from the National Crime Survey, we find the probability per year for a woman [of being raped] is on the order of one in a thousand. I'm certainly willing to admit that there is undercounting here. But even if the under-reporting is fairly large—and I don't believe it is—we're still going to have small numbers.
>
> In the local rape crisis center [in Austin, Texas] they argue that one in three women is raped every year. Those people do good work. I respect it. But they are not criminologists, and they have a vested interest in inflating the numbers to convince people that they provide a necessary service. It's not like it's some innocuous academic debate. It's unnecessarily scaring people and restricting their freedom. (p. 26)

In actual terms, the 1995 Census Department data indicate that 302,091 women were raped in America but when nonreported rapes were added to that figure, the estimate increased to 876,000 rapes and 5.9 million physical assaults (U.S. Census Department, 1998). When the data consider only an intimate partner (current and former spouses, opposite-sex cohabiting partners, same-sex cohabiting partners, dates, and boyfriends/girlfriends), 7.7 percent of all women will experience rape by an intimate and 22.1 percent will experience some form of physical assault during their lifetime. In absolute numbers, 1.5 million women were raped and/or physically assaulted by intimates in 1995. To make the physical assault data more vivid, women are 7 to 14 times more likely to have been beaten, choked, threatened with a gun, or actually had a gun used on them by intimates than men. In actual percentages, women experience 3 times the level of physical assault by intimates than men do, or an assault rate of 22.1 percent for women and 7.4 percent for men. Women are stalked 8 times more often than men. Of the 18 percent of the women facing a probability of being raped in their lifetime, 54 percent will have been raped before the age of 18. Women raped before the age of 18 are significantly more likely to be raped as adults (U.S. Census Department, 1998).

The following data are reported by Greenfeld for the U.S. Department of Justice: In 1995, of the 260,300 cases of estimated rapes and the additional 95,000 threatened or completed sexual assaults other than rape, only 21,655 felony defendants nationwide were convicted of rape; 8 in 10 pleaded guilty (Greenfeld, 1997). For rape defendants, the average sentence imposed was fourteen years. While the average time imposed on rapists has remained stable, the time actually served has increased sixfold from an average of six months served to a little over 3 years served. About 2 percent of convicted rapists received life sentences. Of the 900,000 offenders confined to state prisons in 1994, 88,000 or 9.7 percent were considered to be violent sex offenders (Greenfeld, 1997).

Using U.S. Department of Justice data reported by Greenfeld (1997) since 1980, the annual increase in the number of incarcerated prisoners has been 7.6 percent while the number of prisoners sentenced for violent sexual crimes is almost double that number with the growth in the prison population of violent sexual offenders now at a startling 15 percent. Of the population of sexually violent offenders serving time in prison, their likelihood of having experienced childhood physical and/or sexual abuse while growing up was geometrically higher than that of offenders in prison for nonsexually related crimes. Between 1976 and 1994, there were 317,925 murders in the United States where the circumstance were known. Of the known circumstances, an estimated 4,807 murders or 1.5 percent of all known murders involved rape or other sexually violent offenses. For both 1994 and 1995, the percent of rape reported to the authorities was 32 percent of all estimated rapes and violent sexual offenses. The most common reason given for reporting the crime was to prevent further crimes by the offender against the victim. The most common reason cited by victims of rape for not reporting the crime was that it was considered a personal matter. In 1994 there were about 1 reported rape/sexual assault per 270 females in the general population 12 years of age and older. The rate for males aged 12 or older was 1 per 5,000 males. The group most at risk of being raped were females 16 to 19 years of age, in low-income residences, and urban residents. There is no significant difference defining rape by race or ethnicity (Greenfeld, 1997).

Continuing on with the data reported by Greenfeld (1997), the majority of rape victims (70 percent) report that they took some form of self-protective action during the crime. This usually took the form of running from the offender or struggling with the offender to try and hold that person off. While 4 percent of the victims of violence needed medical attention, 6 percent of the known rape victims required medical attention. This does not factor in the numbers of rape victims who are unknown to us and who seek medical and psychological services after the rape, but the estimates are that more rape victims seek medical and psychological services than the population of victims of violent crime, and that those services are used for a much longer period of time. Seven percent of all victims of sexual violence report losing time at work. Just over 60 percent of all rapes take place in the victims' residence. One in three rapes were by strangers while nine of ten rapes were by family members. About 12 percent of all rapes involved the use of a gun or knife while 80 percent of all rapes involved the use of physical force. Offenders were 5 times more likely to use a weapon in stranger rape. About 40 percent of the victims of violent sexual abuse suffered injuries with 5 percent suffering major injures such as fractures, internal injuries and concussions (Greenfeld, 1997).

Greenfeld (1997) also reports that 31 percent of female rape victims use immediate follow-up medical help although 36 percent report being injured as a result of the assault. Most of the female victims sustaining injuries report more minor injuries such as scratches, bruises, and welts. Relatively few sustain more serious injuries such as broken bones, dislocated hips, concussions, lacerations or knife and gun wounds. It is important to note that the women who do use medical help after a rape use it for multiple reasons and that the number of medical visits involving physical therapy, dental work, emergency room and overnight stays exceeds the amount of medical care needed for physical assaults without rape, attesting to the emotional and physical trauma related to rape (Greenfeld, 1997).

Legal Definitions of Sexual Violence

The following definitions of sexually violent acts are a compilation of terms used by a number of reporting groups including the National Crime Victimization Survey (NCVS), The Uniform Crime Reports (UCR), and The National Incident-Based Reporting System (NIBRS). The definitions are taken from the U.S. Department of Justice Report entitled *Sex Offenses and Offenders* (Greenfeld, 1997, pp. 31–33).

> *Forcible rape*   The carnal knowledge of a person forcibly and/or against their will or where the victim is incapable of giving consent because of their age, mental status or physical incapacity. Assaults and attempts to commit rape by force or threat of force are also included, however, statutory rape without force and other sex offenses are excluded.
>
> *Statutory rape*   The carnal knowledge of a person without force or threat of force when the person is below the statutory age of consent.
>
> *Forcible sodomy*   Oral or anal sexual intercourse with another person, forcibly and against their will, or where the person is unable to consent because of age, mental or physical incapacity.
>
> *Sexual assault with an object*   When the offender uses an instrument or object to unlawfully penetrate the genital or anal opening against their will.
>
> *Forcible fondling*   Touching the private parts of another person against their will for the purpose of sexual gratification.
>
> *Incest*   Non-forcible intercourse between persons who are related to one another defined as not permitting marriage.
>
> *Lewd acts with children*   Includes fondling, indecent liberties, immoral practices, molestation and other indecent behaviors with children including attempts.

The Physical and Emotional Impact of Sexual Violence

Emotional Impact

Sexual traumas, including rape, have serious emotional consequences for victims. Those consequences include depression, social isolation, fear of intimacy, a persistent feeling of disinterest in sexual activity, an inability to be touched, alcohol abuse, eating disorders, panic attacks, continual feelings of apathy and lethargy, and post-traumatic stress disorder with physical problems that are often psychosomatic in origin but cause very real symptoms to the victim. There is a general sense that the more violent the rape, the more serious and lasting the emotional symptoms will tend to be.

Many women report that rape results in the loss of relationships with the men in their lives, including their husbands. Often men, while outwardly sympathetic, believe that in some subtle way, the woman either encouraged the rape or did too little to stop it. Some men even obsess that the woman actually enjoyed the rape and will ask obsessive questions to try and find out if this is true. Intimacy is often a problem for victims following a rape and this can lead to problems in relationships. Often the victim can't fully explain her feelings and the relationship suffers from a nonspecific lack of communication that ends in distancing and hurt feelings between both partners.

Post-traumatic stress disorder is the most common emotional problem related to sexual violence. PTSD may occur whenever a person experiences a "traumatic event that is outside the range of usual human experience" (American Psychiatric Association, 1987). DSM-IV (American Psychiatric Association, 1994) defines PTSD as "the development of characteristic symptoms following exposure to an extreme stressor involving direct personal experience of an event that involves actual or threatened death or serious injury" (p. 424). In a sense, the traumatic event "tears up the individual's psychological anchors, which are fixed in a secure sense of what has been in the past and what should be in the future" (Gilliland & James, 1993, p. 163). As a result, the victim is thrust into a state of crisis until the victim is able to reorganize, classify, and make sense out of the experience. During the time of crisis, the rape victim may experience a number of symptoms that are consistent with post-traumatic stress disorder.

The symptoms of PTSD fall into four general categories: (1) re-experiencing the traumatic event, (2) avoidance of stimuli associated with the event, (3) numbing of general responsiveness, and (4) increased arousal (American Psychiatric Association, 1987). Reexperiencing the trauma can occur in many forms. One of the most common forms is frequent nightmares (Goodwin, 1987). Many victims of sexual trauma have difficulty falling asleep because they find that this is a time when their mind is idle and their thoughts wander back to the traumatic event. However, once they do fall asleep, they often dream about the traumatic event and frequently wake up during the night. Often the victim may have reoccurring dreams that center around the physical and emotional trauma of the sexual assault. As a result of nightmares, many victims of sexually traumatic events suffer from sleep deprivation. To help them sleep, victims of sexual assaults may use alcohol or drugs to relax. The dependence on alcohol and drugs to help with sleep deprivation may lead to drug and alcohol abuse.

Another form of reexperiencing the event is through intrusive or obsessive thoughts. Intrusive thoughts may take the form of images that are introduced by sights, sounds, smells, or sensory experiences that bring the memory of the sexual assault into awareness (Gilliland & James, 1993). Some sexual trauma victims may repeatedly replay the sexual assault in their mind as they search for more positive outcomes of the experience (Goodwin, 1987).

Victims of sexual assault may avoid thoughts or feelings about the event that could potentially bring up further memories of the event (the second symptom of PTSD). For example, someone raped in an elevator may avoid taking elevators and may walk up many flights of stairs despite the inconvenience (Furey, 1993).

A third symptom of PTSD is a diminished responsiveness to the outside world, also referred to as *psychic numbing* or *emotional anesthesia* (American Psychiatric Association, 1987). The victim may feel isolated from other people, lose the ability to be interested in previously enjoyed activities, or experience difficulty with emotions associated with intimacy, tenderness, and sexuality (American Psychiatric Association, 1987).

The fourth category of PTSD symptoms is increased arousal. Many rape victims experience increased pulse rate, high blood pressure, or other forms of physical arousal when they are exposed to a situation that reminds them of the sexually traumatic event (Furey, 1993). They may also experience hyper-vigilance, difficulty in concentrating or completing tasks, irritability, and fear of losing control (American Psychiatric Association, 1987).

While there are a number of general symptoms related to PTSD, there are also a number of related symptoms. Rape victims often experience depression (American Psychiatric Association, 1987; Furey, 1993; Goodwin, 1987). In addition to depression, victims of sexual trauma may feel isolated from friends, peers, and family members believing that others won't understand their emotional pain or that they will blame the victim for what has happened. It is not unusual for close friends and family members to be hyper-critical of the rape victim for the way they are coping with the rape and, ultimately, to blame the victim for the rape itself (Furey, 1993).

And finally, rape victims often experience anger over the changes that the event has caused in their lives and over the unfairness of the event. The anger may result in outbursts over the slightest and most insignificant events, or it may result in physical complaints including headaches, stomachaches, generalized feelings of ill health, and flu-like symptoms, are just a few examples. Victims of sexual assaults may feel physically and emotionally fragile for weeks and even months after the assault.

Blaming the Victim

There have been many positive changes in the treatment of crime victims in the last two decades, but the problem of blaming the victim still exists (Sank & Caplan, 1991). This is particularly true in sexual assault cases where there is a continued belief that victims encourage the assault by being overly provocative even when this possibility is extremely remote (Sank & Caplan, 1991). Blaming the victim is a serious psychological distressor to victims because they are victimized twice; first by the perpetrator who robs them of their self-worth and then, often, by the families, friends, lovers, and the communities that fail to be empathic and then may blame them for the sexual assault and feelings of emotional distress that may follow.

Although many victims are still treated badly by the police, the courts, families, and friends, there has been a significant increase in the number of programs and services provided to victims of crime. These include victim/witness and victim assistance programs, financial compensation, victim impact statements, and education regarding the victims' emotional responses and counseling for victims

(Roberts, 1990). Changes also include the Victims' Bill of Rights and state constitutional amendments (Sank & Caplan, 1991).

Victim/witness assistance programs were developed in the mid-1970s by prosecutors' departments. These programs are usually located in a district attorney's office. The main role of the victim/witness program is to provide guidance, support, and counseling for emotional problems as the victim moves through the court system. The objective of victim services is to reduce the trauma of the assault and the subsequent legal proceedings (Roberts, 1990). The services provided by these programs include: (1) an explanation of the court process, (2) referrals for medical, social and emotional help, (3) providing court escorts, (4) helping the victim with compensation applications, (5) public education on the impact of sexual assaults and ways of coping with the trauma, (6) assisting with the victims' employers, (7) providing transportation to and from court, (8) providing crisis intervention, (9) providing child care, and (10) providing emergency financial help (Roberts, 1990).

Although many victim programs are located in prosecutors' offices, others are located in police departments, nonprofit social service agencies, or county probation departments (Roberts, 1990). While some of the services offered by victim/witness programs are also offered in victim assistance programs, there is a difference. Victim assistance programs mainly provide crisis intervention, social services, and/or referrals to community services (Roberts, 1990).

The aftermath of a sexual assault can take on many forms. The victim not only has physical and emotional traumas from the crime, but may have to cope with emotionally distancing behavior from those closest to the victim including friends, family, spouses, and intimates (Sank & Caplan, 1991). Emotional reactions by victims to sexual assaults often consist of three stages: (1) the acute crisis stage, involving shock and immediate rage or terror; (2) the emotional effort to survive, involving anger, depression, illness, and grief; and (3) a stage that might best be termed as "living after death" (Sank & Caplan, 1991). Intimates and family members of sexual assault victims may experience anger at the police and the courts for the way they handle the feelings of survivors and because of their inability to charge or convict perpetrators, even when the case seems clear-cut to the victim and the family (Sank & Caplan, 1991).

Sank & Caplan (1991) suggest that the reaction of the public is sometimes to "shun, ostracize, and stigmatize" victims. Victims often have to cope with isolation and blame. Many victims complain that employers and other significant people in the victim's life fail to understand that victims don't immediately get over their trauma and that for many victims of sexual assault, the process of coping may take a very long time to resolve and, in some cases, may never be completely resolved (Sank & Caplan, 1991).

Case Study of a Victim of Sexual Violence

Carla Evens is a nineteen-year-old Caucasian sales clerk and part-time student at an urban community college. On the way to her car after attending classes, Carla was raped by a male student from one of her classes who had offered to escort her to her car. The rape took place in Carla's automobile. When Carla opened her door, she was shoved into the car, her mouth was covered by the rapist's hand, and she was quickly raped with the rapist using physical force without threats. She sustained bruising around her face, arms, breasts, buttocks and vagina.

Carla drove herself to the emergency room of a local hospital where she was treated for shock and where a rape kit was used to obtain sperm, pubic hair, and other physical evidence that could be used in finding and prosecuting the rapist. She was treated prophylactically for sexually transmitted diseases and for pregnancy. Her HIV test came back negative. There were no signs of herpes or HIV six months after the rape.

The police were called to the emergency room and Carla gave a description of the rapist. She did not know his name, only that he was a student in her class. The police took her to a shelter where she spent several nights before returning to work. She was initially very frightened and withdrawn, but gradually returned to her normal state and was able to continue on with her work and her educational endeavors. Contact with the college failed to confirm that the rapist was a student. A description of the rapist and a drawing were circulated around campus and the immediate area. Like many mobile rapists, the perpetrator had likely left the area and was not apprehended.

Carla seemed to be doing well when, four months after the rape, she began experiencing nightmares, intrusive thoughts, fear, high levels of anxiety, and depression. She was unable to continue dating a boyfriend and found sexual intimacy difficult. Her parents were very critical, repeating that Carla should not have let someone she didn't know walk her to her car. In effect, they made Carla feel that the rape was her fault. She entered a crisis group run by the shelter and has made some progress. The group uses a cognitive approach focusing on improving her social functioning. There are also opportunities to discuss her rape and to describe her emotional state as a result of the rape. Carla finds the ability to talk openly about her experience to be very helpful. The other women are very supportive and she has made several good friends. She is still very leery of men, has dropped out of school because the school and the surrounding area frighten her, and she fears that she could be raped again. She is withdrawn and depressed but she continues to work. She has begun using alcohol and prescription drugs to numb her feelings. She reports sleeping problems with occasional panic attacks.

Discussion of the Case

The length of time it took for Carla to begin experiencing strongly intrusive symptoms is not unusual. This is not to say that she wasn't experiencing problems immediately after the rape. Like many victims, she believed that she could handle the problems by herself and may have been experiencing a "numbing" of feelings. Her desire to cope with the physical and emotional impact of the rape by herself was reinforced by the generally negative responses she was receiving from her friends and family. Most of her support network concentrated on blaming her for the rape. Carla's experiences reinforce a growing belief that rape creates a crisis, not only for the victim, but for her loved ones of the victim, many of whom have stereotypic views of victims as unconsciously wanting to be raped or of doing too little to prevent and stop it from happening. These often hurtful responses by loved ones suggest a need for family involvement in treatment to help develop ways the family can best help the victim.

The use of alcohol to numb her feelings and the lack of interest in relationships are all negative signs of recovery and suggest that Carla may need a more intensive form of individual therapy with alcohol counseling and a psychiatric evaluation to temporarily prescribe medication to help her with her primary symptoms: sleeping problems, withdrawal, fear, and panic attacks. The college, like most educational facilities, was lax in not making certain that the rapist was actually a student and in not giving women strict instructions regarding safety on the campus. A safe escort service should always be available to women in any facility.

The prognosis for Carla's recovery is guarded. Her group therapist notes a certain immaturity in the way she deals with life and writes, "While making slow but steady progress, Carla is hampered by an unsupportive family and by her own inability to develop more constructive ways of dealing with her symptoms. She feels great comfort from the group and attends it regularly. However, she is passive in the group, seldom comments and, when she does, tends to use clichés rather than anything insightful or appropriate to the other group members and their emotional pain. My sense is that Carla will, in time, resolve her current crisis and return to her more usual level of functioning. She remains, however, a fairly uninsightful young woman who is getting support, not treatment, from the group. Time will likely be her best therapy."

Treating the Victims of Sexual Violence

In many ways, the treatment methods for victims of sexual crimes are similar to those used with people in crisis. But treatment may also vary because of the type of sexual crime experienced. Rape victims, for example, usually experience distinctly different problems from a family whose loved one has been murdered. However, the feelings of pain, anger, and depression are universal.

Methods used for assisting victims in recovery are both traditional and nontraditional. Two-thirds of the victim programs in 1984 provided crisis intervention to victims. According to Roberts (1990), brief crisis intervention with victims and their families can help reduce the length of time to resolve the trauma of sexual crimes if provided soon after the assault has been committed. As with almost all crises, the longer the delay in providing services, often the less effective the recovery.

Victims of sexual assault may feel guilty or responsible for the assault. Crisis intervention should help the client resolve feelings of guilt and responsibility and assist the victim to become a more active participant in attempts to prosecute the perpetrator. Having a perpetrator caught and punished can be a powerful step in the recovery process. Because victims are frightened of perpetrators and believe that prosecuting the perpetrator could result in further harm to them or their families, active involvement in the prosecution of the perpetrator becomes an important aspect of crisis work with victims of sexual crimes.

Victims are generally very frightened after the crime. Crisis workers often find that victims appear lethargic and withdrawn. The first contact with a victim of sexual assault should help the victim cope with the assault. It should be supportive and fairly nondirective. The client should be allowed to tell the story of the assault in a way that is most appropriate. Members of the family should be allowed to sit in on this session. Their input may be helpful in the recovery process. In future sessions, the crisis worker should be able to concentrate on helping the victim deal with feelings of fear and depression. In the initial session, the worker should focus on helping the client move back to normal life routines as quickly as possible. Recovery might be seriously compromised by suggesting that the client take a long break from normal routines that includes work, family responsibilities, and outside interests. Changes in a client's routine life patterns may increase the probability of depression and guilt since the client has additional unstructured time that may lead them to obsess about their experience or about the way they handled the sexual assault. Many clients start to believe that they were responsible for the crime or that they handled it in a way that demonstrated bad judgment or cowardice. To be able to get the client back into a routine and into treatment may help reduce feelings of guilt and self-blame.

Some victims may require longer forms of treatment than brief crisis intervention. Feelings experienced in a sexual assault may release unconscious memories of early victimization of rape or child molestation. The feeling of powerlessness after a crime may touch off similar unconscious feelings of powerlessness that define the client's emotional state as a child, a state the client has worked hard to resolve in adulthood. Victimization may touch off memories of parents not advocating for the child when something was done to them that required the parent's assistance.

Typically, victims of sexual violence come for treatment once they have entered the *intrusive-repetitive* stage of PTSD. This is the third stage of the disorder after the *emergency-outcry* stage and the *emotional numbing and denial* stages. The intrusive-repetitive stage occurs when victims begin having intrusive nightmares and mood swings coupled with panic attacks and high levels of anxiety and depression. It is also the stage in which stress has become so overwhelming that the victim is forced to seek treatment because of overwhelming stress (Gilliland & James, 1993). Gilliland and James (1993) also note the importance of determining if the client is having homicidal or suicidal thoughts and evaluating the seriousness of the client's plan to harm self, the perpetrator, or, in some cases, others who remind them of the perpetrator.

Once the victim has been stabilized, group treatment is recommended (Williams, 1987). In terms of the effectiveness of group therapy in treating PTSD,

Boehnlein and Sparr (1993) found that changes in self-esteem and social interaction might be achieved through the use of group treatment using a cognitive-behavioral approach. Recovery from PTSD is a process that involves support, education, and an environment to work through suppressed thoughts and emotions. Group treatment is often effective with victims of PTSD because it helps victims share their experiences, provides an atmosphere of support, and reduces the social stigma of the assault, and may improves self-esteem.

Often, group therapy is used with individual therapy when treating victims of sexual violence. One of the goals of individual therapy is to reduce the degree of stress experienced by the assault victim. This may be done by reducing the anxiety associated with the sexually violent trauma (Gilliland & James, 1993). Many times, this is done by using techniques that might include relaxation therapy, stress management, meditation, hypnotherapy, and biofeedback (Brom, Kleber, & Defares, 1989; Gilliland & James, 1993; Keane, Gerardi, Quinn, & Litz, 1992). Brom et al. (1989) examined the effectiveness of trauma desensitization, hypnotherapy, and psychodynamic therapy in treating PTSD and found that clients who received trauma desensitization, hypnotherapy, and psychodynamic therapy were significantly lower in PTSD symptoms following treatment than the control group. However, the study also found that these approaches were not beneficial for all clients. Sixty percent of the treated clients had clinically significant improvement while 40 percent failed to improve or actually got worse. The reasons for failure to improve, offered by the authors, may be related to lateness in starting treatment after the assault and the level of physical and emotional damage done by the assault.

Many rape crisis centers use cognitive approaches in treating sexual traumas. Most have found that the earlier the victim seeks help and follows through on treatment, the less debilitating and long-term the trauma. Unfortunately, many sexually traumatized victims fail to follow through with treatment directly after the trauma believing that no one will understand, that the trauma isn't really that bad, or that they can resolve the situation on their own. The time delay in follow-up treatment can be considerable. It is often felt that the longer the delay, the more intrusive the symptoms, although there is some reason to believe that all treatment can only be effective when the client is motivated to seek help. This may mean that seeking help can only take place when the victim is feeling anxiety or depression that has reached the point where the client feels emotionally out of control.

The Psychological Makeup of Perpetrators of Sexual Violence

The dynamic of rape is complicated by an almost paradoxical explanation of this violent offense against women. While the act of rape is sexual, the dynamic behind it is often extreme hostility toward women. In fact, many rapists cannot achieve an erection during the rape. It should be noted that women are raped five times more often than men. Most men often experience rape by other men while rape to women is almost always done by men. In the case of rape to women, 93 percent of the rapists are male. In the case of rape to men, 23.3 percent of the rapists are female (Greenfeld, 1997). The treatment of rape now includes medical castration implying that rape is a physical aspect of sexual need out of control. However, many writers believe that rape has emotional roots that include controlling and humiliating women. In fact, castrated men still rape women. Rape, from this point of view, is about domination, control, and humiliation. Sexual need is largely secondary to the hostile feelings the rapist has toward women.

While rape is never a predictable or easily categorized crime, Glicken (1997) notes the following progression in the rapist's assaults on women:

1. Situational Rape

This type of rape occurs as a situation presents itself. An example might be a woman working alone late at night where no one else is in the building to protect her, or to offer help. The rapist takes advantage of the situation and has forcible sex without consent. Many rapes are one-time-only occurrences where the rapists may be using alcohol or another substance. The rapist may be a coworker or someone with legitimate access to a building. The rape may not be reported because of the nature of the relationship to the rapist (it may be a superior of the victim or someone who has been harassing her without any protection from the company. Or the rapist may suggest repercussions that frightened the victim). Force may not be used and proving that the rape wasn't consensual may be difficult. Situational rape may also happen in nonwork environments and is often done without the use of weapons. The purpose of the rape is sexual gratification and, as it is always a secondary aspect of rape, humiliation and control over the victim. Many men are capable of situational rape. In many ways, situational rape may be related to date rape and other forms of sexual assault where the perpetrator believes that the victim may actually enjoy the experience and fails to perceive the rape as being wrong, even though it may do serious physical and emotional harm to the victim.

2. Rape with Threats

A second type of rape involves verbal threats and the use of weapons, usually knives, to intimidate and frighten the victim. Rape with threats may be done over a period of hours and is usually about humiliation. Since rapists often cannot sustain an erection during the rape, they may use objects, hands, mouths, or anything available to invade the woman's body. Generally, physical harm is not done although there may be bruising to many parts of the body, particularly the breasts and the vaginal areas of women rape victims. There is no rule, however, in terms of parts of the body the rapist may harm. Mutilation is unlikely at this stage in the rapist's development of his pathology. One can never be sure, however, and the transition from situational rape to mutilation rape may be swift and may bypass this stage. Some rapists stay fixated at this stage. Rapists who now use humiliation, threats, and knives to coerce and frighten the victim are clearly pathologically hostile toward women. Rape is now more about hurting and badly frightening victims than about sexual gratification. The length of the rape may progress over many hours. Victims may be threatened repeatedly and told that if they report the rape to the police, that the rapists will find the victim and mutilate or kill her. Threats may be made against the victim's family. Often victims have been stalked for days so that the perpetrator may know a great deal about the victim and her family. The rapist will probably demonstrate what he will do by graphically describing it to the victim or by running a knife over the parts of the body of the victim he intends to mutilate.

The victim may be tied up and the rapist may use a hood or a mask to hide his identity. Rapists at this stage in the progression of their violent behavior may have planned the rape by stalking the victim over a period of time and are usually attracted by aspects of the victim's looks, job, or personality that represent associations with women from the perpetrator's past. They might also just look for a certain type of woman by age and appearance, as likely targets. Rapists will frequently interact with victims at stores or other places and many victims often have the vague memory of having seen the rapist before.

3. Rape with Mutilation and Torture

In the next progression in the development of the rapist's pathology, all of the above are part of the rapist's behavior during the rape with the addition of physical mutilation of the victim's body. Favored places to mutilate are the breasts, the vaginal area, the stomach, particularly if the victim is pregnant, and the face. Choice of weapons may include knives, glass, and broken bottles. Guns may be used to subdue the victim. The length of the rape may now take many hours with the rapist torturing the victim, physically and emotionally. In addition to being assaulted and seriously hurt, the victim is terrorized and may immediately go into shock and post-traumatic stress disorder, making identification of the rapist very difficult. Rapists at this stage may be unable to have erections and may humiliate the victim by telling her how ugly she is and how he made a mistake in choosing her because of some anomaly in her body. Actually, what is happening is that the sexual pleasure is no longer physical but has become interlocked with the humiliation and abuse of the victim. The rapist is now getting sexual gratification from the violence and not from the sexual act itself. Rapists at this stage may not progress to the next stage of mutilation and death, but frequently they do. Death, for them, is now the end-stage in the sexual gratification they achieve by causing pain to women. The rape and torture of intimates also forms a large number of reported rapes. This may occur as an escalation of domestic violence or because of changes (divorce, breakup, or separation) in the victim's relationship to the perpetrator.

4. Rape with Mutilation, Torture, and Death

The progression of the violence has now reached a point where women are stalked, captured, tied up, humiliated verbally, tortured, mutilated, and finally murdered. By not getting caught, the rapist discovers the sexual stimulation he achieves from killing his victims. Thankfully, rapists who kill their victims are still a minority of rapists since they either get caught, come too close to getting caught, or have been accused of rape without enough evidence to convict and discontinue their raping. Serial killing rapists may move around the country and can be inordinately difficult to find and convict. At the same time, a large number of rapists seem to live fairly close to the where victims live.

A somewhat different classification to define the stages of rape is sometimes offered by law enforcement behavioral profilers. Summarizing their work, rapists may be placed in the following categories:

1. Affirming Masculinity through Rape

In this category of rape, the rapist sexually assaults women to affirm his masculinity but is usually not assaultive and sometimes even shows concern for his victims. These rapists might even expect the victim to have an orgasm and to thank the rapist for the pleasure he has provided. Often this type of rapist fantasizes that the victim wants to be raped and that the rapist is taking care of unmet sexual needs of the victim.

2. Rape as a Way to Control Women

In this category, rape is a way to assert control and dominance. These rapists are usually not physically violent and rape to increase their self-esteem, although they may sometimes be threatening and use tactics of humiliation and fear.

3. Rape as a Show of Force

In this category, the rapist uses speed but can also threaten and frighten the victim. These rapists use terror to rape and to gain an advantage. When force is used, it is usually to terrorize the victim into submission. There may be threats, but the threats are usually more suggestive than completed.

4. Rape as an Act of Terrorism

In this category of rape, the rapist uses threats, mutilation, and terrorism. Here, the issues defining the rape have to do with dominance, control, humiliation, terror, and sometimes mutilation and death. These are the most dangerous rapists and often the terrorist tactics used with victims may go on for many hours and even days. Psychological humiliation and physical dominance characterize these rapists who also have very deep-seated hostility toward women. Sexual gratification is tied to humiliating and terrorizing victims and may be disassociated from the physical act of sex. Sexual gratification is usually dependent upon the fear they've created in their victims. Often perpetrators are unable to have erections or to have orgasms and will use foreign objects to penetrate and mutilate the client.

This form of rapist is usually serial and preplans the rape by getting to know the victim and her routines through stalking.

In a 1990 report (FBI Law Enforcement Bulletin), the FBI classified serial rapists (those described as using rape as an act of terrorism) in the following way:

> The majority of serial rapes were premeditated.
>
> Minimal force was used in the majority of cases.
>
> Slightly more than a third of the rapists experienced a sexual dysfunction that interfered with penetration and intercourse.
>
> Low levels of sexual pleasure were reported by the rapist in association with the rape.
>
> The rapists tended not to take precautions to protect their identities, relying on tone of voice and verbal threats.
>
> About a third of the perpetrators had consumed alcohol prior to the rape.

Another FBI report (FBI Law Enforcement Bulletin, February 1992), in describing the serial rapist who gets pleasure out of terrorizing his victims, noted that serial rapists who are sexual sadists "become sexually excited in response to another's suffering . . . to the sexual sadist, it is the suffering of the victim that is sexually arousing" (p. 8).

Case Study of a Rapist

Gerald Goines is a twenty-seven-year-old Caucasian construction worker. He is a serial rapist who first dates women and then breaks into their homes where he tortures, rapes, and mutilates them. He is a very handsome man and women tend to go out with him with very little knowledge of his background. Gerald was physically abused and tortured by his mother, a paranoid schizophrenic whom Gerald killed when he was 14 in what was clearly a case of self-defense. The mother tried to decapitate Gerald's head with a chain saw. Gerald is filled with hatred against women, but he is very careful never to let it show until he rapes. He prefers women who are tall and blond since that is what his mother looked like when she was young. He always meets his victims in bars, dates them three or four times, never has sex with them because he is unable to have intercourse unless he is in the midst of raping them and even then, he is often unable to have an erection sufficient to achieve intercourse with penetration. When Gerald is unable to have an erection, he uses objects including bottles and knives. He likes to give pain to women. It makes him happy to pay women back for the pain he received as a child.

Gerald stalks the women he dates and is aware of the break-in possibilities of the homes his dates occupy. He has tools from the construction work he does and breaking in is never a problem. The women Gerald dates think he's gentle and generous and he has never been a suspect in any of their rapes. He wears a mask that makes his speech muffled and hard to identify. He never wears cologne or anything he would normally wear on a date. When he breaks into the victim's home, he places electrical tape over the mouths of his victims and tells them he is going to kill them by cutting deep into their vaginas until they bleed to death. If they urinate or defecate out of fear, Gerald is deliriously happy and immediately becomes erect. He cuts their clothes off with a knife, verbally terrorizes them, has intercourse, and then mutilates their breasts and vaginal areas with his knife. He's taken to crudely writing words that demean women on their bodies. After seventeen rapes and mutilations in four states, Gerald was caught leaving a victim's home in a routine police patrol of the neighborhood. He is currently in state prison on a 20-year sentence for first-degree rape, mutilation, and terrorism.

Discussion of the Case

Gerald's anger at women should have been dealt with long ago had child protective services and the mental health establishment done their jobs. No one who is as badly disturbed as Gerald gets through life without some contact with the police and with helping professionals, including family physicians. They should have seen the risk to Gerald and done something about it. A thorough evaluation of Gerald's abuse should have led to foster care and treatment. To be fair, however, the damage may have been done so early that no one could have successfully changed the direction of Gerald's anger.

Gerald's incarceration includes mandatory segregation from other prisoners. Rape and child molestation are unpopular crimes in a prison population and more advanced facilities find it best to separate this population and to offer some forms of treatment. Gerald is being seen by a counselor from a local mental health clinic that contracts with the prison to offer therapy for sex-related crimes. The goal of therapy is to help Gerald verbalize his angry feelings toward his mother for her abuse, to see a connection between his violent activity as a rapist and his mother's abuse, and to help Gerald frame women in a more accepting and less violent way. The work is slow and Gerald has almost no empathy for the women he's raped.

The prison has an empathy-training group for women victims and male perpetrators of sex crimes to meet together to help the perpetrators understand the harm they've done. Some of the perpetrators are shocked and ashamed about their behavior, and it helps them change their thinking about women and their desire to ever rape or physically abuse a woman again. Other perpetrators, like Gerald, are unaffected. He believes that women are the reincarnation of the devil. Gerald's mother, to understand his feelings better, had oral sex and then intercourse with Gerald from age 4 and on. She whipped him with a horsewhip in angry tantrums when her schizophrenia was at its most uncontrollable stage. He has permanent scars on his back and legs that look like deep black welts. His mother also tried to cut his penis off with a butcher knife and forced him to eat her feces when he was a child. Gerald's distance from feeling empathy for victims is geometric. He feels nothing except an abiding sense of the unfairness at being in jail for doing something to others while he endured fourteen years of torture by his mother.

His therapist sees a gradual engagement in discussions about his mother and some developing awareness of his dysfunctional and violent belief system. The therapist does not feel that Gerald will be able to be in contact with women for years, if ever. Other than his violence toward women, Gerald is a good worker. He is easy to get along with, stays out of trouble, is considered a loner but can be engaged in discussions about current events and sports. He tests at an IQ of 120 and has begun to train as a medical assistant in the prison hospital. He knows a lot about the body and isn't at all squeamish about pain or blood.

Treating the Perpetrators of Sexual Violence

A number of treatment approaches have been used with perpetrators of sexual violence including those molesting children and perpetrators of rape of intimates and of strangers. The literature suggest that the primary approaches used in various treatment settings include the following traditional and less traditional approaches: insight-oriented individual psychotherapy, group psychotherapy, family therapy, psychoeducational skills training, behavioral treatments, chemical castration, sexual addiction twelve-step recovery programs, relapse prevention, parents united, and several model approaches that combine each of the above. Insight-oriented therapy, behavioral therapy, and group therapy are discussed in Chapter 10. Several of the therapies used with sexual predators are provided here.

Chemical Castration

This controversial treatment is used to decrease sexual obsessiveness by significantly lowering libido, erotic fantasies, erections, and ejaculations. One commonly used drug is Depo-Provera, a testosterone-suppressing agent. Side effects of the drug include weight gain, lethargy, cold sweats, nightmares, hot flashes, hypertension and elevated blood pressure, high blood sugar, and shortness of breath. Berlin (1982) reported an 85 percent effectiveness rate in eliminating deviant sexual behaviors, "as long as the medication was taken on a regular basis. It is not a cure and relapse often follows discontinuation of medication and is not recommenced as an exclusive treatment" (Brown & Brown, 1997, p. 347). Furthermore, the motivation to rape is often less sexual than it is hostility toward women. Consequently, perpetrators may continue to rape even though they lack any sexual desire to rape.

Psychoeducational Skills Training

Because sexual offenders as a group tend to be uninformed about human sexuality (Groth, 1978) and often have difficulty expressing their feelings, skills training groups focus on "multiple aspects of assertiveness skills, including making eye contact, duration of reply, latency of response, loudness of speech and quality of affect are often taught offenders" (Becker et al., 1978, in Brown & Brown, 1997, p. 345). Rosen and Fracher (1983) also recommend teaching offenders tension reduction and anger management in those offenders who may experience anxiety and anger before the assault. Groth (1983) believes that the majority of offenders have very little awareness of the short- and long-range impact of sexual assault on their victims and suggests the use of empathy training to help offenders understand the impact of the offender's behavior on the victim.

Behavioral Treatments

These treatment approaches include covert sensitization, electrical aversion, odor aversion, chemical aversion, and suppression and satiation techniques. *Covert sensitization* is a procedure where the therapist describes a deviant sexual scene followed by an aversive scene. The aversive scene may include going to jail, blood, odors, community responses, and other aversive stimuli the therapist has determined effective in a screening interview. Scenes last about ten minutes and two scenes are presented at each session (Mayer, 1988). This same concept can be used with the addition of unpleasant odors or electric shock with the aversive scene. In *satiation procedures,* the offender is told to masturbate to nondeviant fantasies and then ejaculate. The client is then asked to continue masturbating to deviant fantasies for 45 minutes. Throughout, the client is asked to verbalize his fantasies that are recorded and monitored for client compliance. Satiation procedures attempt to destroy the erotic nature of deviant urges by boring the client with his own fantasies (Johnson et al., 1992).

Dating Violence and Acquaintance Assault

A study by Frinter and Rubinson (1993) at a large Mid-western university indicates that 27 percent of the college women in the study had experienced sexual assault, attempted sexual assault, sexual abuse without penetration, or had been subjected to battery, illegal restraint, or intimidation. Eighty-three percent of the women knew the person who assaulted them. Fifty-six percent of the victims and 68 percent of the offenders had been drinking at the time of the assault. Regarding the perpetrators, Malamuth (1989) indicates that male sexual perpetrators have high scores on scales measuring dominance as a sexual motive. They also have hostile feelings toward women, condone the use of force in sexual relationships, and often have an inability to appraise social interactions and have frequently been the victims of prior parental neglect or physical and or emotional abuse early in life. Drugs and alcohol are commonly associated with sexual aggression. Of the men identified as having committed acquaintance rape, 75 percent had taken drugs or alcohol just prior to the rape (Koss & Dinero, 1988).

Behaviors of perpetrators identified by the University of Nebraska (1996) suggest that perpetrators have the following characteristics:

> They easily lose their tempers; they often abuse alcohol or drugs; they have committed acts of violence against objects and things (sometimes animals) rather than

people; they show extreme jealousy and become enraged when their advice or opinions are discounted; they often need to know where the person they're dating is all of the time and tell that person how to dress and how to wear their hair and makeup; they often follow, stalk or end up at the same places the person they're dating is to the point of the victim feeling as if they're being watched; they have slapped, pulled the victim's hair, twisted her arm, jabbed her in the ribs, pushed or shoved or knocked her around, and they are often physically or verbally abusive at home or have parents who appear to be physically and emotionally violent. (p. 3)

The University of Nebraska report (1996) also warns women to be aware of men who: "Ignore their wishes, attempt to make the victim feel guilty, or accuse the victim of being uptight, act excessively jealous or possessive, ignore personal boundaries, don't listen or disregard what the other person says, abuse alcohol or drugs and, get angry and hostile when the other person says, 'No'" (p. 4).

The University of Nebraska (1996) reports that stalking is common among sexually violent men and notes that many sexually violent men stalk victims or follow them as a way of making certain that the other person is being faithful and as a means of controlling the other person through intimidation. As the report notes, "Stalking can be very frightening particularly when the victim thinks the other person is following them but isn't able to verify it" (p. 4). The stalking becomes more of a sense of the other person's presence with the stalker frequently showing up wherever the victim finds herself. This is often a "clue" that the victim is being stalked, although the perpetrator might deny the use of the word *stalk* and in its place "indicates that they end up in similar locations because they share many of the same interests" (p. 4). The stalking may increase when the victim is trying to leave the relationship. It is at this point when sexual violence is most likely to happen, although from the many reports of women who experience date and acquaintance sexual violence, "there may have been prior instances where the perpetrator has forced the victim into sexually compromising situations that fall under the definition of rape" (p. 4). Victims often define their willingness to have sex as semiconsensual, indicating that they may have sex to reduce the risk of serious physical violence. Again, it should be noted that sexual violence among intimates and acquaintances frequently occurs when both the victim and the perpetrator have been drinking and that boundaries are often blunted and full intent may be difficult for both the victim and the perpetrator to define. Restraining orders may be necessary when stalking begins, although to be fair to victims, the police seldom enforce restraining orders unless there is actual physical contact where some form of abuse has taken place.

Case Study of a Victim of Dating Violence

Jolene Andrews is a nineteen-year-old Caucasian college sophomore in a reputable Mid-western liberal arts college. She is a gender studies major and considers herself to be a grounded, practical, and spiritual person who accepts the ideals of liberalism and the social responsibility of educated people to do good deeds in life. Jolene began dating Robert, a mysterious, poetic, and slightly glamorous Caucasian senior from the same college. He had a reputation as a romantic and disarmingly sensuous young man. Jolene was flattered that he asked her out and was immediately taken with him. He was gentle and nonphysical in their early dates. After several months, they began an intimate and sexually consensual relationship. Just as he had been before they were intimate, he was gentle and tender in his lovemaking. Jolene was happily and crazily in love.

What Jolene didn't know, and what apparently only a few college officials knew, was that Robert had accidentally killed his family in a traffic accident when he was 16. The impact of the accident resulted in a prolonged stay in a psychiatric facility where Robert was treated for over a year for severe depression requiring medication, therapy, and electro-convulsive shock therapy. Robert came out of the experience severely traumatized and suffers from post-traumatic stress disorder (PTSD). When stressful or frightening experiences occur, Robert can become disassociative and violent. He transferred to his current college after terrorizing a young woman he had been seeing. Unfortunately, a minor auto accident while Jolene was driving (Robert refuses to drive) sent him into a disassociative state and Robert held Jolene hostage in the car for hours until the police, with the help of a social work police negotiator, freed her. Robert was sent to a forensic mental health holding facility for evaluation while a badly frightened Jolene spent several nights in the mental health wing of a local hospital. She is back in school and has been assured that Robert won't return. He has sent her notes telling her how genuinely sorry he is for what happened, but Jolene wants nothing to do with him and has been staying home with her roommates making certain that she walks everywhere with companions.

Discussion of the Case

The college, like many institutions of higher learning, was remiss in allowing Robert admission to the school knowing his background. Robert needs close mental health supervision and should be in a more structured setting than a liberal arts college. Jolene thinks she might sue the college. Her social worker thinks that she has a case and that it might be beneficial to her recovery. She has gone from being a happy, committed person to someone who feels unsafe, frightened, and uncertain about her liberal philosophy. She is taking self-defense classes and has begun learning to use a gun. Her therapy consists of helping her work through the trauma she experienced. Robert didn't harm her physically but he held her in the car with a knife to her throat and threatened to maim her if she said anything. He rambled on for hours about his role in killing his family and told her he'd often thought that killing someone deserved that he be killed. He wondered if he killed Jolene, whether the state would finally do what it should have done in the first place. During the time she was held hostage in the car, he repeatedly cut his arm and wrist with the knife saying that if he had the guts, he'd really kill himself. The wounds were superficial.

The therapy Jolene is receiving is cognitive-behavioral with a focus on helping her overcome the trauma of the experience with Robert. It is somewhat successful in that she is less fearful than she was immediately following the traumatic event. She has stopped dating completely and has begun to put on weight and not caring about her appearance. Her therapist has referred her to a group for victims of date violence but Jolene reports that most of the discussion centers around negative feelings about men and Jolene comes out of group more angry and hurt than ever. The therapist thinks that time and continued therapy will break the current cycle she is in. Jolene isn't so sure. She thinks she's been violated and that it could have been prevented if the college had been more diligent in its job of providing a safe environment for women. Her lawsuit was settled privately and Jolene is now a very wealthy but emotionally distraught and unhappy young woman whose career choice has changed from social work to criminal justice. She is thinking of becoming a probation officer and has begun lifting weights to toughen herself up.

Preventing Sexual Violence

There are a number of positive steps that can be taken to prevent sexual violence, some of them happening as a result of the increased awareness of the seriousness of domestic violence. More sexually violent men than ever are serving jail sentences and for a much longer period of time than just five years ago. Obviously, sexual violence is increasingly seen as a serious concern in all of its manifestations. We would add the following prevention strategies to reduce the threat of sexual violence:

1. More research into the cause and the treatment of sexually violent perpetrators. Currently, our treatment strategies are primitive, relying on approaches to treatment developed for nonsexually violent perpetrators. The lack of treatment options for sexually violent perpetrators often limits us to prison sentences that seldom include effective treatment for problems that do not go away during and after incarceration. Those lingering problems include violent feelings toward victims, issues of control and dominance, very low self-esteem, and sexual addictions and gender confusion that result in sexual violence from an intense need to prove masculinity.

    These are problems of a serious nature that cannot be treated effectively by jail sentences or by the limited treatment approaches we have described in this chapter. Sexual violence is often reestablished when men are released from prison and when new victims are identified and assaulted. And, it continues to affect countless victims through harm done to children as they deal with direct and indirect sexual violence in the form of domestic violence, spousal rape, and child molestation.
2. More research needs to be done on ways of helping the victims of sexual violence. At present, only a third of all adult victims of rape seek medical help

for sexually violent acts. A much lower number seek psychotherapy or counseling. When victims *do* seek help, the treatment is often done by nonprofessionals or by other victims in support groups. We lack a body of data to support the effectiveness of the treatment approaches currently used with victims, many of whom have been victimized continually from an early age.

3. A much more serious campaign needs to be enacted against binge drinking, the defining reason in the majority of sexually violent acts related to date rape. Binge drinking is at an epidemic stage on many college campuses where a good deal of sexual violence is committed. Furthermore, we need a "no-tolerance" policy on campuses that assures victims that perpetrators will be prosecuted and that sexually violent behavior will result in termination of university status. The current policies are so contradictory and weak that many victims of sexual violence on campus find themselves sitting in classes next to violent young perpetrators who believe that sexual exploitation and violence are acceptable behaviors and that nothing of consequence will ever happen to them.

4. We hope more victims will come forward and that more perpetrators will be prosecuted. However, as long as sexual violence is considered a private matter, as it so often is in the case of intimates, or as long as we blame the victim for acts of sexual aggression, it will be a slow process to take the many sexually violent people off the street who need supervised treatment to control their violent sexual behavior.

5. Signs of sexual aggression are evident fairly early in a person's development. It goes without saying that childhood victims of physical and sexual abuse are at risk of becoming perpetrators as well as victims of sexual violence. They should be offered substantial help when their abuse is discovered. Similarly, perpetrators of sexual violence tend to begin acting out sexually well before they do substantial harm. Their behavior should not be excused and treatment and supervision are necessary at early stages of development of sexual violence to reduce the serious potential risks to victims.

6. We live in a society where sexual violence is glorified in the music videos and lyrics of all too many songs young Americans hear. It is not okay for the mass media to use sexual violence as a way of selling music. While we don't agree with censorship, certainly we have reached a point in time when common sense suggests a more proactive approach to the use of sexuality and the mistreatment of women in advertising, videos, films, and in the lyrics of music. The lyrics of all too many songs, glorifying violence to women and suggesting that women are inferior to men, can't help but encourage and escalate sexual violence.

7. We need all states to enact laws that require hospitals and physicians to act as mandatory reporters of sexual violence to identify victims, to offer them needed services, and to prosecute sexual perpetrators. It makes little sense to have mandatory arrest laws for domestic violence, which may be less traumatic and serious, and not to have mandatory reporting and arrest laws for

victims of sexual violence, an act that is always extremely traumatic and serious.

8. Finally, we have a society that is much too lax in its recognition of the harm done by sexual violence. It is a society overloaded with sexual messages that blunt the serious nature of violence. Much more needs to be done to report the harmful impact of sexual violence and to make communities aware that lax enforcement of restraining orders, an unwillingness to prosecute cases of sexual violence, and badgering of victims in court where their character becomes more of an issue than the behavior of the perpetrator, all of this leads to more violence.

Case Study with Integrating Questions

Seana Fernandez is a twenty-one-year-old single Hispanic woman who has been dating her boyfriend, John Garza, 23, also Hispanic, for over a year. The couple has had a stormy relationship and quarrel a great deal. There has never been any serious violence, although John shoved Seana once during an argument and is often verbally abusive. When he gets angry with Seana, he calls her a "whore" and a "bitch." John is intensely jealous and believes that Seana is seeing other men. He often follows her home after a date or watches her house to make certain that she isn't with other men. Although Seana has denied that she sees other men, John is still extremely jealous and sees the existence of infidelity whenever he is with her.

While driving to a party, John and Seana got into an argument and John began to hit her. The fight centered around the fact that Seana was reluctant to have intercourse with John unless he wore a condom. John believes that condoms are for "sissies" and feels that Seana is being insulting by asking him to wear one. He also thinks that if Seana really loved him, she would use some other form of birth control that wouldn't require a condom. Making him wear a condom confirms for John that Seana is unfaithful since a condom also protects against sexually transmitted diseases. Since John is being scrupulously faithful to Seana, it confirms his suspicion that she is seeing other men.

During the fight, John drove to a side street, tore Seana's clothes, and attempted to rape her. She resisted and was able to leave the car and run to a nearby home. Seeing Seana's torn clothing and bloody face, the people at the house she ran to called the police (against Seana's expressed desire). The police took her to the emergency room for treatment. Seana sustained a cut on her face that required seven stitches, a dislocated jaw, and a broken nose. She also had cuts along the top of her breasts and she had been vaginally penetrated by keys on a key chain that John used in the struggle, creating deep cuts in and around her vaginal area.

John was arrested and was held in jail pending an initial hearing. Seana was immediately seen by a crisis worker at the hospital. Her primary concern was that John wouldn't see her again because he was sent to jail for something that was a private matter. The crisis worker tried to show Seana that such acts of violence only escalate and that she should take a "time out" from the relationship and allow the legal system to do its job and refer John for counseling. All Seana would say was that once she was released from the emergency room, she was going to the jail and that she would pay John's bond so they could get on with their relationship. They would, she said emphatically, work their problems out by themselves.

Attempts to refer Seana for counseling failed and Seana began seeing John again after he was placed in a diversion project for a year of mandated treatment in lieu of a three-year deferred jail sentence for attempted rape and assault. Seana has continued to see John during this period of treatment and there is talk of marriage. Seana spoke to John's counselor in the diversion project and told him that John is still verbally abusive and continues to be highly jealous of her, constructing more and more elaborate and outrageous scenarios to confront Seana about her suspected infidelity. They can't go to parties anymore because John thinks Seana is making nonverbal contact with men at the party and that she sees other men when John isn't around. John won't let Seana speak to men in his presence and insists that she stay by his side at all times. Seana believes that marriage and children will put an end to John's jealous outbursts and that John's jealousy just proves how much he loves her.

Seana confided in the counselor that her own parents fought continually throughout her early childhood and that her father finally left the home and has been estranged from the family for many years after almost killing her mother in a fight. Seana's father was a heavy drinker and Seana thinks that since John doesn't drink, that the likelihood of John being as violent as her father is minimal. Seana also told the counselor that John's father was very violent and that he ended up in jail for beating his wife and children. She doesn't know much more about the family since they live far away.

Seana also told the counselor that she likes it when John gets angry with her. She thinks it's a sign of love and that he cares so much for her when he loses his temper. She likes the times after a fight when they make up and thinks that John is at his best when he is remorseful. "It's because he loves me so much," she says, "that he gets so mad. He just has so much love inside of him for me that sometimes he just can't control his feelings."

When told by the counselor that John was still a very angry and potentially dangerous man and that she needed to be careful around him, Seana was adamant that John was a good man and that all he needed was to have a family on which to focus all of his loving feelings. "Once he sees his children and we're together as a family," she told the counselor, "then John will love me even more and he won't get mad at me unless I deserve it. He'll be a good father to our kids."

John is in the sixth month of a mandatory treatment group where he continues to express the belief that women like men who control them. He believes that a little violence is permissible, once in a while, to keep a woman in line. He often tells the group, "Women love it when you push them around and slap them once in a while. It just shows them who's boss, and everybody knows that women like the man to be the top dog."

The men in the group say nothing when John speaks about violence to women, but after the group, they praise him for staying true to his ideals. Several of the men see John as a person to respect and ask him questions about their own stormy relationships with their wives and girlfriends. John always tells them the same thing: "A woman wants a man to be in control and to be a real man. Don't listen to that crap about sensitive men. A woman only respects a man when she knows that if she get out of line, there will be hell to pay."

Integrative Questions

1. Seana and John have a relationship that seems very troubled. Why do you think they continue on in a relationship that is so marked by violence that John faces the possibility of jail time if he abuses Seana again?
2. Seana believes that men who are controlling, jealous, and occasionally violent are expressing their love for her. Where do you think that belief comes from in her background and why do you think the belief continues on even after a violent episode in which she was badly hurt?
3. Remorse after an abusive episode is common among perpetrators of dating violence. There are some writers who believe that victims stay in abusive relationships because the honeymoon period, after the abuse, is the best part of the relationship. Do you agree with this notion?
4. The men in the diversion group don't seem to really be getting better. They listen to John after the group and agree with him while sitting passively in the group and saying nothing whenever John justifies his violent and abusive beliefs. Do you think it's possible that these men are getting better even though they often agree with John outside of the group?
5. John believes in the superiority of men and that women like men to be controlling and abusive at times. Is this a portrayal of men that you frequently hear in your lives through friends, family, or through the popular culture?

Sexual violence is a very serious problem affecting large numbers of victims. A great deal of sexual violence is committed by intimates, or familiar acquaintances. Binge drinking is unfortunately also associated with sexual violence and all too frequently occurs on American campuses. Issues related to the cause and the treatment of sexual violence were noted, particularly treatments that involve medical castration and other forms of medical treatment to prevent sexual violence in offenders. Evidence regarding the use of medical approaches to preventing further sexual violence is still uncertain.

REFERENCES

American Psychiatric Association. (1987). *Diagnostic and statistical manual of mental disorders* (3rd ed. rev.). Washington, DC: American Psychiatric Association.

American Psychiatric Association. (1994). *Diagnostic and statistical manual of mental disorders* (4th ed. rev.). Washington, DC: American Psychiatric Association.

Bayley, J. E. (1991). The concept of victimhood. In D. Sank and D. I. Caplan (Eds.), *To be a victim* (pp. 53–62). New York: Plenum.

Becker, J. V., Blanchard, E. B., Murphy, W. D., & Coleman, E. (1978). Evaluating social skills and social aggression. *Criminal Justice and Behavior, 514,* 357–367.

Berlin, F. S. (1982). Sex offenders: A biomedical perspective. In J. Greer and I. Stuart, *The sexual aggressor: Current perspectives on treatment* (pp. 83–126). New York: Van Nostrand Reinhold.

Boehnlein, J. K., & Sparr, L. F. (1993, Spring). Group therapy with WWII ex-POWs: Long-term post-traumatic adjustment in a geriatric population. *American Journal of Psychotherapy, 47*(2), 273–283.

Brom, D., Kleber, R. J., & Defares, P. B. (1989). Brief psychotherapy for post-traumatic disorders. *Journal of Consulting and Clinical Psychology, 57*(5), 607–612.

Brown, J. L., & Brown, G. S. (1997). Characteristics of incest offenders: A review. *Journal of Aggression, Maltreatment and Trauma, 1*(1).

Cooper, N. A., & Clum, G. A. (1989). Imaginal flooding as a supplementary treatment for PTSD in combat veterans: A controlled study. *Behavior Therapy, 20,* 381–391.

Dunn, A. (1994, April 10). The fear of violence. *L. A. Times,* 26–29.

Erez, E. (1990). Victim participation in sentencing: Rhetoric and reality. *Journal of Criminal Justice, 18,* 19–31.

FBI Law Enforcement Bulletin, 1990.

FBI Law Enforcement Bulletin, 1992.

Frinter, M., & Rubinson, L. (1993). Acquaintance rape: The influence of alcohol, fraternity membership and sports teams. *Journal of Sex Education and Therapy, 19,* 272–284.

Furey, J. A. (1993). Unknown soldiers: Women veterans and PTSD. *Professional Counselor, 7*(6), 33–34.

Gilliland, B. E., & James, R. K. (1993). *Crisis intervention strategies.* Pacific Grove, CA: Brooks/ Cole.

Glicken, M. (1997). *Sexual predators.* Course material for a course on human sexuality. San Bernardino: California State University.

Goodwin, J. (1987). *Readjustment problems among Vietnam veterans.* Cincinnati, OH: Disabled American Veterans.

Greenfeld, L. A. (1997, February). *Sex offenses and offenders: An analysis of rape and sexual assault.* Publication NCJ-163392. Washington, DC: U.S. Department of Justice.

Groth, N. A. (1983). Treatment of the sexual offender in a correctional facility. In J. Greer & I. Stuart (Eds.), *The sexual aggressor: Current treatment* (pp. 160–176). New York: Van Nostrand Reinhold.

Groth, N. A. (1978). Patterns of sexual assault against children and adolescents. In A. Burgess, A. Groth, L. Holstrom, and S. Sgroi, (Eds.), *Sexual assault of children and adolescents* (pp. 3–24). Lexington, MA: D.C. Heath.

Hansen, J. C., Stevic, R. R., & Warner Jr., R. W. (1986). *Counseling: Theory and process* (4th ed.). Boston: Allyn and Bacon.

Jay, J. (1991, November/December). Terrible knowledge. *The Family Therapy Networker,* 30–37.

Johnson, P., Hudson, S. M., & Marshall, W. L. (1992). The effects of masturbatory reconditioning with nonfamilial child molesters. *Behavior Research and Therapy, 30,* 559–561.

Keane, T. M., Gerardi, R. J., Quinn, S. J., & Litz, B. T. (1992). Behavioral treatment of post-traumatic stress disorder. In S. M. Turner, K. S. Calhoun, and H. E. Adams (Eds.), *Handbook of clinical behavior therapy* (2nd. ed.) (pp. 87–97). New York: John Wiley & Sons.

Koss, M. P., & Dinero, T. E. (1988). A discriminate analysis of risk factors among a national sample of college women. *Journal of Consulting and Clinical Psychology, 57,* 133–147.

Leymann, H., & Lindell, J. (1988). Social support after armed robbery in the workplace. In E. C. Viano (Ed.), *The victimology handbook* (pp. 285–303). New York: Garland.

Makler, S., Sigal, M., Gelkopf, M., Kochba, B. B., & Horeb, E. (1990, July). Combat-related, chronic post-traumatic stress disorder: Implications for group-therapy intervention. *American Journal of Psychotherapy, XLIV*(3), 381–395.

Malamuth, N. M. (1989). Predictors of naturalistic sexual aggression. In M. A. Prigg-Good and J. E. Stets (Eds.), *Violence in dating relationships: Emerging social issues* (pp. 219–240). New York: Praeger.

Mayer, A. (1988). *Sex offenders: Approaches to understanding and management.* Holmes Beach, FL: Learning Perspectives.

McShane, M. D., & Wiliams III, F. P. (1992). Radical victimology: A critique of the concept of victim in traditional victimology. *Crime and Delinquency, 38,* 258–264.

National Institute of Justice Center for Disease Control and Prevention. (1998, November). *Research in brief..* Washington, DC: National Institute of Justice Center for Disease Control and Prevention.

Parsonage, W. H. (1979). The victim as a focus of criminological interest. In W. H. Parsonage (Ed.), *Perspectives on victimology* (pp. 7–20). Newbury Park, CA: Sage.

Peterson, S. R. (1991). Victimology and blaming the victim: The case of rape. In D. Sank and D. I. Caplan (Eds.), *To be a victim* (pp. 171–177). New York: Plenum.

Roberts, A. R. (1990). *Helping crime victims.* Newbury Park, CA: Sage.

Roberts, R. W., & Nee, R. H. (1970). *Theories of social casework.* Chicago: University of Chicago Press.

Rosen, R. C., & Fracher, J. C. (1983). Tension-reducing training in the treatment of compulsive sex offenders. In J. G. Greer and I. Stuart, *The sexual aggressors* (pp. 144–159). New York: Van Nostrand Reinhold.

Sank, D. (1991). What hope for victims? The need for new approaches and new priorities. In D. Sank and D. I. Caplan (Eds.), *To be a victim* (pp. 425–437). New York: Plenum.

Sank, D., & Caplan, D. I. (1991). *To be a victim.* New York: Plenum.

Scherer, J. (1982). Overview of victimology. In J. Scherer and G. Shepherd (Eds.), *Victimization of the weak* (pp. 8–26). Chicago, IL: Charles C. Thomas.

University of Nebraska. (1996). *Dating violence and acquaintance assault.* Nebraska Cooperative Extension NF 95–244. Available: <http://www.lanr.uni.edu/pubs/family/nf244.htm>.

U.S. Department of Justice. (1992a). *Sourcebook of Criminal Justice Statistics.* NCJ-139563. Washington, DC: U.S. Department of Justice.

U.S. Department of Justice. (1992b). *Uniform Crime Reports.* Washington, DC: U.S. Department of Justice.

U.S. Census Department. (1998). United States Census Department Report. Washington, DC: U.S. Census Department.

Williams, T. (1987). *Post-traumatic stress disorders: A handbook for clinicians.* Cincinnati, OH: Disabled American Veterans.

7 Juvenile Violence

Crime and violent acts committed by at-risk or delinquent juveniles is a very serious problem confronting society today. Certain forms of youth delinquency and violence have recently become more violent and damaging to people and to society. Kingery, Coggeshall, and Alford (1999) explain that "conflicts that used to result in fist fights and end with bloody noses, black eyes, and the occasional chipped tooth now result in the drawing of weapons and often end with life-threatening lacerations and occasional gunshot wounds" (p. 309). Fraser (1996) suggests that although only 20 percent of violent crimes are attributed to juveniles, they have become noticeably more involved in violent acts over the last ten years (p. 347). Chinn (1996) notes that "during the past decade, violent crime committed by juveniles has increased . . . [and] the juvenile and young adult population has grown disproportionately more violent" (p. 70).

Warner, Weisst, and Krulak (1999) report in a 1991 Center for Disease Control (CDC) study that violent "crime rates for those 18 and younger have increased astronomically since 1983" (pp. 52–53). Fraser (1996) specifies that "between 1984 and 1993, the number of juveniles arrested for murder rose 168 percent, and weapons violations rose 126 percent" (p. 347). Using work from Snyder and Sickmund (1995), Howell (1995) reported that "from 1988 to 1992, juvenile violent crime arrests increased 47 [percent]" (p. 2). Juvenile arrests increased for specific offenses, such as a 51 percent arrest increase for murder, 17 percent increase for rape, 50 percent increase for robbery, and 49 percent increase for aggravated assault (Howell, 1995, p. 2). As discussed below, these rates have decreased since the mid-1990s; however, they are still 49 percent higher than in 1988. In outlining methods of intervening with these youthful offenders, the federal Office of Juvenile Justice and Delinquency Prevention has given them the designation SVJ, serious and violent juvenile offenders (Bilchik, 1998).

Firearm-Related Problems

Firearm-related violence and aggression committed by juveniles is one of the worst problems for society. Haynie, Alexander, and Walters (1997) report that "while adolescent deaths from other causes declined the past 20 years, death rates from interpersonal violence increased dramatically" (p. 165). Gun possessions and weapons carrying are associated with the trend during the late 1980s and early 1990s of increased juvenile violence (Page & Hammermeister, 1997). In fact, the second leading cause of death for juveniles is gun violence, and is the leading cause of death for male African American youths (Haynie, Alexander, & Walters, 1997). Injuries to youth from firearms results "in greater loss of potential life years than cancer and heart disease combined" (Page & Hammermeister, 1997, p. 506). "According to Page and Hammermeister (1997), in 1990, 82 [percent] of all homicide victims aged 15 [to] 19 . . . and 76 [percent] of victims aged 20 [to] 24 . . . were killed with guns" (p. 506). According to Dohrn (1997), "the United States now has 75 percent of all child murders in the industrialized world" (p. 46). As a result, Bullock, Fitzsimons, and Gable (1996) report that "the problem of aggression and violence . . . has reached such a serious level that the Centers for Disease Control refers to it as a 'national epidemic'" (1991, p. 34).

Juvenile Crime Prediction Problems

Experts predict that youth violence may get worse if the increased rate of juvenile violence and crime continues because the population of juveniles is supposed to increase by 22 percent over the next ten years (Fraser, 1996). It is, nevertheless, often difficult to predict juvenile violence and crime trends. Part of the prediction and estimation problem is related to the way studies are conducted. Studies may define violence or crime differently, which may affect comparison between study findings. Different data collection methods, coupled with variations in the wording of survey questions, sometimes make it difficult to interpret and compare research findings. Self-reported survey findings, which are often more reliable than valid, might be inaccurate and not useful for prediction. The way survey findings are aggregated and crimes are combined may make it difficult to understand the prevalence of certain types of juvenile crime or violence. Also, findings for studies of juvenile crime and violence are often only applicable to the period of time for which data were gathered. Beside considering potential definition, data collection, and other testing problems, it is important to be careful when drawing conclusions or making predictions about juvenile crime or violence trends when evidence is weak or not relevant.

It is also often difficult to predict who will become part of the serious and violent juvenile population (Bilchik, 1998). Prediction is made more difficult because "many SVJ [serious and violent juveniles] are never arrested, and the majority . . . have only one officially recorded violent crime" (Bilchik, 1998, p. 5). It is important to remember that "research demonstrates that a small proportion of juveniles account for the bulk of serious and violent juvenile delinquency" (Howell, 1995, p. 29; Wolfgang et al., 1972). It is often difficult to identify the small percentage of youth who commit many of the serious and violent crimes. More needs to be done within the field of criminal justice to try and identify the youth that are part of the small group of youth that commit many of the worst types of crimes or engage in the most serious forms of illegal behavior. Besides influencing changes in youth that could transfer into improved life outcomes or reductions in recidivism, those that fail in intervention and/or prevention programs may be more likely to be part of this small group of criminal or violent youth. If identified, resources should be better targeted at these criminal or violence prone juveniles.

Community-based offender programs designed for these chronic high-risk juvenile offenders represent one of the most critical points in justice system processing (see Cavender & Knepper, 1992). Traditionally, these individuals represent a high risk for reoffending—all too often within the first 90–180 days after release into the community (Altschuler & Armstrong, 1991; Jackson, 1982; McArthur, 1974). Many chronic juvenile offenders released from secure facilities exhibit additional problems that need specialized treatment. A number of studies indicate that in addition to a history of alcohol and/or illicit drug use and abuse, many display emotional and cognitive problems that hinder normal postadolescent development (Krisberg & Austin, 1978; Jackson, 1982; Palmer, 1991). The central issue, according to Altschuler and Armstrong (1991), is that "these youths have a poor prognosis for successful community reintegration and adjustment unless their problems are responded to in an appropriate fashion through specialized programming and service provision during early parole reintegration" (p. 52).

Recent Reductions in Youth Violence and Crime

On the other hand, more recent sources indicate that youth violence and crime has gone down. Snyder (1999) indicates that the increase in violence and crime by juveniles during "the late 1980s peaked in 1994" (p. 1). According to the Federal Bureau of Investigation (FBI), crime index offenses, such as murder, forcible rape, robbery, and aggravated assault declined for juveniles during the four years from 1994 to 1998 (Snyder, 1999, pp. 1–11). Snyder and Sickmund (1999) indicate that "serious violence by juveniles dropped 33 percent between 1993 and 1997" (p. 62). While juvenile arrests for violent crimes were reduced by 19 percent during this period, "the number of juvenile violent crime index arrests in 1998 was still 15 [percent] above the 1989 level" (pp. 1–4). When comparing the 1988 juvenile arrest rate for violent crime with the rate in 1997, Bilchik (1999) indicates that the 1997 rate "was still 49 percent higher than in 1988" (p. 15). In 1998, according to Snyder (1999) "juveniles were involved in 12 [percent] of murder arrests, 14 [percent] of aggravated assault arrests, 35 [percent] of burglary arrests, 27 [percent] of robbery arrests, and 24 [percent] of weapons arrests" (p. 11). Therefore, crime and violence committed by juveniles in the United States continues to be a serious problem (Bilchik, 1999, p. 15). Some improvements have been made in recent years. In contrast to many of the late 1980 and early 1990 sources, at least juvenile violence and crime is not spiraling out of control at this time, as predicted earlier. As Fox (1996) reminds us, however, teenage populations ages 14 to 17 are increasing through 2005 by 20 percent, and, as a result of poor parenting to guide their development, we "likely face a future wave of youth violence that will be even worse than that of the past ten years" (p. 1).

Most Juvenile Crime Is Minor

A substantial amount of youth misbehavior results in minor violations against accepted societal norms, values, and practices. To describe the characteristics and prevalence of such misbehavior, Emler and Reicher (1995) suggest that "delinquent action is rarely creative, frequently self-destructive, mostly mundane and still a minority pastime among adolescents as a whole" (p. 2). Of those juveniles that are arrested for any reason, "the vast majority . . . are arrested for property crimes and other less serious offenses—not crimes of violence" (Howell et al., 1995, p. 2). With respect to violent delinquent behavior, Dohrn (1997) relies upon Snyder and Sickmund (1995) to confirm that "less than one-half of 1 percent of all juveniles in the United States were arrested for violent offenses . . . [and that] only 5 percent of youth ages 10 [to] 17 were arrested for anything, and of that 5 percent, only 9 percent were arrested for a violent crime" (p. 3). In Abraham Blumberg's *Law and Order: The Scales of Justice*, Lemert (1973), with the following, clarifies the nature of typical youth delinquency in relation to life processes and changes: [thus] "most youths outgrow their so-called predelinquency and their law flouting; they put away childish things as they become established in society by a job, marriage, further education, or by the slow growth of wisdom" (p. 222).

Undocumented Juvenile Delinquency

A significant amount of juvenile delinquency and crime goes undocumented. Dryfoos (1990) points out that official statistics underrepresent the prevalence of juvenile crime and violence in society (pp. 30–31). Even though the U.S. Department of Justice attempts to keep track of the number of cases that end up in juvenile court, not very many of the juvenile arrests turn into cases that can be documented for official statistical purposes (Dryfoos, 1990). Not very many of the juveniles that are even arrested are actually taken into custody (Dryfoos, 1990). Even though FBI arrest statistics represent the number of juveniles arrested for particular crimes, the statistics do not accurately account for the total number of crimes committed by young people (Snyder, 1999). The FBI data underrepresents the level of youth crime because police departments may report to the FBI that a crime is cleared when a person is arrested and turned over for prosecution, but clearance by arrest does not signify that a person is guilty, does not imply that a person will be convicted, does not indicate that only one youth was involved in the offense, and it does not designate that only one offense was committed (Snyder, 1999).

Youth Crime Statistics Problems

The problem with official statistics generated by the police and sent to the FBI pertains to the probability that data may be inaccurate, omitted from reports, based upon different crime definitions, or missing because police only report the crimes that they come to know about (Snyder, 1999). With less than serious juvenile crime or delinquency, often no official statistical documentation occurs because such youth misbehavior is perceived to be not serious enough for police involvement. Kvaraceus (1966) provided another reason why notable delinquency goes unreported, when it is suggested that "a kind of screening which tends to shelter or protect the offender against becoming a court statistic often takes place in the average community; this accounts for the so-called hidden delinquency which is never recorded but which, nevertheless, is very real" (p. 33). He suggested that this "antisocial and illegal behavior among youth may be considered tantamount to a cultural pattern" (Kvaraceus, 1966, p. 33).

Therefore, the levels of both secondary youth deviance and misbehavior and primary crime and violence are probably more widespread in society than found in official sources. However, most youth illegal behavior is not severe—most arrests do not involve serious crimes or violence. Much youth misbehavior only violates conventional societal norms and values, and it generally does not impact society in any extremely dangerous way. And, as noted, studies indicate that a small group of youth commit a majority of the most serious types of offenses.

With certain forms of serious juvenile crime and violence there have been significant rate reductions in the United States in recent years. However, juvenile crime and violence is still a problem that requires effective public attention and response because it continues to produce a variety of negative consequences for individuals and within society generally. Recent spates of violent drug-related youth crime, car jackings, and acts of school violence around the nation support this concern.

Reasons for Juvenile Violence

The factors associated with youth violence have been researched from a variety of perspectives including biological, ethological, anthropological, and sociological frameworks. Unfortunately, none of these theoretical approaches have been found to sufficiently explain youth violence (Borduin & Schaeffer, 1998; Henggeler, 1989; Kazdin, 1995; Loeber & Farrington, 1998; Ollendick, 1996; Stoff, Breiling, & Maser, 1997). Generally, a number of studies have looked at potential risk factors associated with family, peers, community, culture, race and attributes of the individual. A summary of that research is presented here.

Individual Variables Predictive of Violence

Personal characteristics associated with violent behavior in juveniles include a difficult temperament during infancy which has been associated with aggressive behavior during childhood and adolescence. Another personal risk factor is the initiation of delinquent and violent behavior early in a child's life (Howell, 1995). Some researchers have suggested that difficult temperament in a child predisposed them toward violence and is a result of the interaction between the child's biological predisposition and the parents' behavior toward the child. Some researchers have noted physiological correlates of violence such as low resting heart rates (Raine & Jones, 1987), low serotonin activity in the central nervous system (McFarlin, Kruesi, & Nadi (1990), low cortisol (Lahey, McBurnett, Loeber, & Hart, 1995), and high testosterone (Olweus, Mattsson, Schalling, & Low, 1988) in aggressive children and adolescents. Other biological factors, such as perinatal difficulties, minor physical abnormalities, and brain damage, have also been implicated (Howell, 1995).

Higher levels of cognitive problems have been found in violent youth including lower levels of moral reasoning (Arbuthnot, Gordon, & Jurkovic, 1987), problems in abstract thinking (Seguin, Pihl, Harden, Tremblay, & Boulerice, 1995), and problem solving (Seguin et al., 1995) than in nonviolent youth. Researchers have generally identified low verbal IQ scores among aggressive youth (Farrington, 1991) and a tendency to interpret the behaviors of others as hostile in the absence of true hostile intent (Crick & Dodge, 1994). This may be associated with prior child abuse or molestation.

Gender is also felt to be a predictor of violent behavior, with boys under eighteen years of age arrested five times more frequently for violent crimes than were girls in the same age group (Federal Bureau of Investigation, 1996). However, the rate of increase in violent crimes by female offenders has risen twice as fast as those of male juveniles over the past decade (Federal Bureau of Investigation, 1998).

Peer Variables

Children and adolescents with poor relationships with friends may react by being verbally and physically aggressive (Dodge & Frame, 1982; Dodge, 1993). Rejection by peers may drive aggressive children and adolescents toward more aggressive peer affiliations.

Affiliation with very aggressive peers is a strong predictor of antisocial behavior in youth (Borduin & Schaeffer, 1998). Juvenile gang members report that they gain a sense of control because of gang affiliation (Walker, Schmidt, & Lunghofer, 1997). Hughes (2000) notes that members of gangs often remain in gangs long after they reach an age when gang affiliation may be gang inappropriate just to continue the sense of affiliation and friendships originally developed in the gang.

Community and Cultural Variables

Several community-related variables have been associated with youth violence including the availability of firearms and drugs (Burkstein, 1994) and alcohol (Moss & Kirisci, 1995). Researchers have found that the number of youth carrying guns or other weapons has significantly increased over the past fifteen years. Juveniles who carry guns or other weapons commit more violent acts than those who carry no weapons (DuRant, Getts, Cadenhead, & Woods, 1995). Youth who use street drugs commit more violent offenses than delinquent peers who do not use such drugs (Kingery, McCoy-Simandle, & Clayton, 1997). Very early use of alcohol has also been linked to higher rates of aggression (Moss & Kirisci, 1995) and sometimes serves to facilitate violent acts.

Violence in the media has also been associated with aggressive behavior (Donnerstein, Slaby, & Eron, 1994). Continued exposure to violence through media reporting may also serve to perpetuate violent behavior in youth. Poor and disorganized neighborhoods also experience high rate of youth violence (Hawkins, 1995). Exposure to violence in the community (witnessing or personally experiencing violence) increases violent adolescent behavior (Farrell & Bruce, 1997).

Family Variables

A family history of criminal behavior and substance abuse, family management problems, family conflict, and parental attitudes favorable toward crime and substance abuse have been associated with youth violence (Howell, 1995). Parents of violent youth often encourage and support aggressive behaviors in their children which may lead to youth violence (Widom, 1989). Abusive use of corporal punishment may also be linked to violent behavior in juveniles (Farrington, 1991). Insufficient monitoring of the child may be linked to aggressive behavior in children (Loeber, Stouthamer-Loeber, VanKammen, & Farrington, 1991). Families of aggressive children and adolescence often show low levels of warmth (Henggeler & Borduin, 1990), low levels of cohesion (Gorman-Smith, Tolan, Zelli, & Huesmann, 1996), and high levels of marital discord (Jouriles, Bourg, & Farris, 1991).

Patterson (1982) noted that families of aggressive youth often socialize their children into aggressive behavior by modeling violence in the way the family interacts and the use of approaches to punishment (Kashani & Allan, 1998). Adolescents who were abused as children and grow up in families with multiple problems of violence (child abuse, domestic violence, sexual abuse, emotional abuse, alcohol related abuse) commit more violent acts than adolescents who were not maltreated as children (Thornberry, Lizotte, Krohn, Farnworth, & Jang, 1994).

School Violence

School campuses are settings for criminal activity, interpersonal violence, and student fears. Bullock, Fitzsimons, and Gable (1996) rely upon Sautter (1995) and the U.S. Department of Justice to confirm "that three million crimes—or about 11 [percent] of all crimes—occur each year in or around schools" (p. 34). Based upon findings from the National Center for Education Statistics (1995), around 160,000 students are absent from school every day because they do not want to become victims of violence (Bullock et al., 1996). To characterize the violence generated by youth in the school setting, Haynie, Alexander, and Walters (1997) rely on the 1993 Youth Risk Behavior Survey to report that "among grade 9 [to] 12 students surveyed nationwide, 42 [percent] report having fought in the previous 12 months, 16 [percent] report having fought on school property. . . 22 percent reported having carried a weapon the past 30 days, 7 [percent] having done so on school property" (p. 165). According to the *Christian Science Monitor* (June 13, 1998), "over 6,000 students were expelled last year for bringing guns to school" (p. 16). To further understand school-based weapon possession problems, Page and Hammermeister (1997) indicated the extent to which youths report that they possessed weapons at school, or that they could easily get weapons:

> [Thus] according to the 1990 Youth Risk Behavior Survey, 1 in 20 senior high school students carried a firearm, usually a handgun, and 1 in 5 carried a weapon of some type during the 30 days preceding the survey (Centers for Disease Control, 1991). A survey of 10 inner-city high schools in four states found that 35 [percent] of male and 11 [percent] of female students reported carrying a gun (Sheley, Wright, & McGee, 1992). . . . A poll of students in grades six through twelve conducted by Louis Harris for the Harvard School of Public Health in 1993 found that 59 [percent] said they could get a handgun if they wanted one, and 21 [percent] said they could get one within the hour. (p. 505)

Several factors related to the school environment have been linked with aggression in youth, including strict and inflexible classroom rules, teacher hostility (Pratt, 1973), and lack of classroom management. In addition, youth in overcrowded schools are more aggressive toward peers than are adolescents attending uncrowded schools. Within the classroom, aggressive children have been observed to be more disruptive and off-task than nonaggressive peers (Dodge, Coie, & Brakke, 1982). Furthermore, low academic achievement, academic failure, lack of commitment to school, and school dropout rates have been associated with delinquent and aggressive behavior (Hinshaw, 1992).

School Crime Statistics Problems

Official school disciplinary or expulsion statistics, however, may not accurately capture the true level of criminality, violent behavior, or gun possession problems at schools. Because most school-based crimes are customarily resolved as disciplinary offenses rather than matters that are resolved by authorities outside of the school, rates of violence and weapon possessions at schools may be greatly underestimate such levels because official tracking mechanism are inadequate (Morley & Rossman, 1996). For example, students and teachers may not report violent incidents or weapon possessions because they are afraid of reprisals or they might feel that they will incur official criticism (Morley & Rossman, 1996). Schools are relatively safe places in comparison to estimates of aggregate juvenile crime and violence numbers; nevertheless, school-based levels of crime and violence are underestimated. School environments today are places where too much violence, crime, and weapon carrying does occur, and student fears concerning violence and crime are real and they adversely impact student school attendance and learning. Schools need to try and better arrest juvenile aggression, violence, and weapon possession problems. They also need to try and improve how they handle student behavior problems and fears.

Although violent deaths on school campuses have declined from 54 in 1992 to 1993 to just 9 in 1999 to 2000 school years (National School Safety Center, 2000), fears about such violence were considerably heightened with the slaying of thirteen children at Columbine High School in Colorado on April 20, 1999, by two disaffected teenagers, Eric Harris and Dylan Klebold. This story made the cover of *Time Magazine* (1999, December) with the revelation that these youth had made a videotape describing what they planned to do and why. It was a "revolution of the dispossessed" who were acting out in a rage against all "niggers, spics, Jews, gays, f__ing whites . . . the enemies who abused them and the friends who didn't do enough to defend them" (*Time*, 1999, p. 42). Moreover, what seemed predictable based on their behavior, and possibly preventable, was neither predicted nor prevented.

Case Study: A Victim of School Violence

Lynne is a nine-year-old African American girl who was present at her school when a black former student at her school and a gang member walked into the school and killed the female principal. He'd had a longstanding dispute with the principal for suspending him several times and blamed the principal for the continuing problems he'd experienced since with the school system. On the way out of the school, the young man shot and killed two Asian students. When a janitor came to see what was happening, the killer took a knife out and slit the janitor's throat. Lynne happened to be in the hallway and witnessed the three killings. As the killer turned to Lynne, he laughed and said, "You a lucky bitch today," and walked past her and calmly out of the front door of the school.

Lynne seemed rational and oriented after the shooting and gave the police a description accurate enough for them to catch the killer. In reality, she was in deep shock and an hour after the shooting stood rigid and motionless until her parents came to school and brought her to the emergency room where she was diagnosed with shock and post-traumatic stress disorder. She was placed on tranquilizers and hospitalized. A crisis worker came to see her during the four days she spent in the mental health unit of the hospital offering supportive therapy and grief counseling. He also focused on trying to get her back to the normal rhythms of her life and encouraged her not to think about the killings but to focus more on school, her family and her friends.

Upon release from the hospital, Lynne complained of headaches, sleeping problems, and a fear that the killer, or one of his friends, would find her and kill her for helping the police identify him. Six months after the killings, Lynne is frequently frightened and has regressed at home and in school where her grades have dropped dramatically. She is in treatment with a therapist who specializes in post-traumatic stress disorder as a result of gang killings. The therapist is using systematic desensitization, a form of behavior modification where clients are taught to systematically reduce their level of anxiety over a trauma. The approach helps to reduce fear and anxiety about an issue by imagining the issue and by cognitively lowering the level of anxiety related to the issue. The therapist is also using cognitive behavioral therapy to lessen her level of fear, but Lynne has been very traumatized and after six months has been nonresponsive to treatment. She tells her therapist, "They're gonna get me when I'm not even thinking about them. Maybe at a movie, or in the mall, or maybe in my backyard at home. The gang leaves signs all over with my name on it. My parents are too poor to move. We're scared all the time. My family is mad at me for talking to the police. They say that he didn't hurt me and I should have respected him for that."

Discussion of the Case

Lynne is in a real quandary. She has ample reason to fear retaliation from the killer's gang associates. Retaliation is a daily occurrence in parts of Los Angeles and talking to the police is considered a certain reason for retaliation by a gang. While she is receiving help, she still feels very unsafe. The family's sense that she violated gang etiquette by talking to the police after her life was spared makes them all targets for gang violence. Their home has already been shot at. Police response was so slow to the shooting that the police actually ended up sending a volunteer to the house to talk to them. This lack of action by the police signals to Lynne and her family that the police think she's marked for a killing and do not want to be around when it happens.

Lynne should move to a safer environment but the family lacks resources and can't really move anywhere in the community and feel safe from gang reprisals. The gang has affiliates all over the metropolitan area who feel obligated to fulfill a contract for a member gang when "squealers" are involved. Gangs operate on the belief that fear creates anonymity. If someone breaks that belief, the offender has to be punished so the belief is reactivated. It creates a form of silence that Lynne violated.

Lynne needs a sense of safety to help her get over the trauma of the event and her fear of retaliation. She needs the family to support her moral action in identifying the perpetrator and she needs to be able to return to the normal activities of a nine-year-old girl. Like all too many inner-city children, however, she has to make do with the possibility of death and try to survive the best way she knows how: by developing a tough skin, shutting out the world, and developing a cynical attitude toward everything middle-class America believes. A year after the killing, Lynne is a behavioral problem in school. She acts out in class, gets into fights, and is considered the toughest girl in her class. The gang recruiters have watched her over the year and have decided that she has qualities they admire. She will be asked to join a gang who will protect her and offer her friendship and a sense of affiliation that her family has all but eliminated. The young naive girl who witnessed a killing has become the cynical tough survivor soon to be a gang member and soon, herself, to experience the feeling of killing someone and knowing that nobody will identify her, whatever she does.

Youth Gangs

Youth gang involvement is not a new phenomenon in the United States. Gangs have been known to exist in our country since the eighteenth century. Philadelphia was trying to devise a way to deal with roaming youth disrupting the city in 1791. Officials in New York City acknowledged having gang problems as early as 1825 (National School Safety Center, 1990). The gang problem is not likely to go away soon or to be eliminated easily.

Young people join gangs for a variety of reasons, some of which are the same reasons children join other prosocial groups such as 4-H and Boy Scouts or Girl Scouts. Walker, Schmidt, and Lunghofer (1997) state that some of the reasons for joining a gang may include a search for love, structure, and discipline; a sense of belonging and commitment; the need for recognition and power; companionship, training, excitement, and activities; a sense of self-worth and status; a place of acceptance; the need for physical safety and protection; and a family tradition.

As Lisbeth Schorr has noted in her book *Within Our Reach* (1989), "No one circumstance, no single event, is the cause of a rotten outcome . . . But each risk factor vanquished does enhance the odds of averting later serious damage" (p. 32). At-risk youth entering a gang may have encountered several risk factors, including both personal and institutional racism (i.e., systematic denial of privileges). Gang youth may feel they have been denied access to power, privileges, and resources, and will often form their own anti-establishment group; a sense of hopelessness can result from being unable to purchase wanted goods and services. Young people living in poverty may find it difficult to meet basic physical and psychological needs which can lead to a lack of self-worth and pride. One way to earn cash is to join a gang involved in the drug trade.

Gang members often come from homes where they feel alienated or neglected They may turn to gangs when their needs for love are not being met at home. Risks increase when the community fails to provide sufficient youth programs or alternatives to violence; media influences. Television, movies, radio, and music all have profound effects on youth development. Before youth have established their own value systems and are able to make moral judgments, the media promotes drugs, sex, and violence as an acceptable lifestyle.

However, not all children who are at risk for gang affiliation actually join gangs. Common characteristics among children living in poverty and adverse situations who seemed to be stress-resistant and avoided gang affiliation appear to be: (a) the children were well-liked by peers and adults, and they had well-developed social and interpersonal skills; (b) they were reflective rather than impulsive about their behavior. They had a high sense of self-esteem, self-efficacy, and personal responsibility; (c) they had an internal locus of control, that is, they believed they were able to influence their environment in a positive manner; (d) they demonstrated an ability to be flexible in their coping strategies. They had well-developed problem-solving skills and intellectual abilities.

Reasons for Gang Involvement

To understand gangs, we need to understand the cities where gangs exist. Gangs vary considerably by city, ethnic group, and gender. Taylor (1990) believes that the family is essential to the development of the child's social, emotional, and physical needs. If the family is the source of love, guidance, and protection that youths seek, they are not forced to search for these basic needs from a gang. Taylor also believes that young people benefit from strong education and training and that those who successfully participate in and complete education have greater opportunities to develop into reasonable adults.

While gang membership continues to be studied in considerable detail, few people are objectively looking at the many former gang members who transition into productive lives and are good parents, citizens, and role models. Hughes (1997) has done qualitative studies of a small group of ex-gang members who have successfully made the transition. She reports four reasons for the change: respect and concern for children; fear of physical harm, incarceration, or both; time to contemplate lives, unfortunately, often done in prisons; and support and modeling by helping professionals and community indigenous helpers.

The most promising reason for the transition from gang life, according to Hughes (1997), appears to be respect and concern for the safety of children. Many gang members have fathered children and as their children begin to grow, fathers experience concern for their welfare. Furthermore, former gang members have begun to share similar concerns with at-risk youth in their communities and mentor them away from gang involvement. Using this notion of concern for children as a reason for transitioning from gang life, it would be very useful to find out when that concern for the safety of children begins and how social service organizations can use this information to facilitate the transition from gang involvement.

Father to Father, a national initiative supported by Vice President Gore, was begun in 1997 for the purpose of strengthening the bond between fathers and sons. Nationally, numerous programs have joined this initiative and have developed specific programs focused on fatherhood, an idea that could help gang members use their concern for the safety of children to leave gang life. While these programs have promising anecdotal rates of success, none have been studied with any degree of objectivity.

Gang Violence

A common theme to explain the existence of gangs is that they offer a substitute for dysfunctional families, neighborhoods, and communities (Hughes, 1997;

Morales, 1982). Many inner-city gangs, in particular, offer the member a safety net in an environment that is filled with potential violence. Gang membership does not necessarily suggest individual pathology, although the gang member may be asked to do things which are personally repugnant, including extreme acts of violence. Repetitive acts of violence in fulfilling gang expectations develop a type of hardness and antisocial attitude that may, if begun early enough in life, foster extremely antisocial attitudes and a deep commitment to violence as a way of handling conflict and attainment of goals.

Morales (1982) provides the following reasons many helping professionals prefer not to work with gang members:

- The belief that antisocial personality disorders and/or gang members are untreatable;
- the therapists' fear of violent people and the assumption that all gang members are violent;
- a belief in the lack of psychological capacity for insight of poor and uneducated people, a cohort usually associated with gang activity;
- an over-appreciation of the value of treatment and a belief that every gang member can benefit;
- the opposite belief that gang members can't be treated and that all gang members are manipulative and dishonest;
- a belief that the therapist has the power and hence will control the interview. (Morales, 1982, p.142)

The gang member entering treatment may have conscious and unconscious issues that must be understood by the therapist before work can be considered effective, including:

- a distrust/dislike of authority figures, often the result of prior negative experiences with parents, teachers, and police;
- a strong resentment to being forced into treatment involuntarily as the result of legal mandate;
- a feeling of discomfort with the therapist, who might be of a different ethnic/racial group;
- a sense of a generational, cultural, and perhaps language gap with the therapist;
- looking forward to winning yet another struggle with a social control agent or the notion of the therapist as Freudian cop. (Morales, 1982, p. 143)

Case Study: A Successful Transition from Gang Involvement

Ray Albinos is a nineteen-year-old Hispanic and former member of one of the most feared gangs in East Los Angeles, a place with very high and often very violent gang involvement. Ray was present when some tourists lost their way and accidentally drove down a street that Ray's gang had designated as gang territory. While trying to get directions back to the freeway, Ray's companions opened fire on the car, killing a three-year-old child and wounding several other people in the car. Ray's son lived across the street and bullets from the gang shooting came perilously close, almost killing the child and his mother. Ray was appalled by what happened. He had spent nearly four of the last eight years of his young life in juvenile facilities with hard-core young men who used violence in jail and who generally seemed evil to Ray.

> You join a gang at 12 or somebody kills you. I joined and I acted tough and I did some pretty bad crap, but the more time I spent in jail, the more I wanted to be with my kid and his mom. I couldn't see no point to the gang life. It was for kids with all the codes and crap like that. So when I got out, I told my girlfriend that I was quitting and that we was moving somewhere else and then this killing happened and that made up my mind.

Ray went to a Catholic Church in the area that provided counseling to gang members. He began talking to Cruz, an ex–gang member volunteer who pretty much summed up the way Ray felt about his life:

> Cruz said to me that I wasn't gonna make it to see my kid go to school and that I'd leave him without a dad just like my dad left me. My dad got killed in a gang fight and I was proud of it, but now it seems crazy when I got a kid of my own who loves me and I love him. We snuck out of the house one night and moved to El Centro [a farming community about one hundred miles from Los Angeles] and it's been sweet since. I'm learning a trade with my uncle who's a mechanic. He pays good and we have a good life. I miss the gang, sure, it could be funny and exciting, but I don't miss jail and I don't miss hurting people and I got the love of my family. It's pretty nice, you know?

Discussion of the Case

These personal transformation come to gang members at times when they are most aware of the dangers of gang life. The correct professional response is to be available to help them process feelings and to help solidify decisions about life. In order to do this, it means the worker must go at the client's pace and respect the multiple forces that attract young gang members to gang life and yet make them vulnerable to fear some levels of violence, both at the receiving and the giving ends.

What has happened to Ray happens to most gang members. Perhaps it happened sooner with Ray, but at some point in time, most gang members transition out of the gang while a small number move into lives of crime and violence. The transition may not be a smooth one or always complete. Some gang members vacillate between gang and straight life but most, like Ray, worry about death and further incarceration. Notions that juvenile facilities are more pleasant than the homes gang members come from should be dispelled by visits to juvenile facilities across the nation.

In understanding Ray and the pull toward gang life, one must remember that there are parts of the United States that are third-world in their appearance, functioning, and in the way the authorities treat residents. Schools are often very poor and young people score so low on basic tests that school officials sometimes feel a sense of hopelessness, which transmits itself to the school-aged child. By twelve, Ray had begun to believe that his best hope for making it out of the inner city alive was through affiliation with a gang. The more violent the gang, the more "juice" it would carry in his own self-preservation. This need to affiliate with violence should not be seen as a sign of dysfunction as much as an indication of a strong impulse to survive. Just as many of us may have a moral base that objects to violence, we may also understand that someone's moral base and the need to survive may be at odds with one another. Gradually, as with Ray, survival needs and moral beliefs collide with age and life experience. And like Ray, most gang members become citizens with families, live productive lives, and make contributions to the community. The healthy societal response to gang violence is to provide a sense of opportunity to young children at risk of entering the gang life. Without a feeling of optimism about the future, what other options does the young potential gang member have to survive the next few tumultuous years of his life?

Treatment Issues and Violent Juvenile Crime

The Rationale for Prevention and Intervention

Prevention is a reasonable strategy because it can save money by improving future youth outcomes. It is a more humane way to try and rehabilitate or habilitate youth rather than trying to do it at the incarceration stage. The U.S. Justice Department Office of Juvenile Justice and Delinquency Prevention (OJJDP), according to Wilson (1994), recognizes that "prevention and early intervention programs for first-time offenders are the most cost-effective strategies for deterring youths who are at risk of becoming serious, violent, or chronic career criminals" (p. 118). Wilson (1994) goes on to state that "waiting until a juvenile must be incarcerated is far too expensive" (p. 118). Enough funding, however, needs to go into prevention programs for programs to make a large enough impact across the country. In many jurisdictions millions of dollars are going into building incarceration facilities, but in these same communities, well-run and working private programs are having to struggle just to remain open.

It seems very unlikely, nevertheless, that the federal government will develop a radical urban renewal policy that would change broad societal conditions like poverty, homelessness, racial discrimination, city deterioration, or economic dislocation. Such efforts would be extremely costly and too politically difficult.

Such problems adversely impact the social development of large numbers of children, so federal sponsorship of delinquency prevention efforts need to be further enhanced. Sources should provide more resources for private community-based prevention or intervention programs. Community-based programs are a good alternative to incarceration and they cost much less. For example, "on average, about one-third of those confined in long-term corrections facilities could be safely provided treatment in less secure, and less expensive, community-based programs" (Howell et al., 1995, p. 276).

Even though the federal component is only one among many possible sources of funding, federal efforts need to be further enhanced because the national government is in a better financial position to do so, compared to local communities and states. Greater national involvement in delinquency prevention efforts is also important because "delinquent behavior remains a significant social and personal problem in the United States" (Vazsonyi & Flannery, 1997, p. 271).The national government should play a better fiscal role in prevention because it has a responsibility to do so. Again, it is unlikely that the national government alone will provide enough funding for preventive solutions because there exists fiscal constraints, and because some politicians mistakenly do not want to be associated with measures that are void of get-tough connotation. Some politicians do not believe that it is the government's responsibility to fund prevention efforts because they are ideologically against the idea of big government in general, even though these same politicians are not against big government when it comes to toughening juvenile laws or building more incarceration facilities. Perhaps these politicians are against prevention efforts that may be perceived to be related to social service or welfare.

Youth violence and delinquency is a problem that concerns all of us in society. If youth are not adequately socialized into well-adjusted adults, then these dysfunctional youth could experience years of struggle and disappointment. It may take them many years to overcome their deficits, and if they do, at some point they may be shocked by the realization that many important years have been lost in their lives. But prior to getting beyond their delinquent, criminal, or violent ways, they may cause a variety of harm to others. They may even serve as negative examples for others, thereby propelling others into harmful or unproductive activities. The overall results could destabilize society, and they could produce a new generation of people that exhibit less concern for other human beings, appropriate values and norms, and appropriate attitudes and behaviors. Indeed, it is vital for troubled youth to become whole because "the values and structures of a social order can only survive beyond the present generation through the socialization of the next" (Emler & Reicher, 1995, p. 1).

To have a safer and stronger society that consists of well-adjusted and productive adults, it is important for preventive efforts to receive improved funding sponsorship, especially so that at-risk youth can acquire positive and appreciable skills, knowledge, attitudes, values, habits, beliefs, interests, morals, and ideals. If at-risk youth can be treated, then many can increase their long-term outcomes by the fact that they will have obtained appropriate personalities, role preferences, self-esteem, goals, direction, meaningful accomplishment, and character. It is cost-effective for at-risk youth to attend preventive programs and schools because soft costs (community welfare, general relief, and loss of productivity) can be saved when youth are influenced to positively change their lives earlier than otherwise. It is logical to invest in juvenile delinquents now so that hard societal costs can be avoided—crime costs, law enforcement costs, incarceration costs, and expensive job training costs. It is well known that reducing the dropout rate will substantially save expenditures related to welfare, crime, incarceration, and unemployment insurance payments. It is too costly in lost taxes, misspent revenues, lost productivity, and lost lives to ignore the impact that delinquent and dropout teenagers have on the economy and society.

Comprehensive Interventions

Juvenile delinquency is a complex phenomena that results from a variety of influences that operate mostly in combination with each other. It is often difficult to determine the correct sequencing of factors that produce delinquency. With many of the variables there may be spurious relationships revealed. Each risk factor plays a role in producing delinquency. A combination of factors often operate together to produce youth delinquency. Risk factor combinations may be different because individual lives are different. So, preventive efforts need to be designed in a multifaceted way so that the variety of youth problems can be addressed. In fact, Howell (1995) confirms that "serious, violent, and chronic offenders are the product of cooccurring, multiple problems . . . requiring comprehensive solutions" (p. 30). Preventive efforts also need to include thorough risk assessments so that treatments can be tailored to fit juvenile needs, and so that preprogram risk assessment measures can be compared to postprogram measures to determine if treatment modalities have be effective at reducing youth delinquency or youth delinquency risk.

In addition, based on Lipsey's (1992) review and analysis of four hundred treatment/prevention programs, Howell (1995) find that "the common features of effective delinquency treatment programs [are] those that (a) address behavioral, training, and social skills; (b) consists of multiple treatment modes; (c) include close monitoring, supervision, and implementation of the treatment plan; and (d) provide for extensive service delivery in concrete, structured approaches" (p. 28). Juvenile violence and delinquency prevention efforts should also focus upon reducing delinquency risks that exist within communities, families, peer associations, and schools (Fraser, 1996).

Prevention efforts in communities should be based upon a community risk assessment (Fraser, 1996). From an assessment communities can determine their own risks (Fraser, 1996). Prevention efforts may vary among communities because communities are often different (Fraser, 1996). For example, in some communities gang problems may be present; therefore, community resources could be geared towards reducing gang involvement or gang activities (Fraser, 1996). In other communities, gun possessions may pose an extreme threat; therefore, laws may need to be made tougher to hinder youth gun possessions, or community prevention services may need to work with local law enforcement to reduce the youth gun risk (Fraser, 1996). Community risk prevention strategies should also identify the factors that promote societal security and stability (Fraser, 1996). Protective factors should be promoted to involve more youth with constructive activities (Fraser, 1996).

Preventive efforts in families should promote appropriate problem-solving behavior, whereas conflict resolution should not consist of abusive or violent behaviors (Fraser, 1996). Cooperation and quality parent-child interaction should be developed (Fraser, 1996). Policies that strengthen families should be instituted (Fraser, 1996). Family activities that promote quality and healthy relationships should be undertaken (Fraser, 1996). At-risk youth should be removed from unhealthy family environments when family situations are serious enough to impair youth development and life chances (Fraser, 1996).

In terms of peer association, prevention services should encourage association with peers that adhere to conventional and healthy attitudes, beliefs, and aspirations (Fraser, 1996). Skills training should promote appropriate decision making so that youth will decide to associate with peers that present prosocial attitudes and behaviors (Fraser, 1996). Skills training should also promote information that will help youth make correct decisions, especially in difficult social situations (Fraser, 1996). Parents and teachers whenever possible should promote healthy peer interactions by communicating values and standards that will uphold the importance of appropriate peer associations (Fraser, 1996).

Dusenbury et al. (1997) advocates nine effective or successful program components to prevent juvenile violence and delinquency in schools:

1. A comprehensive, multifaceted approach that includes family, peer, media, and community components.
2. Programs should begin in the primary grades and be reinforced across grade levels.
3. Developmentally-tailored interventions are important.
4. Programs content should promote personal and social competencies.
5. Interactive techniques such as group work, cooperative learning, and discussions facilitate the development of personal and social skills.
6. Ethnic identity/culturally sensitive material should be matched with the characteristics of the target population.
7. Staff development/teacher training ensures that a program will be implemented as intended by the program.
8. Activities designed to promote a positive school climate or culture.
9. Activities should be designed to foster norms against violence, aggression, and bullying. (pp. 410–412)

Mental Health Solutions

A wide variety of treatment approaches have been implemented by mental health professionals in an attempt to address one or more of the many psychosocial risk factors associated with youth violence. These approaches include cognitive-behavioral skills interventions with seriously aggressive or violent youth, cognitive restructuring techniques, role plays, therapist modeling, and behavioral assignments. These approaches attempt to reduce violent behavior by directly addressing psychosocial risk factors within individual youth (e.g., ineffective problem solving, deficits in moral development). Unfortunately, little to no significant impact on long-term recidivism (i.e., recurrence of violent offenses) has been demonstrated with these interventions (Borduin & Schaeffer, 1998).

Parent training models to help parents learn effective communication skills, conflict resolution, family problem solving, contracting, positive reinforcement, mild punishment, and modeling, are effective in reducing child noncompliance and aggressive behavior among preschool and elementary school children. These models attempt to reduce aggressive behavior by addressing the psychosocial risk factors that occur at the family level (e.g., poor parental monitoring and discipline practices, coercive family interactions). However, only minimal improvements in family functioning occur in families of violent youth, and again, no significant reduction in recidivism rates have been demonstrated (Kazdin, 1995).

Overall, most mental health treatments have been most effective with younger, nonviolent, or mildly aggressive youth (Henggeler, 1989; Kazdin, 1995). However, they have been largely ineffective in reducing or preventing further violence with more serious or chronically violent offenders. As a result, many professionals and nonprofessionals are skeptical that the juvenile justice system and the mental health profession can rehabilitate violent youth (Tocci-Lynn, McWilliam, Sideris, & Melton, 1997). It has been argued that the approaches previously reviewed have not been successful for two main reasons: First, they have included interventions that focus on only one or two psychosocial risk factors associated with youth violence (e.g., individual cognition, family relations) and have failed to simultaneously address the many other factors (i.e., peer, school, neighborhood) that contribute to youth violence (Mulvey, Arthur, & Reppucci, 1993). Second, these interventions take place in only one location, such as a mental health clinic or juvenile incarceration facility, and fail to address the other influences on violent behavior such as home life, school, or neighborhood (Henggeler, 1989; Zigler, Taussig, & Black, 1992).

One notable advance in the treatment of violent juvenile behavior is multisystemic therapy (MST) (Henggeler & Borduin, 1990; Henggeler, Schoenwald, Borduin, Rowland, & Cunningham, 1998). MST is a departure from the more traditional approaches such as residential and inpatient treatment, detention and incarceration, and outpatient or clinic-based services (Henggeler, 1997). MST is offered in the juvenile's home, school, and neighborhood, and the interventions are flexibly tailored to the psychosocial needs of each client and his or her family. MST targets the family system (improving family emotional bonding and parental discipline strategies), the school (increasing parent-teacher communication and child academic performance), peers (promoting involvement in extracurricular activities, structured sports, or volunteer organizations), and community agencies (eliciting help from social service agencies) (Henggeler & Borduin, 1990; Henggeler et al., 1998).

Henggeler et al. (1998) argue that this multisystem approach is more effective than traditional approaches since it occurs in the client's natural environment. MST is fairly brief with treatment usually lasting twenty to thirty sessions over a four- to six-month period (Henggeler & Borduin, 1990; Henggeler et al., 1998). Success rates for those involved in MST appear to be quite good as defined by lower recidivism rates, improved family and peer relations, decreased behavioral problems at home and school, lower rates of out-of-home placements and, ultimately, decreased rates of violence (Henggeler, 1997). This success rate may be due to the fact that therapies which offer immediate help to youth in crisis in their natural environments are generally much more effective than approaches to treatment which are formal, structured, and usually not offered where the client lives, plays, and is educated (Borduin & Schaeffer, 1998).

Conclusions

While evidence suggests that violent juvenile crime has decreased since 1993, there is anecdotal evidence from a number of large, urban areas in the United States that shows that juvenile violence is once again increasing. The U.S. Surgeon General (Youth Violence, 2001) reports that only one in ten acts of violence by juveniles can be officially accounted for, calling into question officially reported violence rates. While juvenile violence appears to be increasing with the juvenile population increase, there are still relatively few effective treatment approaches noted in the literature. (Chapter 11 reports on a number of promising programs to treat and prevent juvenile violence.) It remains unclear whether communities will be willing to accept the added costs of treatment and prevention programs given the lack of clear data on their success rates. Areas of concern for juvenile violence remain the school place, gang-related violence, and juvenile violence that stems from unresolved conflicts between peers.

Case Study with Integrating Questions

Jose Fernandez is a fourteen-year-old immigrant from central Mexico who came to the United States to be with his father after his parents divorced. Jose has been having a difficult time in the United States learning English and adjusting to the sometimes chaotic atmosphere of public school in southern California. He has been called a number of racial names and is sensitive to the fact that he is small in stature and more dark-skinned than many of the other Latino students. One of his classmates has been unmercifully cruel to Jose and has made fun of him over the past two years that Jose has been in school. The name-calling culminated in a fight in which Jose beat the other boy to unconsciousness. The school and the county juvenile court have a "no-tolerance" policy toward violence and much to his amazement, Jose found himself in the county juvenile treatment facility, a place usually reserved for gang bangers and highly violent youth. In responding to the placement, Jose felt that he had only defended himself and that he'd shown great restraint in doing nothing to this point. Were it not for his immigrant status and his passivity in not fighting the "system," Jose feels that he would have never been sent to such a rough and dangerous place.

Jose has no juvenile record, is a mediocre student, and is quiet and somewhat withdrawn in class. The court report, prior to sentencing, suggested that Jose had potential for more violence and the judge, on the basis of the report, sentenced him to up to a year in the treatment facility. It has been a blessing in disguise. Both of his social workers are students at a local graduate social work school and both are bilingual and Latina. They decided to take a special interest in Jose since they felt that it was his ethnicity and not his crime that brought him to the facility. They see this type of injustice all of the time and have decided that the Latino youth who get railroaded into facilities just because of their ethnicity deserve extra special help.

The first thing the student social workers did was to bring the father into the case. The father works three jobs to make ends meets and in a tearful reunion at the facility, the father cried and told Jose that his lack of time with Jose was responsible for his trouble. Jose cried as well and told his father that he felt that he was being a burden to the father and his new family. The father hugged his son and told him that this could never be true. He loved his son, he said, and to show it, would come to visit every day. He has held true to his promise and sees Jose daily. Often he brings his wife and baby so that his son will feel more a part of his American family. The two graduate social work students see Jose every day as well. They report that he has a wonderful sense of humor and that he loves puns. Since his Spanish is better than theirs, it often takes them hours to figure out how he's used puns as a sort of loving put-down.

Jose misses his family in Mexico. The student social workers took up a donation in class so that they could arrange a conference call to Mexico during Christmas and allow Jose to speak to his extended family. The call was also a form of family therapy by telephone with everyone involved including both his American and Mexican extended families. Both families assured Jose that he was loved and that when he left the facility, that they would be behind him completely. An uncle in Mexico who is also a doctor has used his influence in America to move Jose to a different school close to his home. It turns out that Jose has writing talents no one knew about and the school he will attend is for teenagers with special artistic abilities.

Jose has gone from being a mediocre student to an excellent student and a leader in his age group at the facility. He has blossomed in the facility and the two graduate students are proud of the work they've done with him while careful not to forget their indignation that the "no-tolerance" rules for violence seem to affect children of color much more frequently than they affect other children. They also think their familiarity with the culture and their facility in Spanish made the difference in the work they did with Jose. "Everyone who works with Latino immigrants should know Spanish," one of them said, "it makes a big difference in the work you can do. Kids who can't speak English just don't get the same services.

It's lucky we were here for Jose or he'd have been even angrier and withdrawn after being in the facility then he was when he came."

Integrative Questions
1. Jose received special services from his social workers because they felt his sentence was unfair. Do you think the sentence was unfair and do you think Jose was entitled to special consideration from the students?
2. An argument can be made that being in the facility was helpful to Jose since he would not have received the help he needed had he not been there. What do you think about this argument?
3. In states with large Latino populations, do you think that workers should know Spanish and be able to provide services in that language?
4. Jose is one of many bright, but forgotten, immigrant children who come to America and are in many ways invisible. What might we in the helping professions do to help immigrants to America adjust to the language, mores, and culture of their new country? Do you feel the burden of this responsibility should be left to the helping professions or should others share in the work as well?

REFERENCES

Altschuler, D. M., & Armstrong, T. L. (1991). Intensive interventions with high-risk youths. In T. L. Armstrong (Ed.), *Intensive interventions with high-risk youths: Promising approaches in juvenile probation and parole* (pp. 45–85). New York: Criminal Justice Press.

Arbuthnot, J., Gordon, D. A., & Jurkovic, G. J. (1987). Personality. In H. C. Quay (Ed.), *Handbook of juvenile delinquency*. New York: John Wiley & Sons.

Armstrong, T. L. (Ed.). (1991). *Intensive interventions with high-risk youths: promising approaches in juvenile probation and parole*. New York: Criminal Justice Press.

Bilchik, S. (1998, May). *Serious and violent juvenile offenders*. Washington, DC: Office of Juvenile Justice and Delinquency Prevention, U.S. Department of Justice.

Bilchik, S. (1999). Minorities in the juvenile justice system. *1999 National Report Series*. Washington, DC: Office of Juvenile Justice and Delinquency Prevention, U.S. Department of Justice.

Blumberg, A. S. (1970). *The scales of justice*. Chicago: Aldine.

Borduin, C. M., & Schaeffer, C. M. (1998). Violent offending in adolescence: Epidemiology, correlates, outcomes, and treatment. In T. P. Gullotta and G. R. Adams (Eds.), *Delinquent and violent youth: Theory and interventions. Advances in adolescent development: An annual book series*, Vol. 9 (pp. 144–174). Thousand Oaks, CA: Sage.

Bullock, L. M., Fitzsimons, A. M., & Gable, R. A. (1996). Combating youth violence: An "all hands on deck" approach to making schools safe again. *Preventing School Failure, 41*(1), 34–38.

Burkstein, O. G. (1994). *Treatment of adolescent alcohol abuse and dependence*. Washington, DC: U.S. Superintendent of Documents.

Cavender, G., & Knepper, P. (1992). Strange interlude: An analysis of juvenile parole revocation decision making. *Social Problems, 39*(4), 387–399.

Centers for Disease Control and Prevention. 1991. *Weapon-carrying among high school students: United States, 1990*. Atlanta, GA: CDC.

Centers for Disease Control and Prevention. 1991. *Morbidity and Mortality Weekly Report, 40*(40), 681–684.

Chinn, P. A. (1996). The long-term effects of Feuerstein's Instrumental Enrichment on the reasoning, intelligence, high school graduation rate, and post-school adjustment of 12- to 15–year-old students with educable mentally handicapping and learning disabled diagnoses. *Dissertation Abstracts* 56(9–A):3506.

Christian Science Monitor. (1998, June 12). *Christian Science Monitor,* p. 16.

Crick, N. R., & Dodge, K. A. (1994, January). A review and reformulation of social information-processing mechanisms in children's social adjustment. *Psychological Bulletin, 115*(1), 74–101.

Dodge, K. A. (1993). The future of research on the treatment of conduct disorder. *Development and Psychopathology, 5*(1–2), 311–319.

Dodge, K. A., & Frame, C. L. (1982). Social cognitive biases an deficits in aggressive boys. *Child Development, 53,* 620–635.

Dodge, K. A., Coie, J. D., & Brakke, N. P. (1982). Behavior patterns of socially rejected and neglected preadolescents: The roles of social approach and aggression. *Journal of Abnormal Child Psychology, 10*(3), 389–409.

Dohrn, B. (1997). Youth violence: False fears and hard truths. *Educational Leadership, 55*(2), 45–47.

Donnerstein, E., Slaby, R. G., & Eron, L. D. (1994). The mass media and youth aggression. In L. Eron and J. H. Gentry (Eds.), *Reason to hope: A psychosocial perspective on violence and youth* (pp. 219–250). Washington, DC: American Psychological Association.

Dryfoos, J. G. (1990). *Adolescents at risk: Prevalence and prevention.* New York: Oxford University Press.

DuRant, R. H., Getts, A. G., Cadenhead, C., & Woods, E. R. (1995, October). The association between weapon-carrying and the use of violence among adolescents living in or around public housing. *Journal of Adolescence, 18*(5), 579–592.

Dusenbury, L., Falco, M., Lake, A., Brannigan, R., & Bosworth, K. (1997). Nine critical elements of promising violence prevention programs. *Journal of School Health, 67*(10), 409–415.

Emler, N., & Reicher, S. (1995). *Adolescence and delinquency.* Cambridge, MA: Blackwell.

Farrell, A. D., & Bruce, S. E. (1997). Impact of exposure to community violence on violent behavior and emotional distress among urban adolescents. *Journal of Clinical Child Psychology, 26*(1), 2–14.

Farrington, D. P. (1991). Childhood aggression and adult violence: Early precursors and later-life outcomes. In D. J. Pepler and K. H. Rubin (Eds.), *The development and treatment of childhood aggression* (pp. 5–29). Hillsdale, NJ: Lawrence Erlbaum.

Federal Bureau of Investigation. *Crime in the United States.* (1996). *Uniform Crime Reports for 1996. www.fbi.gov/ucr/96clus.htm.*

Federal Bureau of Investigation. *Crime in the United States.* (1998). *Uniform Crime Reports for 1998. www.fbi.gov/ucr/98clus.htm.*

Fox, J. A. (1996, March). *Trends in juvenile violence: A report to the United States Attorney General on current and future rates of juvenile offending.* Washington, DC: Bureau of Justice Statistics, U.S. Department of Justice.

Fraser, M. W. (1996). Aggressive behavior in childhood and early adolescence: An ecological-developmental perspective on youth violence. *Social Work, 41*(4), 347–357.

Gorman-Smith, D., Tolan, P. H., Zelli, A., & Huesmann, L. R. (1996, June). The relation of family functioning to violence among inner-city minority youths. *Journal of Family Psychology, 10*(2), 115–129.

Hawkins, J. D. (1995). Controlling crime before it happens: Risk-focused prevention. *National Institute of Justice Journal, 229,* 10–18.

Haynie, D. L., Alexander, C., & Walters, S. R. (1997). Considering a decision-making approach to youth violence prevention programs. *Journal of School Health, 67*(5), 165–170.

Henggeler, S. W. (1989). Delinquency in adolescence. *Developmental and clinical psychology and psychiatry, 18.* Newbury Park, CA: Sage.

Henggeler, S. W. (1997). *Treating serious anti-social behavior in youth: The MST (multisystemic therapy) approach bulletin.* Washington, DC: Office of Juvenile Justice and Delinquency Prevention, Office of Justice Programs, U.S. Department of Justice.

Henggeler, S. W., & Borduin, C. M. (1990). *Family therapy and beyond: A multisystemic approach to treating behavior problems of children and adolsecents.* Pacific Grove, CA: Brooks/Cole.

Henggeler, S. W., Schoenwald, S. K., Borduin, C. M., Rowland, M. D., & Cunningham. (1998). *Multisystemic treatment of antisocial behavior in children and adolescents: Treatment manuals for practitioners.* New York: Guilford Press.

Hinshaw, S. P. (1992). Academic underachievement, attention deficits, and aggression: Comorbidity and implications for intervention. *Journal of Consulting and Clinical Psychology, 60*(6), 893–903.

Howell, J. C. (Ed.). (1995). *Guide for implementing the comprehensive strategy for serious, violent, and chronic juvenile offenders.* Washington, DC: Office of Juvenile Justice and Delinquency Prevention, Office of Justice Programs, U.S. Department of Justice.

Howell, J. C., Krisberg, B., Hawkins, J. D., & Wilson, J. J. (1995). *A sourcebook: Serious, violent, and chronic juvenile offenders.* Thousand Oaks, CA: Sage.

Hughes, M. (1997, June) An exploratory study of young adult black and Latino males and the factors facilitating their decisions to make positive behavioral changes. *Smith College Studies in Social Work, 67*(3).

Jackson, P. (1982). *The paradox of control.* New York: Prentice-Hall.

Johnson, L. (1999, August). Understanding and responding to youth violence: a juvenile corrections approach. *Corrections Today, 61*(5), 62–64.

Jones, M. A., & Krisberg, B. (1994). *Images and reality: Juvenile crime, youth violence, and public policy.* San Francisco, CA: National Council on Crime and Delinquency.

Jouriles, E., Bourg, W., & Farris, A. M. (1991). Marital adjustment and child conduct problems: A comparison of the correlation across subsamples. *Journal of Consulting and Clinical Psychology, 59*(2), 354–357.

Kashani, J. H., & Allan, W. D. (1998). The impact of family violence on children and adolescents. *Developmental Clinical Psychology and Psychiatry, 37.* Thousand Oaks, CA: Sage.

Kazdin, A. E. (1995). *Conduct disorders in childhood and adolescence* (2nd ed.). Thousand Oaks, CA: Sage.

Kingery, P. M., Coggeshall, M. B., & Alford, A. A. (1999). Weapon carrying by youth: Risk factors and prevention. *Education and Urban Society, 31*(3), 309–333.

Kingery, P. M., McCoy-Simandle, L., & Clayton, R. (1997, February). Risk factors for adolescent violence: The importance of vulnerability. *School Psychiatry International, 18*(1), 49–60.

Krisberg, B., & Austin, J. (1978). *The children of Ishmael: Critical perspectives on juvenile justice.* Palo Alto, CA: Mayfield.

Kvaraceus, W. C. (1966, May 3). *The urban school and the delinquent.* Published proceedings of the Annual Invitational Conference on Urban Education. New York: Yeshiva University.

Lahey, B. B., McBurnett, K., Loeber, R., & Hart, E. (1995). Psychobiology. In G. P. Sholevar (Ed.), *Conduct disorders in children and adolescents* (pp. xviii, 392). Washington, DC: American Psychiatric Press.

Lemert, E. M. (1973). Juvenile justice, quest and reality. In A. Blumberg (Ed.), *Law and order: The scales of justice* (2nd ed.) (pp. 219–303). New Brunswick, NJ: Transaction Books.

Lipsey, M. (1992). Juvenile delinquency treatment: A meta-analytic inquiring into the variability of effects. In T. D. Cook (Ed.), *Meta-analysis for explanation: A casebook.* New York: Russell Sage Foundation.

Loeber, R., & Farrington, D. P. (1998). *Never too early, never too late: Risk factors and successful interventions for serious and violent juvenile offenders.* Thousand Oaks, CA: Sage.

Loeber, R., Slouthamer-Loeber, M., VanKammen, W., & Farrington, D. P. (1991). Initiation escalation and desistance in juvenile offending and their correlates. *Journal of Criminal Law and Criminology, 82,* 36–82.

McArthur, A. V. (1974). *Coming out cold: Community reentry from a state reformatory.* Lexington, MA: Lexington Books.

McFarlin, K. E., Kruesi, M. J., & Nadi, N. S. (1990, April). RBC contamination and amino acid concentration in the CSF of children. *Psychiatry Research, 32*(1), 99–101.

Morales, A. (1982). The Mexican American gang member: Evaluation and treatment. In R. Bicera and M. Karno (Eds.). *Mental health and Hispanic American clinical perspectives*. New York: Grune and Stratton.

Morley, E., & Rossman, S. B. (1996, August). Cities in schools: Supporting school safety through services for at-risk youth. *Education and Urban Society, 28*(4), 473–491.

Moss, H. B., & Kirisci, L. (1995). Aggressivity in adolescent alcohol abusers: Relationship with conduct disorder. *Alcoholism: Clinical and experimental research, 19*(3), 642–646.

Mulvey, E. P., Arthur, M. W., & Reppucci, N. D. (1993). The prevention and treatment of juvenile delinquency: A review of the research. *Clinical Psychology Review, 13*(2), 133–167.

National Center for Education Statistics. (1995). http://www.ncei.com.

National School Safety Center. (1990). http://www.nssc1.org/index2.htm.

National School Safety Center. (2000). http://www/nssc1.org/index2.htm.

Ollendick, T. H. (1996, Fall). Violence in youth: Where do we go from here? Behavior therapy's response. *Behavior Therapy, 27*(4), 485–514.

Olweus, D., Mattsson, A., Schalling, D., & Low, H. (1988, May/June). Circulating testosterone levels and aggression in adolescent males: A causal analysis. *Psychosomatic Medicine, 50*(3), 261–272.

Page, R. M., & Hammermeister, J. (1997). Weapon-carrying and youth violence. *Adolescence, 32*(127), 505–513.

Palmer, T. B. 1991. Intervention with juvenile offenders: Recent and long-term changes. In T. L. Armstrong (Ed.), *Intensive interventions with high-risk youths: Promising approaches in juvenile probation and parole* (pp. 85–120). New York: Criminal Justice Press.

Patterson, G. R. (1982). *Coercive family processes*. Eugene, OR: Castalia.

Pratt, J. E. (1973). Comparisons of linguistics perception and production in preschool stutterer and nonstutterers. *Dissertation Abstracts International, 34*(2–B):913.

Quinn, J. F., & Downs, B. (1995, Spring). Predictors of gang violence: The impact of drugs and guns on police perceptions in nine states. *Journal of Gang Research, 2*(3), 15–27.

Raine, A., & Jones, F. (1987). Attention, autonomic arousal, and personality in behaviorally disordered children. *Journal of Abnormal Child Psychology, 15*(4), 583–599.

Sautter, R. C. (1995, January). Standing up to violence. *Phi Delta Kappan, 76*(5), K1–K12.

Schorr, L. (1989, Spring). Early interventions to reduce intergenerational disadvantage: The new policy context. *Teachers College Record, 90*(3), 362–374.

Seguin, J. R., Pihl, R. O., Harden, P. W., Tremblay, R. E., & Boulerice, M. (1995, November). Cognitive and neuropsychological characteristics of physically aggressive boys. *Journal of Abnormal Psychology, 104*(4), 614–624.

Sheley, J. F., Wright, J. D., & McGee, Z.T. (1992, June). Gun-related violence in and around inner-city schools. *American Journal of Diseases of Children 146*(6), 677–682.

Snyder, H. N. (1999). *Juvenile arrests 1998. Bulletin*. Washington, DC: Office of Justice Programs, Office of Juvenile Justice and Delinquency Prevention, U.S. Department of Justice.

Snyder, H. N., & Sickmund, M. (1995). *Juvenile offenders and victims: A focus on violence*. Washington, DC: Office of Juvenile Justice and Delinquency Prevention, U.S. Department of Justice.

Snyder, H., & Sickmund, M. (1995, August). *Juvenile offenders and victims: A national report*. Washington, DC: Office of Juvenile Justice and Delinquency Prevention, U.S. Department of Justice.

Snyder, H. N., & Sickmund, M. (1999). *Juvenile offenders and victims: 1999 national report*. Washington, DC: Office of Justice Programs, Office of Juvenile Justice and Delinquency Prevention, U.S. Department of Justice.

Spergel, I. (1995). *The youth gang problem: A community approach*. New York: Oxford University Press.

Stoff, D. M., Breiling, J., & Maser, J. D. (1997). *Handbook of antisocial behavior*. New York: John Wiley.

Taylor, Carl S. (1990). *Dangerous society*. East Lansing: Michigan State University Press.

Thornberry, T. P., Lizotte, A. J., Krohn, M. D., Farnworth, M., & Jang, S. J. (1994). Delinquent peers, beliefs, and delinquent behavior: A longitudinal test of interactional theory. *Criminology, 32*, 47–83.

Time Magazine. (1999, December 20). The Columbine Tapes (12-20-99), p. 40.

Tocci, L., McWilliam, R. A., Sideris, J., & Melton, S. (1997). *Families' reflections on their experiences with early intervention services. Early Childhood Research Institute: Service Utilization Findings*. Chapel Hill: University of North Carolina.

Vazsonyi, A. T., & Flannery, D. J. (1997). Early adolescent delinquent behaviors: Associations with family and school domains. *Journal of Early Adolescence, 17*(3), 271–293.

Walker, M. L., Schmidt, L. M., & Lunghofer, L. (1997). Youth gangs. In M. I. Singer, and L. T. Singer (Eds.), *Handbook for screening adolescents at psychosocial risk* (pp. 400–422). New York: Lexington Books.

Warner, Weisst, & Krulak. (1999). Report in a 1991 Center for Disease Control (CDC) study that violent crime rates for those 18 and younger have increased astronomically since 1983 (pp. 52–53).

Widom, C. S. (1989). The cycle of violence. *Science, 244*, 160–166.

Wilson, P. R. (1994). Recidivism and vocational education. *Journal of Correctional Education, 45*(4), 158–163.

Wolfgang, M. E., Figlio, R. M., & Sellin, T. (1972). *Delinquency in a birth cohort*. Chicago, IL: University of Chicago Press.

Youth Violence. A report of the Surgeon General. (2001). *http://www.surgeongeneral.gov /library/youthviolence/youvioreport.htm*.

Zigler, E., Taussig, C., & Black, K. (1992). Early childhood intervention: A promising preventative for juvenile delinquency. *American Psychologist, 47*, 997–1006.

8

Workplace Violence

With the exception of the marital relationship and the stressors experienced by people in relationships of intimacy, few life experiences have more potential for crisis than the workplace. OSHA (1998) data suggest that a fourth of all workers report stress from the workplace serious enough to affect their functioning on and off the job. After years of concern for such workplace issues as low morale, job dissatisfaction, and worker burnout, we now have the culmination of these issues with the problem of workplace violence. As Studs Terkel (1974) noted in his book *Working,* the effects of work can be as varied as drinking too much, marital fights, kicking the dog around, and now, harm to coworkers resulting in workplace disputes that increasingly include violent behavior.

The workplace is where we spend our day. It is the place that provides feedback about our worth. It differentially rewards us for our labor and, from that reward, society attaches a status to our importance. It is above all a place to schedule our time. Without work, we often lack direction and meaning. The unemployed tell us that, aside from the loss of pay, the worst thing about not working is the inability to organize time and the endless experience of boredom. Unemployment can literally drive normal and well-functioning people to acts of violence. Many recent violent episodes in the workplace have been related to workers who have been laid off, downsized, given a temporary unpaid leave of absence, or any of the more creative euphemisms for being fired.

Without work, men and women lose status, income, the ability to organize their day, and their sense of self-worth. With work that is below competency or that is filled with conflict and tension, men and women experience constant feelings of anxiety and depression that, in the minds of many people, results in job-related stress and difficulties in personal lives (Glicken, 1977; 1986a; 1986b; 1986c).

The workplace is a rich place to study work-related violence because there is so much of it. The American workplace has become a breeding ground for discontent and malice. It seethes with anger and violence. It is surely one of the most well-studied arenas for the development of emotional problems to the worker. In its worst form, it contributes to alcohol and drug abuse, anxiety, depression, marital discord, and now, violence within the workplace between workers (*Work in America,* 1973). That violence should move to the workplace is not difficult to understand. For years, researchers have seen the connection between spousal and child abuse and problems on the job. Researchers have also known of a connection between problems on the job and health problems including ulcers, headaches, back problems, and more severe forms of emotional trauma (*Work in America*, 1973). As workers are unable to resolve personal problems experienced in the workplace through the use of supervision, mediation, or union grievances, many workers have begun to carry the anguish, despair, and anger they feel directly to those whom they believe are the cause of their unhappiness at work: bosses, coworkers, customers, and the random innocent bystanders who are often in the wrong place at the wrong time.

Workplace dissonance is felt most strongly in the minority community. Even when black males, for example, begin to achieve in the workplace, and incomes for middle-class black males are nearly equal to that of other middle-class Caucasian Americans, Akbar (1991) suggests that, "As cruel and painful as chattel slavery was, the slavery that captures the mind and incarcerates the motivation, perception, aspiration, and identity in a web of anti–self-images, generating a personal and collective self-destruction, is more cruel than the shackles on the wrists and ankles." This lack of a sense of freedom in the workplace prompts many African American men to question the value of their lives and the lives of others, regardless of their educational achievements or economic gain. Supporting this view that even when black men have achieved workplace success, the price is considerable, Hochchild (1995) writes, "They [African American males] have grown disillusioned and embittered with the American dream."

When unemployment becomes a problem for black men, as it does for a third of all black men, many take to the streets to find employment. But when black men *do* find work, Houk and Warren (1991) write that "marked economic and social disparities among Americans contribute to the etiology of violence [in the workplace] in fundamental ways. . . . joblessness, and the lack of real employment opportunities promote violence by generating a sense of frustration, low self-esteem, and hopelessness about the future" (p. 228).

Workplace Violence Data

Violence in the workplace includes assaults from people outside of the workplace as well as assaults by employees of an organization who assault one another. Risk factors for assault from people outside of the workplace have been described in previous research (Bureau of Justice Statistics, 1998; Davis, 1987; Davis, Honchar, & Suarez, 1987; Kraus 1987; NIOSH 1993, 1995), and include the following: contact with the public; exchange of money; delivery of passengers, goods, or services; a mobile workplace such as a taxicab or police cruiser; working with unstable or volatile persons in health care, social service, or criminal justice settings; working alone or in small numbers; working late at night or during early morning hours; working in high-crime areas; guarding valuable property or possessions; and working in community-based settings such as recreational facilities, play grounds, and parks.

Among workplaces, retail trades had the highest number of occupational homicides (2,787) during the period 1980–1989, and services had the second highest number (1,275). These two workplaces accounted for 54 percent of all occupational homicides during this period (NIOSH, 1993). Three workplaces had homicide rates that were at least double the average annual rate (0.7/100,000) for the United States: retail trades, public administration, and transportation, communication, and public utilities. Workplaces with the highest rates of occupational homicide were taxicab establishments, liquor stores, gas stations, detective/protective services, justice and public order establishments (including courts, police protection establishments, legal counsel and prosecution establishments, correctional institutions, and fire protection establishments), grocery stores, jewelry stores, hotels/motels, and eating/drinking places. Taxicab establishments had the highest rate of occupational homicide—nearly forty times the national average and more than three times the rate of liquor stores, which had the next highest rate (NIOSH, 1993).

These data are consistent with workplace violence statistics for 1992 to 1996 (BJS, 1998). However, for this later period of time (1992 to 1996), as reported by the U.S. Department of Justice Bureau of Justice Statistics (BJS, 1998), of the two million reported cases of workplace violence, law enforcement experienced almost 250,000 violent victimization while teachers had almost 150,000 violent victimization, further reinforcing our concerns that American schools are dangerous places. Medical personnel experienced almost 150,000 violent victimizations while the mental health field experienced more than 75,000 reported victimizations. Workers during the 1992 to 1996 period of time, as reported by the Bureau of Justice Statistics reports (BJS, 1998), experienced 51,000 rapes and sexual assaults, 400,000 aggravated assaults, and 1.5 million simple assaults.

According to the Bureau of Labor Statistics Census of Fatal Occupational Injuries (CFOI), there were 709 workplace homicides in 1998, accounting for 12 percent of the total 6,026 fatal work injuries in the United States. Workplace violence appears to be on the rise according to Robinson (1996).

In 1992, the Bureau of Labor Statistic (NIOSH, 1992) reported that 43 percent of all women who died on the job were victims of violence, compared to 18 percent of the men. Occupational homicides were most common to victims between the ages of 25 to 44. But workers 65 and older had the highest rate of occupational homicide. The rates of occupational homicide among African American workers and other ethnic groups were more than twice the rate of white workers. Homicide is the third leading cause of occupational death for men and the number one cause of occupational death for women. Seventeen percent of all occupational deaths are work related; five or six homicides per month are directed against managers and employees; 80 percent of the victims are males while 20 percent of the victims are female.

During the period of 1980 to 1989, nearly 7,600 U.S. workers were victims of homicide in the workplace. Homicide was the leading cause of occupational death from injury for women, and the third leading cause for all workers. The actual number of occupational homicides is probably higher than reported because methods for collecting and reporting death certificate data tend to underestimate the total number of deaths (NIOSH, 1993). National Traumatic Occupational Fatalities (NTOF) data indicate that for the period 1980 to 1989, the average annual rate of occupational homicide was 0.7/100,000 workers (NIOSH, 1995). (See Jenkins, Laynes, & Kisner, 1992, for an overview of work-related homicides based on NTOF data for 1980 to 1988.) Although data are not available to report nonfatal assaults in the United States, such intentional injuries to workers occur much more frequently than occupational homicides.

Of the 7,600 homicide victims during the period 1980 to 1989, 80 percent were male. The homicide rate for male workers was three times that for female workers (1.0/100,000 compared with 0.3/100,000). Nonetheless, homicide was the leading cause of death from occupational injury among women, causing 41 percent of all such deaths among women compared with 10 percent among men. (See Bell, 1991, for an analysis of NTOF data on occupational homicides among women.) These data are consistent with statistics for the years 1992–1996 (BJS, 1998).

Nearly half of the occupational homicides occurred among workers aged 25 to 44, but workers aged 65 and older had the highest rate of occupational homicide (2.0/100,000). During the period 1980–1989, 75 percent of occupational homicide victims were white, 19 percent were black, and 6 percent were other races (NIOSH, 1993). However, the rate of occupational homicide among black workers (1.4/100,000) and other races (1.6/100,000) was more than twice the rate for white workers (0.6/100,000). Guns were used in 80 percent of all occupational homicides from 1992 to 1996 (BJS, 1998). Knives and other types of cutting and piercing instruments accounted for only 14 percent of these deaths during this period.

Information on death certificates does not allow identification of the circumstances of homicide in the workplace. However, the types of high-risk workplaces and occupations identified suggest that robbery is a predominant motive. In addition, some homicides are caused by disgruntled workers and customers or by domestic violence disputes that spill over into the workplace.

From 1980 to 1989, homicide was the third leading cause of death from injury in the workplace, according to data from the NTOF Surveillance System (NIOSH, 1993). Occupational homicides accounted for approximately 7,600 deaths during this period—or 12 percent of all deaths from injury in the workplace. Only motor vehicles and machines accounted for more occupational deaths from injury.

Case Study: A Potential Perpetrator of Workplace Violence

Jack Warren is a twenty-six-year-old Caucasian student in math at a large public university on the west coast. He went to student counseling services and was seen by a social worker on staff for obsessive thoughts about killing people. The thoughts are random, very powerful, and continual. He sometimes thinks about sneaking up behind people and slitting their throats. The social worker conferred with the clinical psychologist on staff and both felt that while Jack's obsessive thoughts were real, that he had never acted on them and that coming for treatment was a positive sign.

The treatment staff was concerned about potential danger to university employees, students, and visitors. With the client's consent, they contacted the university police department to discuss the case. The client had no particular victim in mind so the rule of forewarning a threatened person didn't apply. He had never actually done anything harmful to anyone and looked and acted like a respectable member of the university community. His grades were good and in conversations with his parents, with whom he lived, no evidence of dangerous behavior was noted. He was not psychotic and there was no evidence of any medical problem. The counseling team urged him to have a complete physical because of their concern for a possible brain tumor, just to rule out medical problems.

The obsessive thoughts of violence began in junior high and have escalated since. He admits that he logs on to the Internet a great deal and interacts in chat rooms with others who also have violent fantasies. He finds it helpful to know that there are other people like him who have violent thoughts, but don't act on them.

The client is frightened about these obsessive thoughts and has sought help because the thoughts are so intrusive. He has no history of child abuse or any other type of serious problems in the past that might explain his obsessive thoughts of violence. The treatment team doesn't believe that he is a current danger to himself or others but worries that he might feel compelled to act on his obsessions of violence at some point in time. They feel frustrated that they can't find a cause and that treatment has failed to lessen the strength of his obsessive thinking. The social worker is using a cognitive approach in which he is trying to teach the client to tune out his obsessive thoughts. The approach is not very successful and the client is becoming frustrated with the limited progress he is making. The client has begun to speak of being possessed and is wondering if an exorcism might be the best way to resolve his obsessive thoughts of violence.

Discussion of the Case

This is a troubling case since the treatment team believes that Jack will act out his obsessive thoughts at some point. With the cooperation of his parents, Jack had a neurological workup that revealed no indication of pathology. Jack was placed on a medication that has worked in the past with many clients to reduce obsessive thinking. It had no impact on Jack and his obsessive thoughts were as frequent and strong as ever. Jack is thinking of institutionalizing himself to reduce the risk of harming others. With so little to go on, the treatment staff at the university considered the possibility of brief hospitalization as a possible way of preventing a serious incident that might affect other students or employees at the university.

One afternoon, Jack came into the student-counseling center on an emergency basis to complain that he was becoming dizzy and suffering from short-term memory loss. The social worker at student counseling immediately called the neurologist who had done the initial examination. He found this new information fascinating and suspected that the neurological examination had failed, as it sometimes does, to find seizure patterns that are sometimes associated with obsessive thoughts. "They are very uncommon but occasionally one reads case studies," he said. Jack was brought in for further evaluation by the neurologist. The client was placed on a very mild antiseizure medication that worked almost immediately to eliminate both the seizure like symptoms and the obsessive thoughts about killing people.

Jack has lost interest in the Internet and has indicated no further thoughts of harming others. He is progressing normally in his university studies, but continues on in therapy with the social worker. Many years of obsessive thoughts about harming others has made him socially isolated and he desperately wants to become more socially adept. He has also expressed an interest in dating. This time, the cognitive behavioral approach seems to be effective. Jack is also in a treatment group where he is able to talk about issues of relevance and to interact easily with others. He sees his neurologist monthly just to make certain that the medication is working and that his symptoms haven't changed.

Coping with Workplace Violence from Perpetrators outside of the Workplace

Commonly used ways of reducing assaults on employees by perpetrators who are not company employees include cash-handling policies in retail settings that include procedures such as using locked drop safes, carrying small amounts of cash, and posting signs and printing notices that limited cash is available. It may also be useful to explore cashless transactions in taxicabs and retail settings through the use of machines that use automatic teller account cards or debit cards. These approaches could be used in any setting where cash is currently exchanged between workers and customers (NIOSH, 1993).

Physical separation of workers from customers, clients, and the general public through the use of bullet-resistant barriers or enclosures has been proposed for retail settings such as gas stations and convenience stores, hospital emergency departments, and social service agency claims areas. Consideration must still be given to the ease of conducting business; a safety device that increases frustration for workers or for customers, clients, or patients may actually increase and not decrease violence (NIOSH, 1993).

Visibility and lighting are also important considerations in reducing the potential for violence. Making high-risk areas visible to more people and installing good external lighting should decrease the risk of workplace assaults (NIOSH, 1993). Access to and from the workplace is also an important area to consider. The number of entrances and exits, the ease with which nonemployees can gain access to work areas because doors are unlocked, and the number of areas where potential attackers can hide are issues that should also be addressed. The issue of worker protection and safety of facilities has implications for the design of buildings and parking areas.

Security devices may reduce the risk of assaults against workers and help identify perpetrators. Common security devices in current use include closed-circuit cameras, alarms, two-way mirrors, card-key access systems, panic-bar doors locked from the outside only, and trouble lights or geographic locating devices in taxicabs and other mobile workplaces. Personal protective equipment such as body armor has been used effectively by public safety personnel to lessen the effects of workplace violence.

Practices such as escorting patients and prohibiting unsupervised movement within and between clinic areas are part of the occupational safety codes in many states for medical and mental health settings. Increasing the number of staff on duty may also be useful in service and retail settings. The use of security guards or receptionists to identify persons entering the workplace and controlling entry to work areas may also be a way of controlling external violence.

Routine ways of opening and closing buildings as well as policies related to money drops and pickups should be carefully considered since they might actually increase risk of assault to workers. Practices that include garbage, grease, or food storage or that relate to the transport or storage of money also need careful attention and may inadvertently increase the potential for violence (BJS, 1998).

Policies and procedures should be in place for evaluating and reporting threats of violence to employees that indicate a "zero tolerance" for workplace violence. When employees have been at risk of workplace violence, procedures must be in place for obtaining medical and emotional support following violent incidents (BJS, 1998). As we know from a variety of violent situations, and as we are learning from recent terrorist attacks, workplace violence may affect family members. Services to family members when workers experience the physical and emotional after-effects of violence can be very helpful in facilitating the employee's recovery (Glicken, 1986f; 1986g). Training workers in nonviolence and learning to peacefully and sensitively resolve conflict may also reduce the risk of violence by defusing potentially violent encounters with customers and coworkers.

Case Study: Workplace Violence in a Treatment Facility

Mental health professionals must deal with hundreds of thousands of potentially violent clients each year. Clients and staff are attacked on a regular basis. In forensic facilities such as county jails with mental health units, or in forensic state hospitals that only treat inmates until an improvement in their mental health status permits them to stand trial, that number can be enormous. The following case is from an outpatient mental health facility providing a day program to clients with long-term chronic mental illness. Clients are seen from 8 AM to 5 PM during the week and usually live in board and care facilities catering to small groups of the chronically mentally ill. During the day, clients receive counseling, case management, recreational and social skills development programming, along with individual and group therapy. They also make their own food, provided at the facility, as part of their therapy.

Workplace Violence Involving a Social Worker

Larry is a thirty-four-year-old Hispanic former gang member with a diagnosis of bipolar disorder, or what used to be called manic-depression. Larry was shot in the head during a fight with a rival gang when he was in his late teens. He has a shunt in his brain and also has diabetes. To control his bipolar disorder, Larry takes one of the newer drugs to replace Lithium, called Depakote. He also has occasional seizures because of the brain damage caused in the shooting and takes Dilantin.

Larry weighs 325 pounds, is 6' 2", and is covered with tattoos. He has problems controlling his temper. He is also a master chef and does all of the cooking for the clients in the day program. He has a low tolerance for people disagreeing with his decisions about food and often has arguments with other clients about the menu. Since he is such a good cook, however, the clients give in, but there is animosity among the clients toward him. One day, another patient of equal size began badgering Larry and wanted to taste the food before it was ready. The two argued until Larry took a butcher knife from the kitchen and threatened to kill the other client. Julie, the social worker and director of the day program, walked in on the scene and calmly told Larry to put the knife down. He refused and Julie kept calmly telling him to put the knife down, and that if he attacked anyone, he would go to jail and that would end treatment at the facility, a place he truly loved.

Larry finally gave the knife to Julie, a 100 pound, five-foot-tall worker. He sat in the kitchen and cried. The patients in the facility make up the ethics committee to determine disciplinary responses to infringements of agency policy and immediately met, with Julie present, to determine what would happen to him. Larry had been making very good progress and the clients felt that it was unfair to punish him too severely since the other patient had been belligerent and threatening. Their decision was to suspend him for two months but to continue his therapy and case management at the board and care facility. At the end of the two months, he returned to the day program and was then and continues to be a sweet, gentle man with increasingly positive social skills and the ability to control his angry impulses, according to Julie.

Discussion of the Case

While everyone applauded Julie for her bravery, administration at the facility has a no-tolerance rule for potentially violent behavior. The police are to be called in the first time an indication of violence exists. While Julie wasn't reprimanded, she was told that the safety of the staff and clients was foremost in everyone's mind and that the client could have hurt her and others. She defended her behavior by saying that bringing the police in would have only escalated the violence since Larry has a long police record and the police can sometimes inflame situations that are better dealt with by using tact and professional judgment. Since Larry is making such good progress, it is perhaps one indication that Julie was right. However, the argument between the two clients could have become violent and Julie might have easily become an innocent victim.

This case validates the need for a violence plan. It also suggests that violent clients should not have access to weapons of any kind. A butcher knife is a dangerous weapon and use of the kitchen utensils can lead to confrontations among fragile and sometimes confused mentally ill patients. Staff sometimes forgets that even with patients who are making excellent progress, that chronic mental illness doesn't always allow clients to respond in rational emotional ways. Clients sometime cycle off their medication and begin to show signs of deterioration and potential for violent behavior. A safety plan and a no-violence policy are all essentials for facilities working with clients in varying stages of chronic mental illness.

The disciplinary action by the clients in Larry's case resulted in a much more involved and motivated client. Larry loves the facility and wants desperately to be there every day. He can see that he's getting better and that his life is improving. The patients were right in suspending him and it tells us something about the sophistication of the agency and the commitment of the clients that they could suspend Larry and then welcome him back. Julie should also be commended. She organized and manages the program, and has never had an instance of violence resulting in harm to a staff member or client, in an agency serving clients who have frequently been in jail for violent behavior.

Workplace Violence Committed by Employees to One Another

Many of the perpetrators of workplace violence are disgruntled employees who were terminated, fired, or laid off. Twenty-five percent of the perpetrators of workplace homicide commit suicide after the violent act. Some of the similarities in the employees who committed acts of violence at work as reported by Robinson (1996) from FBI and Department of Labor data include:

1. a history of violence, a fascination with the military, or being a survivalist;
2. white males;
3. age 35 years or older;
4. a loner or an extremist;
5. carries a grudge;
6. difficulty accepting authority or reality;

7. a history of violence toward women; and
8. may have substance abuse problems and/or mental health problems.

The following indicators of potential for workplace violence by coworkers have been identified by the Federal Bureau of Investigation's National Center for the Analysis of Violent Crime, Profiling and Behavioral Assessment Unit in its analysis of past incidents of workplace violence (BJS, 1998):

> Direct or veiled threats of harm to others in the workplace; intimidating, belligerent, harassing, bullying, or other inappropriate and aggressive behavior; numerous conflicts with supervisors and other employees; bringing a weapon to the workplace, brandishing a weapon in the workplace, making inappropriate references to guns, or fascination with weapons; statements showing fascination with incidents of workplace violence, statements indicating approval of the use of violence to resolve a problem, or statements indicating identification with perpetrators of workplace homicides; statements indicating desperation (over family, financial, and other personal problems) to the point of contemplating suicide; drug and or alcohol abuse; and, very erratic behavior with serious mood swings. (p. 4)

Each of these behaviors is a clear sign that something is wrong and none should be ignored. Some behaviors require immediate police or security involvement while others constitute misconduct and require disciplinary action or an immediate referral to an employee assistance program. It is not advisable to rely on "profiles" or "early warning signs" to predict violent behavior. "Profiles" often suggest that people with certain characteristics, such as "loners" and "men in their forties," are potentially violent. Stereotyping does not help predict violence and may lead to unfair and destructive treatment of employees. The same must be said of the use of "early warning signs" such as assuming that anyone in therapy or those experiencing marital difficulties may be at risk of workplace violence. Most of us experience emotional turmoil, but very few of us become violent.

If an employee displays a significant change in behavior or suddenly becomes hostile, it is important to find out why the change has occurred. A referral for counseling may determine the cause of the problem and treatment may reduce the risk that symptoms will turn into workplace violence. However, employees who are acutely unhappy and blame others for their problems may be at risk for workplace violence. Generally, the difference between chronic unhappiness and risk of violence takes place when an employee makes threatening comments or actually physically confronts another employee. If this happens, an evaluation of potential violence must be made with a referral to a mental health professional.

Workplace threats need to be taken seriously. Organizations should have written policies outlining the procedures for reporting all threats of violence. Those procedures should also describe the actions that will be taken in cases of workplace violence. Threatened employees have a right to know what an organization will do to protect them and what measures they need to take to protect themselves. Since it is impossible to know whether a threat is going to be carried out, the organization should always treat threats in a serious manner and act as though the person making the threat will carry it out.

Glicken and Ino (1997) describe the progression in the development of violent behavior in the workplace as follows.

Level 1

A preoccupation by a worker that he or she has been mistreated. A tendency by the worker to blame others for their lack of success on the job and to obsessively complain about how badly they have been treated in the workplace. At this stage, the problem should be evaluated and an attempt should be made to try and resolve concerns the worker has openly shared with supervisors, other workers, or with personnel departments. These concerns, if voiced irrationally or if illogical, are particularly problematic and need to be dealt with in a proactive way by encouraging counseling or by trying to help the worker develop a more accurate perception of the problem. Employee assistance programs (EAPs) or mediators can help at this early stage in the worker's preoccupation with his or her mistreatment on the job. If the worker is unwilling to become involved in counseling, mediation, or some other form of conflict resolution, the worker needs to be clearly told about the organization's "no-tolerance for violence" rules. There must also be an agreement from the worker to accept a no-violence contract so that any future concerns will be dealt with in a violence-free atmosphere. It may also be wise to provide the worker with an advocate or an ombudsman to help in future disputes. The advocate represents the interests of the worker in all contacts with the organization and is recognized as the worker's ally.

Level 2

The worker has obsessive thoughts about a plan to pay others back for the way the worker believes they have been treated. The plan may be diffuse and nonspecific, or it may be elaborate. The plan is often shared with others on the job who may incorrectly think that the angry worker is just venting anger. Usually, others do not take the plan seriously. This is a considerable mistake often made by organizations since it is at this point in time that workers begin to obsess about revenge. The reason for the progression to level 2 is that organizations often badly handle the worker at level 1. The way the worker is dealt with initially can have significant meaning for the progression, or the lack of progression, of violent impulses. All threats, plans, indications of payback, obsessive thoughts, and preoccupations with unfairness should be seen as problematic by the organization and every attempt should be made to deal with the problem through the use of an EAP, mediation, or some conciliatory process to logically resolve the problem. If the worker is being laid off, it should be done with notice, with respect, and with some semblance of concern for the worker's long-term well-being. Stories of the way organizations lay people off, in cruel, insensitive, and often rude and disrespectful ways, suggest reasons for the development of anger in workers and dramatically increase the risk of violence.

Level 3

The violence plan is now articulated to others. Potentially violent workers will share their violence plan with others they trust or find sympathetic. At this stage, if threats are not taken seriously and if something isn't done to deal with them, the anger grows and workers become victims of their own inability to control emotions that are now clearly out of control. Most perpetrators of workplace violence have discussed their plan with others in a position of authority. Some managers act on this information, but all too many ignore it thinking it best not to make problems for the worker, or worry that any report of the plan might end in a court action by the worker. For whatever reason, most workplace homicides have been articulated clearly by perpetrators. It often doesn't come as a surprise when perpetrators actually end up killing someone. When one hears about a workplace killing, it is almost always followed by statements from coworkers saying that they didn't take the worker's threatened violence seriously or that they misjudged the degree of the anger. This is the moment in time to make formal reports to the police or to company security so that action can be taken to protect other workers.

Level 4

Actual threats are made to people on the job. These threats may be made to those directly involved in the worker's obsessional system or they may be made to anyone who is handy. The worker's anger is now increasingly more difficult to control since he or she has made a decision to confront others as a release for intense feelings of anger at the organization. At this moment in time, the worker has clearly lost control. Coworkers begin to complain to superiors who often do nothing to control the behavior or who may terminate the worker without necessary professional help or police involvement. The worker at level 4 is now ready to commit an act of violence. In almost all cases of workplace violence, supervisors, personnel departments, and union stewards were forewarned about problematic employees but did nothing to ensure that help would be given or that the problem would be resolved. When threats are made, it may be necessary to bring in the police and to file charges against a violent employee. While this may end in a trial or in a prison sentence, it may also end in mandatory treatment and the safety of a number of innocent people. Remember that many perpetrators of workplace violence injure innocent bystanders who may not be part of an organization. They may also kill their own family members, often in despair over what they intend to do at work.

Level 5

The worker acts out his or her violent thoughts and commits violent acts on the job. When workers say that they are going to kill someone or commit an act of violence to coworkers, take it seriously. Threats are more than words. They are acts about to take place and are often the worker's unconscious attempt to have the act stopped. When a threat is made and nothing constructive is done to help the worker, violence is very likely to follow. The violence may be directed at specific people but more often than not it is random and affects people who have nothing to do with the worker's grievances against the organization.

It should not surprise us that many workers move to level 5 in the development of violence. Far too many managers and supervisors worry about lawsuits or union actions if they intervene and they become inactive when violent behavior begins to show itself. Nor should it surprise us if workers show none of these levels and act out their violent thoughts without seeming provocation. These are the anomalies of the workplace and the individual workers within the workplace. By and large, however, workers give advanced notice of potentially dangerous behavior. When that behavior is dealt with badly by organizations, violence is likely to result. In the next section we will see how intervening in all work-related problems is a much more effective way of dealing with unhappiness on the job than doing nothing.

Intervention Strategies to Prevent Workplace Violence

When problems in the workplace begin to surface, managers should meet with the workers, and find out what is bothering them. If the problem is beyond their ability to resolve, professional help should be sought. Many problems, however, can be dealt with by the organization. Work assignments can be varied to prevent burnout. Promotional and salary decisions can be made equitably to ensure that all workers feel treated with dignity and respect. References of workers can be checked carefully with the added protection of having potential workers undergo careful screening and evaluation before they are hired to identify those applicants with obvious emotional problems or histories of violent behavior on other jobs. Disputes between workers can be mediated informally before they become serious problems. When workers feel diminished, and no longer believe that the organization cares about them, the potential for workplace problems grows in severity.

When companies are responsive to their workers, many of the problems that lead to workplace violence can be resolved. In these companies, Employee Assistance Programs (EAPs) are used to offer workers an alternative way of resolving problems that may be difficult to resolve for managers and supervisors. Companies using EAPs offer a variety of alternatives to workers. Some EAPs are located in the organization and are readily available. In these organizations, managers, workers, and treatment personnel work closely together to resolve the problem. In other organizations, the worker might go to a social agency or counseling center with which the organization has contracted. The services provided may be time-limited and supportive, or they may be longer-term and designed to meet the individual needs of the client (Glicken, 1988; Glicken, 1996).

Often workplace problems have their origins in the personal lives of workers. Resolving personal problems is important, but keeping the worker employed supercedes the resolution of a personal problem. Organizations often complain that workers do not improve on the job after treatment is provided. This complaint is valid but organizations also need to be made aware of how long it may take for the worker to improve. Problems such as addictions to substances are slow to respond to treatment and may take months to improve with the added possibility of a need for residential treatment. Just as employers give workers time to mend after an illness or surgery, employers need to give workers time to mend when they have emotional problems (Glicken, 1988; Glicken, 1996).

Workers have aspirations and dreams for the future. It is the organization's responsibility to know what those dreams and aspirations are and to respond to the worker with loyalty and generosity. Far too many healthy and able people in America feel dead-ended in work early in their lives. The hopes and dreams of youth are replaced by cynicism and despair because workers often see that they have no opportunity to use their abilities. The stress and strain of work should not lead to workers who are burned-out in their forties, or to workers in their early fifties who have been permanently downsized because an organization feels so little about their contribution that it has stopped caring about a worker's future life. This discounting of older workers is one of the keys to the development of violence in the workplace. Imagine how someone in mid-life may feel when they have given twenty years of their life to an organization only to be laid off. They will never have the same opportunities in the workplace because age is now a negative factor in finding new and equally challenging work.

According to Robinson (1996), training is a critical component of any prevention strategy since it permits employees to become acquainted with experts within the agency who can help them when potentially violent situations arise. Robinson further suggests that "employees and supervisors seek assistance at a much earlier stage when they personally know the agency officials who can help them" (Robinson, 1996, p. 6).

Other forms of prevention suggested by Robinson (1996) and others include a confidential background check on new employees, which at the very least would include a check on the applicant's criminal, credit, and employment history, and driving record. Once an applicant is hired, it is important to track and record observable and relevant changes in behavior and take the proper steps toward intervention. Most experts suggest a zero tolerance for threats, intimidation, and any act of violence, which should be included in the personnel policies of all organizations. The organization should have assigned personnel to investigate threats or acts of violence. This might be similar to the way many organizations handle complaints of sexual harassment. Ongoing training and education and easy access to grievance procedures are also important aspects in preventing violence.

Some organizations also use ombudsman programs, facilitation, mediation, and other methods of dispute resolution to identify and prevent potential workplace violence. These strategies are often most useful before the threat of violence becomes serious enough to require a formal workplace action. The following is a short description of some preventative techniques suggested by Robinson (1996) and others (NIOSH, 1992; NIOSH, 1993) that organizations have found useful in dealing with workplace violence problems at their beginning stages.

Ombudsmen

Ombudsmen are employed by an organization and use a variety of strategies to resolve workplace disputes. These strategies include counseling, mediation, conciliation, and fact-finding. An ombudsman may interview all the parties involved in a dispute, and review the history of the problem and the organization's personnel policies to see if they have been correctly applied. He or she might offer suggestions and alternative ways of resolving the dispute to the workers involved in a disagreement. An ombudsman does not impose solutions but may suggest alternative strategies to resolve it. Workers involved in a dispute may refuse options offered by the ombudsman and are free to pursue other remedies or strategies including legal ones.

Facilitation

The facilitator focuses on resolving the dispute and is most helpful when the level of emotions about the issues is fairly low. Facilitation is most effective when the parties involved trust one another so that they might develop acceptable solutions.

Mediation

Mediation uses a third party who is not a member of the organization and is free of bias in the situation. The mediator can only recommend, although some organizations accept binding mediation as a way of resolving disputes. Mediation may be helpful when the parties involved in a dispute have reached an impasse and the situation is potentially dangerous. A mediator may offer advice, suggestions, and options to help resolve the problem. The authority the mediator brings to the dispute is neutrality and expertise. Hopefully, those involved in the dispute will accept suggestions made by a mediator.

Interest-Based Problem Solving

Interest-based problem solving attempts to improve the working relationship between the parties in dispute by using rational and focused ways of resolving problems and by reducing emotions among the people involved. Techniques suggested for use in interest-based problem solving include brainstorming, creative alternative solutions to a problem, and agreed-upon rules to reach a solution.

Peer Review

Peer review involves the evaluation and possible solution of a problem recommended by fellow employees. Because these suggestions come from peers, they may have more impact on the involved parties. However, peer reviews are subject to concerns about objectivity, composition of the review panel, and conflicts of interest. They are usually only helpful if done with the complete confidence of the parties involved. Review panels in sexual harassment cases might be a good example to explain this approach. Sexual harassment review panels have a mediocre to poor record of objectivity and recommendations to upper management are often rejected because of due process issues and concerns regarding objectivity. On the other hand, courts have been reluctant to overturn decisions made by organizations when review panels are used in sexual harassment investigations.

Employee Training

All employees should understand the correct way to report potentially or actively violent and disruptive behavior observed in other workers. Robinson (1996) suggests that the following topics should be included in all workplace violence prevention training:

> Discussion of the organization's workplace violence policy; a willingness of employees to report incidents; suggested approaches to preventing or coping with potentially violent and hostile behavior; conflict resolution training; training in managing stress and anger; training in the location and operation of alarm systems; personal security measures; and, understanding the various programs offered by organizations including employee assistance programs, the ombudsman, and mediation. (p. 6)

Supervisory Training

Special attention should be paid to effective training of supervisors so that they know how to identify, evaluate, and resolve workplace problems that may lead to violence. This includes the use of personnel policies to provide accurate evaluations of performance and reports that correctly identify a worker's behavior with fair and well-thought-through disciplinary actions provided. Skills necessary to prevent workplace violence by managers may include the ability to screen applicants for potential for violence, crisis management and conflict resolution skills, and encouragement of other workers supervised by the managers to share incidents of observed violence or potential violence in coworkers.

Security Measures

Workers need to feel safe on the job. Organizations can increase this feeling of safety by providing weapons checks, employee identification badges or cards with pictures, immediate response by the police if threats have been made, and assurance of the safety of workers who have been threatened or assaulted by coworkers. All organizations need to have a no-tolerance policy against all forms of weapons with immediate suspension if a weapon is found on a worker. Reports of weapons must be immediately shared with the police or with the security officer of an organization or company.

Preemployment Screening

Before a worker is officially offered a position, the personnel department should be contacted to find out what preemployment screening techniques (such as interview questions, background and reference checks, and drug testing) are permitted by federal and state laws and regulations for the position. These screening techniques should be used with all workers before a position is offered to a potential employee.

Working with Potential Perpetrators of Workplace Violence

When treatment is required for potential perpetrators of workplace violence, the literature on short-term crisis work would suggest the use of cognitive-behavioral approaches (Glicken, 1986a). These approaches, developed by Ellis, Glasser, Beck, and Wolpe, are designed to help workers understand the ideas and self-perpetuating sentences used to convince themselves that a problem exists when, with practice and help from an outside person, the nature and the seriousness of the problem may be rethought and the problem may then lessen in severity. The behavioral aspect of this approach to treatment is that it is geared to changing behavior through practice, or through what Albert Ellis calls the completion of "Homework Assignments."

Ellis (1963) has a list of irrational ideas that usually, in the extreme, get people into emotional difficulty. Taking the example of the person who has been bypassed for a promotion that he thinks he deserved, his analysis of the situation may be that the promotion went to someone else because of a personal preference by the manager. The idea that someone would be chosen for a promotion because of personal whim festers and grows in the worker until it becomes an obsessive thought that leads to unmanageable anger at the manager who made the decision and at the worker who received the promotion. It further develops as hostility toward the entire organization for allowing the inequity to exist in the first place. The hostility that now exists as a result of being passed over for the promotion and the worker's sense of outrage at the organization's handling of the situation now spill over into the workplace, where the worker has become difficult, argumentative, surly, and openly hostile to the manager and to the promoted coworker.

The therapist, using a cognitive approach, may help the client see the damage that obsessive and irrational ideas cause and ask him, as a homework assignment, to go to the manager and find out what his decision to promote someone else was based on. Not surprisingly, the worker may not have done this before. Upon following through, though reluctantly, the worker and the manager have an opportunity to clear the air and develop a plan to help the worker attain a desired promotion.

The use of short-term approaches that utilize advice and homework has revolutionized the treatment of work-related problems. Often, problems that seem to be deeply rooted in the past can be dealt with in just a few sessions. Frequently, however, workplace problems have their origins in a belief that the organization has been unfair to them or has, in some way, treated them badly. These perceptions are often true, unfortunately, and it is the therapist's difficult job to help workers cope with the many slights and attacks to the psyche in the workplace that can be very destructive. This job of helping people cope with painful work situations is difficult, particularly when the organization is unlikely to change. But teaching people to cope does not imply that we help workers become passive. On the contrary, workers can be helped to develop strategies to change their interactions at work so that they control the outcomes of work-related issues more adequately. The benefit of cognitive-behavioral therapy is that it teaches workers to analyze situations rationally and to respond in ways that are logical and productive.

When workers have problems that cannot be helped in a few sessions through an EAP, longer-term treatment may be necessary. This is often the case in alcohol and drug addictions and in personality disorders including anti-social behavior. Many employers have found benefits in employing substance abusers in remission and ex-felons (Glicken, 1986e). Both types of employees can make excellent workers but are more prone than others to emotional and social difficulties including problems away from work that affect workplace performance (marital problems, financial difficulties, feelings of isolation and loneliness). Workers with serious and long-term emotional problems should initially be evaluated for physical causes when their behavior becomes problematic at work. Many emotional difficulties on the job may be caused by medications that have behavioral side effects, undiagnosed illnesses such as diabetes, thyroid problems that may explain hyperactivity or depression, and neurological problems that might explain irrational behavior or problems in cognition. A good criticism of the mental health field is that it often ignores physical explanations for aggressive behavior.

The use of psychotropic medication may be necessary for some workers to function well. The therapist working with organizations should know the major psychotropic drugs and their impact. One of the important tasks of the EAP worker is to monitor the use of medications and to give physicians feedback on the way they appear to be affecting the worker. A second task is to make certain that employees stay on prescribed medications so that a thorough analysis of their effectiveness can be made. It is true that many people fail to use psychotropic medications correctly. Often when clients on psychotropic medications feel better emotionally, they prematurely discontinue the use of the medication. If the medication is having major or minor side effects, they may also discontinue its use before the medication has had time to take effect. Often they fail to tell anyone that they've discontinued the medication. The deterioration in their behavior may be caused by a discontinuation of medication that, if used properly, could be helpful to the worker in controlling emotions that may lead to violence.

The important lesson we are learning about potential workplace violence is that proper evaluation and treatment can be an effective way to reduce its frequency and severity. Organizations that have no plan for providing interventions in potential workplace violence make serious mistakes that result in harm to others and financial losses that more than offset the cost of treatment.

Working with Victims of Workplace Violence

A considerable amount of material is presented in Chapter 6 on post-traumatic stress disorder (PTSD), which directly relates to the impact of workplace violence on victims. Workplace violence has a significant impact on victims because it often happens in settings that most of us consider safe. Much like violence in the home, workplace violence is often random, unexpected, and traumatic.

Workplace disasters caused by accidents are no different in this respect. In studying the impact of the collapse of catwalks over the main floor of the Kansas City Hyatt Regency during a dance when more than one hundred people died, one of the authors (Glicken, 1986d) found that employees were severely traumatized by the accident. Wisely, the hotel corporation brought crisis counselors in to work with employees who had witnessed the accident, many of whom suffered symptoms of PTSD for months following the accident. From that experience and from an earlier fire at the MGM Hotel in Las Vegas, it became evident that immediate mental health intervention was necessary or employees could experience many of the symptoms of PTSD so severely that it affected their ability to continue to work in the organization. Many of the workers in the Hyatt Regency disaster felt guilt over what happened and thought themselves responsible for the accident, although there was no basis in reality for feeling that way. Significant numbers of workers had sleeping disorders, felt ill when they approached the worksite, experienced panic attacks, claimed they could hear the screams of dying people for months after the accident, had eating problems, were often unable to work, and experienced unemployment and relationship problems (Glicken, 1986d).

Regarding the impact of workplace violence on other workers, five hundred managers were surveyed at an American Management Resources Conference in 1994 (65th Annual American Management onsite survey, 1994). The managers surveyed reported that 43 percent of the workers they supervised experienced reduced morale as a result of workplace violence in the prior four years, while 39 percent experienced lowered productivity. There was an 8 percent increase in workers filing disability claims citing workplace violence as a contributor to stress and emotional difficulty, while companies with workplace violence experienced a 10 percent increase in litigation against them for not containing workplace violence. Clearly, workplace violence has a negative impact on organizational life and on workers who experience the end result of violence.

Case Study with Integrating Questions

Jim Kennedy is a forty-five-year-old Caucasian engineer working in the aerospace industry in southern California. For the past two years, Jim and his supervisor have had a running battle over the quality of Jim's work. Jim thinks that his work is fine, as do his colleagues, but the supervisor believes that Jim doesn't follow directions and that his work wanders off into areas that aren't related to his assignments. On several occasions, they have almost come to blows.

Jim was referred to the company's Employee Assistance Program (EAP) and was told by his supervisor that either he would enter counseling or he would be fired. Jim has a wife who doesn't work and two children in college. His salary barely covers his expenses, and many months he lives on credit cards and loans. Quitting isn't a realistic option since a weak business market in the aerospace industry limits his work opportunities. The opportunities to transfer to a different department at work are also limited since what Jim does is highly specialized. At 45, he doesn't want to ruin a very good pension plan. He feels stuck and resents going for counseling. He believes that his problems at work are the supervisor's fault and thinks the supervisor should be in treatment, not him. He is becoming surly and difficult at work. On several occasions, he's written derogatory remarks about the supervisor in the men's restroom and on the company elevator. While no one can prove that Jim is guilty, everyone knows that he is to blame.

In the past six months, Jim has begun to deteriorate physically and emotionally. He often comes to work looking haggard and unkempt. People have begun to find his body odor offensive and wonder if he bathes. His EAP counselor suspects that Jim is drinking heavily and has ordered a random alcohol test.

Jim has made several indirect threats against his supervisor that coworkers have heard but have not reported. They believe that Jim has a grievance and they feel obligated to protect him. The coworkers feel that Jim is going through a midlife crisis but on closer examination, Jim is deteriorating badly. His thoughts, which he confides to his wife and family, have increasingly become violent. He purchased a gun and shoots it in the basement of his home or outside of his home in the desert. The feel of the gun and the sound of the bullets give him a sense of power that he finds intoxicating. He has also begun to drink heavily and had a DWI charge that resulted in the removal of his license and the impounding of his car. He drives anyway, using a second car he purchased in his wife's name.

Jim feels invincible and doesn't think anything will happen to him. Because of his sophistication with the Internet, he has begun sending e-mail messages to everyone at work that imply violence to certain people in upper management. He never mentions the name of the supervisor he hates so much and his e-mails are untraceable. In a company with thousands of people, it's difficult to pinpoint who has made the threats or how seriously they should be taken, but the messages unnerve everyone at work and there is a sense of foreboding in the company that something awful will happen.

Jim's EAP counselor believes that Jim's deteriorating condition is reason to worry about potential violence and has warned the company that he may be at risk of violence. The company fears a lawsuit if they fire Jim. They believe that he will do something serious, but not dangerous enough to fire him. The EAP counselor disagrees. He sees concrete signs of potential serious workplace violence. Those signs include a highly intelligent man who is emotionally deteriorating and who is also demonstrating increasing paranoia and an obsession about getting revenge. The drinking and fondness for guns add to the counselor's sense of potential violence. If the counselor knew of the verbal threats Jim had shared with his coworkers and the fact that Jim is the one making e-mail threats, the counselor would be absolutely certain that Jim's volatile behavior will end in a violent act.

Jim has always been eccentric. His aloofness from people, his disdain for others he considers to have lesser ability, his angry feelings at management for not recognizing his abilities all provide a backdrop to his potential for workplace violence. As an unsupportive supervisor thwarts his ambitions, and as he suffers the indignity of having to go for counseling, Jim has begun to have fantasies of violence. They include going into the management side of the company and randomly killing every manager in sight, starting with his own supervisor. The fantasy is so clear and appealing to him that it has almost taken on sensuous overtones. It is likely that while Jim seems troubled, but functional, he is having moments of irrationality and severe emotional dysfunction that make him highly dangerous.

The EAP counselor is concerned about Jim's potential for danger and has warned the company. Unfortunately, he cannot pinpoint a specific threat or act to concretely suggest that Jim will be violent at work. While Jim seems to be going through a rough stretch, his coworkers aren't seeing the dangerous side of his behavior and believe that like all eccentric people, Jim has a side of him that is different from the rest of the engineers he works with. That side, aloof, uncomfortable with people, egocentric, also makes him a good engineer, probably the best engineer in the group. For these reasons, his coworkers haven't accurately evaluated his level of increasing danger.

A day after a particularly degrading and offensive meeting with his supervisor where Jim was placed on administrative leave without pay because of the deterioration in his work, Jim took his guns to work and shot and killed three managers, including his supervisor. He wounded four others, including several people who had nothing to do with the company and who were just there to deliver packages. The security guards assigned to the company shot and killed Jim in a struggle, and the company is left to sort out the reasons it took them so long to take remedial action and to correctly determine his level of violence. Everyone interviewed believed that Jim was going through a patchy time but he would snap out of it. No one felt that he was excessively dangerous or that he had potential for violence, other than the EAP counselor whose warning to the company went unheeded.

Integrating Questions

1. Do you believe that Jim's company should have taken earlier action to help Jim by suspending him with pay and referring him for counseling in a facility not connected with the company?
2. If you were the counselor, how would you have treated Jim's growing anger at the company?
3. Do you think that companies have the right to fire workers who are not violent but have the potential for violence? How do you think this determination should be made so that it protects the rights of all parties involved?
4. What types of behavior in Jim should the company have seen as possible predictors of violence? Do you think a program to help coworkers and colleagues identify potential for violence would reduce violence in the workplace or might it contribute to increased paranoia and dismissals for potential violence that aren't warranted?
5. As a consequence of unfair dismissals, might a proactive policy actually lead to more violence by people who had no intention of doing anything violent but who now feel so badly treated that violence is now an option they might consider?
6. What is management's role in preventing workplace violence?

The workplace is a primary arena for crisis. Most problems can be resolved by managers who use equity and good judgment in their decision making. When managers fail to use good judgment, or when problems are more serious in nature, many companies refer workers to agencies who provide short-term crisis services to workers. The primary treatment approach used by these agencies is the cognitive-behavioral approach because it helps workers analyze the ideas that prompt emotional problems. As in all emotional problems, care should be taken to make certain that a problem is not caused by medical difficulties that have emotional symptoms. This chapter suggested a number of strategies for dealing with the potential for violence including mediation and the use of an advocate. Most workplace violence can be prevented by early intervention and a concern for the safety of workers.

REFERENCES

American Management Association 65th Annual Human Resources Conference On-Site Survey, San Francisco, 1994.

Akbar, N. (l991). *The chains and images of psychological slavery.* Jersey City, NJ: New Mind Productions.

Bell, C. A. (1991). Female homicides in United States workplaces, 1980–1985. *American Journal of Public Health 81*(6), 729–732.

Bureau of Justice Statistics. (1998, July). Workplace Safety. Bureau of Justice Statistics, U.S. Department of Justice. NCJ 168634.

Chapman, S. G. (1986). *Cops, killers and staying alive: The murder of police officers in America.* Springfield, IL: Charles C. Thomas.

Clark, R. (1970). *Crime in America: Observations on its nature, causes, prevention, and control.* New York: Simon and Schuster.

Cose, E. (1993, November 15). Rage of the privileged. *Newsweek,* 52–63.

Crow, W. J., & Erickson, R. (1989). *The store safety issue: Facts for the future.* Alexandria, VA: National Association of Convenience Stores.

Davis, H. (1987). Workplace homicides of Texas males. *American Journal of Public Health, 77*(10), 1290–1293.

Davis, H., Honchar, P. A., & Suarez, L. (1987). Fatal occupational injuries of women, Texas 1975–84. *American Journal of Public Health, 77*(12), 1524–1527.

Ellis, A. (1963). *Reason and emotion in psychotherapy.* New York: Lyle Stuart.

Gilliland, B. E., & James, R. K. (1993). *Crisis intervention strategies.* Belmont, CA: Brooks / Cole.

Grier, W. H., & Cobbs, P. M. (1965). *Black rage.* New York: Basic Books.

Glicken, M. (1977). *A regional study of the job satisfaction of social workers.* Dissertation. The University of Utah.

Glicken, M. (1986a, January / February). A clinician's guide to stress management. *EAP Digest.*

Glicken, M. (1986b, October.). Identifying worker burnout. *Personnel Management: Policies and Practices.*

Glicken, M. (1986c, October). Treating worker burnout. *Personnel Management: Policies and Practices.*

Glicken, M. (1986d). Work related accidents which lead to post-traumatic stress reactions. *Labor Relations: Occupational Safety and Health.*

Glicken, M. (1986e, March 20). A manager's guide to stress management. *Executive Action Report.*

Glicken, M. (1986f). Post-traumatic stress syndrome and work: Treatment considerations. *EAP Journal.*

Glicken, M. (1986g, September / October). The after-shock of on-the-job accidents. *EAP Digest.*

Glicken, M. (1988, January 24). Resolving office conflict. *National Business Employment Weekly.*

Glicken, M. (1996, February). Dealing with workplace stress. *National Business Employment Weekly.*

Glicken, M., & Ino, S. (1997). *Workplace violence: A description of the levels of potential for violence.* Unpublished paper.

Hochchild, J. (1995, April 29). *The New Yorker,* p. 69.

Houk, V., & Warren, R. (1991). Forum on youth violence in minority communities: Setting the agenda for prevention. *Public Health Reports, 106,* 225–280.

Jenkins, E. L., Layne, L. A., & Kisner, S. M. (1992). Homicide in the workplace: The U. S. experience, 1980–1988. *American Association of Occupational Health Nurses Journal, 40*(5), 215–218.

Kraus, J. F. (1987). Homicide while at work: Persons, industries, and occupations at high risk. *American Journal of Public Health, 77*(10), 1285–1289.

May, R. (l973). *Man's search for himself.* New York: Delta.

Mulvihill, D., Tumin, M., & Curtis, L. (1969). *Crimes of violence: A staff report to the National Commission on the Causes and Prevention of Violence.* Washington, DC: U. S. Government Printing Office.

Myers Jr., S. L., (1983). Estimating the economic model of crime: Employment versus punishment effects. *Quarterly Journal of Economics, 88,* 157–166.

New York City Police Department. (1990). *Safety tips for the taxi driver and the for-hire vehicle driver.* New York: New York City Police Department.

NIOSH. (1992). *Homicide in U. S. workplaces: A strategy for prevention and research.* Morgantown, WV: U. S. Department of Health and Human Services, Public Health Service, Centers for Disease Control, National Institute for Occupational Safety and Health, DHHS (NIOSH) Publication No. 92–103.

NIOSH. (1993). *Fatal injuries to workers in the United States, 1980–1989: A decade of surveillance: National profile.* Cincinnati, OH: U. S. Department of Health and Human Services, Public Health Service, Centers for Disease Control and Prevention, National Institute for Occupational Safety and Health, DHHS (NIOSH) Publication No. 93–108.

NIOSH Alert. (1995, May). *Preventing homicide in the workplace.* Washington, DC: Publication No. 93–109.

Robinson, J. L. (1996). *Ten facts every employer and employee should know about workplace violence: It may save your life!* Smart Business Supersite: *http://www.smartbiz.com.*

Terkel, S. (1974). *Working: People talk about what they do all day and how they feel about it.* New York: Random House.

Washington, J. M. (Ed.). *(1992) Study of safety and security requirements for at-risk businesses.* Tallahassee, FL: Office of the Attorney General.

Work in America. (1973). A Report by the Presidents Commission on Work. Cambridge, MA: MIT Press.

OSHA LINKS TO ADDITIONAL INFORMATION ON WORKPLACE VIOLENCE

1. **Workplace Violence: A Report to the Nation.** The University of Iowa Injury Prevention Research Center. (2001, February), 331KB PDF. This report summarizes the problem of workplace violence and the recommendations identified by participants at the Workplace Violence Intervention Research Workshop in Washington, DC, April, 2000. The workshop brought together thirty-seven invited participants representing diverse constituencies within industry, organized labor, municipal, state, and federal governments, and academia. *http://www.osha.gov/media/oshnews/may00/national-20000509.html*

2. **Workplace Violence for Health Care and Social Service Workers.** OSHA Publication 3148. (1998). Also available as a 168KB *http://www.osha-slc.gov/Publications/Osha3148.pdf.*

3. **Stress at Work.** DHHS (NIOSH) Publication No. 99–101 (1999), thirty-two pages. Job stress poses a threat to the health of workers and, in turn, to the health organizations; this booklet highlights knowledge about the causes of stress at work and outlines steps that can be taken to prevent job stress. *http://www.osha-slc.gov/OshDoc/Speech_data/SP19980428.html.*

4. **Commonsense Recommendations to Reduce Workplace Violence.** *http://scripts.osha-slc.gov/PHP/redirect.php?url=http://www.opm.gov/ehs/workplac/index.htm.*

5. **Dealing with Workplace Violence: A Guide for Agency Planners.** U. S. Office of Personnel Management. (1998). This handbook is the result of a cooperative effort of many federal agencies sharing their expertise in preventing and dealing with workplace violence. It is intended to assist those who are responsible for establishing workplace violence initiatives at their agencies. PDF version is available in two forms: as *http://scripts.osha-slc.gov/PHP/redirect.php?url=http://www.opm.gov/ehs/workplac/index.htm*, individual chapters, and as a single 1.78MB *http://scripts.osha-slc.gov/PHP/redirect.php?url=http://www.opm.gov/ehs/workplac/pdf/full.pdf.*

6. **Workplace Violence, 1992–1996.** U. S. Dept. of Justice. Revised 1998, July 18. Analysis of workplace violence from a crime victimization survey from the Bureau of Justice Statistics: *http://scripts.osha-slc.gov/PHP/redirect.php?url=http://www.ojp.usdoj.gov/ovc/new/directions/pdftxt/bulletins/bltn13.pdf.*

7. **Preventing Homicide in the Workplace.** CDC home page: *http://www.cdc.gov*. Alert—DHHS (NIOSH) Publication No. 93–109. The principal contributor to this alert was Dawn N. Castillo, Division of Safety Research, NIOSH. Comments, questions, or requests for additional information should be directed to Dr. Thomas R. Bender, Director, Division of Safety Research, National Institute for Occupational Safety and Health, 944 Chestnut Ridge Road, Morgantown, WV 26505–2888; telephone (304) 284–5700.

8. **Workplace Violence Initiative.** OSHA (1996). A list of links related to the Workplace Violence Initiative: *http://www.osha-slc.gov/workplace_violence/wrkplaceViolence.intro.html*.

CHAPTER

9

Acts of Random Violence

Probably one of the greatest fears of most Americans is random violence. Most recently, those acts have been carried out in schools and workplaces where the perpetrator may know some of the victims, but the goal of this type of violent act is to make a statement based on some real or imagined injustice that has occurred. Headlines such as "5 slain in Pittsburgh shooting spree," in which a man opened fire in two suburban Pittsburgh shopping centers in a racially motivated shooting, have become commonplace (Spangler, 2000). In this chapter, we will discuss truly random crimes of violence, including both mass murder and serial killings, hate crimes, gang violence, terrorist acts, and workplace and school violence. Many of these acts may be seen as random because the victims are often selected randomly; however, they are targeted with respect to specific groups or organizations.

A term that is being used for recent incidents of workplace and school violence is *rampage* killings, which denotes anger and a recklessness or lack of planning, even though considerable planning may have gone into the event, such as that at Columbine High School in Colorado in 1999. A more useful term might be *situational* or *event-triggered.* It may be more useful to think of random violence on a continuum from impulsive behaviors, such as killing a spouse in a rage, to those that are well-planned and/or done over long periods in time, such as the serial killer. For our purposes, it is probably more likely that individuals on the impulsive end of the continuum can be helped through human services approaches, although the FBI profilers also strongly suggest positive outcomes for preventive approaches with individuals who show the potential to become serial killers or mass murderers. Outside the continuum are the truly insane, who may require more intensive treatment approaches, or may be unaffected by treatment.

Butterfield (1991), reporting on the rise in mass murder in the United States, indicated that eight of the ten largest mass murders in American history have occurred since 1980 with a current average of two mass murders a month in this country. He found that most mass murders occurred in Texas, California, and Florida, which are heavily populated states with a significant influx of migrants. These states are also among those with the largest prison populations, along with New York state and the federal prison system (Beck, 2000). Seeking an explanation, Butterfield (1991) quotes James A. Fox, Dean of the College of Criminal

Justice at Northeastern University and coauthor of *Mass Murder* who concluded that these individuals:

> . . . were unhappy, angry people, and almost always middle-aged white men in their 30s or 40s . . . [and that] Typically mass murderers are men with no previous criminal record or history of mental illness . . . [according to Wolfgang] and their killings "are not really planned." (Butterfield, 1991, B3)

Douglas and Olshaker (1995) distinguish mass murderers from serial killers because they kill two or more people in one act. However, for both types of killings there is usually a precipitating or triggering catastrophic event, termed a *stressor*, which is often the loss of a job or a marital breakup. According to Butterfield (1991), some of the blame for mass murders can be placed on media coverage of similar events, such as the killing of thirty individuals, mostly Southeast Asian refugees, in Stockton, California, in 1989. Also, a growing "culture of hate" for specific groups in society is thought to be responsible for the increase.

A recent example of such a mass murder occurred in California when a man deliberately drove his car into a Costa Mesa preschool playground (Associated Press, 2000a). Two children were killed and five injured. He was convicted in August 2000 for murder and attempted murder. The forty-year-old man, Steven Allen Abrams, said, in confession, "I was executing them . . . as many as I could get. I was aiming for as many children as I could kill" (p. A3). He pleaded insanity, claiming that he heard voices from "brainwave makers" who controlled his thoughts and behavior. The prosecution said he was seeking revenge for a 1994 conviction for stalking his girlfriend, for which he got a jail sentence, and which his defense attorney said confirmed his client's paranoid thoughts about a conspiracy against him.

Communities are concerned about this type of random violence, whether impulsive or planned. In a conference whose theme was understanding youth violence held in Riverside, California, an expert in youth violence indicated that "violence today is random violence . . . schools used to be a safe haven and now that's just not true" (Leedy, 1999). These events are seen as random because they are unexpected and often appear to target no single individual or group. In fact, when such events occur, investigators desperately try to determine *who* the perpetrator was attempting to injure. This understanding would take some of the feared randomness out of the event, and perhaps make it seem more preventable. Also, it would provide some guidance about how to address the problems of the individuals involved.

Gallup polls for the years 1982 to 1999 showed that crime or violence was "the most important problem facing this country today" for 3 percent of all citizens polled in 1982, and rose to a peak of 52 percent in 1994, followed by a decline to 17 percent by May 1999 (Maguire & Pastore, 1999, p. 96, Table 2.1). Nationally, from 1995 to 1998, a public (adult) poll found concern about "fighting/violence/gangs" rising from 9 percent (1995) to 15 percent (1998). Only concerns about use/abuse of drugs rose as sharply (Maguire & Pastore, 1999, Table 2.8).

Citizens were asked in a 1999 Harris poll to indicate what contributed the most to violence in American society in terms of "a lot," "a little," or "not at all." Ninety percent responded "a lot" for "lack of adult supervision of children," followed by 65 percent indicating "Easy availability of handguns," 58 percent "Television," and 57 percent "Movies"; just 39 percent indicated that "Local TV news reports" contributed "a lot" toward violence (Maguire & Pastore, 1999, p. 122, Table 2.43).

Curiously, the role of substance abuse is not included in the response categories, although the relationship between drug use and drug dealing to violence in youth is widely understood. The Harris percentages were fairly uniform across sex, race/ethnicity, education, income, region, and age, with the exception of eighteen- to twenty-four-year-olds, of whom 10 percent fewer (80%) felt that the lack of adult supervision contributed "a lot." This finding is of particular interest after the various school shootings where concerns have been raised about parental supervision of the offenders. The greatest differences were related to political affiliation, where Republicans' percentages were 5 to 10 percent higher for all categories.

Teenagers' responses concerning the most important problems facing people their age (in 1998) indicated that their top six concerns were drugs (29%), social pressures (16%), doing well in school (8%), sexual issues (7%), crime and violence in school (5%), and other crime and violence (4%) (Maguire & Pastore, 1999, p. 98, Table 2.5). Attitudes toward the biggest problem facing people their age placed violence and crime third (7%) after drugs (39%) and peer pressure (15%) (p. 98, Table 2.6). When asked about the biggest problem where they go to school, violence topped the list at 16 percent (18% of males, 13% of females), followed by drugs with 14 percent and discipline with 9 percent (p. 98, Table 2.7).

Violence: Number versus Nature

Acts of violence have seen an overall decline in society, as described in Chapter 2, although these declines may be uneven across various cities. A recent report from the U.S. Department of Justice found violent crime down in the United States, with the 10 percent drop in 1999 one of the largest decreases in decades (Leary, 2000). However, cities such as Los Angeles, Orange County, California, New Orleans, Boston, and even London have experienced increases in murder rates (Monkkonen, 2000).

Even with these sporadic drops in violent crime, it appears to be the *nature* of violence that is taking a toll on Americans, young and old. Crimes by strangers against people they do not know or who are simply part of a group that is seen as a threat to the perpetrator have changed the nature of violence. And, these types of incidents have become more public. Acts of seemingly random violence might more accurately be called "public crimes," or media crimes, because of their high visibility in society, largely through media exposure that was not as prevalent in earlier cases.

The crime classification used discriminates between *stranger* and *nonstranger* perpetrators. If the victim does not know the perpetrator, it is a crime by a stranger, and is often a random act. However, not all acts of violence that appear random are truly "random" with respect to the selection of a target or target population by a perpetrator. Moreover, treatment or intervention with these individuals presents special problems for the helping professions.

Bureau of Justice Statistics (BJS) figures from victim surveys for 1982 to 1984 indicated that:

> Of violent crimes measured by the NCS: rape, robbery, and assault—46 [percent] were committed by total strangers. Another 11 [percent] were committed by persons known to the victim by sight only; 31[percent] were committed by acquaintances and friends; and 8 [percent], by relatives. (Timrots & Rand, 1987)

By 1997, the distribution of perpetrator/victim relationships had changed very little, although the category definitions have varied; 46.5 percent of all crimes of violence were committed by strangers, 15.4 percent by "casual acquaintances," 25.8 percent by those "well known" to the victim, and 8.6 percent by relatives (including a spouse). About 4 percent are unknown. Thus, close to two-thirds of violent crimes are committed by strangers or people not well known to the victim (Bureau of Justice Statistics, 2000).

Much of the definition of random depends on who the victims are and how they are selected. For example, juveniles in gangs often perpetrate acts of violence against members of other gangs, and their violent activities are more often directed at specific targets within their so-called industry, as when illegal drug sales go bad or they come into contact with law enforcement officers. Their violence becomes random when innocent citizens get in the way of these activities. Mass murderers and serial killers represent distinct categories of violent offenders who usually are not known to their victims prior to the event.

Hate crimes, or *bias* crimes, have become a special classification of crimes usually perpetrated against strangers and committed for the purposes of victimizing the target, not for personal gain on behalf of the attacker. A hate crime is a criminal offense committed against a person or property where the motive is a preexisting bias against the group to which that person is presumed or perceived to belong. These crimes are often committed by individuals who identify with or are members of groups such as the Ku Klux Klan, Neo-Nazis, Skinheads, Christian Identity, Black Separatists, and the Aryan Brotherhood. Many of these groups exist within prison walls, such as the Aryan Brotherhood and the Mexican Mafia, and have links to their organizations in the community.[1] The numbers of hate crimes rise and fall at different times. For 1999 hate crimes in Los Angeles had a reported increase of 11.7 percent, with blacks, Jews, and gays the target of most attacks (Associated Press, 2000b).

Another source of seemingly random violence is terrorist groups, although their targets and techniques more resemble those of the serial killer. The nature of all of these groups raises questions about how one manages violent offenders who

operate in an organized fashion. Can one do psychotherapy with an avowed terrorist, or with an organized crime member, as attempted in the popular television
series about a mob family, *The Sopranos*?

Many individuals who are involved in gangs, hate crime groups, terrorism,
or who are mass murderers or serial killers are not good subjects for traditional
forms of intervention or treatment. In their book on serial killers, which is based
on the pioneering work of John Douglas in profiling serial killers, Douglas and Olshaker (1995) raise some concerns about the management of *dangerous* offenders.
Their chapter "Battle of the Shrinks,"[2] especially pages 337, 338, and 357 should
be required reading for human services professionals. They warn that mental
health professionals tend to work with self-reported information from these individuals rather than looking at their actual behavior, or how dangerous they are to
society. The profiler, along with many law enforcement personnel, looks at behavior and makes inferences about personality from that perspective.

Case Study: A Hate Crime with Violence

Jeff Langer is a nineteen-year-old unemployed Caucasian high school dropout. He
lives with his parents in an uneasy alliance and spends much of his time with
friends who abuse alcohol and drugs. Jeff hates gays and lesbians. When he was
six years old, he was sexually abused by an older male relative. He never told anyone about the abuse but has developed an overwhelming anger at gays and lesbians, which has cycled into a level of homophobia that startles his family and
even worries his friends. He sees homosexuality everywhere and frequently ac-
cuses straight people of being gay. The accusations have resulted in fights, with
Jeff usually getting the worst end of the fight. He is filled with a rage against gay
people that permeates his life.

Because Jeff is physically weak and can only show his homophobia when he
is high on drugs or alcohol, he has taken to parking his car outside of known gay
or lesbian bars and clubs. He waits until someone comes out of the club or bar
who appears to be drunk and defenseless. Then he walks out of the car with a
baseball bat and beats them to the point of unconsciousness. He has done this six
times and has gotten away with all six beatings. When he is done with the beatings, he feels empty and cries. What he has done is wrong and he knows it, but
the rage inside drives him on and it only goes away for a while before he beats
someone else. Then, even though he feels remorse, a calm comes over him that
lasts several weeks before it is displaced with a growing rage at gay people.

In a final act of rage, Jeff beat and killed an elderly man who left a bar fre-
quented by gay men after most of the other patrons had left. It turned out to be a
janitor who was straight. When Jeff read about it in the paper the next day, he
cried in his room, went to his bathroom, and slit his wrists. Although he lost a considerable amount of blood, his parents found him and his life was saved in the
emergency room by, ironically enough, a gay doctor. Jeff is in jail now awaiting his
trial. The inmates have decided to have sex with him as much as they can and he

has been anally raped eight times. Since he is on a suicide watch, he is unable to kill himself and the guards are aloof about the rapes. They think he's getting what he deserves and look the other way during the rapes.

Discussion of the Case

Like most hate crimes, there is usually a reason, but homophobia is so rampant in our society that it exists, like racism, often without a logical explanations. It is a shame that Jeff wasn't able to discuss his molestation with someone and get appropriate help. The inability to resolve the emotions related to the experience have surely created deep feelings of humiliation and anger that are now displaced against all gay people.

Jeff was sentenced to twenty-five years to life after a court trial attended by many gay people. The audience in the trial brought signs into the courtroom, which humiliated Jeff. They called him a "Closet Queer" suggesting that Jeff's anger at gays was really a form of denial of his own leanings toward homosexuality. Secretly, Jeff finds himself attracted to men and won't admit it, but in prison, Jeff's closet homosexuality has come out of the closet. He is the "wife" of one of the prisoners who, in exchange for sex, protects Jeff from some of the more brutal inmates.

In a treatment group for perpetrators of hate crimes that Jeff is required to attend, Jeff has admitted to being attracted to men but denies that he's gay. He says that his relationship is based upon the need to survive but that he doesn't enjoy the sexual parts of the relationship. The other men snicker and laugh at Jeff. They've been involved in similar hate crimes. One man hates black people but admits to having had a secret love affair with a black woman before going to jail. All the men know that their hate is an ambivalent sort of hate and that their behavior is inconsistent. Most of the men have had serious physical and sexual abuse in their backgrounds as children. As one inmate told his therapist: "You got to hate somebody for what your pa did to you. I hate Black people. I blame them for everything. My pa drunk his self to death but there are plenty of Blacks out there to hate and I hate everyone. Every time I think about my pa and what he done to me, I hate another Black person worse. They never did nothin' to me that I can think of but when I was a kid, I started seeing that they were the reason my pa beat me and done the other stuff to me. He lost his job to a Black guy so I started feeling that it was their fault that he beat me. Over the years, I got so that I can't be around them at all, I hate them so much."

This tendency to displace anger onto others is very common among perpetrators of hate crimes and is historically one of the best reasons we have for the anti-Semitism and other historical mass forms of bigotry that all too often exist in our world. But we do live in a society of bigotry where even "good" people tell jokes about minorities and gays. Such behavior forms a backdrop for hate crimes because secretly, the bigotry of the society can only find perpetrators who know that what they do often has some acceptance. It is a situation with great potential for harm to all too many people.

The Need for Power

Most serial killers, and probably many other types of individuals involved in acts of violence, especially rape and child molestation, work from a position of power (dominance, manipulation, and control), which makes them not only very dangerous but difficult to treat. They are excellent manipulators of their therapists, as many prison staff and treatment personnel can verify (see Tappan, 1960, p. 140). These individuals do well in managing the system in a well-ordered prison environment. However, their violence is *situational* and can easily emerge again once outside these controls (Douglas & Olshaker, 1995, p. 343). Tappan's case summary of Earnest Jones demonstrates how an inmate can impress and manipulate prison authorities (p. 140), as does the case study of Lionel Brown at the end of this chapter.

Douglas and Olshaker (1995) do not decry the need for intervention, prevention, and ultimately control of these offenders. Their work raises the question of why one would try to treat these individuals at all. At several points they indicate that early intervention may be the *only* good approach to these individuals, which is discussed below in relation to available research. Douglas says "Throughout the study [of serial killers] and my work since then, I've become very pessimistic about anything remotely akin to rehabilitation for most sexually motivated killers. If anything has a hope of working, it has to come at a much earlier stage, before they get to the point at which fantasy becomes reality" (p. 137).

When considering what can be done about individuals who have become dangerous to society, the concern is how to intervene to control mental instability or character defects before it is too late:

> Unfortunately, there's no quick or simple answer. In many instances, law enforcement has become the front line of order and discipline, rather than the family. This is a dangerous situation for society to be in, because by the time we [the FBI] enter it's too late to do any good. (Douglas and Olshakar, 1995, p. 357)

Asking schools and educators to do the job of changing these individuals is seen by Douglas and Olshaker as asking too much of them, although they can help with early identification. One of the FBI agents involved in looking at the future of violent crimes provided some suggestions. He would continue Head Start programs, which were seen as "one of the most effective long-term, anticrime programs in history" (p. 357). He would bring in "an Army of social workers" to provide assistance for battered women and homeless families with children, and find good foster homes for children in trouble, all of which would be backed up with government tax incentive programs.

The Evolution of Random Violence Terminology

Crimes by strangers, or acts of public violence, while having occurred historically, were not classified as such until recently. In Tappan's 1960 criminology text the terms *stranger crime, mass murder, hate crime, serial killer,* and so on, are not used. Crimes are seen as single events wherein the offenders must be understood through traditional psychological and sociological explanations. *Obsessive compulsive* and *impulse neuroses* are discussed: "Many compulsive or impulsive acts are socially innocuous, though they may be painful to the neurotic and may reduce his efficiency and stability" (p. 132).

Certain compulsions are described as extremely dangerous, however, and others produce recurrent criminality (Tappan, 1960, p. 132). Tappan mentions arson (pyromania), compulsive stealing (kleptomania), and compulsive drinking (dipsomania) as common but less severe disorders. More serious crimes are indicated, such as pedophilia. However, Tappan provides the 1947 case of William Heirens, who was the apparent subject of a psychiatric journal article and a book called *Before I Kill More* (Douglas & Olshaker, 1995) because he wrote in lipstick at a murder site "For heaven's sake catch me before I kill more . . . I cannot control myself" (p. 134). Consistent with the much later (forty years) study of serial killers by Douglas and Olshaker (1995) this offender does not fit the conception of a "berserk killer," but that of an organized serial killer. He was an attractive, quiet, college student of middle-class religious parents with no prior history of crime or psychosis. He was found sane at trial and sentenced to life in prison.

Tappan (1960) discusses the frustration of the scientific community in using terms like "psychopathic personality" and "sociopathic personality" to describe "a condition of psychological abnormality in which there is neither psychosis nor psychoneurosis but in which there are chronic abnormal responses to the environment" (p. 137). This very much fits the concept of Douglas and Olshaker, who see these individuals as perhaps mentally ill, although not insane by law. They manifest a "character defect" (Douglas & Olshaker, 1995, p. 338) that prevents them from taking responsibility for their actions even when they know right from wrong. This is why prevention and early intervention may be the best strategy for reducing violent crimes by these individuals.

Adler, Mueller, and Laufer (1995) draw on the definition of sociopath used by Levin and Fox, again consistent with Douglas and Olshaker (1995), by stating that they "do not agree with the hypothesis that all mass and serial murderers are mentally diseased (for example, psychotic), and therefore legally insane or incompetent. On the contrary . . . serial killers are sociopaths, persons who lack internal controls, disregard common values, and have an intense desire to dominate others" (p. 234). They note that Levin and Fox suggest that increases in mass and serial murder are related to the increased publicity surrounding these individuals.

History of Random Violence

Historically, as discussed in Chapter 1, homicides committed in riot situations, mass murder, and serial killing rampages are distinguished from individual incidents of violence against individuals. These types of violence have existed in America for many years. For example, Nat Turner, a black slave, led a slave rebellion in 1831, killing more than fifty whites during a six-week rampage. He and sixteen others were hanged (Graham, Davis, & Gurr, 1969). The Western "social bandits" of the nineteenth-century West included such historically well-known names as Frank and Jesse James and Cole and Bob Younger. William F. Bonney, or Billy the Kid, was idolized by poor villagers of the Southwest and supposedly killed twenty-two men before being shot to death at age twenty-one by a sheriff.

After the Civil War, the Ku Klux Klan operated in the South to deal violently with Negroes. Lynching justice flourished not only in the South but also on the Western frontier of the late nineteenth century. Labor violence was rampant in the U.S. in the early twentieth century. Especially notable was the 1914 Ludlow Massacre in Colorado, when National Guardsmen killed striking miners and set fire to their tents, leaving hundreds of families homeless. A total of seventy-four deaths resulted from this series of incidents, including the smothering deaths by fire of eleven children and two women (Graham, Davis, & Gurr, 1969, p. 332).

Between 1915 and 1919, twenty-two racial disturbances occurred in American cities. The worst was in Chicago in 1919, which was preceded by frequent bombings of Negro residences, and resulted in the death of fifteen whites and twenty-three Negroes. The Harlem riot in 1943 and the 1968 riot following the death of Martin Luther King, Jr. also took several lives, as did the Koon and Powell (Rodney King) trial riots in Los Angeles in 1992. Riots, however, are often spontaneous events involving many angry and frustrated individuals. Other types of random killing sprees, while not well-planned, are usually long-term acts of individuals, such as Bonnie Parker and Clyde Barrow. Bonnie and Clyde were the notorious "public enemies" of the 1930s, but their violence was directed at law enforcement and others who got in the way of their quest for illegal gain. The popular film about their exploits received ten Academy Award nominations.

Leyton (1990) has provided comparative figures for these events from 1920 through 1984. He found only about one or two sets of "multiple murders" per decade from 1920 to 1950, jumping to six per decade in the 1960s, averaging one new killer every twenty months. Seventeen new cases emerged in the 1970s, one new killer every seven months, and twenty-five from 1980 to 1984, one every 1.8 months. Numbers of victims per decade were modest through 1960, ranging from a high of thirty-nine in the 1920s to eleven in the 1950s (p. 209). Seventy were identified in the 1960s, 219 for the 1970s, and 444 for the first *four years* of the 1980s, an annualized rate of *one hundred times* that of the 1950s (the Starkweather-Fugate spree). On a population rate basis these increases are significant, almost tripling the number of victims from the 1960s to the 1970s, with the first four years of the 1980s having five times the victims as the 1960s, twice that of the 1970s, and twenty-eight times that of the 1950s. Leyton suggests that America's changing cultural norms have accounted for these differences.

Perhaps the first "modern" incident of a truly random killer was Charles Starkweather, who terrorized Nebraska in 1958 with his girlfriend Carol Ann Fugate, and killed eleven people. The escapade was fictionalized in the 1980s film

Badlands and the later *Natural Born Killers*, which was not an accurate account, although Fugate's mother, stepfather, and sister were killed by the couple. The Nebraska National Guard was mobilized to find the couple, and martial law was a possibility. The police chief recalled that "The public was up in arms . . . just everybody was frantic, carrying arms. Gun shops sold out, people were on the streets carrying shotguns . . . it was just fortunate that some innocent person didn't shoot some other innocent person" (Schmidt, 1988, p. 2A). Starkweather died in the electric chair in June 1959 for one of the killings. Fugate got life in prison, later reduced, and was paroled under a fictitious name in 1976.

The case of Edward Gein, from a small Wisconsin farm town, was the basis for the novel and film *Psycho* as well as *The Silence of the Lambs*. In the 1950s, Gein wanted to use human female skin, first taken from graves and later from his victims, to drape across his own body to assume the features of a woman (Douglas & Olshaker, 1995). He was found legally insane and died in a mental hospital in 1984.

The list of serial killers and mass murderers is a long one. Adler et al.(1995) state "Between 1970 and 1993 U.S. police know of approximately 125 cases of multiple homicides . . . some recent serial murderers have become infamous" (p. 233). Many have achieved notoriety in our curiously violent American society in that they are the subject of trading cards called *True Crime Series: Serial Killers and Mass Murders* (Eclipse, 1992). There are fifty-four listings on the "Series Two Checklist" alone (Bonnie and Clyde are Card #34; Starkweather and Fugate are card #79); they include:

> Dennis Nilsen (Card #77), a Scottish homosexual who befriended transients and unemployed men in London between 1978 and 1983. He got them drunk and strangled them. He was discovered when human flesh was found in his sewer lines; he claimed more than fifteen victims. Although remorseless and sullen, he was found sane and received life in prison. He said he related to Jeffrey Dahmer (Card #76), who had eleven to seventeen victims, who ate the flesh of some of his victims. (Adler et. al, 1995)[3]
>
> Theodore "Ted" Bundy (Card #88), an illegitimate child who spent the first four years of his life posing as his mother's brother to hide the family's shame. Molested by a male relative, he mutilated animals and spied on girls. He was bright and handsome, but began stalking women in 1972 and raped, battered, and killed a woman in 1974; he killed and brutally mutilated an estimated nineteen to thirty-six young women in five states and was electrocuted in Florida in 1989.
>
> John Wayne Gacy, Jr. (Card #67), beaten and called a "sissy" by his alcoholic father, suffered a head injury that caused him to black out periodically. He was a community activist who entertained young children at hospitals as a clown, even having his picture taken with a First Lady. He was a homosexual who tortured, sodomized, and killed at least thirty-three young men, who were buried in crawl spaces in his home.

Mass murders are now called "rampage" killers in the media. They do not appear to manifest the long-term planning and deliberation found in serial killers. Their killing sprees appear to be triggered by stressful events in their lives. Mass murders by individual rampage-type killers include: Charles Whitman (Card #79), who in 1966 killed sixteen and wounded thirty, shooting from the University of Texas clock tower. Twenty people died in 1984 at the McDonalds in San Ysidro, California, at the hands of James Huberty (Card #100). One of the worst mass murder events in American history was in Texas, where an unemployed man drove his pickup truck through a restaurant window in 1991 and killed twenty-two people (Adler et al., 1995, p. 233). Colin Ferguson killed six and wounded seventeen on a Long Island subway in 1993, for which he was convicted.

These types of incidents were followed by several workplace shooting sprees, usually after the perpetrator had been fired from that workplace. These also appear to qualify as rampage killings, based on anger and impulse, although some minimal level of preparation and some planning was clearly involved. The U.S. Postal Service lost thirty-eight employees to violent incidents during an eight-year period between 1986 and 1993, and has been concerned about developing solutions (Adler et al., 1995). This reaction to work conditions has become known as the "postal response," or "going postal". Some of these shootings are documented by Brownstein (2000), who notes that in one case the act "may have been triggered by a dangerous mix of holiday depression, financial woes and a chronic sense of being victimized and unappreciated" (p. 153). Such responses may result from poor administrative practices and a lack of communication within the agency.[4] Also seen as contributors are job stress and unreasonable management expectations leading to morale problems, coupled with bad security.

Careful analysis finds that, considering the size of the workforce of the postal service (900,000 in 2000), the rate of killings may not be higher than in other work environments. A recent study found that "retail employees were eight times more likely than postal workers to be killed at work, with 2.10 workplace homicides per 100,000 from 1992 through 1998" (*Washington Post, 2000*). In 1998 just 16 of 6,719 workplace homicides were postal employees and nine of them were killed by current or former coworkers, making postal employees one-third as likely as others in the national work force to be victims of homicide: .26 per 100,000 versus .77 per 100,000 (Schmid, 2000). Unfortunately, the incidents that have occurred have been highly publicized, such as the 1986 incident when a letter carrier in Oklahoma killed fourteen coworkers and himself. The retail trade is more dangerous, especially convenience stores. This suggests that all workplaces should be subject to scrutiny regarding violent acts from outside and from within (see Chapter 6).

These incidents occurred in the same time period as a series of school shootings, such as the 1999 massacre at Columbine High School in Colorado, which qualify as rampage killings. Several cases of violence by youthful offenders are documented by Reid (1995). The death of two-year-old James Bulger in England at the hands of two eleven-year-olds, who were subsequently sentenced to "indefinite custody," made the defendants the youngest persons convicted of murder in England in 250 years. In this case, and others mentioned, lack of motives and lack of remorse by offenders for these mostly random murders is seen as a major societal concern.

The school incidents do not appear to be decreasing in number. In one month in March 2001, two incidents occurred at schools in Eastern San Diego County that were not ten miles apart. In the first, a disaffected youth killed two male students in a shooting spree at Santana High School in Santee (March 5), followed by shootings at Granite Hills High School, less than three weeks later (March 23). Fortunately, in the second incident an armed school resource officer was immediately summoned and shot the suspect, wounding but not killing him. The target of that assault appeared to be a vice principal who was seen as responsible for the youth's inability to enlist in the military. This youth subsequently committed suicide while in detention. Several local, state, and national news articles were generated over these incidents.

As noted, the first concern is why the youths acted as they did. News reporters searched for a target that triggered the incidents, followed by speculation and reports of consultation with experts regarding other causes. The findings of a report of the U.S. Surgeon General on the Columbine incident were cited in an *L.A. Times* report (Mestel, 2001). One conclusion was that:

> some popular measures such as funneling juveniles into the adult criminal justice system, counseling youth in groups and prison visit shock programs like Scared Straight may further harden troubled children and increase their involvement in crime and violence. (Mestel, 2001, p. A1)

Studies seem more likely to support aid to low-income pregnant mothers, help to high-risk children to forge stronger ties to school and home, and intervention at many levels with these youth. Several of the risk factors cited in other governmental reports include substance abuse at an early age, and later (ages 12–14) weak social ties, anti-social and delinquent peers, and gang membership. The Santee shooting appeared to be related, in part, to the youth's involvement with drugs and delinquent peers, as well as separation from peers in a former school, as described in a subsequent article (see Gold, Gale, & Marosi, 2001).

Another report sponsored by the U.S. Department of Justice, which was completed after the April 1999 Columbine, Colorado, student massacre, is also relevant. *Safe from the Start* was published in November 2000 (Reno, 2000). The report summarized a National Summit on Children Exposed to Violence. The result was the "action plan" presented in the report.

The report first called for rational analysis of the issues, grounded in facts and using a cross-disciplinary approach. The facts from a 1995 survey:

> indicate that of the Nation's 22.3 million children between the ages of 12 and 17, approximately 1.8 million have been victims of a serious sexual assault, 3.9 million have been victims of a serious physical assault, and almost 9 million have witnessed serious violence. Every day in 1997, six young people (under the age of 18) were murdered; 56 percent of the victims were killed with a firearm. (Reno, 2000, p. xii)

Solutions were similar to those proposed in other governmental reports by the same experts. Prevention, intervention, and accountability are stressed. Prevention means getting to at-risk families early and investing in programs that address methods of managing conflict. Intervention means becoming more responsive to the problems of children in our society, and beginning earlier in the child's life. Accountability means making perpetrators of violence responsible for their acts (Reno, p. xiii).

Finally, the call is for more law enforcement on campuses nationwide. However, even law enforcement officials warn against expecting them to stop every crime on campus because of their limited presence at any time. It seems wiser to try to address causes and develop solutions before the child arrives at the school with a gun. These goals, and others cited in the report, are all tasks that will require dedication and resources. Programs of child protective services and domestic violence prevention operating in several states are cited, along with many other resources for action.

Assessing the Risk from Violent Strangers

In a chapter on crimes against the person, Reid (1995) documents several instances of random violence, including the murder of James Jordan, father of basketball superstar Michael Jordan in 1992, which was described by local authorities as "random violence" (p. 148). Mr. Jordan apparently did not know his killers. In discussing the brutal deaths of five University of Florida students at the hands of Danny Rolling, convicted and sentenced to death, Reid states "The randomness of some victims creates fear in many people that they too might be found in the wrong place at the wrong time and lose their lives" (p. 149). The youthfulness of offenders, the use of torture and other atrocities, and the random choice of victims are seen as major contributors to fear of violence.

Personal safety is critical to everyone, and fear of crime is a concern of many citizens. Charles Silberman's book *Criminal Violence, Criminal Justice* (in Bittner & Messinger, 1980) is an expression of this fear in America. In the chapter "Fear," Silberman refers to "murders by strangers, stranger homicides, as criminologists call them" (p. 368). He states that "Violence at the hand of a stranger is far more frightening than a comparable injury incurred in an automobile accident or fall; burglary evokes a sense of loss that transcends the dollar amount involved" (p. 371). Silberman discusses the physiological aspects of vigilance that may lead to action to avoid violence, pointing to the "paradox" that we may fear strangers, yet we live most of our lives among strangers. Also, there is no clear relationship between the amount of crime in a community and people's fear of crime, or the risks associated with crime.

People make judgments about the conduct of their lives based on what is happening in their world at a given time. As noted above and in Chapter 3, violent crime is a major concern and the basis of fear in American society. It is costly in real and intangible terms. Concerns increase in areas with high crime rates, or in the wake of an urban riot, a mass murder rampage, or after crimes such as the 1999 Columbine High School massacre in Colorado or similar acts that target no one individual in particular. Acts of school violence from 1997 through Columbine in 1999 occurred in Mississippi, Kentucky, Arkansas, Pennsylvania, Tennessee, Oregon, and Idaho in schools that seemed unlikely candidates for such violence (*San Bernardino County Sun*, 1999).

Subsequent to the acquittal of officers in the Rodney King incident in Los Angeles in 1992, cries of racism arose that led to rioting. For many people, after the very costly riots, these cries of racism eventually gave way to a reassessment of the chances for a decent quality of life in parts of Los Angeles, especially for groups such as the Korean Americans, whose businesses were targeted by rioters. In a review of Baldassare's collection of articles on the Los Angeles riots, Debro (1996) pointed out "(1) that conditions of the poor have not improved in Los Angeles since the last riots of the sixties, (2) that black/white tensions remain high because of continuing institutional racism, and (3) that the effects of foreign immigration and economic restructuring are leading to interethnic hostilities" (p. 18). Several efforts at "coalition building" over many years had failed in the city. Under such conditions, people who have the means to will simply move to safer communities. Many Korean Americans who operated businesses in Los Angeles that were targets of the riots have left the city. This decision is not unlike that made by many working and middle-class people when the courts upheld school busing thirty years ago. They did not see their children as safe in these urban schools, and left for the far suburbs, taking their buying power and tax base with them. They did not want to risk violence to their children, even though the risk may only have been perceived as greater.

Most people make decisions based on the probability that things will go well for them and their families, that they and their children will be safe, and that they will have opportunities for education and jobs, and so on. These probabilities are formed by what people see and hear, particularly in the mass media, and may lead to fears, rational or irrational, about rising crime, violence generally, economic conditions, and the like. Everyone makes decisions about relative risk when they buy a house, take a job, or even when they marry. Social scientists see the anticipation of risk as having social costs. What people "choose" to be afraid of depends on what social and practical consequences will flow from that choice, not just on the consequences of the risk itself. That is, "risk" decisions are costly even if the particular result we fear, such as a riot, chemical spill, or whatever, does not happen.

Communities that do not offer safety and opportunity will be abandoned by those who can leave. These communities present a real or imagined fear. Police who then are asked to serve these communities often see the probabilities for their success, much less survival, greatly decreased. There are social costs of many kinds after a riot or major violent incident. People of all colors, politics, and social strata will react as human beings, not as members of a particular group. In Los Angeles County in the 1990s, fears about gang violence were heightened, as in many American cities. Questions were raised about how the burgeoning gang problem was to be managed. What do other jurisdictions do? To what extent is it a police or corrections problem? Or is it a family, social, or educational problem? And, what role does the public have, if any? What have other cities done when faced with these problems?

Then-Sheriff Sherman Block of Los Angeles County did not call for police reinforcements to deal with the gang problem. He called for social programs, which he saw as "absolutely essential" to "stopping the carnage that is paralyzing too many neighborhoods" (*L.A. Times*, 1990, p. M6). As pointed out in an *L.A. Times* editorial, this was a new approach for law enforcement, and a correct one. A summit conference using Block's philosophy received support. Many urban jurisdictions have begun to explore similar solutions, many through initiatives now known as community policing.

Case Study: A Perpetrator of Random Violence

Lionel Brown is a twenty-three-year-old African American male who violently assaulted a sixty-three-year-old man in an attempted carjacking. Lionel had just been released from the county jail in Hennepin County, Minnesota, having served six months of a two-year sentence for a barroom fight, claiming it was self-defense. Since the patron was seventy-one, five-foot-seven, and had been sitting and minding his own business, the court tended not to believe Lionel's story. Lionel is six-foot-five, weighs 270 pounds, and has a history of violence going back to elementary school. He has been in and out of juvenile and adult facilities since he was twelve. His longest time on the outside has been four months. In jail, Lionel is gentle, helpful, and a model prisoner. Out of jail, he is impulsive, drug addicted, and without remorse for his crimes.

After the last violent attack, Lionel was moved to a forensic facility in Minnesota specializing in the treatment of violent behavior. The staff uses insight-oriented therapy to get at the cause of the violence and group therapy to reinforce the insight therapy and to keep prisoners on the hot seat of critical self-examination so that they are unable to con therapists. Group members hardly ever let one another say or do anything that is manipulative or untrue. The staff also provides a therapeutic recreational program where violent interactions, common with the client group served at the facility, are dealt with immediately by supervising the conflict and forcing the prisoners to work the conflict out in a responsible and socially acceptable way. In essence, the clients are being taught social skills they have never had, on the assumption that the better their social and verbal skills and the more trained they are in conflict management, the less likely they will be to act out.

Lionel is a great client. He is impressed with the help he's getting, thankful for the support, happy not to be in the more confined prison environment he's accustomed to, and a hard worker, both at therapy and in the facility where he volunteers frequently for extra assignments. He has never lost his temper or displayed the maladaptive behavior seen when he's released. He is in the facility for a first-degree assault charge carrying a sentence of 5–7 years. After three years of exemplary work, he has been released to the custody of a supervised halfway house in Minneapolis, which has a daily treatment program. Two weeks after his release, Lionel battered a man to death in a mugging. The man had $3.00 in his pocket. When arrested, Lionel seemed happy, cooperative, and calm. "Goin' home," he said, "goin' back to see my friends."

Discussion of the Case

This is a case one the coauthors worked on as a project social worker for a program Lionel was to enter after release. He saw Lionel in the facility three weeks before his release and after the parole board had agreed, on the recommendation of the staff, to release him to our program. Lionel had a very normal-looking Minnesota Multiphasic Personality Inventory (MMPI) when he was seen by the social worker and seemed appropriate, even nice in the interview, but his behavior raised a number of red flags. Lionel was unhappy about leaving jail. He wanted to stay at his home, as he described it. The social worker wrote the prison authorities a long letter urging them not to release Lionel. Prison had become home for him. In prison, he was a model citizen, but out of prison, the lack of structure and detailed directions on how to conduct his life overwhelmed him. He never experienced home life and having been abandoned at birth, was raised in group facilities, or what we used to call "orphanages." He was filled with rage when left on his own and functioned well only when he was confined.

We think of prisons as places people want to leave, but for some institutionalized people, it really *is* home and to leave it brings out the awful inner demons they carry around in their psyches. Lionel looked normal on MMPI because he *is* normal in prison. But be aware that in many prisons, psychological tests are often administered by other prisoners who also do the scoring. For two packs of cigarettes, Lionel bribed the test giver to show a normal MMPI profile, not because he wanted to be released, but because he wants people to see him as an essentially healthy person. Actual MMPI results, from an inventory given after the murder sentence by a qualified psychologist, revealed strong dependency needs, little self-confidence, and, unfortunately for his many victims, a high degree of impulsivity coupled with a very low IQ (65).

Lionel is almost completely incapable of making correct social judgments unless he is first instructed and then supervised to the point of committing them to memory. Lionel understands the rules of institutional life and is perfectly fine when he knows the rules and expectations of life. Lionel needs to be in a facility but could have avoided the awful carnage he was responsible for had someone taken the time early on to do some good diagnostic work with him. Lionel has a life sentence but sits in a solitary cell where he has almost no interaction with other prisoners. He is miserable. He misses people and has tried to kill himself several times. He can't be a star prisoner any more and life just isn't fun the way it used to be. "I wanna go home," he keeps telling the prison staff. "I wanna go back to my home."

What Can Be Done?

Do solutions lie in addressing family, social, or educational problems? As did Sheriff Block, many urban jurisdictions have begun to look beyond their criminal justice systems for answers, an area which will be discussed in more depth in Chapter 11. Hopefully, these concerns will not generate solutions based on simply throwing dollars at the problem, because those dollars are not available and solutions based on social programs alone have had mixed results. We can be hard-nosed and practical in approaching the problem of crime. Offenders must be accountable for their behavior. For example, Chief Reuben Greenberg of Charleston, SC, demands that we should not give offenders "ten chances" to violate the law, opting for punishing first offenders more severely.

A "first offender," in reality, is not usually someone who has committed a first offense, but rather someone who has been caught and charged for the first time. But, why not opt for more meaningful intervention early in the lives of these individuals? Have we totally given up on large segments of our population? It has been suggested for some time that neglect of these segments of the population, mostly black and Hispanic, portends serious social consequences for the long term. Our society must respond with more than punishment to be truly effective.

What is being tried elsewhere? There is an emphasis on increased police presence through neighborhood policing: foot patrols, bicycle patrols, greater use of prevention and community problem-solving techniques, but these are also very expensive. Several national efforts are under way to see if prosecutors working with police can increase involvement with communities and help coordinate the work of various social agencies to address community problems. The hope is that with police help, informal social controls can be reinstituted in some of these communities.

As Douglas and Olshaker (1995) suggest, there is little that can be done after the fact of a mass murder or after the arrest and conviction of a serial killer. Early intervention in the lives of these individuals may be the only answer; however, no one can be sure how many of these offenders have been stopped by programs of early intervention. This is where the difficulty comes in for the human services professions: we must "sell" society on potential solutions to problems that are difficult to prove in the long term. Greenwood, Model, Rydell, and Chiesa (1996) of RAND address the question of using precrime diversion rather than postcrime incarceration to prevent criminal careers from developing and reduce crime in society.

They document the costs and benefits of diverting children from a life of crime by examining four types of interventions for at-risk youth: home visits and day care, parent training, graduation incentives, and delinquent supervision. Conclusions are that:

> When combined with other information . . . three of the four early-intervention approaches compare favorably in cost-effectiveness with incarceration . . . [they caution that] the costs of the four early interventions . . . do not take into account

the savings realized by not having to eventually imprison these youths diverted from criminal careers [and] Because the estimates . . . are the results of limited demonstrations and educated guesses, actual values could vary considerably . . .; however . . . substantial variations in the values do not reverse the cost-effectiveness outcomes relative to the three-strikes law. (Greenwood et al., 1996)

Consistent with the RAND findings, a promising approach to early intervention is being used in Orange County, California. After identification of the juveniles who make up the "chronic 8 percent problem," programs of early intervention have been put in place (Schumacher, 1994). The factors found to contribute to continued delinquency (addressed later) are those that have long been identified with future offending; however, the Orange County study provides outcome (predictive) validity for such factors.

The majority of the problem youth in Orange County were under age fifteen at the time of their original juvenile court disposition. Of six factors evaluated, those predicting chronic offending were drug abuse, dysfunctional families, or failure in school. Over a six-year follow-up period, these chronic cases averaged twenty months of incarceration, each costing Orange County $44,000 in custody costs alone (p. 2) and was based on the research they recommended "targeting younger minors with multiple problem profiles" (p. 2) that include school behavior/performance (attendance, suspensions or expulsions, poor grades), family problems (poor parental supervision), substance abuse, and delinquency factors (stealing pattern, runaway pattern, gang member).

Most importantly, Orange County's preliminary findings were that the juvenile justice system in the county was successful in deterring repeat offenses. For youth receiving intervention services, 42 percent had subsequent petitions filed as compared to 81 percent of the comparison group. Twenty-two percent of the preliminary study group had new law violations compared to 55 percent for the comparison group.

Other approaches have been shown to be effective in managing violent youth, even youth in violent gangs. These were dubbed "mediating structures" by the American Enterprise Institute (AEI): "the institutions of kinship, ethnic and religious organizations, and other bodies that lie between the individual and what these theorists regard as an inevitably distant and bureaucratic state" (Currie, 1985, p. 259). These preventive approaches were outlined by Woodson (1981), who "argues that nonprofessional, community-based agencies that share a common culture with violence-prone youth and stay resolutely clear of entanglements with government bureaucracies offer the best hope for dealing with youth crime in the face of the failure of more traditional juvenile institutions" (Woodson, 1981, in Currie, p. 260). As an example of a nonprofessional approach, Philadelphia's House of Umoja is most often cited.

The House was begun rather informally by "Sister" Falaka Fattah and her husband David in their own home as an effort to help youth involved in violent gang crime, including their own sons. The house created a sense of "family" that instilled a sense of ethnic pride and encouraged youth to make positive decisions about their lives based upon traditional values of work and education. The House received no government funding. Currie has described the problem faced by the volunteer effort when the Reagan administration cited it as an example of the type of "volunteerism" that should replace government-funded programs. This proposed lack of support through public funding produced a major debate about the relationship between volunteer efforts and the need for a commitment by government to support effective volunteer efforts aimed at reducing crime and violence. Curtis, who authored the Eisenhower Commission reports on violence in America, has raised the question about how we can create the type of agency that will provide parental nurturing and discipline and result in a well-functioning family. (1985).

Currie's conclusions regarding the changing needs of youth in American society are instructive:

> Where [community] ties have been broken: by disruptive economic growth, extremes of inequality, and the separation of youths and adults from stable occupational roles: the appeal to the traditional virtues is hollow and often hypocritical. The emphasis on the reconstruction of community responsibility is not wrong; it must be central to any serious strategy against crime. But it needs to be broadened and deepened. (p. 263)

Community approaches to prevention, without some support from public funds, may not be adequate. Stable livelihoods are critical. In summary, it appears that a stable economy, coupled with community and law enforcement cooperative approaches, may represent some of the best first steps in managing violent crime and crime of all types. Community volunteers and service agencies should continue to be full participants in these efforts. The recent emphasis on community policing is a reflection of this strategy. How one "reconstructs" a community may be a far more difficult problem. Until this reconstruction occurs, it must be made clear to the potentially violent offender that acts of random violence, violence against groups, or against their own families will receive societal censure and an appropriate legal response. It is also our obligation to attempt to identify and intervene where we see that an individual may be leaning toward an aggressive or violent solution to a personal problem.

Societal Approaches

In his discussion of the reasons for violence in America, Leyton (1986) states, "If we were charged with the responsibility for designing a society in which all structural and cultural mechanisms leaned toward the creation of killers of strangers, we could do no better than to present the purchaser with the shape of modern America" (p. 211). He contends that America's shifting cultural norms are the primary cause of violent behavior, particularly those that emphasize individualism as opposed to concerns for group welfare. However, he notes that this individualism is celebrated as both necessary and "heroic" in defining personal achievement in American society. This same individualism has led to the search for notoriety in violent acts that achieve this end for their perpetrators. And, the perpetrators have no concern for others.

We may ask what differentiates a businessman, such as Bill Gates of Microsoft, a very tough businessman who has ruined competitors, from a serial killer? The businessman makes his "kill" in a world that must exist for him to survive, and his reward is the profits and a possible satisfaction from the control involved. The violent offender does not need the world or its people to survive, and his reward is in the absolute control exercised over the victim. He feels excluded from society and strikes out. Leyton (1990) puts this in perspective by quoting Ted Bundy, "What's one less person on the face of the earth, anyway?" (p. 211). The rest of society is dehumanized. Certainly, the combat war veteran has to reintegrate into society after being taught to kill, and many have difficulty with this process. Medal of Honor holder and movie star Audie Murphy was said to have spent much of his life trying to deal with his military experiences in which he killed many of the enemy. Police officers who have seen violence may also suffer the same problems.

All of this strongly suggests that efforts must be made to ensure that all individuals are taught respect for others in society. This can be accomplished in many ways, but it can only be done by paying attention to the behavior of children as they grow and develop into adults. The figures on increases in violence suggest that child-rearing practices are breaking down, especially in teaching respect for the social or moral codes (mores, folkways) of society. It may be that mass media representations of society are contributing to this breakdown of social responsibility, perhaps coupled with less attention to the crucial role of parenting in an ever-busy society. When these breakdowns occur, it is difficult for a human services professional to take on the task of reintegrating the individual into society.

This makes the case presented by Greenwood et al. (1996), the Orange County, California, early intervention program (Schumacher, 1994), Douglas and Olshaker (1995), and many others that early and strong intervention in families is a critical role for human services professionals. This intervention must be measured but firm, and should involve law enforcement and the courts, as needed. Where necessary, children should be removed from families that are unable to perform parenting functions; however, the alternatives must not be worse, as sometimes is the case.

Currie (1985) and others present more broadly based solutions to crime and violence that would require leadership from government agencies. Many of these strategies are addressed in Chapter 11. Currie (1985) maintains that criminologists, mostly liberals, have failed to come to grips with the problems of crime and violence in America because they deny the seriousness of the problem. He breaks the problem down into the components of "pathology, community, and political economy" (p. 227). We tend to underestimate "the depth of social and personal *pathology* that criminal violence on the American scale represents" (p. 227).

Because of this misjudgment, he thinks that liberal criminologists, and presumably their political allies who make social policy, have underestimated the resources needed to implement their "poorly conceived, ill-equipped, and superficial programs" that were designed to manage problems which would require intensive and long-term intervention to be successful. And, when these programs failed, the (presumably conservative) critics who opposed them were often delighted, because they once again proved that government-sponsored programs might not be the best answer to social problems.

Currie (1985) believes that this failure of governmental programs was coupled with an inadequate understanding of how economies work to create jobs that may keep individuals out of crime. Liberal criminology failed to confront the need for job creation and the required redirection of public and private investment that this would entail. He says this without discussing the massive community action and employment program attempted in New York City in the 1960s called Mobilization for Youth (MFY), although he does acknowledge the earlier Chicago Area Project, which focused more on community organization than on economic solutions for the problems of youth. The MFY experience supports his position.

Mobilization for Youth

The Mobilization for Youth experience was described in a four-volume series edited by Harold Weissman, one of the administrators of the federally sponsored project. There were five basic program areas: (1) community development or social action, (2) provision of individual and group services, (3) employment programs, (4) educational programs, and (5) the area of justice and the law, as it is applied to the poor. The results are relevant to governmental programs designed to prevent adult and juvenile crime of all types through positive forms of intervention.

The geographic area encompassed by the project was about 67 blocks of New York's Lower East Side; population 107,000, one-third black and Puerto Rican (1961 figures) with 43,030 youths less than 20 years old, 90 percent of them *Black–Puerto Rican*. The area had 62.4 percent substandard housing; unemployment at least double that of New York City overall; 41 percent of the households on public financial assistance; 37 percent of the residents had not completed eighth grade. Delinquency *rates* had gone from "28.7 offenses per 1,000 youths in 1951 to 62.8 per 1,000 in 1960" (Weissman, 1969, pp. 19–20).

In this context, the program began in 1962 after about five years of planning. The theoretical basis for the project came from Richard Cloward and Lloyd Ohlin in a treatise on delinquency and opportunity:

> A unifying principle of expanding opportunities was worked out as a direct basis for action. This principle was drawn from the concepts outlined by sociologists Richard Cloward and Lloyd Ohlin in their book *Delinquency and Opportunity*. [They] regarded delinquency as the result of the disparity perceived by low-income youth between their legitimate aspirations and the opportunities—social,

economic, political, and educational: made available to them by society. If the gap between opportunity and aspiration could be bridged, they believed delinquency would be reduced; that would be the agency's goal. (Weissman, p. 19)

Examination of the reports reveals that as the project progressed the concerns for delinquency and opportunity became submerged in a more general plan for mobilizing the entire community on its own behalf. This shift was best summarized by Cavan:

The program, not limited to delinquents, is directed against poverty, conceived as a basic result of unequal education and opportunity; it is only indirectly concerned with delinquency as a possible end result of a chain that links inadequate education with limited opportunity and indirectly with delinquency. In this orientation, Mobilization for Youth closely resembles the basis for the poverty-reduction programs. (1969, p. 328)

Mobilization's community action program became a pilot project for the "war on poverty" which followed in 1964 with the passage of the Economic Opportunity Act of 1964. Section 202 of this Act was written in terms of "community action programs" which were "to give promise of progress toward elimination of poverty or a cause or causes of poverty through developing employment opportunities, improving human performance, motivation, and productivity, or bettering the conditions under which people live, learn, and work" (Weissman, 1969, p. 186).

MFY lasted from 1962 to 1967 and went through five distinct phases, beginning with hiring, then the development of issues, followed by a shift from small group organization to mass protest over housing conditions, schools, work training programs, etc. By mid-1964 MFY was attacked as riot-producing, communist-oriented, left-wing, and corrupt. A political struggle over who had control of MFY ensued, the director resigned, and all programs were virtually stopped until after the 1964 presidential election. This was followed by a coalition phase, including a reappraisal of programs and direction. Political pressure was still seen as vital to community change and smaller groups were encouraged to unite (coalition plan) to gain greater political leverage; they were most successful in the welfare area. From 1966 to 1967 there was a technical phase. The program movement away from issues, protest, and organization building to a concept of "an intermixture of social services, social protest, and social organization." Staff members were seen as a technical resource in community development, and the importance of community development in all phases of programming was realized.

What happened with MFY, therefore, was that it shifted from a program aimed at opening up opportunity for juveniles and potential delinquents to a much broader program focused on the whole issue of poverty and its consequences for all community residents. What was learned was that social problems need political solutions; however, the extent to which an organization such as Mobilization can participate in such solutions became the overriding issue:

While there is little doubt that in the long run the social problems of the slum are political and must be resolved politically, the extent and manner in which a social agency like Mobilization can participate in such a political process are open to question. First, a politically oriented, controversial social movement cannot long be sustained with public funds. Second, agencies like MFY cannot sanction illegal or antisocial actions. Third, they cannot engage in partisan political activities. (Weissman, p. 185)

Weissman concluded that the role of a social agency in making the public aware of "social issues and potential solutions" might be sufficient in itself. The debate within Mobilization appeared to revolve around how much help a social agency should give a community, short of designating ends for the community action programs (pp. 185–186). In this sense, the battle appears to have been won but the war was lost. In the first six years of its operation Mobilization moved from a highly dynamic, externally oriented, action-producing organization to an organization which was very concerned with its political image, and hence very cautious with respect to how far it would go:

The problem of how to carry out controversial social action with money from public sources still accompanies Mobilization along every step of its action programming. There would seem to be an ill-defined limit to such actions that must constantly be tested through political processes, of which public controversy is one. (Fried, 1969, p. 161)

Weissman provided an appraisal of MFY youth employment programs that indicated a positive outcome (i.e., employed, returned to school, placed in training) for 49 percent (209) of the youngsters in a "typical period" (July 1, 1964 to May 30, 1965). Of the total group of 431, Weissman indicated that less than 25 percent got jobs that promised security and an opportunity for advancement, and about 25 to 30 percent may have achieved increased employability. The problems of determining success were discussed, and the blame fixed for the failure of these types of employment programs:

The Mobilization experience clearly bears out the implication that the emphasis in youth employment programs should not blur the problems that exist in the social structure. The best kind of training in the world will not suffice if the economy does not produce enough jobs and if schools are not providing the skills necessary to master the jobs. Until the schools and the economy work more effectively, youth employment programs will be needed . . . However one evaluates the success of Mobilization's work-training programs, they are a clear statement to the general public that low-income youths need help in finding employment. (Weissman, p. 111)

One of the principal conclusions reached in the MFY project was that overall community organization was important; however, specific programs were *not* found to be especially useful except where contacts with their workers led to *real jobs*, real educational opportunity, and real social responsibility. The MFY program did not have the capability to do these things, lacking both the number and breadth of jobs necessary to satisfy the needs of youth for job training, as well as providing money-producing work for them. It appears doubtful that any single program can provide these opportunities outside the context of improvements in general economic conditions.

It is interesting in this context to see that explanations for recent declines in youth violence are attributed, in part, to improved economic conditions. Citing a one-year decline in violent crime of 16.9 percent, which is part of a four-year decline in violent crime in California, "Officials attribute the drop in crime to several factors, including a heightened police presence in some communities, a bustling economy, and more community involvement and interaction with police in thwarting criminals" (Nelson & Cardona, 2000). Law enforcement has involved the community in crime prevention. All of this suggests that Currie may be right in suggesting that improving the (political) economy by providing real jobs and real employment without special programs may be the best approach, especially as better intervention programs, which are supported by law enforcement, are implemented.

Thus, it would appear that attacking problems of crime and violence at the community level, as suggested by Currie, would require considerable skill. Increasing employability for lower-class youth through job training was a constant feature of the MFY program from 1962 to 1967, and the program was well funded by the federal government. This type of program is probably no substitute for generally improving economic conditions, although job training should be continuous for those requiring such assistance. An apparent inability of both liberal and conservative forces to support and conduct government programs that might improve the lives of individuals leads us to consider individual approaches to prevention and intervention that are required in any type of social or political environment.

Individual Approaches

Based on the work of Greenwood et al. (1996) and Schumacher (1994) and others, the best target for reducing violence, especially random violence resulting in murder, appears to be early intervention in the lives of children who may be prone to such violence. Violent acts by adults that do not result in murder, such as assault or domestic violence, may be managed through the use of human services approaches involving intervention by psychologists, social workers, and mental health workers, often working with the probation and parole officers, and sometimes with law enforcement participation. Sexual assault cases may be far more difficult to work with and must be approached very carefully with respect to the issue of public safety (see Douglas and Olshaker, 1995; see also Chapter 6 of this book).

There is much to do to intervene with individuals who might strike out randomly or in a more direct way with violence against individuals or groups in our society. Approaches range from highly individualized treatments to community efforts to prevent violence through early intervention strategies. Many of the points for needed change touched upon by Currie and by others are part of the two California commission reports summarized in Chapter 11. These two reports, which were produced in 1982 and 1995, summarize what is known about the causes of violent crime, and advance proposals for attacking the problem at all levels. They are relevant to all jurisdictions, many of which have produced similar documents.

Case Study: A Victim of Random Crime with Integrating Questions

Eunice Adler is a fifty-three-year-old Caucasian woman working at a bank in an urban area of the mid-west. Leaving her office late one evening, she was mugged and robbed by a masked assailant. Her car was also stolen and her wedding ring was taken, along with other personal items from her purse. Eunice was found semi-conscious by a motorist in the bank parking lot where she was mugged. She was taken to the emergency room, having sustained some cuts and bruises to her face after the assailant hit her with the butt of a gun. The assailant told her not to report the crime since the assailant had her billfold and identification. If she did, she was told, he would find her and kill her.

The injuries Eunice sustained were minor and she was released from the emergency room that same evening. Eunice is a widow, without family in the area, and went to a local hotel to spend the night. Unable to go to work the next morning because of severe anxiety, Eunice called her physician who diagnosed post-traumatic stress disorder, gave her a mild anti-anxiety medication, and referred her for crisis intervention through her medical plan.

When seen in treatment the next day, Eunice seemed agitated and frightened. She was convinced the mugger would find her and kill her since she had reported the crime to the police through the emergency room visit. Mandatory reporting in her state is required of any visit to a hospital where violence is suspected.

The worker listened to Eunice's fears, worked on developing a safety plan for Eunice to live with a friend from work, and got her to go back to work that same day. While frightened and still agitated, Eunice agreed. In subsequent visits, the worker urged her not to blame herself for what happened, a common problem among the victims of random crime. He also worked on getting her to return to old routines on the assumption that the less the incident changed her lifestyle, the sooner she would be able to return to normal functioning.

As many victims of crime report, over the next few months, Eunice went from a fearful and passive place in her behavior to a more proactive stance. She took self-defense courses, wrote several letters to the editor of the local paper outlining what had happened to her and the need for better policing, and was asked by several groups to discuss victimization and the approach she had taken to resolve her feelings of fear and anger.

While her progress seemed extraordinarily fast (she was back at work almost immediately and went to live in her home after only two nights spent with a friend), the worker feared that Eunice would continue to suffer from PTSD. As it turned out, he was correct. One night, she heard noises at the front door and went into a full-blown panic attack. The police were called and she was seen in the emergency room with heart palpitations and breathing difficulties. The police could find no evidence of tampering with her door. Another night, a wrong number from a man whose voice sounded strangely familiar to her sent her into a similar panic attack with a visit to the emergency room.

Her crisis worker wisely continued seeing her in treatment and referred her to a support group for victims of crime. The approach he used was mainly cognitive-behavioral, focusing on the irrational thoughts she sometimes had that caused her to be anxious, and then the homework she needed to do to keep the intrusive thoughts from causing panic attacks. The worker was able to get state funds for victims of violent crime to offset the limited treatment she was permitted under her medical plan. The treatment continued for almost six months before the worker felt Eunice had made sufficient progress to sustain herself with the occasional follow-up visit for treatment.

Eunice continues to see the worker for "check ups" every month but reports a lingering mild depression which she thinks is linked to the mugging. The worker agrees with Eunice about the cause of her depression but also believes that the mugging initiated fears of death that were a result of having lost her husband to a car accident a year before the mugging incident. He thinks that the mild depression is also related to Eunice's belief that others don't sense how severe the trauma was to her and that she has to deal with the after-effects of the incident on her own.

The worker, using a cognitive-behavioral approach in treatment sessions once a month, treated the lingering depression and Eunice's feelings of loneliness and isolation. The worker also let Eunice talk about her fear of death and how much she missed her husband. She also continued to attend the support group and has sought out other groups in the community for help, including a bereavement group to deal with the loss of her husband.

It has taken Eunice two years to return to a fairly stable emotional state. She views the mugging as one of the terrible things that sometime force people to look carefully at their lives. She believes that she was in a fairly deep depression over the death of her husband when the mugging took place and that the incident forced her to get help. She still experiences hyper-vigilance and panicky feelings from time to time, but she is doing well at work, has a male companion, a new set of friends, and is socially active.

Eunice has made excellent progress, but like many victims of random crime, the impact may never completely go away. A continuation of fearful feelings, particularly when victims are alone in potentially dangerous places, can be anticipated and a loss of feelings of invulnerability is usual in cases of random violence.

Integrating Questions

1. This client received almost immediate help. How do you think the mugging and robbery so soon after the death of her husband would have affected Eunice had she not received help?

2. Post-traumatic stress disorder suggests that traumatic events such as the experience Eunice had will probably occur in most people. Can you think of people who have special coping skills who might not be affected? What do you think these special coping skills would have to be?

3. Eunice was attacked in the parking lot of the bank where she worked. Do you think Eunice will have work-related problems as a result of the lack of safety precautions shown by her employer? What do you think those work-related problems might be?

4. Victim support groups can be very beneficial in helping victims of random crime to better cope with the experience. What conditions within the group should exist for the group to have a positive impact on the client? What might the goals of the group be?

5. Eunice is angry with herself for experiencing the mugging. She thinks that she might have prevented the incident. How would you go about helping her deal with her sense of complicity in the mugging so that she no longer blames herself?

REFERENCES

Adler, F., Mueller, G., & Laufer, W. S. (1995). *Criminology* (2nd ed.). New York: McGraw-Hill.

Associated Press. (2000a, August 25). Convicted killer pleads insanity. *San Bernardino County Sun*, p. A3.

Associated Press. (2000b, August 25). Hate crimes increase 11.7% in L.A. County. *San Bernardino County Sun*, p. A3.

Beck, A. J. (2000, April). *Prison and jail inmates at midyear 1999*. Washington, DC: Bureau of Justice Statistics, U.S. Department of Justice.

Brownstein, H. H. (2000). *The social reality of violence and violent crime*. Boston, MA: Allyn & Bacon.

Bureau of Justice Statistics. (2000). *Criminal victimization in the United States, 1997*. Washington, DC: Bureau of Justice Statistics, U.S. Department of Justice.

Butterfield, F. (1991, October 19). Experts explore rise in mass murder. *New York Times*, p. B3.

Cavan, R. S. (1969). *Juvenile delinquency* (2nd ed.). New York: J. B. Lippincott.

Currie, E. (1985). *Confronting crime*. New York: Pantheon.

Curtis, L. (1985). Neighborhood, family and employment. In L. A. Curtis (Ed.), *American violence and public policy*. New Haven, CT: Yale University Press.

Debro, J. (1996). The Los Angeles riots: Lessons for the urban future. *Criminology, 21*(2), 18–19.

Douglas, J., & Olshaker, M. (1995). *Mindhunter: Inside the FBI's elite serial crime unit*. New York: Scribner.

Eclipse. (1992). *Official true crime trading cards: Serial killers and mass murderers*. Forestville, CA: Eclipse Enterprises.

Fried, A. (1969). The attack on mobilization. In H. Weissman (Ed.), *Community development in the mobilization for youth experience*. New York: Association Press.

Gold, S., Gale, E., & Marosi, R. (2001, March 8). Nightmare evolves from the suburban dream. *L.A. Times*, p. A1.

Graham, H. D., & Gurr, T. R. (1969). *Violence in America: Historical and comparative perspectives*. Washington, DC: U.S. Government Printing Office.

Graham, H. G., Davis, & Gurr, T. R. (1969). *The history of violence in America.* New York: Bantam Books.

Greenwood, P., Model, K. E., Rydell, P. C., & Chiesa, J. (1996, May). *Diverting children from a life of crime: Measuring cost and benefits.* Santa Monica, CA: RAND.

Jones, R. G. (1989). *The mammoth book of murder.* New York: Carroll & Graf.

Leary, W. E. (2000, August 28). Violent crime down. *San Bernardino County Sun,* p. A1.

Leedy, M. (1999, October, 23). Stopping youth violence: Focus on younger kids. *San Bernardino County Sun,* p. B1.

Levin, J., & Fox, J. A. (1991). *Mass murder: American's growing menace.* New York: Berkeley Books.

Leyton, E. (1990). American culture incites serial killers. In D. Bender, and B. Leone (Eds.), *Violence in America: Opposing viewpoints.* San Diego, CA: Greenhaven Press.

Los Angeles Times. (1990, November 18). Gangs keep shooting, people keep dying. *L. A. Times,* p. M6.

Maguire, K., & Pastore, A. L. (Eds.). (1999). *Sourcebook of criminal justice.* Washington, DC: Bureau of Justice Statistics, U.S. Department of Justice.

Mestel, R. (2001, March 7). Triggers of violence still elusive. *L.A. Times,* p. A1.

Monkkonen, E. H. (2000, September 3). The puzzle of murder statistics: A search for cause and effect. *L. A. Times,* p. M1.

Nelson, J., & Cardona, F. (2000, August 17). Violent crime off 16.9%; County shows a steady decrease during last 5 years. *San Bernardino County Sun,* p. A1.

Nguyen, C. (2000, August 10). Letters show Mexican Mafia prison link. *San Bernardino County Sun,* p. B1.

Reid, S. T. (1995). *Criminal law.* Englewood Cliffs, NJ: Prentice Hall.

Reno, J. (2000). *Safe from the start: Taking action on children exposed to violence.* Washington, DC: Office of Juvenile Justice and Delinquency Prevention, U. S. Department of Justice.

San Bernardino County Sun. (1999, April 21). School shootings. *San Bernadino County Sun,* p. A9.

Schmid, R. E. (2000, September 1). "Going postal" is a myth, independent panel says. *San Bernardino County Sun,* p. A5.

Schmidt, J. L. (1988, January 29). 30 years ago, terror ruled as 2 teens went on rampage. *San Francisco Herald,* p. 2A.

Schumacher, M. A. (1994, March). *The 8% problem: Chronic juvenile offender recidivism. Executive Summary.* Orange County, CA: California Probation Department.

Silberman, C. (1980). *Criminal violence, criminal justice.* In E. Bittner, and S. L. Messinger (Eds.), *Criminology review yearbook* (Vol. 2). Beverly Hills, CA: Sage.

Spangler, T. (2000, June 15). 5 slain in Pittsburgh shooting spree. *San Bernardino County Sun.*

Tappan, P. W. (1960). *Crime, justice and correction.* New York: McGraw-Hill.

Timrots, A. D., & Rand, M. R. (1987). *Violent crime by strangers and nonstrangers.* Washington, DC: Bureau of Justice Statistics, U.S. Department of Justice.

Washington Post. (2000, Sept. 1). Going postal is a bad rap, study finds. p. A20.

Weissman, H. (Ed). (1969). *Community development in the Mobilization for Youth Experience.* New York: Association Press.

Woodson, R. (1981). *A summons to life: Mediating structures and the prevention of youth crime.* Boston, MA: Ballinger.

NOTES

1. A recent law enforcement raid in a southern California town found that members of the Mexican Mafia were getting their orders on everything from how to handle drug distribution to whom they should murder from inmates in prisons around the state (Nguyen, 2000).

2. Tappan (1960) refers to this as the "battle of experts" (p. 409).

3. Daumer was not the first to eat the flesh of his victims; Albert Fish, a sixty-year-old mild-mannered father of six cooked and ate the flesh of the children he killed in the 1940s in New York City. While seen as insane by the jury, he was convicted as sane because the jury was convinced he should be in prison (Jones, 1989).

4. From a conversation with Donald A. Sechrest, former postal employee.

CHAPTER

10 Treating Perpetrators of Violent Crime

Case studies and research data on the treatment of violent perpetrators have been provided throughout the book which we hope give direction to the reader. In this chapter, we will expand that discussion by showing how to use primary treatment approaches with actual clients. The research on treating violent behavior suggests that the following approaches are the most widely used at present: insight into past events in life that may affect current behavior; a cognitive understanding of the irrational ways the offender might view situations that lead to violence; understanding role expectations that might explain the way offenders view their roles in life situations which end in violence; the susceptibility of certain people to violent ideas that are translated into violent actions; modifying behavior using classical behavioral shaping techniques; and short-term crisis intervention.

Psychosocial Reasons for Violence

Why do people become violent? Freud believed that violence was a breakdown in the superego. The primitive forces of the unconscious and the violent impulses in the id, according to Freud, were a genetic repository of man's primitive and often violent nature and controlled the issue of violence. Most of us have strong enough superegos to keep our violent impulses in check. But like anything in life, sometimes even the strongest superego can develop cracks and sometimes violence can be the end result. As all too many historical events have shown, when people are placed in violent and inhumane settings such as the prison camps of Andersonville during the Civil War or the killing fields of Indochina, decent people, law-abiding and nonviolent people, can act in ways that suggest that the potential for violence is in all of us.

But this potential to be violent aside, what are the primary reasons from the literature for violent acts by perpetrators? Most can be explained as follows:

1. A trauma early in life such as physical or sexual abuse or early exposure to an environment where violence was common. This is such a common experience for people who are violent that many therapists and counselors believe that it is the major reason for violent behavior. Children become socialized into violence by their perpetrators. They aren't necessarily taught

to be violent but develop strong degrees of unconscious rage over their abuse that is directed at others as a way of releasing anger.

2. A brain malfunction caused by a blow to the head or by repeated blows to the head. Early childhood physical abuse may have been responsible for minimal organic brain damage that leads to violence (Rosenbaum & Hoge, 1989). In that case, it is difficult to say if the emotional damage caused by the abuse in childhood is responsible for later life violence or whether it is the result of the organic brain damage. But in all too many violent offenders, evidence exits of minimal organic brain damage related to child abuse.

3. Development of a personality disorder where violence is a way of getting whatever the offender wants. Whether one develops a personality disorder because of genetic reasons, prior trauma, or socialization by parents without the capacity to bond or provide a nurturing and loving relationship with the child, is difficult to say. Nonetheless, a number of frequently violent people are thought to have personality disorders, which limit the amount of guilt the violent person experiences over their behavior and therefore provides the violent person with few reasons to control their violence.

4. Use of drugs and alcohol that act as disinhibitors and permit violent thoughts and impulses to be realized.

5. A social environment in which children are taught to use violence much in the same way some families initiate their children into crime.

6. Social pressure such as that experienced in juvenile gangs.

7. Situations where rage and impulse come together in otherwise nonviolent people.

8. Biochemical reasons for violence. Mawson (1999) believes that violence can be explained as a series of biochemical interactions driven in part by stimulus-seeking behavior. The higher the arousal rate, the more likely the person is to experience violent behavior.

9. George Will (2001), writing about a Polish village during the second world war in which the Polish population killed almost all Jews in the community (more than 1,600 civilians), believes that this terrible event took place not because of political reasons or an affinity for the Nazi regime, but because the German authorities gave a hateful, deeply anti-Semitic people the opportunity to do so. Will writes, "Why in Jedwabne did neighbor murder their neighbor? Because it was permitted. Because they could" (p. 68). Will believes that when order in a society breaks down, violence may often be the end result.

Working with Violent Perpetrators: Insight-Oriented Approaches

Knowing why we commit violent acts may be a way of getting offenders to connect past events with current behavior. This makes a certain amount of sense and may be useful in explaining patterns of violent behavior that the offender does not necessarily understand. The question is, does providing the perpetrator with insight into his or her behavior lead to a change in the violent behavior? Most researchers would argue that insight alone isn't very effective in changing behavior. In insight-oriented approaches to the treatment of violence, the belief is that emotions come before thought and that they are controlled by unconscious issues that the client has repressed. Certain stimuli that touch on unconscious feelings may serve as catalysts for strong emotions, even violent behavior. Why does the offender get so angry at life situations that, in and of themselves, may seem so benign? The answer is that the conscious situation may remind the client unconsciously of how he or she felt in a similar situation when they were experiencing some severe physical or emotional trauma. Let's consider a case study of a violent child abuser to demonstrate how the unconscious may contribute to violent behavior.

Case Study: Using an Insight Approach

John Berthalemew is a highly educated, forty-two-year old Caucasian professional engineer. He is very successful at work and is well liked in the community. However, his children and wife see another side of him, a dismal and hurtful side. When John is challenged by his children, or when they disobey or argue with him, John goes into a rage. He hits, kicks, punches, beats and hurts without concern for the harm he might do. He has severely harmed all of his children who are now in foster care because of his abuse. They want nothing to do with their father.

When John was a child, his father beat him in a similar way. John is humiliated by the things his father did to him, abusive and vile things that he has difficulty discussing, even as an adult. He has a low self-concept and feels that the last bastion of support is his family. But instead of being supportive, his family is a cantankerous group of bright children who are highly energized and who often say the unsupportive and mildly critical things children sometimes say to parents. When this happens, John's sense of dignity goes out the window. He feels betrayed and attacked. He knows at one level that this is what smart children act like but at the hurting level, the child inside of him has no ability to handle disrespect and he seethes when his children aren't perfect gentlemen in his presence. The lack of respect puts him in the same ego state he was in as a child and he fights back by doing what his father did to him: hurting his children for their lack of respect and support.

John is in therapy with a therapist using an insight approach. He is now aware of the reason he feels so out of control around his children but he can do little to stop the rush of feelings that come over him when his children show disrespect. His therapist has been helpful in showing John the unconscious issues that seem to control his behavior, but John still feels the little unloved child inside of him much of the time. He has understanding but no real direction about how to change his perceptions of life events that seem to bring out a great deal of repressed anger.

The therapist decided to let John use a Gestalt technique in which John moved between chairs, one of which represented him and the other his father. This type of role-play has been helpful in getting John to see that what was done to him was also done to his father. He isn't so angry and he's been able to have supervised visits with the children. They dislike and fear him so much, however, that he can barely stand the emotional pain he has caused them and doesn't really want to go for visits. His wife, who held the family together for a long time, is also in treatment and has decided not to live with John anymore. Like the children, he has abused her badly and she has anger and resentment at him that comes out whenever they're together.

John is also in a perpetrator group that uses insight-oriented approaches. He's come to appreciate the fact that so many of the men in the group are nice and warm on the outside, but angry and violent on the inside. They seethe with anger and resentment. Little conformations in the group bring on rage reactions. Potential fights are always brewing. Little hurts become major hurts. John believes that the damage done to him as a child is irreversible. He doesn't think it will ever go away and knowing why he hurts so much doesn't seem to help at all. He is pessimistic about life and thinks that the best course for him is to stay away from intimate contacts with people. It is a lonely course to follow, but John thinks it is for the best.

Discussion of the Case   Unfortunately, insight alone may not be enough to stop violence. John has a large reservoir of anger sitting deeply in his unconscious. Who can ever understand the depth of his pain or how he tried to explain to himself his father's behavior? John is a violent man. His violence has been limited to the abuse of his family but he admits to road rage and workplace violence. He put his hand through a wall in a dispute with a coworker and ran someone off the road who had been tailgating him on the freeway. He has kept guns out of the house for fear that he might use one, but he has fantasies about them and likes to go to gun stores just to pick them up and run his hand over their cool steel frames. He feels strong when he holds a gun in his hand.

The insight approach has helped John see important connections between his abusive behavior and the abuse done to him. It has, however, left him confused about what to do with his anger. He resents the thought that he's behaving like his father, but harbors strong feelings that the abuse he does to others is a payback for what was done to him. He believes that his abusive behavior is justified and appropriate. He fantasizes about humiliating people. He has no understanding of intimacy and lacks a definition of what a loving relationship between an adult or a child might be. John is a long way from being healthy and the weekly sessions that go over his relationships with his mother and father seem to be going nowhere. He feels frustrated but informed and educated. He knows why he is the way he is but it just doesn't seem to help him change his behavior. More to the point, he has no model of what he wants to be like. If he changes, who will he become? He hasn't a clue.

John is highly intelligent and has begun to ask these questions of the therapist. The response he gets is that delving into the unconscious takes time and that John is making good progress. John doesn't think so. He has begun to seek out other approaches and has decided to try an anger management group, an approach we will discuss later in the chapter with John as our client.

Working with Violent Perpetrators: Cognitive-Behavioral Approaches

The cognitive-behavioral approach is probably the most widely used approach in forensic settings. This approach tries to help perpetrators see their behavior across a continuum of rational to irrational thoughts that may lead to violent behavior. The approach is largely educational and is grounded in the notion that people can be taught to think more clearly. According to cognitive theorists, thought or perception of an event always precedes emotion. If the violent offender can see the illogic of a thought and can then trace the paths he or she took that lead to violence, then the client can be helped in the future not to make the same mistake. Their behavior, in time, will hopefully change. Several primary forces in the cognitive behavioral approach have been Albert Ellis (1962) and Aaron Beck (1976).

Cognitive-behavioral approaches all believe that people think before they act. Thinking is translated into simple sentences that the people tell themselves about any given situation. Jack, a client we will discuss next in a case study, was involved in a workplace problem in which a box he packed with important technical equipment broke in transit. It was clearly Jack's inept job of packing that led to the equipment being damaged. When confronted by his boss, Jack had to leave the room or he would have hit his boss. Jack believed that his boss intentionally humiliated him in front of coworkers and felt demeaned and deflated, a feeling that almost immediately led to rage.

Jack told himself an incorrect set of sentences about the situation with his boss that almost led to violence. He might have said to himself, "Whoops, I messed up. Better listen to the feedback, repack the box, and apologize if I want to keep the job. Make the boss happy and I'll be fine." Most of us would have done just that, but Jack is badly socialized in the ways of resolving conflict. Jack thinks that violence is appropriate for any situation in which his self-worth is threatened. To help Jack lessen his anger and resolve conflict in a less antagonistic way, the cognitive-behavioral approach would teach him the following steps:

1. Thinking always comes before emotions, we might tell him. If we were in a room on the twenty-third story of a building with only one exit and a cocker spaniel was blocking it, we would assume no danger. But in the same scenario, if a lion blocked the exit, we would (most of us, anyway) be filled with fear. Why? Because most of aren't afraid of cocker spaniels but most of us are afraid of lions. Therefore, we think and perceive before we emote.

2. It isn't so much what happens to us in life that makes us upset, it's how we view situations in life that can be upsetting. If we convened a group of people who had just had homes destroyed in a natural disaster we would hear a very different set of perceptions about the event. Some people will see it as the end of their lives while others will see it as a chance to start anew and make different decisions about their lives. Different perceptions of events lead to different emotions.

3. We have all been taught to think irrationally about some things. Being liked by everyone, while impossible, is a goal for some of us. Doing well in every activity in life might be another. These impossible and irrational thoughts permeate our thinking and often make us angry to the point of violence. Jack's anger at his boss is partially a reflection of his belief that if someone criticizes him, they also dislike him and deserve to be punished.

4. If we look at a situation carefully and accurately, we will see that it isn't the way we remembered it at first. This technique, called freeze framing by cognitive therapists, helps people see that their memory of the event may be very inaccurate. We find this often in domestic violence where two people remember the same situation so differently that it doesn't even appear to have happened to the same people. Nietzsche said, "Pride and memory had an argument about what really happened, and pride won."

5. If you can learn to think irrationally, you can also learn to think rationally and to act rationally. This process can be taught through processing events that result in violence and then explaining how the situation might have been handled more rationally. It also involves having the perpetrator practice new behaviors that have successful results and don't end in violence.

6. Whatever happened to us in the past to create our emotional problems doesn't stop us from correcting those problems in the present and continuing to correct them in the future. People are not shaped forever by their past life histories.

Let's consider a brief case to demonstrate the cognitive-behavioral approach.

Case Study: Using Cognitive-Behavioral Treatment

Jack Brown is a twenty-three-year-old Caucasian violent offender who beat his boss to unconsciousness over a workplace dispute. Jack has a long history of problems with violence and has been in and out of incarceration since he was 14. Jack's boss was angry that Jack had incorrectly packed a television set for shipping and told him so. Jack took the feedback personally and hit the boss without warning, beating him to the point of unconsciousness. These are the irrational thoughts Jack translated into self-sentences that lead to his assault on his boss:

1. The criticism of Jack's work was viewed by Jack as a criticism of him. He took the feedback not as an attack on his work, but as a personal attack. The

anger this developed in Jack was immediate. Jack has very low self-esteem and has difficulty taking criticism without personalizing it.

2. Jack's next thought was that since the boss didn't like him and probably wasn't going to keep him employed, that he should get some satisfaction out of the situation and beat up the boss. He didn't think about the consequences of his act. All he could sense was the satisfaction he would get from hurting his boss. After all, as Jack told the therapist, "You gotta act before they do. You gotta let him know who the real boss is. I learned that in the joint." Jack was fired, arrested, and sentenced to a year in jail for assault. He is in a state with a three strikes law. One more violent offense and he faces long-term incarceration.

Let's look at how Jack's irrational thinking got him into trouble and how we might change it using the cognitive-behavioral approach.

Cognitive-behavioral therapy is an aggressive-directive therapy. It tries to show offenders of violence the cognitive distortions in their thinking that lead to violence. In Jack's case, it took over six months before Jack actually understood the cognitive system well enough to use it, and then his ability to use it was often very limited. Jack believes that violence is good. He thinks it makes others give him what he wants. He also realizes the negative consequences of his behavior. Violence results in incarceration. After six months, Jack doesn't want to go to jail again, but he has a difficult time seeing anyone else's point of view in a dispute. Each issue of conflict must be processed again and again for Jack to see the illogical way he looks at situations, but he's finally beginning to understand. He knows that he floods himself with irrational thoughts that usually focus on how others are taking advantage of him. He knows these thoughts aren't always accurate but they are a long-held part of the way he views life. To supplement the cognitive approach, Jack is in a treatment group that forces him to deal with his anger rationally. If he gets mad, he has to calm himself down by rationally discussing whatever made him angry in the group. It's very hard work for Jack. He carries grudges and fantasizes about hurting other inmates when they disagree with him or, from his point of view, put him down. But he's slowly learning to take an emotional time out, process his anger, and come up with other solutions.

The cognitive-behavioral approach also focuses on advice-giving and homework. It's not enough to understand how one's behavior is irrational; we also have to change that behavior. It is at this point that the therapist began providing assignments for Jack to complete, which he must then report on in the next treatment session. As an example, Jack is angry with his wife because she forgot to bring him some food he's been craving while in jail, food not available unless someone brings it to him. He hollered at her during their last visitation and was removed from the visiting area with his visitation rights revoked for two weeks. The therapist gave him a supervised assignment to call his wife on the phone and apologize. His impulse was to scream at her again and to blame her for his loss of privileges. Under the therapist's guidance, he calmly apologized and found the experience so touching (his wife started to cry) that he spoke for a long time in the therapy session about how he just might be learning something useful.

Working with Violent Perpetrators: Behavior Modification

Behavior modification uses learning theory to modify violent behavior (Wolpe, 1958). In learning theory, there are three primary ways to change behavior: positive reinforce where a reward is given for acceptable behavior; negative reinforce where the reward is withheld; and punishment where something physically or emotionally painful is done to stop the unwanted behavior. In the context of violence, behavior modification is often used in forensic institutions to help model behavior which, theoretically, should continue on after the offender is released if the conditioning process is sufficient and if the behavior modification continues after release. Behavior modification believes that change needs to be constantly reinforced. One technique used in behavior modification with violent offenders is token economy. In token economy, the entire approach to the prisoner is to only reward socially acceptable, nonviolent behavior. Negative deviations from acceptable behavior may result in negative reinforcement or punishment. Let's see how token economy might work in an institutional setting with violent juvenile offenders.

Case Study: Behavior Modification Using Token Economy

The Atkins Child Facility in Texas uses token economy with juvenile offenders who have committed violent crimes, including assault with intent to do harm, attempted murder, rape, and a list of crimes with serious and harmful impact to victims. The facility is a locked facility because the offenders are considered dangerous. Some of offenders are as young as 10 but are felt to be seriously emotionally disturbed. The facility uses a strict token economy. Positive behavior has a reward system (positive reinforcement), that includes better food, less work requirements, work that is not strenuous, supervised passes into town to see athletic events or movies, and other privileges denied to any offender whose behavior remains disruptive in the institution, threatening to the staff or inmates, or shows a neutral, passive attitude where only the minimal amounts of change demonstrated.

When behavior is offensive or dangerous, the inmates are placed in special cells where there are no outdoor privileges and where food is bland and basic.

The staff and the inmates construct the reward system and determine how it is to function. One way the token economy works at the facility is that there is a point system in use. For every positive behavior, the inmate earns points or tokens. When the points or tokens reach a certain level, the inmate gets a reward. The rewards are for positive behavior that show good citizenship in the facility and are consistent with the behavior one would look for on the outside. If the inmate consistently is rewarded for positive behavior, his sentence may be reduced.

Jason, a fourteen-year-old Caucasian inmate, beat up his stepfather, sending him to the hospital for two weeks with broken bones, a concussion, and a broken kneecap. The stepfather was abusive to Jason and his family and beat them when he was drinking. Jason used a heavy shovel to pummel his stepfather while the stepfather was asleep. The courts thought that Jason had serious emotional problems, confirmed by expert social work and psychological testimony. The facility was felt to be the correct setting to send him to since it had such a tight and well-functioning token economy that had been helpful in treating other violent juvenile offenders.

Jason learned the reward system quickly. By attending school and doing well, he earned a considerable number of tokens. By joining a treatment group and by being a good participant, he earned even more privileges. Jason worked in the library and developed a way to place the library holdings on the computer. This earned him even more tokens and privileges. Because he has learned the token economy so well, Jason has one of the best rooms in the facility and no roommate. He gets frequent outside privileges and sees movies every weekend. He is allowed to have visits with his girlfriend, although they are not conjugal visits. He is allowed to eat the same food as the staff and he has a loaner computer in his room to do his schoolwork. Jason has learned the system well and has benefited, but has his violent behavior changed? The facility thinks so. Their reasoning is that when a violent juvenile manages to do well in a facility with strict rules and a composition of other violent offenders, the probability is high that he will continue to do well after he leaves the facility, if the reinforcement system continues.

Jason was released after eighteen months in the Atkins facility to a halfway house that uses the same behavior modification approach as the facility. He attends school in town but must return to the halfway house immediately after school. A bus from the facility makes sure that he is back on time. Breaking the rules of the halfway house means that he will be returned to the facility. He also continues on in cognitive-behavioral therapy.

In the quarterly report written to the juvenile court that has jurisdiction over Jason, the counselor assigned to the halfway house who is also the parole officer to the boys in residence wrote: "Jason understands that abiding by the rules of the halfway house results in better living conditions. His self-awareness has improved as a result of his group treatment. He is remorseful over what he did to his stepfather and is aware that he will not be able to return home because the stepfather won't permit it. He is angry that nothing was done to the stepfather for his abuse and feels that what he did to the stepfather was justified. Although he understands that there were other routes for him to take regarding the abuse, a rage came over him and he was unable to control his behavior. We think that he is a good candidate for release to a foster home or to a small, well-structured group home. He is intelligent, does well in school, and is a model resident. As with all violent people, Jason is still capable of violence if the conditions and the situation are right. We believe that if he is released, that he should have regular group treatment and that he should be frequently evaluated for lapses in his management of anger.

Discussion of the Case Behavior modification has, what is called in medicine, a short halflife. That is, unless the behavior is continually being modified, the gains that might have been made become extinguished in time and the client may revert back to violent behavior. While the offender is in a controlled facility, he may function well, but when the scheduled and enforced rules of the facility are not present after release from the facility, many professionals believe that the violent behavior returns. The structure of any facility may be very easy for offenders to learn and to navigate. But life on the outside is chaotic for many offenders and most professionals believe that treatment must be continued for a considerably long period of time if the violent behavior is to be controlled.

Techniques of Treatment with Violent Offenders

Several techniques, as opposed to theories of behavior for treatment of violent offenders, seem to have relevance. They are: the use of stories, the men's group, anger management, the selective use of role-plays, empathy training, and crisis intervention.

The Use of Stories

Allen and Laird (1993) suggest that one potential approach to treatment is to permit men and women who use violence in their families and intimate relationships to tell stories about their lives. They note that: "[People] have been denied their domestic stories. We know little of their places in family life and they are often at a loss for words about the intimate environs of family life" (p. 441).

The use of stories in treating violent offenders can be a powerful way of understanding underlying themes in their lives. While reality is sometimes manipulated when stories are told, stories serve as an ideal way of helping offenders to remember important life events and to identify themes in their lives that may continually be repeated. Stories may also serve to explain definitions of masculinity and femininity and the confusion that may lead to dysfunctional relationships.

One of the author's clients, in trying to summarize an act of violence, told him the following story:

> My father was an FBI agent. A very macho guy. The strong one. In fourth grade he took to driving me out into the country and telling me how useless his life was. He'd have a drink and then he'd take his service revolver out and put it to his temple. "If I had the guts," he'd tell me, "I'd pull the trigger." He never did until I was in tenth grade. By then, he'd lost his job because of his drinking. We never did know what the trouble was. By the time he killed himself, I wasn't surprised, I was relieved. I vowed that I'd never be the wimp that *he* was and here I am at 38 with the same preoccupation with death, beating the hell out of my wife and kids, and

getting into fights at work. I guess you grow up with violence, it does something to the way you act in life. It makes me feel weak and then it makes me feel strong. I guess that's the way my dad felt right before he pulled the trigger.

This story doesn't tell us directly why the offender chose to become violent. Perhaps it was his own inability to stop his father from killing himself, or perhaps the father's pathology was internalized by the son. Violence to the self is often thought of as the other side of the coin of violence to others. Both are dictated by extreme anger. Using this initial story, the worker asked the client to tell a story about his mother. The worker wondered if perhaps the lack of information he was getting in the work with this client about his mother was indicative of something deeper in terms of the driving force to hurt his wife and children. This is the story he told us.

My dad used to intimidate my mom. He never hit her but he was nasty to her when he drank and he made fun of her in front of the kids. One time he came home drunk and he made her take her clothes off so we could all see how fat she'd become. He showed us her stomach and she was crying and all (the client starts to weep) and then he made her sit on the toilet seat so we could see how her behind hung over the toilet. She sat there crying and pleading with him to stop but he kept on making fun of her calling her a "sow" and a "fat slob". And then he'd pass out and the kids would help comfort my mother, but I hated her. I hated her so much I started to treat her like my dad did, and she let me. She was so worn out by his tormenting her that she'd just given up. One day she left and we never saw or heard from her again. It was like she never was there to start with. My dad wouldn't even let us mention her name. I find myself doing the same thing to my wife. I don't want to, but I do it anyway.

We can see in this story the depth of the client's anger at both his mother and father and his sense of impotence in not being able to stop the abuse or the suicidal tendencies of his father. One of the fascinating aspects of working with people is that no one can say for certain whether a client who grows up with violence will choose to become violent. It's certainly a good bet, of course, that it will happen. With this client, the abuse didn't start until he was married and began having children. And then some free-floating anguish was let loose and the violence kept escalating until it came to the attention of the police and he was sent for treatment. The stories he was urged to tell formed a large part of his understanding of his anger and, with group support and some long-term cognitive therapy, he began the slow but sure cessation of his violent behavior.

It is common among offenders to tell stories that may have metaphorical meaning. Often, however, offenders fail to see the broader meaning of a story. This is where the therapist might help the client find themes and connections in a story the violent offender has chosen to tell. Stories in our society are often considered safe ways of sharing feelings. They may be literal and straightforward or they may contain hidden messages that are often unclear to the client but, at some level, may seem to have relevance. Never assume that a story is literal but look to the context and the intent of the story to help the client see important connections. This is the way offenders learn. . . . By being helped to see and connect disparate behaviors, themes, and life experiences.

Using Offender Groups to Change Violent Behavior

Offender groups have been widely used in the treatment of family and dating violence. Their effectiveness seems to suggest that they might work equally as well with a wide variety of forms of violence, Eisikovits and Edelson (1989), for example, in an evaluation of studies of men in groups treating domestic violence, note that treatment success has been as high as 65 percent. They concede, however, that methodological issues make effectiveness evaluation difficult.

The following conditions appear to be the necessary attributes of successful treatment groups with violent offenders:

1. An accepting environment where bonding and social interaction are emphasized. In successful offender groups, indigenous leaders play an important role in group interactions by the group.
2. A therapeutic environment that emphasizes the strengths and positive behaviors of group members and where participants do not feel demeaned for their emotional problems.
3. A nurturing but no-nonsense therapeutic approach that allows offenders to feel that being vulnerable may, in fact, lead to important change.
4. A type of emotional outreach that makes offenders feel wanted, accepted, and valued.
5. A reframing of issues of violence where life problems are not explained by using a pathology model but are understood in a social context that emphasizes the positive and healthy components of a group members behavior.

Using Group Interaction as a Way of Deterring Violence

In offender groups, members are permitted to discuss highly emotional and often heretofore undiscussed issues. In one group, for example, a female offender discussed her father and his contribution to her violent temper that resulted in the death of a spouse during an argument. She had never before discussed her father.

> He abused me for as long as I can remember. And then after he abused me, he'd call me a slut for letting him do it. I had to take care of him after he had a stroke and it was all I could do not to kill the son-of-a-bitch right there in his bedroom. He made my life hell. I've been damaged goods since. What kid wants to have sex at seven with a man? He groped me and prodded me and filled me with pain since I can remember.

Relatives in their homes, including fathers, had themselves sexually abused many of the women in the group. They were able to offer support and a safe place for the client to share her feelings and to provide feedback suggesting that their offenders did many of the same things to them that the client's father did to her. The group was able to take the issue one step further, however. They were able to help the client see that the anger she had for her father wasn't being channeled properly by the free-floating rage she felt toward everyone else. It was better, they told her, to deal with the rage she felt at her family for allowing the abuse to continue than to take it out on others who weren't responsible. In time, the client was able to do this by discussing the fact that everyone in the family knew she was being abused but did nothing to prevent it or to protect her. In fact, the abuse she experienced resulted in less abuse to them. In a way, the client was the scapegoat for the father's pathology, saving the others from similar abuse.

When the client was able to see the connection between her rage at her family and the freewheeling hostility she felt toward the world, she was able to make movement in the group and became less angry and volatile in her life in prison. The group had helped her see connections, make changes in her thinking, and support her during a rare moment of painful self-disclosure. That's what groups do best. She told the group after a year of treatment and many backwards steps:

> You [the group] helped me to see that being mad at everyone was making me even angrier. I've begun to work out my feelings about members of my family, one by one. The more I've done that, the less angry I am at the world. I'm still damn angry, you understand, because someone should have stopped this from happening, some teacher or doctor, but I won't kill anyone again and that's what it's all about. Maybe I'll get better in time and maybe I won't be angry at all. I'll be an old lady when I get out of here but at least I won't be a mean old lady. [The group members applauded.]

Case Study: Using an Anger Management Group   The core idea behind anger management is that violence can be controlled by understanding the illogical things we say to ourselves that create angry feelings. Anger management groups help people learn to identify those illogical self-statements and then to practice new ways of viewing issues of anger in the group. This is done both in the context of the group experience and as homework assignments that the client must complete between group meetings. Group members in anger management groups help one another confront angry feelings by learning to provide feedback and helpful suggestions.

John, the highly intelligent engineer who has been receiving insight-oriented therapy and was described earlier in the chapter, joined an anger management group. The group didn't focus on why he was violent but rather stressed the idea that he could learn to manage and control his angry feelings. The focus of the anger management group, much like the cognitive-behavioral approach itself, was on identifying flawed thinking that led to violent emotions. The particular group that John was in always gave the members assignments and forced them to resolve angry confrontations between group members, which were frequent.

John feels that the approach is overly simple but seems to be responding well to it. He's learned some anger management steps that help him cool down when he starts becoming angry. He knows how to analyze the reason for his anger in most situations and he's learned to recognize when he's calm enough to discuss his reaction to others who have made him angry. Sometimes it takes him as much as an hour to calm down enough to talk to any group member who has made him angry. Sometimes he can't do it for a week or two and broods about the upsetting thing that was said to him, imagining all sorts of ways of hurting the other person.

Gradually, however, the anger management techniques have given him a sort of aloofness from which he can operate without feeling rage. Using these techniques, he seems much more calm than he really is. Knowing why he gets angry (which he learned through insight therapy) and knowing how to deal with his anger (which he's learned from anger management) have given him tools with which to manage his rage. To be sure, his anger is close to the surface and John is in a constant struggle not to lose his temper. He thinks of these anger management techniques as ballast to keep him afloat in a sea of rage and he has learned, at some basic level, to use the techniques as tools. He is not, however, a convert to his knowledge about controlling his anger. He still feels that he's entitled to his anger and sometimes likes to think about the people he's angry at and what he might do to them if he could.

It would be nice to say that anger management is a way of controlling violent emotions and that it works well, but like most therapy approaches with very angry and violent people, anger management is a tool and it can never completely substitute for the intense damage done to people who have suffered the indignity of childhood abuse and maltreatment at the hands of violent adults. It can, however, provide guidance in the ways of keeping very angry feelings from moving into violent behavior.

Empathy Training or Moral Development to Treat Violence

The notion that one can teach violent offenders to empathize with their victims has been used to a considerable extent. This approach believes that violent offenders lack moral development and that they fail to possess the internal controls necessary to control their impulsivity. Empathy awareness uses actual victims of crime to meet with offenders so that the offender might better understand the long-term impact of violence on their lives. By understanding and feeling remorse for their personal involvement in violence, according to this approach, the violence will lessen and the offender will develop better internal controls. Empathy training also uses other devices including lectures, discussions, films and videotapes, and values clarification to teach offenders ways of controlling their violent impulses.

Let's consider a case example of an encounter between a victim and a perpetrator in an empathy training group held in a prison in the Midwest. Note that the victim and perpetrator don't know one another, although there are instances when the perpetrator and the actual victim do meet under supervision.

Case Study: The Use of Moral Development   Judith Parsons, a twenty-seven-year-old Caucasian female, was raped and terrorized by a perpetrator three years ago. The rapist was never found and Judith has been alternating between severe depression and panic attacks ever since. Her long-term relationship with her boyfriend ended soon after the rape because the boyfriend couldn't accept the rape and felt that it somehow made Judith a "sinful" woman. Judith has continued to work as a paralegal, but a promising career that she hoped would result in eventually becoming a lawyer, has ended. Her few friends are supportive but find it difficult to cope with Judith's "dark" moods. She hasn't dated since the rape and finds the thought of intimacy repulsive. She has agreed to be part of a victim awareness group at a local state prison facility believing, on the advice of her therapist, that the group experience will be helpful by indirectly confronting her rapist. This empowerment technique will hopefully help resolve her fear of her rapist. She also believes that confronting a rapist might change his behavior and the behavior of other sexual offenders in the victim awareness group. The group is composed of eight female victims of rape and eight male rapists. It is conducted by a licensed clinical social worker trained in forensic social work. The following is an excerpted exchange between Judith and Ken, a convicted rapist sentenced to five years for raping and terrorizing a sixteen-year-old young woman.

> JUDITH: How could you do such a thing? Don't you know how it destroys women?
>
> KEN: I never thought about that. All I thought about was that I was horny and angry and that someone was gonna pay for it.
>
> JUDITH: So why not go to therapy and get it worked out?
>
> KEN: I was in therapy since I was 8 and my dad was having sex with me and my brothers and sisters. It just made me madder.
>
> JUDITH: Did you have any idea of what it would do to your victims?
>
> KEN: I hoped it would hurt them real bad.
>
> JUDITH: How can you feel that way?
>
> KEN: Someone had to pay. The county wouldn't do nothing and the old man could do anything he wanted to us. How is that fair? Why didn't somebody help us? They knew he was a molester and they didn't do nothing about it.
>
> JUDITH: Can I tell you what it did to me, the guy who acted like you did?
>
> KEN: I guess.

JUDITH: I have no life anymore. I'm scared all the time that he's going to find me and kill me because I told the police. I don't want anyone to touch me. I'm depressed all the time. I can't sleep.

KEN: And so I feel the same way too.

JUDITH: Aren't you even sorry now after all this time in prison?

KEN: Yeah, I am. I'm sorry for them and I'm sorry for me. We're all ruined people. But yeah, I shouldn't have done it. I been raped in prison, if you want to know. It's pretty humiliating.

JUDITH: Would you do it again?

KEN: I don't know. I hope not, but sometimes these urges come over me and I can't stop myself.

JUDITH: [Takes her jacket off and exposes a long knife wound. Ken looks at it and lowers his head.] He did this to me all over my body. He tortured me for two days. He said vile things about me and used everything he could find to get inside of me. Do you know what I mean? (Ken nods his head.) He couldn't get it up and he got mad at me and blamed me and then he'd say these things and cut me and threaten to kill me. I thought he would. I think he still will. Do you know how that feels to have that done to you? They call it post-traumatic stress disorder after it's over but they should call it hell because that's where you are. You're in hell.

KEN: [Looks away.] I never done that to nobody.

JUDITH: Did you ever talk to your victim?

KEN: I seen her in court and she couldn't look at me, but when she testified, she cried most of the time. I thought maybe she liked me and enjoyed what we did. Maybe that was sort of f—ed up for me to think that.

JUDITH: Do you still feel that way? Do you think the women you rape and terrorize enjoy it?

KEN: Sometimes I have thoughts like that, yeah.

JUDITH: Well they don't. It destroys them. They hate you for what you did. I hate you. Men think women like to be treated rough. We like to be treated with respect and love. Isn't that what you want?

KEN: Yeah, I do. I just don't have no idea of how to get that from a woman except forcing her. The women I go with are cold and hard and they don't give me nothing. My mother used to watch my dad screw us and she'd laugh. She was happy it wasn't happening to her, I guess.

JUDITH: Well, it's too bad what happened to you but you're an adult now and you could have stopped or gone for help. You want to be mad at women, write about it or talk to other men but don't do this shit to women anymore.

KEN: Yeah, I can see what it done to you. Maybe we can talk some more about it next time.

Discussion of the Case   While victim awareness approaches have been widely studied, there is only a limited indication that they work with violent offenders. The reason for this may have more to do with the psychopathology of the offenders and that many have severe and long-term personality disorders where moral development has not taken place in childhood. Moral messages are often scoffed at by the perpetrator. The question that might be asked is whether moral development works for the victims of violence? Perhaps this is the ultimate benefit of empathy training.

Working with Violent Perpetrators: Brief Crisis Work

Stages in the Development of Crisis

Golan (1978) has helped us understand the progression of events that characterize crisis and that can be particularly helpful in the short-term treatment of violent perpetrators. She notes five components of crisis.

1. The Hazardous Event   The event may be the act of violence or it may be an accumulation of other events leading to violence, including the death of a loved one, a natural disaster, loss of work, financial crisis, a relationship gone bad, or any number of events that place the perpetrator in a heightened state of arousal.

2. Vulnerable State   A vulnerable state suggests a moment in time when the perpetrator's coping mechanisms are at their lowest point. Fatigue, failure at work or in their personal lives, lingering illness, rejection by a loved one, or a host of other temporary and generally changeable events may exist just as the perpetrator experiences a hazardous event. Once again, the state of vulnerability may be as obvious as the weakened emotional state experienced when we work too hard or it may be as subtle as the short-lived moment when we grieve for someone who died some years ago. The weakened or vulnerable state we are in may serve to severely limit our ability to cope with a hazardous event.

3. Precipitating Factor   Perpetrators may be in a weakened state when a hazardous event occurs and still not experience crisis. The precipitating factor is the linkage between the hazardous event and the vulnerable state. The precipitating factor puts the perpetrator over the brink and directly leads to the crisis state where violence is most likely to take place. The important question to ask in understanding the progression to violence is what significance the precipitating factor has for the perpetrator. To a large degree the important question we might as at this stage is, *why now?* It is a question we must ask, particularly when the client has successfully dealt with hazardous events in the past that are as serious in nature as the current hazardous event.

Let's review the progression of events leading to a state of crisis.

1. The perpetrator is in a weakened or vulnerable state caused by fatigue, illness, failure, or a host of other temporary and situational events.
2. The perpetrator, in his or her weakened state, experiences a hazardous event that creates vulnerability to crisis.
3. The precipitating factor moves the perpetrator into a state of crisis and answers the question, *why now?*

4. Active Crisis State   The active crisis state occurs when the perpetrator's ability to cope with the hazardous event begins to deteriorate and the steady state that typically characterizes the client's behavior becomes marked by extreme emotional upheaval. To cope with an active crisis state, the perpetrator first uses normal coping mechanisms to deal with the rise in tension related to the onset of the crisis. When those coping mechanisms fail to work, the perpetrator uses unusual coping mechanisms set aside for difficult situations. Friends may be brought in for advice, over-the-counter medication may be used to reduce anxiety, alcohol or illegal drugs may be consumed, or the perpetrator may flirt with impulsive behavior on the assumption that a shock may help alleviate the symptoms he or she is experiencing. The use of substances coupled with impulsive behavior dramatically increases the risk of violence.

Caplan (1964) suggests that the active crisis state in which the client is in severe emotional imbalance lasts no more than four to six weeks. But, as Golan (1978) points out, the client may have coped with a crisis within some degree of acceptable limits for a long while, giving rise to Korner's term *exhaustion crisis,* (1973, p. 31–32). A sudden shift in life issues may create the state of *shock crisis* in which Korner suggests an immediate breakdown in coping mechanism leading to a severe crisis reaction and, in the case of the perpetrator, violent behavior.

An additional factor to consider in the length of an active crisis state is the long-term debilitating condition known as an *existential crisis*. In this form of crisis, the hazardous event creates a growing lethargy similar to burnout that may last for a very long time. A severe illness, divorce, or death of a loved one may serve to lessen coping skills and the debilitating crisis state they experience may not only last for a very long time, it may not be particularly responsive to treatment. Workplace and random violence are serious examples of people in existential states of crisis where the meaning of life has become so confused that acts of violence sometimes seem to be the only logical form of expression left to cope with a crisis. This final belief that options to resolve a crisis are limited to violence often exist in people whose wishes, expectations, and desires have largely been unmet. In people with very long-term existential crisis, violence may appear to be the only way to make a statement reflecting the client's anguish. Senseless random killings, acts of violence out of character for the otherwise nonviolent perpetrator, and school violence whose perpetrator is quiet, withdrawn, and passive may be perfect examples of violence related to existential crisis.

5. Reintegration   Movement back to the steady state may include adaptive or maladaptive coping approaches whose outcomes suggest growth or continued dysfunction. Adaptive approaches may include the use of social support networks, professional help including prescribed medication, correct cognitive perceptions, and a host of other logical ways of resolving the crisis so that minimal harm results and the potentially violent person returns to his prior steady state.

Maladaptive approaches the perpetrator may continue to use include alcohol or drugs to achieve homeostasis (steady state or balance) or the perpetrator may run away from the crisis situation and try to develop a new life. This is particularly true in domestic and workplace violence. The perpetrator may also use abusive behavior to regain control of his emotions, or to blame others for the crisis state and the difficulty experienced in regaining more normal functioning. This is a time when clients strike out at others in an attempt to reduce anxiety. Violence is very common at this stage of development of the crisis.

Steps in Brief Crisis Work

Rapoport's (1970, pp. 267–311) discussion of treatment may help us in understanding ways to address crisis states in perpetrators. She suggests the following steps or guiding principles for crisis work.

1. Relief of Symptoms   This may be accomplished through the use of supportive therapy, medication to reduce anxiety, stress management techniques including behavior modification, rest, planned time-outs from work or the crisis situation, and a host of relief-inducing techniques that serve to lower high levels of anxiety that may accompany a crisis state and that may lead to maladaptive approaches to reducing pain. Brief hospitalization may also be recommended if the perpetrator is likely to cause damage to self or to others.

2. Restoration to Precrisis Levels of Functioning   This notion suggests that we move the client back to work and family life as quickly as possible. While this may sometimes be difficult for the perpetrator who has committed an offense and faces jail time, an important finding is that the more quickly the perpetrator returns to normal routines, the more likely they are to achieve homeostasis. Remember that the person may still be in a crisis state, in which lessened coping skills are the norm. Still, moving the client back to his or her usual routine may go a long way to resolve the crisis state and to help the client return to precrisis levels of functioning. When violence takes place, this may not, of course, be possible. The client may be arrested and placed in jail for a considerably long period of time. But when it is possible for the client to return to normal routines in which the safety of others is not at issue, it is wise to do so.

3. Insight into the Cause of the Crisis Clients should be given information in treatment that serves to explain why the crisis occurred. This may be superficial and relatively benign without consideration of unconscious factors. The purpose of this technique in treatment is to help the client cope with very intense stress. Basic information may be useful, particularly if the client has limited awareness of the situation or, in general, lacks insight. This may often be the case when violence is used, but the perpetrator has a poor understanding of the progression of events leading to the crisis state and to the violent behavior.

4. Remedial Measures for Family and Community We may ask for the family to keep an eye on the perpetrator and report very troublesome behaviors. We may also refer the perpetrator to a recreational facility for physical exercise or a mental health facility for supportive therapy. Enlisting the help of other social support networks, including self-help groups, is a reasonable way of strengthening the treatment options that extend beyond our brief contact. Use of medication to lower levels of anger and impulsivity may also be recommended. If clients are using substances, substance abuse counseling is absolutely essential.

5. Connecting the Current Stresses with Past-Life Experiences and Conflicts An in-depth understanding of the crisis state is very important or we risk a post-traumatic repetition of the crisis event whenever conditions exist that create another crisis state. Affective approaches that use role-playing and self-awareness techniques are particularly helpful. They include Gestalt therapy, encounter groups, redecision therapy, and other approaches that give the perpetrator an immediate understanding of prior life conditions that may serve to contribute to crisis responses on a frequent basis.

6. Initiating New Modes of Perceiving, Thinking, Feeling, and Developing New Adaptive and Coping Responses That Can Be Useful Beyond the Immediate Crisis Situation The completion of crisis work includes helping the perpetrator modify his life to prevent another crisis. Self-help and support groups may aid in this process. Use of cognitive techniques that emphasize a planned and logical approach to problem solving and decision making are also very likely to help.

Models of Crisis Intervention

Caplan (1974) notes that the essential elements of crisis intervention that have stood the test of time are that: "(a) it advocates immediate short-term interventions; (b) it emphasizes increased receptivity and susceptibility to influence . . . during periods of temporary upset precipitated by a sudden, significant, situational change, and (c) it draws attention to the arousal of motivation to intervene among "third parties" (xiii).

Golan places her model of crisis intervention into the structure of beginning, middle, and ending phases. The model is flexible in that these phases "may all take place within a single three-hour interview or may be spaced out over several months" (Golan, 1978, p. 81). In this approach, the beginning phase is where contact is established, and assessment of the crisis takes place. In the middle phase, tasks are identified and carried out, new coping styles are established, and limited goals are set. The most important objective is that the client regain autonomy of the ego, so that this and future difficult situations can be resolved. In the final or termination phase, the intervention is reviewed and special attention is paid to the work accomplished and the new coping patterns that have been developed. Golan stresses that throughout the intervention all possible support systems and community resources should be accessed (Golan, 1978, p. 82).

Bellak and Small's (1978) model is designed as a five-session psychotherapy format. This was decided on from statistical data indicating that clients often stop treatment voluntarily after about five sessions. The intervention is fast-paced; the authors recommend that by the end of the first session, planning should have evolved regarding the areas of intervention, the method of intervention, and the sequence of both. History-taking constitutes most of the first session. The second session in the model focuses on the perpetrator's reactions to the first session and further development of the problem explanation. Bellak and Small suggest that improvement in the client should be noticeable by the third session and that termination should be briefly mentioned at this point. By the fourth session, the client is often worse, as previous problem development, separation anxiety, and other difficulties are encountered. The fifth session is composed of summarizing and termination. If the client is inappropriate for termination at that point, treatment may be continued as deemed necessary.

Gilliland's (Gilliland & James, 1993) six-step applied model of crisis intervention is divided into three listening activities (steps 1–3), and three action behaviors (steps 4–6). Gilliland stresses, however, that the worker utilizing this approach must be flexible. In step 1, *defining the problem*, the worker tries to comprehend the client's problem from their point of view by utilizing listening skills. The second step, *ensuring client safety*, helps the worker consider the danger to the client and others, not just at this point in time, but throughout treatment. At step three, *providing support*, the worker demonstrates their acceptance of the client in an unconditional and positive way. The fourth step of Gilliland's model stresses the *examination of alternatives*, in regard to resources within and outside of the client. The fifth step, *making plans*, continues naturally from step four as actions are taken to identify resources and strengthen the client's coping mechanisms. Finally, at the sixth and final step, *obtaining commitment*, the client accepts responsibility for handling the situation before termination takes place. Gilliland points out the need for the client to regain equilibrium throughout the process of the treatment (Gilliland & James, 1993, pp. 27–32).

While all of these approaches have merit and value to the field of crisis intervention with violent perpetrators, the most progressive therapists consider it wise to maintain an eclectic approach in their practice. As Gilliland and James note, "all people and all crises are unique and distinctive, and all people and all crises are similar" (1993, p. 22).

Working with Violent Perpetrators: The Hot Seat Method

One effective way of helping violent people is to help them see an issue from another point of view. This may be accomplished by assuming another person's view of that issue. In the hot seat approach, attributed largely to the work of Gestalt therapist Fritz Perls (1969) the client changes chairs as he or she changes identities. Let's look at this technique as it was used with Robert, a very violent twenty-seven-year-old Caucasian mugger who beats and torments his victims.

> CLIENT AS SELF (SITS IN CHAIR A): It makes me laugh at how scared them people get when I mug them. Some of them are bigger than me and they could probably hold their own but when they see me, they become wimps. I think it's pretty funny.
>
> CLIENT SWITCHES CHAIRS AND IS NOW A VICTIM: Yeah, it's pretty funny all right. It made me pee in my pants that's how funny it was.
>
> CLIENT AS SELF: What a wimp. You see? Just another scared chicken. Puck, puck, puck!
>
> CLIENT AS VICTIM: Listen you shit, who do you think you're calling a chicken? You have a gun and I don't. What's so brave about that?
>
> CLIENT AS SELF: If you weren't so stupid, you'd never let me get the draw on you. What were you doing in that dark alley anyway? [Chuckles to himself.]
>
> CLIENT AS VICTIM: It's you who's the chicken. It's you who needs the gun. Big brave mugger.
>
> CLIENT AS SELF: [Turns to therapist]: I don't like this game. I want to stop.
>
> THERAPIST: So who told you that you had to play the game?
>
> CLIENT: I don't know what you mean.
>
> THERAPIST: Nobody made you become a mugger, or did they?
>
> CLIENT: What are you talking about?
>
> THERAPIST: It's a game you play, mugging. No one made you do it or did they?
>
> CLIENT: I don't like this game at all.
>
> THERAPIST: Who made you become an angry, violent person, Robert? Tell that person how it feels to be a mugger.

Robert goes on to continue the role-play pointing out a series of vicious beatings he received from his father and other members of his family. He alludes to sexual abuse but doesn't come right out and admit it. He also speaks about long-term problems he has had containing his violent feelings and how he tends to be most violent when he's feeling insecure. He can't control his behavior anymore and feels that he's going down a black hole that will lead to death. He isn't sure that death isn't the best answer for him. This initial role-play was important in helping Robert begin the long and painful journey toward controlling his violent impulses, a process that took more than two years in prison before his therapist felt that he had even made a semblance of improvement. Robert is awaiting parole and until he's released, no one will know for sure how he will conduct himself in the community. In prison and in his work in and around the prison, he has become a model prisoner. Whether this will continue on as he faces the pressures of life away from the security of jail is anyone's guess.

Treatment Guidelines in Work with Violent Behavior

The following guidelines for treatment of violent offenders were reported by Glicken (1995) in a study of abused men. In the Glicken study, 400 social welfare workers were asked to develop guidelines for work with violent offenders. These are the guidelines they developed:

1. People who are violent often do not self-disclose easily. Their violence is embarrassing to them and they often want to deny that it even exits. Warm-up periods and false starts are likely to take place initially because many violent people (and men in particular) believe that therapy is feminizing and unmasculine.

2. Treatment may require a less direct path with considerable opportunity given to the violent client to brag, tell self-aggrandizing tales, and deny culpability in their violent behavior. But in time and with patience, most violent people reach a point where they are willing to self-disclose and work on change. Pollack (1990) says that therapists must learn to reach out to male clients, in particular, mindful of the man's need to "save face" in the process of self-disclosure and intimacy.

3. Because of prior abuse in their lives and because of the shame associated with their behavior, violent people do not bond easily and are generally suspicious of attempts to form relationships before they are emotionally ready. Do not assume an intimate therapeutic relationship with a violent client even when the client suggests that it exists. Violent people often live in an environment of distrust and are most fearful of getting hurt when they begin developing, almost against their will, the desire to trust the worker.

4. Violent people have seldom learned healthy outlets for their emotions and are often unable to discuss emotional difficulty. Consequently, emotions tend to build and may be released in treatment in torrents of anger and rage, often directed against the therapist. One goal of treatment may be to help the violent client learn to use language as a way of releasing rage before it contributes to violent behavior.

5. Violent people feel weak when they are forced to admit to being in pain, particularly emotional pain. Asking them to admit that they hurt will often be met by denial since they have learned that succumbing to pain often makes them feel weak.

6. Men will often try to manipulate female workers but, in the process, they may work hard to please and may make significant gain as a result. The same is often true of violent female offenders working with male workers.

7. While violent offenders may not want to talk about their emotional distress, they love to talk. Let them talk about anything, even things that may seem insignificant. In time, they will often indirectly bring up important issues in their lives for discussion relating to their violent behavior.

8. Because violence is such a disorderly behavior, violent people often need order in their lives. Structure therapy carefully so that it has a logical set of steps to achieve an end result with a predictable point in time when it will end.

9. Praise the violent client for their accomplishments. Keep the discussion on strengths and positive behavior. Most violent people have very low self-worth and may be reluctant to discuss negatives issues unless they feel they are operating from a positive emotional position.

10. Most violent people do not like to be categorized. Never use diagnostic terms with negative implications or the client will feel demeaned and resentful. This goes for all violent clients. The diagnostic category may be true but it certainly will not help the client to know it.

11. Treatment of violence may be most effective when it is offered in the client's natural environment (where he or she works, lives and plays). Furthermore, treatment offered when the client needs it rather than at times convenient for treatment personnel (evenings, weekends, holidays, and during moment of crisis) may be most useful to the client. Treating violence may require a completely different concept of when, where, and how we offer services.

12. Like everyone else, most violent people have intimacy needs that can be used in treatment by developing positive, affirming, and supportive relationships. Even though the perpetrator may have directed violence against loved ones (spouses, mates, children, and parents and relatives) this doesn't mean that they don't develop feelings of love or that they aren't saddened by their violent outbursts. These feelings of regret can be used in a positive way to develop goals in treatment that negate violence.

13. Not every violent person can benefit from talking therapy. Studies of violent perpetrators in domestic violence situations noted in Chapter 4 estimate that upwards of 70 percent of all domestic violence perpetrators can benefit from talking therapy. Thirty percent seem to be nonresponsive to treatment and may require institutionalization with attempts at therapy while institutionalized.

Case Study with Integrating Questions

Xavier Brown is a sixteen-year-old African American high school student who was arrested for beating a homeless man after Xavier had spent the day drinking with friends. He claims that he blacked out and that the next thing he remembered was being placed in the patrol car by a police officer. He has no memory of assaulting the homeless man. He says he comes from a religious family where violence isn't permitted. This is the third time in four months that Xavier has assaulted someone after a long bout of drinking. He is currently in a county juvenile detention facility where he is awaiting a nine-month placement in a residential facility specializing in the treatment of juvenile offenders with drug and alcohol problems.

There is a history of drinking problems in Xavier's family, although no one has been involved in violence. Xavier was introduced to liquor at the age of ten by an uncle and has been using it, with frequency, since he was thirteen. He says that he can go for weeks without a drink but then something happens and he just can't stop drinking. He doesn't understand the blackouts and is never sick after a bout of drinking. He doesn't know why he assaults people when he has been drinking. He considers himself to be a religious young man and he has a personal code that negates violence. He does well in school where he is seen as a quiet and respectful student earning average grades. He is a skilled athlete and many people at his high school think he has the ability to play major league baseball. His future seems bright except for his drinking and the violence it seems to precipitate.

One of the authors of this book was field liaison to the juvenile court forensic (mental health) unit, a division of the county mental health department and unaffiliated with the juvenile court. The presence of mental health in juvenile court is unpopular with court personnel, but it is required to meet state law that offenders with emotional problems be provided mental health services while incarcerated. The field liaison met with the graduate social work student carrying the case and his supervisor, a licensed clinical social worker. Xavier has been seen three times in four months by the student because of arrests for assault in conjunction with his drinking. Since the relationship between the forensic unit and the probation department is strained, plans are made for Xavier that often fail to include the recommendation of treatment personnel.

The liaison wondered why Xavier blacks out and then commits crimes rather than passes out the way many people do when they have too much to drink, but the supervisor believes that this is common among many adolescent alcoholics and that it is the way many of them came into the juvenile justice system—the student feels that Xavier may have some other problems, perhaps neurological in nature. Xavier was hit by a car at age seven while walking across the street. He spent a number of weeks in the hospital. Xavier has no memory of the event and since he was living with grandparents out of state, the entire affair is sketchy. It raises the issue, however, of minimal organic brain damage and the possibility that the blackouts may be more the result of a neurological problem induced by alcohol and less the result of alcohol addiction.

The graduate social work student feels that the placement in a drug and alcohol facility is a mistake without first doing a complete medical workup. But since the decision to place Xavier is the authority of the probation officer who has never actually met Xavier and who carries a caseload of 200 juvenile offenders, the student has accepted that the forensic unit is there to calm violent offenders while in the juvenile detention facility and not to actually do any meaningful treatment or to be involved in discharge planning. As the graduate student said when the conference ended, "Dr. Glicken, these people think social work is a joke. They figure the only way to treat offenders is to be even meaner than the juvenile. I don't know, but it seems to me Xavier's going to kill someone soon with his blackouts and here I am trying to warn people and no one wants to listen."

Integrative Questions
1. Why would there be such animosity between the mental health department (forensic unit) and the probation department?
2. Do you think the two approaches—mental health and probation—have very different philosophies in the treatment of violent behavior? What do you think those differences might be?
3. How do you feel about the issue of people blacking out after drinking and then committing crimes for which they have no memory? Do you think it actually happens or do you think it's just a way of manipulating the legal system by removing blame for violent behavior from the perpetrator and restating the cause of violence as medical in nature?
4. In addition to neurological reasons for blacking out, are there other medical/psychological reasons to explain selective amnesia in the commission of a crime?
5. The graduate student is opposed to sending Xavier to a facility treating substance abuse and thinks the client needs a complete physical workup before any treatment decision is made. Do you agree with this assessment? What if a neurological problem were found—doesn't Xavier still have a substance abuse problem that needs to be treated?

In this chapter, we have included the most prominent approaches to the treatment of perpetrators of violence. We have not included chemical treatments, some of which may be found in Chapter 6. However, we should point out that much more research needs to be done on the treatment of violence and that other than behavior modification and the cognitive approaches, all too little is known about the effectiveness of treating violent perpetrators using traditional techniques of the talking therapies.

REFERENCES

Adams, D. (1988). Counseling men who batter: A profeminist analysis of five treatment models. In K. Yllo and M. Bograd (Eds.), *Feminist perspectives on wife abuse* (pp. 176–199). Newbury Park, CA: Sage.

Allen, J., & Laird, J. (1993). Tales of the absent father: Applying the "story" metaphor in family therapy. *Family Process, 32*(4), 441–458.

Bagley, C. (1990). Development of a measure of unwanted sexual contact in childhood, for use in community mental health surveys. *Psychological Reports, 66,* 401–402.

Beck, A. T. (1976). *Cognitive therapy and emotional disorders.* New York: International University Press.

Bellak, L., & Small, L. (1978). *Emergency psychotherapy and brief psychotherapy.* New York: Grune & Stratton.

Bernard, J. L., & Bernard, M. L. (1984). The abusive male seeking treatment: Jekyll and Hyde. *Family Relations, 33,* 543–547.

Brannon, R. C. (1976). No "sissy stuff": The stigma of anything vaguely feminine. In S. Sailid, and R. Brannon (Eds.), *The forty-nine percent majority.* Reading, MA: Addison-Wesley.

Brooks, M. (1994, July 17). Interview in Cuernavaca, Morelos, Mexico.

Caplan, G. (1961). *An approach to community mental health.* New York: Grune & Stratton.

Caplan, G. (1964). *Principles of preventive psychiatry.* New York: Basic Books.

Caplan, G. (1974). *Support systems and community mental health.* New York: Behavioral Publications.

Carlson, K. A. (1990). A personality test for Spanish-literate offenders: The Psicologico Texto. *Journal of Offender Rehabilitation, 16.*

Chafetz, J. (1979). *Masculine/feminine or human.* Ithica, IL: Peacock.

DeMaris, A. (1989, March). Attrition in batterers' counseling: The role of social and demographic factors. *Social Service Review.*

Deschner, J. P., McNeil, J. S., & Moore, M. G. (1986). A treatment model for batterers. *Social Casework, 67*(5).

Dewhurst, A. M., Moore, R. J., & Alfano, D. P. (1992). Aggression against women by men: Sexual and spousal assault. *Journal of Offender Rehabilitation, 18.*

Driscoll, J. M., Meyer, R. G., & Shanie, C. F. (1973). Training police in family crisis intervention. *Journal of Applied Behavioral Science.*

Dodge, K. A., Bates, J. E., & Peteit, G. S. (1990). Mechanisms in the cycle of violence. *Science, 28.*

Dodge, K. A., & Richard, B. A. (1986) Peer perceptions, aggression and peer relations. In Pryor and Day (Eds.), *The development of social cognition* (pp. 35–58). New York: Springler-Verlag.

Duluth Domestic Abuse Intervention Project. (1983). *Hamline Law Review, 6,* 247–275.

Dutton, D. G., & Edelson, J. L. (1986). The outcome for court mandated treatment for wife assault: A quasi-experimental evaluation. *Violence and Victims, 1*(86), 163–175.

Eisikovits, Z. C., & Edelson, J. L. (1989, September). Intervening with men who batter: A critical review of the literature. *Social Service Review.*

Ellis, A. (1962). *Reason and emotion in psychotherapy.* New York: Lyle Stuart.

Feazell, C. S., Mayers, R. S., & Deschner, J. (1984). Services for men who batter: Implications for programs and policies. *Family Relations, 33,* 217–223.

Franklin, A. J. (1992). Therapy with African American men. *Families in Society, 73.*

Gilliland, B., & James, R. (1993). *Crisis intervention strategies.* Pacific Grove, CA: Brooks/Cole.

Glicken, M. (1991, October). *Resolving male problems in therapy.* Social Work Board of Clinical Examiners Annual Meeting. Washington, DC.

Glicken, M. (1995). *Abusive men: A research report.* Unpublished Monograph.

Goff, C. (1994, July 23). Interview in Cuernavaca, Morelos, Mexico.

Golan, N. (1978). *Treatment in crisis situations.* New York: The Free Press.

Harris, J. (1986). Counselling violent couples using Walker's model. *Psychotherapy, 23.*

Harrison, J., Chien, J., & Ficarratto, T. (1989). Warning: Masculinity may be dangerous to your health. In M. Kimmel and M. Messner, *Men's lives.* New York: MacMillan.

Jouard, S., & Landsman, M. (1969). Cognition and the "didactic effect": Men's self-disclosing behavior. *Merrill-Palmer Quarterly, 6,* 176–184.

Korner, I. M. (1973). Crisis reduction and the psychological consultant. In G. A. Spector and W. L. Claiborn (Eds.), *Crisis intervention.* New York: Behavioral Books.

Lerman, L. (1984). A model state act: Remedies for domestic abuse. *Harvard Journal on Legislation*, *21.*

Linquist, C. U., & Telch, C. F. (1984). Violent versus nonviolent couples: A comparison of patterns. *Psychotherapy, 21.*

Linquist, C. U., Telch, C. F., & Taylor, J. (1983). Evaluation of conjugal violence treatment programs: A pilot study. *Behavioral Counseling and Community Intervention, 3.*

Longress, J., & Bailey, R. (1979, January). Men's issues and sexism: A journal review. *Social Work, 26–32.*

Los Angeles Times. (1994, August 11). Domestic violence.

Mawson, A. R. (1999). Stimulation-induced behavioral inhibition: A new model for understanding physical violence. *Integrative Physiological & Behavioral Science, 34(3),* 21.

Mirande, A. (1977). The Chicano family: A reanalysis of conflicting views. *Journal of Marriage and the Family, 39,* 747–756.

Mulvey, E. P., & Repucci, M. D. (1981). Police crisis intervention training: An empirical investigation. *American Journal of Community Psychology, 9.*

Nedig, P. H., Friedman, D. H., & Collins, B. S. (1985). Domestic conflict containment: A spousal abuse treatment program. *Social Casework, 66.*

O'Neil, J. M. (1981). Patterns of gender role conflict in: Sexism and fear of femininity in men's lives. *Personnel and Guidance Journal, 60.*

Osherson, S., & Krugman, S. (1990). Men, shame and psychotherapy. *Psychotherapy, 27.*

Osherman, S. (1986). *Finding our fathers: The unfinished business of manhood.* New York: The Free Press.

Pagelow, M. D. (1984). *Family violence.* New York: Praeger.

Parad, H. J. (1971). Crisis intervention. In R. Morris (Ed.), *Encyclopedia of social work* (16th issue, 1). New York: NASW.

Perls, F. (1969). *Ego, hunger and aggression.* New York: Random House.

Pirog-Good, M. A., & Stets, J. (1986). Programs for abusers: Who drops out and what can be done. *Response, 9(2).*

Pollack, W. (1990). Men's development and psychotherapy. *Psychotherapy, 27.*

Rapoport, L. (1970). Crisis intervention as a mode of brief treatment. In R. Roberts, & R. Nee (Eds.), *Theories of social casework.* Chicago: University of Chicago Press.

Robertson, J., & Fitzgerald, L. (1990). The mistreatment of men: Effects of client gender role and life style on diagnosis and attrition on pathology. *Journal of Counseling Psychology, 37(1),* 3–9.

Rosenbaum, A. (1986). Group treatment for abusive men. Process and outcome. *Psychotherapy, 23(4).*

Rosenbaum, A., & Hoge, S. K. (1989). Head injuries and martial aggression. American *Journal of Psychiatry, 146,* 1048–1051.

Rosenfeld, A. (1972). Why men die younger. *Readers Digest,* 121– 124.

Roth, J. A., & Moore, M. H. (1995, October). Reducing violent crimes and intentional injuries. *NIJ Research in Action.*

Roy, M. (Ed.). (1982). *The abusive partner: An analysis of domestic battering.* New York: Van Nostrand Reinhold.

Sakai, C. E. (1991, November). Group intervention strategies with domestic abusers. *Families in Society.*

Salgado, N. (1994, July 22). Interview in Mexico City, Mexico.

Scher, E., & Stevens, M. (1985). Men and violence. *Journal of Counselling and Development, 65.*

Scher, M. (1990). Effect of gender role incongruencies on men's experiences as clients in psychotherapy. *Psychotherapy, 27,* 322–326.

Schuerger, J. M., & Reigle, N. (1988). Personality and biographic data that characterize men who abuse their wives. *Journal of Clinical Psychology, 44(1).*

Sherman, L. W., & Berk, R. A. (1984). The specific deterrent effects of arrest for domestic assault. *American Sociological Review, 49,* 261–272.

Sonkin, D., Martin, D., & Walker, L. (1985). *The male batterer: A treatment approach*. New York: Springer.

Snyder, R. (1994, July 19). Interview in Cuernavaca, Morelos, Mexico.

Straus, M. A. (1978). Sexual inequality, cultural norms, and wife beating. *Victimology: An International Journal, 1*, 54–70.

Taylor, J. W. (1984). Structured conjoint therapy for spouse abuse cases. *Social Casework, 65*.

Tiller, P. (1967). Parental role division and the child's personality. In E. Dahlstrom (Ed.), *Changing roles of men and women*. Boston: Beacon.

Tollman, R. M., Beeman, S., & Mendoza, C. (1987, July). The effectiveness of a shelter sponsored program for men who batter, preliminary results. Paper presented the Third National Conference on Family Violence Research, Durham, New Hampshire.

Widon, C. S. (1989). Does violence beget violence? A critical evaluation of the literature. *Psychology Bulletin, 106*, 3–28.

Waldo, M. (1987). Also victims: Understanding and treating men arrested for spousal abuse. *Journal of Counselling and development, 65*.

Waldron, I., & Johnson, S. (1976, September). Why do women live longer than men? *Journal of Human Stress*.

Wiederholt, I. C. (1992). The psychodynamics of sex offenses and implications for treatment. *The Haworth Press, 18*, 19–24.

Will, G. F. (2001, July 9). *Newsweek*, p. 68.

Williams, O. J. (1992). Ethnically sensitive practice to enhance treatment participation of African American men who batter. *Families in Society, 73*.

Wolpe, J. (1958). *Psychotherapy of reciprocal inhibitions*. Stanford, CA: Stanford University Press.

PART III

In Part III of the book, we consider the ways in which America has attempted to cope with violence through the use of a number of sometimes controversial programs. We will discuss the future and why we believe that violence, reportedly in decline for the past eight years, will once again show signs of serious growth.

In Chapter 11, we discuss the many attempts to reduce rates of violence through special programs in the community, in residential treatment, and through attempts to redistribute resources to those most at risk of becoming violent offenders. We also discuss more recent attempts to reduce crime through three strike laws, longer prison sentences, and more prisons. These recent programs have often been thought to be the reason that crime and violent crime have fallen dramatically in the past few years. As we will note in Chapter 11, however, the decline in crime rates have not been related to comparable declines in fear of crime or in reports of crimes by perpetrators. Quite simply, we do not believe that violence has decreased. Rather, we believe that it will increase in the coming few years.

In Chapter 12, we present a scenario for the future that includes a dramatic increase in violent crime. We believe that declines in reported rates of violence have leveled off and that there are indications of increased violence in many areas of the country and, particularly, among youthful offenders. We also believe that many of our institutions, but particularly the mass media, have made violence such a primary subject that even small children are inundated with violent messages. In Chapter 12, we present an argument for what needs to be done to prevent dramatic increases in violent crimes. We believe that too little is being done to prevent serious harm to children. These troubled, abused, and neglected children form a large part of the population of violent perpetrators who act out their own abuse on others. We also think that punitive laws, including those laws that place many nonviolent people in jail for life after three prison sentences, result in increasing numbers of jails and prisons that threaten other important institutions —education, for example. We think the sevenfold increase in the number of prisons in America since 1969 has becomes economically burdensome. We also believe that prisons have little rehabilitative value and do little to reduce the potential for violent behavior. Many of our prisons are little more than warehouses with few resources to help perpetrators cope with substance abuse problems or anger management. The result will be a massive infusion of violent people into the society as a poor economy is unable to sustain the cost of running so many newly built jails and prisons.

We hope that we are wrong, but terrorism is increasingly a threat to the

United States. We believe that it will have a long-term negative effect on the economy. Lower employment and safety concerns that limit travel and needed opportunities to relax may result in increased domestic violence and child abuse. The cycle of violence will continue, we fear, unless we put our minds and hearts together to resolve violence as a growing way of life in the United States.

11 Societal Responses to Violence

People familiar with the problems of crime and violence in American society generally agree that solutions do not lie solely in the use of increased law enforcement and prison space. Even with the advent of three strikes laws designed to incarcerate serious offenders for long periods, most offenders are not deterred by the prospect of a prison sentence, and they often come out worse than they went in.

Increased arrests, harsher sentencing, more prison space, or more police officers on the streets will not have a long-term deterrent effect if violent and aggressive individuals cannot receive needed help or find satisfaction through legitimate alternatives in society. These problems are often deeply rooted social problems that will not yield to simplistic notions of punishment. Without the help of their family and/or the community, and without addressing social problems emanating from poor schools, unemployment, poverty, and racial discrimination, there is little likelihood that significant progress will be made against crime or violence. Young men and women without resources, and possibly violating the law, require well-rounded, community-based programs that will assist them in growth at home, in school, and in finding and financing training for jobs. This is especially true as available jobs increasingly require technical skills that can only be provided by a concerned society.

To manage the problem of violence in the United States, a variety of responses, approaches, or solutions must be pursued. Certainly, for many adult and juvenile violent offenders, incarceration away from society is the best answer, sometimes for a long time, particularly where public safety is at issue. There is evidence, however, that many programs for youthful violent and adult offenders work well when using a period of incarceration followed by closely supervised community follow-up. For adults, various approaches such as anger management and domestic violence counseling are useful. Rosenberg (1995) sees the need for a radical shift in our ways of thinking about violence that emphasizes primary prevention. People must think in terms of solutions, such as providing shelters for battered women and their children, in an effort to prevent further violence. This chapter will explore solutions targeted at individual behavior as well as those that involve broader social policies.

Absent of professional expertise, political or policy-driven solutions may be lacking in effectiveness. Professionals often get frustrated in their efforts to get the attention of policy makers. For example, Jeffrey, Myers, and Wollan (1991) argue that drug addictions and violence can be prevented and treated: "We should focus our attention on the 5 percent who become career criminals with a history of violence and drug/alcohol abuse. We should also focus on early childhood and developmental factors. Age birth to six is the time to prevent crime, not age 15 to 18" (p. 5). They note that the law often prohibits early intervention by not allowing compulsory treatment, while demanding compulsory punishment. Breakthroughs in modern genetics and biotechnology have opened up new possibilities for intervention, coupled with a concern for the legal and ethical issues involved. Even the prediction of dangerousness may be possible.

This chapter offers a range of potential solutions to the problems of violence in the United States, ranging across social policy and community responses to violence, efforts at prevention, and specific programs designed to work with individuals who have committed a violent act. Informed policy solutions require that a broad range of options be developed, from long-term incarceration of dangerous individuals to very dedicated efforts to work with early juvenile aggressiveness and violent behaviors. The authors suggest that within this framework, individuals, adults, and juveniles who become involved in violent behavior of many kinds can often be managed through sound human services approaches operated by trained professionals. Since a major concern is early intervention with juveniles, several approaches to the management of aggressive and/or violent youth are discussed. The chapter begins by looking at a community and concludes with a case study of a juvenile who might have benefited greatly from some type of intensive, focused intervention.

Prevention: A Proactive Approach to Violence

While individuals must be held accountable for their actions, society has a responsibility to these individuals, but especially to its citizens to prevent and control violent behavior and its consequences. Efforts to prevent violence may target the individual, his or her family, community initiatives, and the attitudes and values expressed in society generally. As discussed in the following sections, California's Lungren Commission Report (1995) outlines three areas of prevention: primary, secondary, and tertiary:

> *Primary prevention* fosters and maintains healthy individuals, families and communities . . . *Secondary prevention* intervenes with individuals, families, and communities to address the attitudes, behaviors, conditions and environments that place them at risk of violence or expose them to violence . . . *Tertiary prevention* targets violent populations and their victims to reduce or prevent the risk of continued violence through treatment or determent.

An integrated approach to understanding and preventing violence was presented in the same year in a report issued by Rosenberg (1995), a physician and director of the National Center for Injury Prevention at the Centers for Disease Control and Prevention. He states that methods to reduce violence requires the:

> determination of causation and risk factors to shed light on the patterns of violence and the effects on subgroups . . . targeted programs aimed at specific high-risk populations . . . youth violence intervention programs must focus on young children and their parents, often children themselves, to prompt appropriate changes in knowledge, skills, and attitudes. (p. 102)

In order to address the problem scientifically, Rosenberg developed categories of violence that can be used to determine common patterns. These included self-directed violence (e. g., suicides), interpersonal violence (sexual assault, robbery), drug-related violence, group or gang violence, domestic violence, child abuse, and elder abuse (p. 103). Using these categories and related definitions, underlying patterns of violence since 1968 were assessed. For example, since 1988 the perpetrators and victims of homicide have been getting younger, and we are faced with the problem of children killing children. Once such a pattern is found it can be addressed.

Rosenberg maintains that it is necessary to identify these patterns to begin to develop effective methods of prevention and intervention. We can determine the types of programs needed to address specific problems within specific groups in society. For example, since many parents are not far from being children themselves, they will need training in child rearing that will teach coping skills designed to avoid frustration and aggressive responses. Also, peer mediation in schools is an intervention that can assist in violence reduction. And, mentoring programs that provide positive role models to youth can help the mentor as well as the recipient.

While the CDC has initiated youth violence prevention programs at sixteen sites nationally, it is costly and takes time to do the research necessary to determine successes. This frustration with solutions often yields to a "learn-as-we-go" approach that uses available techniques and evaluates them in a learning context. Most important, however, is asking the right questions: What is the problem? Why is it happening? What works? How do you implement a plan? The goal of succeeding sections is to provide a sampling of the types of programs that have been tried, and the approaches that appear to have the most success with juveniles and adults involved in aggressive and/or violent behavior.

Community/Societal Responses to Violence

The California Response

Responses to the problems of crimes of violence vary by state and local jurisdictions. Recent increases in violent crime in Los Angeles have local officials quite concerned, especially with the news that violent crime has been dropping nationally:

> Alarmed by a sharp rise in violent crime, Los Angeles Police Chief Bernard C. Parks huddled with top LAPD officials Monday on how to arrest a trend that has pushed homicides up 23.5 percent so far this year . . . murder, rape, robbery, and aggravated assault jumped 10.9 percent in the city from Jan. 1 to August 19 compared to the same period a year ago. (Rabin & Newton, 2000)

Chief Parks indicated that most of the additional crimes were committed by fourteen- to twenty-four-year-olds during the evening hours in certain areas of the city, and speculation was that relatively more murders than assaults were recorded because of the increased use of weapons. The questionable aspect of the debate is how effective the police can be in preventing violence. Street murders are "repressible" but not those that occur in homes. These types of increases again raise questions about both individual and broad scale societal approaches to the problem of violent crime.

As have many states and localities, two California commissions were formed to address the problems of crime and violence and make recommendations about the types of responses that are needed. These two reports, which were produced in 1982 and 1995, reviewed what is known about the causes of violent crime and advance proposals for attacking the problem in California. Their findings are relevant to the problem throughout the United States. The 1982 report (hereafter called the Roden Commission Report) addressed topics such as parenting, early childhood development and family violence, economic factors and institutional racism, schools and educational factors, biochemical factors, biological factors, parent-infant bonding, violence and the media, sexual violence, government and violence, and youth gang violence. Recommendations are made throughout.

The Roden Commission Report, completed in 1982, begins with the admonition that most current approaches to violence address its symptoms, and in doing so, accept the inevitability of a certain amount of violence in society. The report concludes that the United States ranks as most violent among western, industrialized democracies; however, it states that the problem can be confronted. Certain negative aspects of our social and cultural condition encourage violence "which, when identified, can be remedied. At the least we can begin to take scientifically-grounded action *to prevent* violence" (p. 1).

An important conclusion by the Roden Commission was specific to the U.S. Attorney General's 1981 report to the nation in the Task Force on Violent Crime, which stated that the wave of serious, violent crime reflects a breakdown of the social order, not the legal order. The Roden Commission (1982) responded that while it supported efforts to improve the effectiveness of the criminal justice system:

> The criminal justice system is not, cannot be, the loving parent to our children, the teacher of humane values, nor the leveler of economic inequities. Thus, short-term

approaches to bolster the criminal justice system must be combined with long-range efforts to eliminate the root causes of violence. (p. 2)

This statement is consistent with the conclusions reached by law enforcement and behavior science experts (see Douglas & Olshaker, 1995; Greenwood, Model, Rydell, & Chisea, 1996). The Roden Commission confined itself to issues of interpersonal violence, rather than large-scale social violence, although noting some of the inherent dangers in focusing only on the individual who acts violently rather than examining environmental influences.

Understanding these dangers was seen as important for the purpose of developing a societal response to violent behavior. The first danger lies in not understanding the total social, historical, and cultural context of the individual's life, or the environmental influences that might lead to an understanding of the causes of the violence. Another danger, on the opposite side, is that by addressing environmental influences on behavior individual responsibility may be discouraged, that is, individuals may not be seen as accountable for their actions. The focus of the Roden report was on the interaction between individual and environmental factors. The report contains a section on Californians working together to prevent violence.

Synopsis of the Roden Report

The family was seen as critical to personal development because it structures and "determines the nature and quality of subsequent social relations" (Roden, p. 6). Related to, and flowing from a poor family environment was their conclusion that "lack of self-esteem, negative or criminal self-image, and feelings of distrust and personal powerlessness are prevalent among violent offenders and highly recidivistic criminals" (p. 6). Certainly the profilers (Douglas & Olshaker, 1995; Ressler & Shachtman, 1992) would agree that an attempt to regain or assert power is inherent in almost all crimes of violence.

The report further highlights findings that lead to aggression and violence, noting that the family is the first and critical area of training in the values, rules, attitudes and skills necessary for forming sound social relations with others. Short of stating a clear cause-and-effect relationship, a strong association was found between rejection, abuse, and lack of love and affection as key elements in producing violent individuals, especially childhood physical abuse and parental neglect. Methods of discipline that do not involve corporal punishment are seen as more effective in reducing aggressive consequences.

Economic factors and institutional racism are cited as factors in higher arrest rates for violence within some minority groups. Links between race and socioeconomic status exist. Denial of participation in "mainstream American life, economically and politically" (p. 10) can lead to alienation and feelings of powerlessness that may manifest themselves in violent reactions.

School crime and fear of crime was addressed in the report, but lacked the depth of analysis available with current reporting systems. The need for clearly defined and enforced rules was linked to issues of perceived fairness in the schools. School failure may result from the perceived (or real) lack of upward mobility through education. Issues of diet and drugs were also addressed in the report, as were the influence of biological factors. Other themes were addressed, such as the influence of the media on violent behavior, youth gang violence, governmental violence, and sexual violence. The typology of the rapist that is used describes three basic components: "power, anger and sexuality . . . either power or anger dominates. . . [rape] is the use of sexuality to express power and anger" (p. 16).

The social policy recommendations of the report cover the areas described above. Great emphasis is placed on the training of family members in child rearing, even suggesting a course in parenting prior to issuance of a marriage license. Early intervention for troubled families is recommended, including promulgation of methods of nonviolent resolution to family conflicts and reduced use of corporal punishment. Many of these goals are designed to reduce "the risk that aggressive, combative attitudes and values espoused by parents may encourage aggressive behavior on the part of their children"(p. 27). Methods for reducing spousal abuse and related sexist attitudes are provided. Recommendations are also provided in the other areas of concern: school violence, drugs and biochemical factors, biological factors, violence and the media, sexual violence, and gang violence. These types of recommendations seem quite sensible and are reiterated in other reports of this type.

The Lungren Report

The second California report on violence prevention was produced in 1995 by the Policy Council on Violence Prevention under the direction of Attorney General Lungren (1995). Other than a brief chapter on contributing factors to violence, this report did not explore the causes of violence to any great extent. And, consistent with the life of commission reports, no significant mention was made of the 1982 (Roden) report or its recommendations. However, considerable attention was given to national increases in violence rates. Violence was defined as the "threatened or actual use of physical force or power against another person, against oneself, or against a group or community that either results in, or has a high likelihood of resulting in injury, death, or deprivation" (p. 63). From an individual perspective, it was seen as learned behavior that emanated from "a complex array of factors" (p. 51). These factors included media, firearms, alcohol, corporate promotion (media, sales, sports), poverty, hopelessness and isolation, educational decline, lack of responsibility, and mental health problems, including biological and physical causes.

Solutions proposed in the Lungren report were based on its approach to prevention stated earlier. Specific goals range from the adoption of violence-free values in society to strength-based approaches to community building. Asset- or strength-based models or approaches appear to represent a recent attempt to package behavior modification techniques in a way that avoids the negative aspect of aversive conditioning. Reinforcement of positive behavior is emphasized rather than punishment of negative behavior. The paradigm shift is to look at positive approaches to improving communities, youth, and families, rather than just assessing risks and punishing offenders. Society must reinforce areas of individual and community competence. Individuals should be empowered to help themselves, and individuals should be treated as resources rather than problems, especially youth (p. 65).

Ten major common ground initiatives were presented by the council. Most of these are general goals and are followed by individual chapters stating specific initiatives, or "recommendations for action" in each area. Most of the recommendations are not unique and were addressed in the 1982 (Roden) report. A more useful goal for the council would have been to assess the progress made in the ensuing twelve years to implement the initiatives outlined in the 1982 report. In fact, many major reports have been produced in the areas addressed. These include reports by the Berkeley Media Studies Group (Dorfman & Schiraldi, 2001), which is concerned with the exaggerations of violent crime in the media that drive crime policy, especially for juveniles.

The Management of Juvenile Violence

In their call for action in combating juvenile violence and delinquency, the Office of Juvenile Justice and Delinquency Prevention (OJJDP) made a profound prediction in 1996: "Demographic experts predict that juvenile arrests for violent crimes will more than double by the year 2010, given population growth projections and trends in juvenile arrest over the past several decades" (p. 1). While these projections did not materialize by 1998, with the juvenile violent crime index reaching its lowest level in ten years in 1998, 30 percent below the peak year of 1994 (Snyder, 1999), the projected increases in juveniles in the violent crime-prone age group suggests that this projection may yet materialize. As pointed out in Chapter 7, there is cause for concern: "The proportion of juvenile murders that involved a juvenile offender increased from 21 percent in 1980 to 33 percent in 1994, the peak year for all murders by juveniles" (Bilchik, 1999a). A recent report on juvenile crime trends notes that "despite a decrease in murders of teens (25 percent . . . from 1991–1997), homicide remains a leading cause of death for juveniles . . . juvenile violent crime continues to be of concern to the general public" (Criminal Justice Research Reports, 2000).

The OJJDP report suggests that there is hope for managing juvenile violence and delinquency, in that only about one-half of one percent of youth are arrested for violent crimes each year. Several approaches are suggested, which are delineated below.

To some extent, societies have always feared their young. The problem of youthful aggression and violence has been a concern in America since the first days of the juvenile court in 1899. Violent and aggressive juveniles are a pervasive problem in schools and in the communities in which they live. Fagan (1990) states that the debate about what to do with juveniles, especially those who are violent, is ongoing, with complex social and policy implications. This policy debate affects the way these youth are treated at home, in their schools, and in the juvenile court. Should these youth be given the benefit of a benevolent juvenile court, with programs of treatment and rehabilitation, or should due process and retributive approaches be emphasized (see Fagan, 1990)? Judicial waiver to transfer violent youth under age eighteen to trial in adult court has increased in many states, some as low as fourteen years of age. In the heat of the debate, questions were raised about the effectiveness of programs of rehabilitation in the face of concerns about rising juvenile violence rates, and many people feel that incarceration is the best, if not the only, solution to the problem. Evidence of this attitude can be found in the vote (by proposition) in California in 1999 to increase juvenile detention space yet not lower the approval factor for voter approval of new schools.

Citing the uneven quality of past research on program effectiveness, Fagan (1990) has summarized recent empirical evidence on effective interventions for juvenile offenders, much of which is supported by the OJJDP action plan for combating violence and delinquency published six years later. The programs cited were generally "small, community-based projects with intensive supervision and reintegration efforts . . . studied in a variety of correctional populations, in diverse areas of the country, and in varying social and economic contexts" (Fagan, 1990, p. 95).

Institutionalization was not found to have better results than nonincarcerative, community-based programs, although successes were not always as great as hoped. A problem with many of the studies, however, was that they did not often separate the effects of treatment of violent youth and youth involved in other types of crime. This situation was confirmed in California when one of the authors (Sechrest) did a study of violent youth recidivists in fifty-eight California counties for the California Assembly. With the support of the Chief Probation Officers of California, all fifty-eight counties were asked to supply data on programs for violent offenders. Only one responded with such a study. Just a few could, or would, provide data on their serious, violent juvenile offender population. No reasons were given for this lack of information, although with cutbacks in services it is possible that most offenders are considered serious and discriminations are difficult to make.

Fagan (1990) documented the results of the Violent Juvenile Offender (VJO) program, which confirmed the relationship of therapeutic integrity to recidivism; that is, programs that were well-implemented produced lower recidivism rates. Conducted in urban juvenile courts in four states for youth identified as violent by virtue of their crimes (completed or attempted homicide, aggravated assault, armed robbery, and forcible rape), the crux of the effort was to address treatment needs in the critical months after their return to the community, when most failures occur. Experimental and control groups were used. Where there was strong program implementation, lower rearrest rates were found and time at risk before rearrest increased. Conclusions from the VJO study were that:

> the social integration factors that initiate or maintain delinquency may be unrelated to its cessation . . . Intervention had little discernable effects on the social indicators of school, work, or family, nor did it strengthen the social bonds thought

to be part of the etiology of delinquency. Yet there were indications of reduced re-cidivism for experimental youths. Accordingly, there is reason to believe that some aspects of program participation may have contributed to these effects, though without significantly altering the social status or social integration of the partici-pants. (Fagan, 1990, p. 100)

What then, did work? Consistent with evidence from earlier "classic" studies, the consistency of support over a long period of time appears to be critical. The VJO and Serious and Violent Juvenile Offenders (SVJ) reports are discussed in Chapter 7, inclusive of the predictors of SVJ. These themes are reiterated here from the OJJDP summaries of these approaches in 1998 and the 1999 OJJDP report to Con-gress on juvenile violence research (Bilchik, 1998, 1999b).

Treating Violent Juveniles

Alexander (2000) provides a chapter on the treatment of juvenile offenders that addresses several problems of juveniles. A principal concern is violent behavior because, along with substance abuse, it is one of the greatest concerns in looking at youthful behavior. He cites the need for specialized programs for African Amer-ican males, and notes that treatment may be more successful with youth who commit violent acts as the result of disputes against relatives or peers. Several spe-cific approaches are discussed as to their application; however, most professionals (91 percent) who work with aggressive and/or violent youth use techniques that address anger or aggression management.

Alexander (p. 216) notes several points that should concern the professional involved in the treatment of violent juveniles. These include a determination of (1) the best setting for treatment, (2) the safest and most effective treatment that will decrease the juvenile's violent impulses, (3) which systems are necessary to the process (family, school, etc.), and (4) interventions appropriate to comorbid con-ditions, and whether these interventions can be applied in the residential setting used. Following Cornell, Benedek, and Benedek (1987), specific typologies of ju-venile murderers are presented: psychotic (mental disorder), conflict (parental, gang disputes), and crime-related. As noted above, the best candidates for treat-ment are seen as juveniles whose offense has resulted from a situation of conflict.

Hospitalization or long-term residential care is recommended in order to shield the juvenile from society's enmity, to help the youth understand his or her behavior, and to teach new coping skills for stress and anger. Aggression Re-placement Training (ART), as developed by Goldstein and Glick (1996), is recom-mended for professionals working with aggressive children including teachers, counselors, social workers, and child-care workers. ART consists of three compo-nents: skillstreaming, anger control, and moral education, each taught weekly.

Skillstreaming involves the teaching of fifty skills characteristic of prosocial be-haviors . . . [in] six areas . . . These skills are taught in group counseling [groups of] about six to eight juveniles [through] modeling, role-playing, performance feedback, and transfer training. (Alexander, 2002, p. 217)

Anger control techniques developed by others are incorporated into ART in a ten-week period designed to teach responses to anger-provoking incidents. Principles of moral education stress the development of an increased sense of justice, fairness, and concern for other's rights. However, Goldstein and Glick do not see this aspect as effective in reducing aggressive behaviors without the skills training.

Alexander also describes the somewhat different approach of Varley (1984) as an appropriate method for working with aggressive juveniles. This approach appears to rely more on positive and negative reinforcement to accelerate the development of prosocial behaviors. Alexander devotes an entire section of his text to behavioral theories and related therapies. As noted, these types of therapies are now beginning to appear under the rubric of strength-based approaches, probably to avoid the stigma of punishment. These are sometimes called "cultural competence" programs for minorities. They can result in strength-based courts, such as the drug courts used mostly with adults. Successful programs of "contingency management," or the pairing of a reward (often a token) with desired behavior, are described (Alexander, 2000, p. 77).

Unfortunately, the effectiveness of programs for aggressive and violent offenders have been mixed. However, Greenwood, Model, Rydell, and Chiesa (1996) document successful programs directed at prevention and early intervention, most of which involved working with families. They cite Lipsey's (1992) meta-analysis of more than four hundred juvenile program evaluations that:

> found that behavioral, skill-oriented, and multi-modal methods produced the largest effects, while some methods actually produced negative effects, such as deterrence programs [like] "shock incarceration" and "scared-straight" techniques . . . Positive effects were larger in community rather than institutional settings. (p. 13)

This study found that the mean "effect of treatment" in comparison with untreated control groups was to reduce recidivism by 5 percent. In an update of this analysis using two hundred studies, Lipsey, Wilson, and Cothern (2000) addressed effective intervention for serious juvenile offenders by asking two questions: (1) can intervention programs reduce recidivism rates among serious delinquents, and if so, (2) what types of programs are most effective?

For this new database, Lipsey et al. (2000) examined 200 experimental or quasiexperimental intervention studies for noninstitutionalized and institutionalized serious offenders. The majority of the adjudicated delinquents were involved in person or property crimes or other more serious delinquent acts. Subjects were largely male, mostly white or of "mixed" ethnicity, with an average age of fourteen to seventeen years. Treatment providers varied, with one-third receiving treatment from juvenile justice system personnel, one-fifth mental health personnel in public or private agencies, and the remainder other counselors, laypersons, or researchers.

Institutional programs emphasized counseling and skill development for periods of one to thirty weeks, with contacts ranging from once or twice per week to daily for half an hour to ten hours per week (p. 2). Random assignment was used in about half the studies. Recidivism included new police contacts, if available, or other types of comparable system contacts. Institutionalized and noninstitutionalized databases were created for analysis.

Of the 200 studies analyzed by Lipsey et al., 83 dealt with programs for institutionalized youth; 74 were in juvenile institutions, and 9 were in residential facilities under private or mental health administration. Researchers examined the same four clusters of variables as in the sample of studies with noninstitutionalized offenders. "The clusters associated with the largest variation in method-adjusted effect size were, in decreasing order of magnitude: general program characteristics, treatment types, treatment amount delivered (e. g., total number of weeks and frequency of treatment, and other ratings of treatment effectiveness), [and] juvenile offender characteristics" (p. 3).

Based on the small number of studies done for serious noninstitutionalized juveniles, three types of treatment showed the strongest and most consistent evidence of reducing their recidivism: "interpersonal skills training (based on three studies), individual counseling (based on eight studies), and behavioral programs (based on seven studies)" (p. 3).

Regarding the effectiveness of treatment types by institutionalized and noninstitutionalized juvenile programs (see Lipsey, et al., 2000 p. 5, Table 1), results were ranked by type of effect and strength of evidence. For noninstitutionalized juveniles these were individual counseling (one-on-one, reality therapy; multisystemic treatment for sex offenders), interpersonal skills (drama, videos, commitment to community projects), behavioral programs (family counseling, contracting), and multiple services (varied techniques, intensive probation, intensive case management).

Programs for institutionalized juveniles included interpersonal skills (social skills training), teaching family homes (community-based, family style, behavior modification in group homes, token economies), behavioral programs (cognitive meditation in small discussion groups, stress inoculation training, peer counseling in reinforcement therapy), community residential programs (advocacy, counseling, educational support, vocational support/assessment and training, groups), and multiple services (probation camps, multiple service cottages).

Operation New Hope

As discussed in Chapter 7, community-based offender programs designed for chronic high-risk juvenile offenders represent one of the most critical points in justice system processing because these individuals represent a high risk for reoffending, all too often within the first 90 to 180 days after release. Many chronic juvenile offenders released from secure facilities exhibit additional problems that need specialized treatment. A number of studies have indicated that in addition to a history of alcohol and/or illicit drug use and abuse, many of these individuals display emotional and cognitive problems that hinder normal postadolescent development. They have a poor prognosis for successful community reintegration and adjustment unless their problems are responded to in an appropriate fashion through specialized programming and service provision during early parole reintegration.

One program evaluated by the authors that addressed the management of serious youthful offenders in the community was Operation New Hope "Lifeskills '95." This postprison program was designed to provide 115 California Youth Authority parolees with the basic skill levels necessary to survive the demands of early reintegration. Research assessed an attempt to support the reentry process using data collected and analyzed on two groups of these parolees. The area chosen for this study was a parole region in Southern California. Eligibility criteria for inclusion in the study were developed and applied to all paroled youthful offenders assigned to the CYA's Inland Parole Office (Riverside and San Bernardino Counties), between February and December 31, 1995 (Josi & Sechrest, 1999). The program was successful in significantly *reducing recidivism* for youthful parolees during the period of program participation as compared to a group of parolees in the same office who did not get the program.

Data for statistical comparison on this and other background characteristics were retrieved from the individual's family history profile—reported by the "precommitment clinical assessment team" as part of the ninety-day medical evaluation screening conducted on all youth authority wards prior to institutional assignment—and from data accumulated during the parole intake process. The mean age of the two groups was very similar—20 years for the experimental versus 20.2 years for the control group. Members of both groups had served about the same mean number of months in institutions prior to their most recent parole (22.7 for the experimentals versus 23.3 for the controls) and had approximately equal time remaining in youth authority parole jurisdiction (time remaining on parole) as of December 31, 1995 (41.6 months versus 40.0 months, respectively).

About 90 percent from both groups had one or more previous criminal convictions; 43 percent of the experimental group and 46 percent of the control group had four or more previous convictions. Eighty-seven percent of those assigned to the experimental group and 86 percent from the control group were incarcerated for more than twelve months in a secure institution immediately prior to parole; 45 percent and 52 percent, respectively, served more than twenty-four months. For the two groups, gang association (81 percent of the experimentals versus 76 percent of the controls) and weapon use (during crime of commitment) (66 percent versus 60 percent, respectively) were about the same.

More than six in ten (63 percent of the experimentals and 63 percent of the controls, respectively) were committed for violent crimes against persons; and, 46 percent of the experimentals versus 36 percent of the controls, did not exhibit any remorse for their victims. More than eight in ten (89 percent of the experimentals versus 85 percent of the controls) were considered a high security risk at the time of their commitment.

A large majority from both groups had a previous history of alcohol and illicit drug use/abuse. Seventy-six percent of the experimentals and 71 percent of the control group members admitted to the daily use/abuse of alcohol. Seventy-eight percent from both groups admitted to the daily use/abuse of illicit drugs. Approximately four in ten from both groups (42 percent of the experimentals and 38 percent of the controls) admitted to "being under the influence" of either alcohol or drugs at the time of their commitment offense. Less than half of all participants (39 percent from the experimental group and 46 percent from the control group) admitted to being "poly" or multiple drug abusers.

Less than 10 percent from either group had a history of previous work experience; less than two in ten had any marketable skills. Forty-six percent of the experimental group and 41 percent of the control group scored below a sixth grade level on a TABE (Test and Objectives Performance Evaluation Report) functional development test. More than 80 percent of the two groups had not received a high school diploma or GED prior to the beginning of this study.

Family socialization patterns for both groups were the same. Less than one in five participants assigned to the experimental group (19 percent) and about one in four control group participants (26 percent) were raised within an intact family structure (both biological parents present). Approximately three in ten experimental (29 percent) and one in four control (24 percent) participants' parents had never married. A large majority of all participants (80 percent) were raised in a family environment situation described by staff psychologists as "severely dysfunctional." Furthermore, a number of the participants' biological parents had an extensive history of alcohol and illicit drug use/abuse. Approximately one-third of the biological fathers had abused alcohol (32 percent experimental and 30 percent control, respectively); more than one in ten had abused drugs (16 percent experimentals and 15 percent controls, respectively). Approximately 10 percent of the biological mothers from both groups had abused alcohol; 20 percent had a sustained history of drug abuse.

The program's creator, Bill Degnan, used six principles representing thirteen counseling modules (consolidated from the original thirty-nine used in an institutionally-based program), with a total twenty-nine program subtopics. Each module represents a three-hour program—1.5 hours for lecture and 1.5 hours for group discussion (Degnan, 1994). The thirty-nine-hour program should be completed in thirteen consecutive weekly meetings.

By design, "Lifeskills '95" is a completely interactive program without an independent start-finish. According to Degnan (1994), the program modules are sequenced to enhance an individual's understanding of the lifestyle process; however, each topic is considered an independent stand-alone unit. Individual participation at one session is not dependent upon attendance at the preceding session to understand, nor to progress through the program. Degnan insists the information covered in each topic is as relevant to the "first timer" as it is to the long-term participant.

An unanswered question concerning the "Lifeskills '95" program is why it appears to work. It was not possible to determine which of the program's components are most effective in reducing the high-rate of short-term parole failure and which are least effective. In comparison with other juvenile offender programs, however, several of its features stand out and deserve consideration as likely contributors to its apparent success, and are reflected in the discussion of programs presented later.

Perhaps the most noticeable feature or characteristic of the "Lifeskills '95" program was its decidedly positive, upbeat atmosphere. Absent was the typical preprogrammed rhetoric taught by individuals who lack appropriate training and a clear understanding of their target audience. It appears that the program elements, developed by Bill Degnan, because of both their substantive content and number, created a program for serious, often violent young men that kept them occupied with positive expectations and experiences.

A second notable feature was the intensive individualized treatment orientation encompassing socialization and self-esteem training, substance abuse awareness and treatment aftercare, and community reintegration counseling. A third feature was the program's intensive job training efforts. Twice as many Lifeskills' participants, compared with those assigned to the control group, were either employed or enrolled in an academic training program at the end of this study. A fourth feature was the unintentional relocation of about four in ten of these parolees to the San Bernardino/Riverside area from Los Angeles County, which may offer a number of potential advantages. Removal from the negative influences of a dysfunctional family, renewed contact with sibling offenders, substance abusing associates, and negative peer gangs together with the long-term effects of socioeconomic isolation and abject poverty, may be the necessary catalyst for those who seek a positive change in their lifestyle and are sincere in their desire to "make it."

The last feature highlights the question of the long-term significance of the reentry program on these parolees lives, particularly in contrast with the forces at work in the disadvantaged communities to which they are returning (e. g., the limited resources and opportunities in poor communities). If the major reasons for reentry failure do indeed reside in an essentially closed and unresponsive opportunity structure, then what lasting significance can the reentry program itself have in the context of this larger social reality?

An important finding for these individuals was that there was no "honeymoon period" at release. There was immediate struggle and difficulty for virtually all of these individuals. The major characteristics of the initial reentry experience were disorientation, estrangement, and alienation. The parolees were largely unprepared for the shift from avoiding trouble and staying out of jail to a "how do I fit in" mentality. They had not set foot outside the institution prior to walking out the front gate on the day of release. They were completely inside one day and completely outside the next. Thus, several areas of functioning during the reentry process were found to be critical to effective reintegration. These included employment, which may be the most pivotal issue of the whole reentry period. Most of these parolees were forced to rely on their own initiative and resources in getting jobs.

Another major concern was substance abuse. By the end of the third month of parole, about three out of every ten members of the experimental group (Lifeskills participants) and more than half of the control group were suspected of at least occasional drug use. For many of the parolees, family relationships were the most positive part of the transition period. Overall, comparison figures for family relationships were significantly better for the experimental group.

Recidivism was the primary outcome measure. While the important question of whether Lifeskills had an impact on long-term parole failure has not been answered definitively, the quasiexperimental data obtained for this evaluation suggest that the Lifeskills program did have a positive impact on the short-term rates of recidivism. At the end of three months, the control group of 115 (non-ONH) parolees were more than *three* times as likely to have failed parole (38% versus 11%) than their counterparts in the experimental group of 106 parolees.

Clearly, the kinds of postrelease adjustments made will, in the long run, depend fundamentally on the kinds of opportunities available to parolees. If meaningful opportunities for productive adjustments are not available, then satisfactory adjustments obviously cannot occur. Any discussion of the impact of the Lifeskills reintegration program on parolees, however, must not be allowed to hide the specific responsibility of correctional agencies for the immediate problems of reentry. A critical issue of reentry concerns the negligence of the responsible correctional agency and its respective service component, institutions and parole officers who created many reentry problems and took little responsibility for helping the parolee manage the reintegration process.

Youthful offenders have little influence over those correctional practices that contribute to their difficulties and have limited ability to create opportunities where they do not already exist. If the situation they confront is one in which the social realities do not come close to meeting their legitimate needs and aspirations, then the major responsibility for meeting those needs rests squarely on those institutions that have the resources and leverage necessary to this task. It is for this reason that the reluctance of the juvenile justice system to assume this responsibility becomes a major issue of parole reentry. And, because the reintegration model recognizes this responsibility when it asserts that crime is as much a reflection of social failure as personal failure, a discussion of correctional neglect of reentry cannot be divorced from the more general issue of the juvenile justice system's commitment to the reintegration model.

The critical question is why does this institutional neglect for these potentially violent offenders continue. Programs for parolees as well as other offenders must begin with the assumption that most of these individuals are genuinely intent on changing their lives. Reintegration programs must begin working with clients several weeks in advance of release and they must recognize that a primary source of reentry difficulties are the parolees' life situations in addition to their own personal limitations, attitudes, or emotional difficulties. A major focus of these efforts must be on providing meaningful opportunities that provide alternatives to previous lifestyles rather than supervision or adjustment-oriented counseling. The returning parolee needs a helping relationship with someone whom he or she feels is committed to his interests and believes in the parolee. This person should be much more an advocate than a counselor.

Parole reintegration, as well as other types of programs for difficult offenders, need to recognize the extent to which change in one life sphere influences others. Help with family relationships is especially critical. Families are an important resource during reentry and a major source of conflict and stress. Developing postrelease vocational and educational placements with the potential for meaningful future opportunities may be critical to a program's ability to direct the parolee to a new lifestyle. Finally, reentry programs should involve agencies and people from the parolee's community. It should be understood that the fundamental problem of parole reentry is the lack of responsiveness of our social institutions to the legitimate needs and aspirations of the offender. This lack of responsiveness may be a factor in the management of many youth and adults who are involved in serious, violent behavior.

Treatment Approaches: The Problem of Serious Chronic Juvenile Offenders

The extent of serious juvenile crime has been discussed in previous chapters. Since the early 1990s, there has been a decline in serious crimes in the United States Among juveniles, the rates of violent offenses, especially homicide and gun-related crimes, increased dramatically from the mid-1980s to 1994, but there has been some decline since then (Snyder & Sickmund, 1999). Regardless of the statistics, public concern with violent crime and the level of fear of crime remain high. Similarly, public support for harsh punishments continue to be strong. Many legislators, politicians, and criminal justice officials attribute the decline in crime rates to the "tough on crime" policies that were introduced since the 1970s, starting with the "war on crime" and continued with the "war on drugs" campaigns. These policies influenced the legislation of more severe penal measures. The last two decades witnessed a host of mandatory imprisonment and three strikes laws, habitual offender and career criminal programs, and an increased use of the death penalty. The results were very significant. The prison population in the United States has grown from less than a quarter of a million in 1975 to over 1.3 million in mid-1999 (Beck, 2000).

There were major changes in the approach to juvenile delinquents as well. These changes had an impact on the juvenile justice system. From its inception, the philosophical foundation of the juvenile justice system in America and in most industrialized countries was based on two divergent traits: treatment and punishment. Thus, the juvenile system became a hybrid of a social welfare agency and a penal institution. The contradictory ideas of rehabilitation on the one hand and punishment on the other that characterize juvenile justice often come into sharp conflict, creating situations that contribute to the controversial nature of this system.

For decades during the twentieth century, the rehabilitation ideology was the guiding principle of the juvenile justice system and the juvenile court was seen as the "rehabilitative court." With the changes in the general approach to crime, social control, and punishment, strong criticisms were leveled against the rehabilitative orientation of the juvenile justice system. The main claims were that it became too lenient, allowing too many hard-core violent delinquents get away with a slap on their wrist without having any deterrent effects.

Since the 1970s, there are persistent efforts to bring the juvenile system closer to the adult criminal justice system. Thus, according some observers, the juvenile justice system is in a process of changing its orientation from a rehabilitative one to a punitive one. This trend is reflected in an increasing number of transfers of juvenile cases to adult criminal courts. Currently, under various provisions "all states allow juveniles to be tried as adults in criminal courts under certain circumstances" (Snyder & Sickmund, 1999, p. 102).

Recently, several researchers predicted a steep increase in juvenile violence starting at the beginning of the twenty-first century. Predictions about changes in violent offenses are usually based on demographic factors when the defining variable is the size of the age cohorts most prone to be involved in violence, namely the young age groups.

It has been stated for many years that based on juvenile incarceration rates and criminal activity, the public correctly demands protection from juvenile crimes, and especially from the serious and/or chronic juvenile offender. This concern appears to be supported by the fact that the number of juveniles in the courts and in custody has increased over these years. For example, "Juvenile courts handled 1.8 million delinquency cases in 1996, 600 more cases each day than in 1997" (Snyder & Sickmund, 1999, p. 144). The number of cases involving juvenile detention increased 35 percent from 1987 to 1996, and the number of crimes against persons for these detainees has risen from 19 percent to 27 percent over this period (Snyder & Sickmund, 1999, p. 153).

Programs for Serious Chronic Juvenile Offenders

Hamparian found that fewer than half of the juveniles adjudicated delinquent for violent offenses receive probation or a juvenile corrections sentence (Hamparian, 1985, p. 181; C. P. Smith, et al., 1979; D. Smith, et al., 1981). She documented a recent trend away from the traditional practice of treating juveniles adjudicated for violent offenses in the same way as other juvenile offenders. However, she concluded that the juvenile justice system is becoming an offense-based—rather than offender-based—system, with harsher penalties being imposed for violent offenses. She noted the trend of waiving juvenile status and treating older youth as adults. The adult criminal justice system now handles a significant percentage of juveniles arrested for violent offenses (Hamparian, 1985, p. 181).

In a follow-up to her book *The Violent Few,* Hamparian, Davis, Jacobson, and McGraw (1985, p. 9) presented evidence that serious, chronic youthful offenders would become adult offenders; 59 percent of the violent juveniles in her cohort study were arrested at least once for an adult felony offense between age 18 and their 23rd to 27th birthdays. These individuals are more likely to be male, first arrested at 12 or younger, more likely to have been chronic "index violent" juvenile offenders, and have been committed to a state juvenile facility in the past. Prevention of future crime by these youngsters requires better programs for them.

Control and Treatment of Serious Juvenile Offenders

The primary goals of programs for all juveniles apply equally to programs for highly active serious and chronic juvenile offenders. Many of these goals are applicable to programs for adults involved in violent behavior. Hamparian (1985, pp.181–182) cited several goals and related techniques for the development of successful programs for violent juvenile offenders, many of which have been discussed more fully by Mann (1976). Goals for treatment of these youth include:

1. the need to reduce their incidence of subsequent criminal and/or violent behavior for their benefit and to protect the public;
2. to operate programs that provide positive role models;
3. to provide activities that will assist in the reduction of subsequent criminal and/or violent behavior.

Program techniques include:

1. specification of realistic goals for each youth and rewards for meeting agreed-upon goals;
2. maximum involvement by youth in decision making about their treatment plan, inclusive of the community reintegration period;
3. community reintegration programming through home visits, community trips, etc.;
4. programs that have a helping role, with staff committed and involved in these programs;
5. job placement in the reintegration phase based on remedial education and job training.

Operational issues include concern about staff burnout and subsequent high turnover rates; there should be continued use of well-monitored contract services from private agencies, with assurance that there will be no abuse of the youths in these facilities. Vachss and Bakal (Hamparian, 1985, p. 178) provide a model for such a secure treatment program.

Programs to Manage Violent Juvenile Offenders

Programs to manage and rehabilitate both nonviolent and violent juvenile of-fenders have been tried in many settings using many techniques. Some of these rely on system-wide changes, others on specific types of programs within sys-tems. Many are fads, such as Scared Straight and boot camps, and, upon careful evaluation, are not found to be as successful as their creators say they are. There-fore, we should proceed carefully in looking at new programs for adults or juve-niles. The Guided Group Interaction or Positive Peer Pressure and Positive Peer Culture programs that began in the 1950s in Highfields, New Jersey, and Min-nesota are examples. The technique was implemented in residential facilities of youth ages 8 to 12 and relied on verbal and sometimes physical peer pressure on participants to make them confess and describe past sins.

A careful evaluation of legislatively mandated programs in California found that 44 percent of 4,000 males released from custody in 1961 reoffended within five years causing enthusiasm to wane (p. 239).

Behavior modification returned with Achievement Place, in Kansas, which was a widely-replicated method of providing points for positive performance and lost points for poor performance. It was done in units of six to eight youth in "teaching-family homes" operated by married couples. "Delinquent activity was reduced only while the youths were living in the teaching family homes. A year following treatment there was no significant difference between them and youths from comparison groups" (Baker, 1995, p. 246).

State juvenile services organizations have approached the problems of the vi-olent, chronic, juvenile offender in a variety of ways. Major concerns are to deter-mine the effectiveness of incarceration as opposed to the use of community treatment approaches, or to see how they work in combination, often with intensive casework approaches. One of the best known of these programs has been the Massachusetts experiment in deinstitutionalization that began in 1972 and reduced the training school population from about 1,000 to about 100 very difficult offend-ers, which is now closer to 300. In 1979 the Massachusetts Department of Youth Services (DYS) had 10 secure treatment units for juveniles with a total of 123 beds. Admissions were carefully screened to ensure that no youth who could succeed in an open setting was placed in the secure facilities. Many services were provided on a purchase of services basis by private providers. Programs included clinical, edu-cational, vocational, recreational, and family therapies tailored to the needs and strengths of each youth. Efforts were made to incorporate day work programs into the treatment. Local gyms and swimming pools were used for recreation.

The DYS Violent Offender Project is a systematic treatment approach con-sisting of a secure treatment phase using a thirty-three-bed facility with five staff. This was followed by a nonsecure residential phase and intensive casework su-pervision upon return to the community. The program was seen to "significantly curtail the delinquent activities of those youths who had completed the program," with the claim that 79 percent of the participating youths were able to find un-subsidized employment as compared to 29 percent of the control group (Loughran, 1987, p. 17).

Reasons given for the success of these programs were the assignment of a case manager to each child, who develops a treatment plan and arranges for post-discharge tracking and service planning. The diversity of housing options allows for highly individualized placements. Violent and chronic offenders are 15 percent of the juvenile population and are confined in fifteen-bed facilities followed by placements in community programs; violations of liberty lead to secure confinement. One of these facilities is the Butler Center for Emotionally Disturbed, a fifteen-bed secure treatment program for youth who exhibit significant emotional disturbance, many having juvenile records that include crimes of violence and/or sexual deviancy. It has an extensive clinical component and individualized and facility therapy session designed to motivate youths to openly confront their problems (Loughran, 1987, p. 17).

Overall, the programs for juveniles in Massachusetts appear to have been successful. Their successes indicate that in 1972, the beginning year of deinstitutionalization in Massachusetts, a total of 35 percent of the persons committed to the Department of Corrections had previous experience with their Department of Youth Services, but that by 1985, this had dropped to 15 percent (see National Council on Crime and Delinquency, 1991).

Unified Delinquency Intervention Services

The Unified Delinquency Intervention Services (UDIS) program in Illinois was perhaps the most innovative experiment in examining the relationship between incarceration and community programs for serious juvenile offenders. Started in 1974, UDIS was originally designed to serve youths who were at risk of being committed or recommitted to juvenile institutions including probation and parole violators and repeat delinquent offenders. It later came to involve mostly serious juvenile offenders; of 211 juveniles served in the initial project year, 55 percent had been charged with major felonies such as murder, rape, armed robbery, arson, and burglary (Hamparian, 1985, p.173). Differences were found for the 583 youth over a two-year period. Prior to the training school sentence they averaged 13.6 arrests, with 8.2 arrests for UCR index offenses and 5.4 nonindex offenses (Hamparian, p. 218). Of the 583, 317 were sent to state training schools, or youth prisons, and served an average of 10.86 months. The remaining 266 were sent to community alternatives. These were "reasonably comparable groups on socioeconomic status and personal variables" (Hamparian, pp. 218, 224).

The UDIS program used a brokerage system, allowing for purchase of services, coupled with a case management approach. Clients could agree to individual counseling, family counseling, educational and tutoring services, vocational testing and job placement, specialized foster care, group home care, temporary living arrangements, wilderness stress programs, and private residential treatment programs. Youth participated as a condition of probation with the goal being to keep them in the community and reduce the unnecessary use of institutions for them. The evaluation of the program by Murray and Cox (1979) found it successful in reducing recidivism (7 percent reductions in the first year; Mann, 1976, p.

43). There were large declines in the rate of offending for youth placed in well-managed and intensive community-based programs, but minimal reductions among youth placed in traditional probation programs. This was the most controversial finding: *Youth committed to Illinois training schools showed less recidivism than youth placed on traditional probation.* Findings of success, however, were subject to some controversy due to a suspected "regression effect," that is, the youths involved were high rate offenders upon admission and their rates would have dropped even without the program (McCreary et al., 1979). Several organizational factors are cited as part of the success of UDIS, especially a committed board, a good monitoring/tracking system, and a flexible staff (Mann, 1976, p. 44).

The finding that youth sent to training schools had lower recidivism rates than those kept in traditional community programs led to the conclusion that the threat of institutionalization, the "suppression effect," worked to reduce recidivism rates one year after the program (cf. Siegel & Senna, 1985, p. 515).

Hamparian, Schuster, Dinitz, and Conrad (1975) argued that institutionalizing chronic offenders actually diminished the number of months between arrests after release but *increased the seriousness of subsequent crimes.* Most evidence leads to the conclusion that secure treatment of violent, chronic juvenile offenders simply reinvolves them in crime (Siegel & Senna, 1985, p. 515). The key point appears to be that, no matter the type of program, *interventions must be sufficiently intensive and salient to youth to reduce future youth crime* (Krisberg, 1987, p. 47). Interventions do not have to be just institutionalization; although, for chronic, serious, and violent juvenile offenders it may be required as a first, albeit brief, step.

Institution-Based Programs

In contrast to the community supervision emphasis of UDIS, the Green Oak Center of Michigan Department of Social Services, Institutional Services Division, was designed for serious offenders who had to be institutionalized. It is a maximum security, special treatment unit for 100 males between the ages of twelve and nineteen. These youths have been found guilty of serious crimes against persons and have been in serious trouble from an early age. Small group techniques, principally Guided Group Interaction, were used. These techniques involve the use of confrontation and peer pressure to help residents learn to show concern for themselves and others, and to make more informed decisions about their behavior (cf. Mann, 1976, pp. 34–39). An evaluation of the program's impact on subsequent recidivism found nearly two-thirds had avoided further imprisonment in thirty months after release, although as Hamparian (1985, p. 175) pointed out, the severity of subsequent offenses was reduced more than their frequency.

A program that begins with an institutional component is the Minnesota Serious Juvenile Offender program, begun in 1978. This program serves fifteen- to eighteen-year-old youths adjudicated for murder, first-degree arson, second-degree manslaughter, or first- or second-degree assault, and other specified felony history criteria. The program starts with an institutional stay followed by "graduation" to less restrictive community placements. Youths contract for a treatment plan within a continuous case management treatment model. An evaluation of the first seventy-six program participants found that sixty-two had not been adjudicated for a new felony or gone AWOL since being admitted to the program. This was over a two-year period, with about six months in the institution prior to release (Hamparian, 1985, p. 171).

Utah's youth corrections system includes two thirty-bed high-security units for violent and chronic offenders that are linked with assessment and observation centers and community programs. An NCCD study concluded that these "well-structured community programs . . . represent an important new range of treatment options for handling serious and chronic juvenile offenders (Schwartz, 1989, p. 54; Van Vleet, Rutherfore, & Schwartz, 1987, p. 28). Much of the success of this program was attributed to the use of "an excellent risk screening system that directed the most high-risk and violent offenders into secure beds" (Krisberg, 1987, p. 48).

Pennsylvania went through a period of deinstitutionalization similar to Massachusetts. A total of seven programs for 230 serious juvenile offenders were established after the closing of the state correctional institution at Camp Hill. All but two of the programs serve twenty or fewer youths. One unit serves the mentally regarded or those with problems of maladaptive behavior, and the other serves mentally ill juvenile offenders. These programs are supplemented by private agency programs operated by RCA, Inc. One of these programs is the Weaversville Intensive Treatment Unit that RCA operates under contract with the Pennsylvania Department of Welfare (Krisberg, p. 180). Professional staff serve as positive role models to the youths in the program and operate educational and vocational programs in these facilities. The Cornwell Heights Intensive Treatment Unit, opened in 1975, serves about fifty youths in Pennsylvania. It is operated by the Office of Children of the Department of Public Welfare on the grounds of the Cornwell Heights Development Center. It attempts to mainstream children into the educational program established for the center and operated by RCA, Inc. (Blackmore, Brown, & Krisberg, 1988).

Different Models of Treatment

Several models of treatment can be applied to the problems of serious juvenile offenders, including the use of private agencies, joint mental health and corrections models, and wilderness programs. The private for-profit sector has been involved for many years in programs such as the one in Pennsylvania. Another such program is Elan One in Poland Spring, Maine. This is a residential center for "incorrigible" adolescents between ages of fourteen and twenty-five. The program receives state agency referrals for youth who cannot be treated elsewhere, the "end of the road" youth—and "disturbed" youth placed there by their parents (Hamperian, 1985, p. 177). Elan is designed as a complete, continuous therapeutic community in which juveniles with out-of-control behavior problems come to understand the causes and consequences of their behavior. This is done through the use of group techniques and a carefully designed "reinforcing social structure" that provides absolute support while promoting change. Meritorious performance yields "promotions" in the organization and more privileges. Illegal behavior is not tolerated: no drugs, violence, or sex. Violators are punished immediately (Hamparian, 1985, p. 177). Many former residents work in the program.

Another model for working with serious juvenile offenders is the joint mental health corrections model. The New York City Department of Mental Hygiene and the Division for Youth created the Bronx Court Related Unit (CRU). The CRU had two components: a secure ten-bed in-patient diagnostic unit operated by mental health and a long-term treatment unit operated by juvenile corrections. Youth had to meet rigid criteria for mental illness and to have been adjudicated as guilty of a serious crime. A comparison group of youth who met program criteria but were not admitted was used to examine program effectiveness. Recidivism rates somewhat favored CRU participants (62.2% versus 75.8%), as did average re-arrest rates (2.8 versus 3.3), and those CRU youth that were rearrested did fewer violent crimes (38.9% versus 43.5%). Results were considered encouraging, although high costs, agency strains, underutilized bed space, and philosophical problems with "get tough" advocates led to its termination (Hamparian, 1985, pp. 176–177).

Similar programs have operated in Pennsylvania including the Southeast Secure Treatment Unit (SESTU), which is devoted specifically to the treatment of small groups of mentally retarded, violent teenagers. In Colorado the Closed Adolescent Treatment Center (CATC) worked with hard-core juvenile offenders using behavior modification techniques.

Additional models for managing serious juvenile offenders can be found in the challenge programs, or wilderness programs, many of which are now being carefully evaluated by RAND researchers (cf. Krisberg, 1987, p. 49). Logan (1989) provides an overview of these programs in a federal report on the uses of "shock incarceration" for young offenders. The original challenge program was Outward Bound, founded in 1960, which has been successfully replicated in many states. The approach is based on providing youth a physically and emotionally challenging experience in a wilderness environment with progressive greater challenges.

Research shows that this experiential approach can improve self-esteem and is correlated with performance variables such as better grades, interpersonal competence, and improved work responsibilities (Logan, p. 58). The physical fitness aspect alone appears to improve behavior. A comparison-group evaluation in Massachusetts found a 20 percent recidivism rate for Outward Bound participants and 42 percent in a matched comparison group of youths over a one year period, which was statistically significant. A five-year follow-up revealed 38 and 58 percent rates, respectively (Logan, p. 59). Another study of great importance was the Violent Juvenile Offender (VJO) program of the OJJDP, which has been discussed previously. This program contained all of the core ingredients identified in previously successful community-based efforts.

The Florida Environmental Institute (FEI) program is another example of a successful program for violent and chronic juveniles. "The Last Chance Ranch" is located in the Florida Everglades (cf. Weaver, 1989). It has twenty-two residents and twenty nonresidential cases, and has served 173 youths in the 15 to 18 age range since 1982. The average program length is eighteen months, with six months of this in a nonresidential community setting. There are two residential phases. Phase I emphasizes work and education—they live in a dormitory with no air conditioning, television, or other amenities; points are earned for graduation to phase II. The youth function at the fifth-grade level or below.

Phase II focuses on continuing work and education, emphasizing environmental projects. Toward the end of phase II they earn the right to return home with their community coordinator to find work and begin reintegration with family and friends. The third phase is aftercare and concentrates on job and family problems. There are twenty-two direct service employees at the camp who accept a two year "tour of duty"; cost per day is $102, residential, $20 nonresidential. The program is committed to the concept that education lowers recidivism, and research on the program indicates a recidivism rate of 45 percent compared to a training school population rate of 60 percent (Weaver, 1989, pp. 32, 37). This research was completed by the Florida Department of Health and Rehabilitative Services, and states that 80 percent of the training school population had less serious criminal histories than FEI youth.

Additional successful violence prevention programs have been identified by Mihalic, Irwin, Elliott, Fagan, and Hansen (2001). Of over 500 they studied that were systematically reviewed, eleven model programs, or "blueprints," were identified as "effective in reducing adolescent violent crime, aggression, delinquency, and substance abuse and predelinquent childhood aggression and conduct disorders" (p. 1). Drug use deterrence and/or delinquency reductions were also considered in weighing effectiveness. As with other meta-analyses, experimental or quasiexperimental designs with matched control groups were evaluated. It was required that effects be sustained for at least one year beyond treatment. Another nineteen programs were identified as "promising." Cost-to-benefit ratios were also considered, as were various mediating factors in violence prevention. The programs studied were considered cost effective and effective in reducing recidivism.

Programs designed for juvenile offenders had the largest and most consistent economic returns (e. g., Functional Family Therapy, Multisystemic Therapy, Multi-dimensional Treatment Foster Care) (Michalic et al., p. 4). Programs targeting younger juveniles not in the criminal justice system had smaller returns in system savings. Problems related to program weaknesses ("challenges") are cited as are program strengths. The need for continued support at all levels is made clear: administrative, supervisory, staff, and community.

The types of programs described should be considered by anyone developing a program for serious, violent, and/or chronic youth. In fact, sound replications of these types of programs would be most helpful in the ongoing process of determining what works with these individuals.

Critical to the issue of understanding and managing violent behavior in American society is the issue of the societal responses to violence. Clearly, solutions do not and cannot lie solely in the use of increased law enforcement and prison space. Most offenders are not deterred by the prospect of a prison sentence, and both youth and adults often come out of correctional facilities worse than they went in. We are seeking long-term effects. Communities must address deeply rooted social problems that will not yield to simplistic notions of punishment. They must develop programs designed to work with families. They must seek to address social problems emanating from poor schools, unemployment, poverty, and racial discrimination. Various approaches have been presented.

At the individual level, after the failure of family and community in prevention, remedial steps must be taken in order to make progress with individuals who resort to crimes and/or violence. This chapter has presented some of the types of programs that can achieve long-term effects, if properly implemented.

REFERENCES

Alexander, Jr., R. (2000). *Counseling, treatment, and intervention methods with juvenile and adult offenders.* Belmont, CA: Brooks/Cole.

Beck, A. J. (2000). *Bureau of Justice Statistics Bulletin. Prisoners in 1999.* Washington, DC: U.S. Justice Department.

Bilchik, S. (1998, May). Serious and violence juvenile offenders. *Juvenile Justice Bulletin.* Washington, DC: Office of Juvenile Justice and Delinquency Prevention.

Bilchik, S. (1999a). *Juvenile offenders and victims: 1999 national report.* Washington, DC: Office of Juvenile Justice and Delinquency Prevention.

Bilchik, S. (1999b, July). *Report to Congress on juvenile violence research.* Washington, DC: Office of Juvenile Justice and Delinquency Prevention.

Blackmore, J., Brown, M., & Krisberg, B. (1988, May). *Juvenile justice reform: The bellweather states.* Ann Arbor, MI: Center for the Study of Youth Policy.

Bureau of Justice Statistics. (1989, May). *Children in custody, 1975–85.* Washington, DC: U.S. Justice Department.

Cornell, D. G., Benedek, E. P., & Benedek, D. M. (1987). Juvenile homicides: Prior adjustment and a proposed typology. *American Journal of Orthopsychiatry 57,* 383–393.

Criminal Justice Research Reports. (2000). *Trends in juvenile crime and juvenile justice.* http://virlib.ncjrs.org/juvenilejustice.asp.

Curtis, L. (1985). Neighborhood, family and employment. In L. A. Curtis, (Ed.), *American violence and public policy.* New Haven, CT: Yale University Press.

Degnan, B. (1994). *Lifeskills post-parole treatment program.* Sanger, CA: Operation New Hope.

Dorfman, L., & Schiraldi, V. (2001). *Off balance: Youth, race & crime in the news.* Washington, DC: Berkeley Media Studies Group, Public Health Institute, Justice Policy Institute.

Douglas, J., & Olshaker, M. (1995). *Mindhunter: Inside the FBI's elite serial crime unit.* New York: Scribner.

Fagan, J. (1990). Social and legal policy dimensions of violent juvenile crime. *Criminal Justice and Behavior, 17*(1), 93–134.

Goldstein, A. P., & Glick, B. (1996). Aggression replacement training: Methods and outcomes. In C. R. Hollin and K. Howells (Eds.), *Clinical approaches to working with young offenders* (pp. 151–179). Chichester, England: John Wiley & Sons.

Greenwood, P. W., Model, K. E., Rydell, C. P., & Chiesa, J. (1996). *Diverting children from a life of crime: Measuring costs and benefits.* Santa Monica, CA: RAND Corporation.

Hamparian, D. M. (1985a). Control and treatment of juveniles committing violent offenses. In L. Roth, (Ed.), *Clinical treatment of the violent person.* Washington, DC: U.S. Department of Health and Human Services, Public Health Service, Alcohol, Drug Abuse, and Mental Health Administration.

Hamparian, D. M., Davis, J. M., Jacobson, J. M., & McGraw, R. E. (1985, June). *The young criminal careers of the violent few.* Washington, DC: Office of Juvenile Justice and Delinquency Prevention.

Hamparian, D. M., Schuster, R., Dinitz, S., & Conrad, J. (1975). *The violent few: A study of dangerous juvenile offenders.* Lexington, MA: Lexington Books.

Jeffrey, C. R., Myers, L. B., & Wollan, L. A. (1991). Crime, justice, and their systems: Resolving the tension. *The Criminologist, 16*(4), 1, 3–6.

Josi, D., & Sechrest, D.(1999). *Report on treatment effectiveness of Lifeskills '95' program.* Riverside, CA: Riverside County Board of Commissioners.

Krisberg, B. (1987, January). Preventing and controlling violent youth crime: The state of the art. In *Violent juvenile crime: What we know about it and what can we do about it?* (pp. 35–54). Ann Arbor, MI: Center for the Study of Youth Policy.

Lipsey, M. W. (1992). Juvenile delinquency treatment: A meta-analysis inquiry into the variability of effects. In T. D. Cook, H. Cooper, D. S Cordray,. H. Hartmann, L. V. Hedges, L R. J. Light, T. A. Louis, and F. Mosteller (Eds.), *Meta-analysis for explanation: A casebook,* (pp. 83–127). New York: Russell Sage.

Lipsey, M. W., Wilson, D. B., & Cothern, L. (2000). *Effective intervention for serious juvenile offenders.* Juvenile Justice Bulletin. Washington, DC: Office of Juvenile Justice and Delinquency Prevention, U.S. Department of Justice.

Logan, W. (1989). Description of challenge programs. In *Shock incarceration: An overview of existing programs* (pp. 57–59). Washington, DC: National Institute of Justice.

Loughran, E. J. (1987, January). Juvenile corrections: The Massachusetts experience. In *Reinvesting youth corrections resources: A tale of three states* (pp. 7–18). Ann Arbor, MI: Center for the Study of Youth Policy.

Lungren, D. (1995). *Violence prevention: A vision of hope.* Attorney General's Policy Council on Violence Prevention. Sacramento, CA: Crime and Violence Prevention Center.

Mann, D. (1976, July). *Intervening with convicted serious juvenile offenders.* Santa Monica, CA: RAND Corporation.

Mathias, R. A., DeMuro, P., & Allinson, R. S. (Eds). (1984). *Violent juvenile offenders: An anthology.* San Francisco, CA: National Council on Crime and Delinquency.

McCreary, R., Gordon, A., McDowall, D., & Maltz, M. (1979). How a regression artifact can make any delinquency intervention program look effective. In L. Sechrest, M. Philips, R. Redner, S. West, & W. Yeaton, (Eds.), *Evaluation studies review annual* (Vol. 4.) (pp. 626–665). Beverly Hills, CA: Sage.

Mihalic, S., Irwin, K., Elliott, D., Fagan, A., & Hansen, D. (2001). *Blueprints for violence prevention.* Juvenile Justice Bulletin. Washington, DC: Office of Juvenile Justice and Delinquency Prevention, U.S. Department of Justice.

Murray, C. A., & Cox, L. A. (1979). *Beyond probation: Juvenile corrections and the chronic delinquent.* Beverly Hills, CA: Sage.

National Council on Crime and Delinquency. (1988, May). *Facts about violent juvenile crime.* San Francisco, CA: National Council on Crime and Delinquency.

National Council on Crime and Delinquency (1991). *Unlocking juvenile corrections: Evaluating the Massachusetts Department of Youth Services.* San Francisco, CA: National Council in Crime and Delinquency.

Rabin, J. L., & Newton, J. (2000, August 29). Parks, top staff, map response to surge in crime. *L.A. Times,* p. B1.

Reno, J. (1996, March). *Combating violence and delinquency: The National Juvenile Justice Action Plan, summary.* Washington, DC: Coordinating Council on Juvenile Justice and Delinquency Prevention.

Ressler, R. K., & Shachtman, T. (1992). *Whoever fights monsters.* New York: St. Martin's Press.

Roden, S. (1982). *Ounces of prevention, toward and understanding of the causes of violence.* Final Report to the People of California 1982. Sacramento, CA: State of California Commission on Crime Control and Violence Prevention.

Rosenberg, M. L. (1995). Violence in America: An integrated approach to understanding and prevention. *Journal of Health Care for the Poor and Underserved, 6*(2), 102–113.

Schwartz, I. M. (1989). *(In)Justice for juveniles: Rethinking the best interests of the child.* Lexington, MA: D. C. Heath.

Siegel, L. J., & Senna, J. J. (1985). *Juvenile delinquency, theory practice and law.* St. Paul, MN: West.

Smith, C. P., Alexander, P., Kemp, G. L., & Lemert, E. (1979). *A national assessment of serious juvenile crime and the juvenile justice system: The need for a rational response.* Sacramento, CA: American Justice Institute.

Snyder, H. N. (1999, November). Juvenile arrests 1998. *Juvenile Justice Bulletin.*

Snyder, H. N., & Sickmund, M. (1999). *Juvenile offenders and victims: 1999 national report.* National Center for Juvenile Justice. Washington, DC: Office of Juvenile Justice. and Delinquency Prevention, U.S. Department of Justice,

Steketee, M. W., Willis, D. A., & Schwartz, I. M. (1989, November) *Juvenile justice trends, 1977–1987.* Ann Arbor, MI: Center for the Study of Youth Policy, University of Michigan School of Social Work.

Thomas, D. (1989, September). *Fact sheet on children held in public facilities.* Washington, DC: Office of Juvenile Justice and Delinquency Prevention, U.S. Department of Justice.

Vachss, A., & Bakal, Y. (1979). *The life-style of the violent juvenile.* Lexington, MA: Lexington Books.

Van Vleet, R., Rutherford, A., & Schwartz, I. M. (1987, January). *Reinvesting in youth corrections in Utah, in reinvesting youth corrections resources: A tale of three states* (pp. 23–32). Ann Arbor, MI: Center for the Study of Youth Policy.

Varley, W. H. (1984). Behavior modification approaches to the aggressive adolescent. In C. R. Keith (Ed.), *The aggressive adolescent: Clinical perspectives* (pp. 268–298). New York: The Free Press.

Weaver, R. S. (1989, November). The last chance ranch: The Florida Environmental Institute program for chronic and violent juvenile offenders. In *Programs for serious and violent juvenile offenders* (pp. 27–39). Ann Arbor, MI: Center for the Study of Youth Policy.

Wolfgang, M. (1987). Youth crime. In *Violent juvenile crime: What we know about it and what can we do about it?* (pp. 7–22). Ann Arbor, MI: Center for the Study of Youth Policy.

CHAPTER

12   Future Directions

In this chapter, we will discuss future issues in the treatment and prevention of violence in America. We have some strong beliefs about the future. We believe that the decrease in violent crime reported since 1994 has reached its bottom level and that we will begin to see increases in violence in the coming years. This belief is reinforced by preliminary figures from the Uniform Crime Reporting program (UCR), a nationwide compilation of crime in America published by the FBI. Data for 2000 indicate that violent crime rates remain unchanged from the year before (FBI Press Office, 2001). Another indication that declines in violent crime may have reached their bottom point is the Surgeon General's Report on Youth Violence (2001) that asks youth if they have been involved in violent juvenile crime. The U. S. Surgeon General's report (Satcher, 2001) notes that:

> Since 1993, when the epidemic of juvenile violence peaked, youth violence has declined steadily nationwide as signaled by downward trends in arrest records, victimization data, and hospital emergency records. But the problem has not been resolved. Another key indicator of violence . . . youth's confidential reports about their own violent behavior . . . reveals no change since 1993 in the proportion of young people who have committed physically injurious and potentially lethal acts. Moreover, arrests for aggravated assaults have declined only slightly and in 1999 remained nearly 70 [percent] higher than the preepidemic years of 1982 [to] 1993. (p. 1)
>
> Arrest records give only a partial picture of youth violence. For every youth arrested in any given year in the late 1990s, at least 10 were engaged in some form of violent behavior that could have seriously injured or killed another person. (p. 1)

We also believe that the amount of random violence from terrorism could increase, although we certainly hope not, raising a fear of violence that affects our sense of safety and limits travel and recreation, necessary outlets for work and home-related tensions. As a result, we believe that domestic and dating violence could increase. As a further result of the fear of random violence and the limits on recreational and travel as an outlet, we are concerned that an increase in substance abuse will follow. Substance abuse is one of the key catalysts in violent behavior.

An area of terrorist activity that is often ignored is the impact of terrorism on surviving victims and their families. One report in *Newsweek* (Cowley, 2001) notes that of the number of victims of the World Trade Center attacks, an estimated 40,000 people, including survivors, witnesses, and emergency personnel, suffered serious psychological trauma during the attack on the Trade Center (p. 50). Most, the article goes on to say, will cope with the experience in time but "past experience suggests that a third or more of the people touched directly by the events will develop post-traumatic stress disorder. For those people, every day will be September 11" (p. 50). The *Newsweek* article (Cowley, 2001) goes on to note:

> Dr. Carol North, a professor of psychiatry at Washington University in St. Louis, has studied more than 2,000 survivors of a dozen disasters. Of the tragedies she has analyzed, the highest rate of PTSD was Oklahoma City, where 34 [percent] of the survivors went on to develop it. (p. 50)

The symptoms of PTSD, described in more detail in Chapter 8, include "feelings of intense fear when recollecting the event; insomnia, loss of appetite, headaches or chest pains; anxiety, excessive worry about the safety of loved ones; feelings of hopelessness and indifference and isolation resulting in intrusive memories, hyper-vigilance with panic attacks and social withdrawal" (Cowley, 2001, p. 52).

Since reporting on terrorism is such a new area for American academics, it is difficult to know precisely what impact terrorism will have on violent crime. *Newsweek* (2001) reports that crime in New York was down 14 percent two weeks after the September 11, 2001 terrorist attack and crime in Washington, DC, was down 23 percent one week after the attack. Obviously, no one can predict with certainty whether terrorism will increase or decrease violence. Our educated guess, however, is that violence will increase as a result of terrorism. One certain conclusion is that guns were purchased in higher numbers after the September 11 attacks. Availability of guns is often a predictor of fear of violence.

Another area that we think will show an increase in violence as a result of the impact of terrorism is child abuse. An economy in recession often brings with it unemployment and the unwanted side effects of family violence. Our urban child protective agencies have not been functioning well and we fear that as child abuse increases, the response, both in terms of quantity and quality of services provided by our agencies treating children, will decline. An additional troubling problem facing us in the future is the reduction of trained workers for our child protective service and mental health systems. The number of people entering educational programs in the social services has been stagnant for the past several years, and the number of trained professionals (Lennon, 2001) able to work with our most troubled children decreases as rates of child abuse increase across the nation.

Because of the numbers of babies born addicted to substances, particularly crack cocaine and alcohol, we believe the physical damage done to many American children by the addictions of their mothers increases the potential for impulsive behavior that sometimes leads to violence. As the numbers of drug-affected children reach adolescence, we think that increasing levels of violence will force a reevaluation of current laws related to emotional instability and the proper sentencing for children who, through no fault of their own, have developed behaviors that are related to addictions that often lead to violence.

New York City currently requires violent mentally ill men and women to reside in supervised halfway homes where their medications are administered nonvoluntarily. While the program raises civil rights issues, the attempt to control violence among emotionally unstable perpetrators will likely be used in other communities where the mentally ill, living in squalid conditions in the inner city, often deteriorate and commit crimes they would probably not have committed in a supervised setting. The treatment of violent mentally ill citizens, as we will point out in several case studies in this chapter, is often inconsistent, and sanity pleas are seldom easy to correctly evaluate.

We wonder if the current economic recession, a result of a declining economy and the recent acts of terrorism, will result in a long-term depression creating problems with unemployment. We doubt that the economy will make a rapid recovery because of fears of continued terrorism. Millions of Americans are facing downsizing and a reduction in salary and the quality of their home and work lives. A bad economy may increase the amount of crime and with it, the amount of random violence. We suspect that a bad economy could also increase racial and ethnic conflicts and that hate crimes may increase as people blame others for the nation's difficulties.

Unfortunately, in this sad scenario we see for the future, the angry and violent men and women who are the tenants of our nation's prisons, many of them nonviolent when they entered prison, will soon be returning to American communities. We believe that prisons are breeding grounds for violence and that many nonviolent offenders will return to the streets of America angry, embittered, and fully capable of violent acts that may have been unthinkable before they were imprisoned. We hope that this tendency to jail nonviolent offenders and place them with violent offenders will lead to a more enlightened approach to the nonviolent population of perpetrators with an emphasis on alternative sentencing and rehabilitation, but we doubt it. There is almost nothing in the literature of the affluent years behind us to suggest a willingness to fund expensive alternative programs and to stay with those programs if they show promise. One thing is clear, however: In a declining economy, the money to build more and more prisons that demonstrate negligible results will force us to consider alternative sentencing laws and alternatives to incarceration.

The mass media of America continues to rely on violence as its primary topic of entertainment for television and film viewers. The reliance on violence and the over-emphasis of violence reporting by the news media have created both an obsession with violence and a sense of apathy toward its consequences. This deadens people's willingness to deal with violence. In this chapter, we will urge a more rational policy toward violence in mass media. The obsession with violence by the media cannot help but have a negative impact on many of our more impressionable citizens.

While this scenario is a pessimistic one, we think it also provides an opportunity for America to use its national resources and know-how to concentrate on the reduction of violent behavior, which will bring with it a greater sense of safety in its people. Fear of violence should not affect the way millions of Americans make important life decisions.

Violence: A Look at the Future

For almost eight years now, the reported rates of violence in America have been declining. Between 1999 and 2000, the National Crime Victimization Survey conducted by the U.S. Department of Justice noted a 15 percent decline in violent crimes in America reaching, according to the NCVS, the lowest level in violent crimes in NCVS history (October 1, 2001). Yet no one in America feels safer and most people who examine the data are unable to determine any one reason for the decreased rates of violence. While the three strike laws, tougher sentencing, and more prisons have been suggested as possible explanations for decreasing violent crime rates, Americans fear violent crime at levels over 120 percent higher than they did in 1969 (Eisenhower Commission, 2000). If violence is really declining, then why does fear of violence still trouble Americans?

Fear of violence troubles Americans a great deal and results in behaviors that often significantly increase individual and family stress. As a result of inner-city violence, many Americans have chosen to live in suburban areas that often require long, impossible drives to work because violence is perceived to be lower in suburbia. While violence is lower in suburbia, the absence of parents because of work and long drives has dramatically increased the numbers of unsupervised children and adolescents, many of whom become involved in crime, drugs, and violence. This is the core of children involved in violence, but not caught, that makes the recent U.S. Surgeon General's report on youth violence so troubling.

Out of the fear of violence, Americans have agreed to such ill-advised laws as the three strikes laws that incarcerate all too many nonviolent offenders. Bond issues are passed permitting jails and prisons to be built at an alarming pace so that more people than ever, at an incredible cost, are now involved in the criminal justice system. If crime and violence are down so dramatically, then why the need for more prisons and tougher laws that are often overly punitive and unjust?

The building of more prisons has created a system of inequity in the way our tax dollars are spent. In California, the prison system costs more to run than its higher education. Ironically, the most untolerated among us, criminals, are provided with more resources than the most admired among us, the young students attempting to better themselves through higher education. As the weight of the prison system drains resources from other state-run institutions, one can anticipate a time when more rational minds will prevail and alternatives to an expensive and often unproductive prison system will be replaced by more creative and effective ways of dealing with violence.

American violence is often random. It is difficult to predict and it affects every strata of our society. To the extent that one can use a comparison to terrorism, it functions as a terrorist act and keeps otherwise safe people from feeling at ease. It can't be entirely avoided by staying in safe areas. We all drive the freeways of America where a good deal of random violence occurs. Cars permit violence to cycle from unsafe areas of the community to otherwise safe areas. And certainly, as the data become clearer, violence has been on the rise even in the midst of an excellent economy and reduced racial and ethnic tensions. One area of clear increase is violence to women as reflected in rape and sexual assault rates which increased 13.3 percent in 1999 (Bureau of Justice Statistics, 2000). Another area of increase in violence is in the higher number of violent crimes in the urban areas of the fifty largest American cities (Eisenhower Commission, 2000).

We think people are correctly assessing the random nature of violence and fear violence for rational reasons. No one who enters the inner cities of America should feel safe. These are crime-ridden and violent areas. They are underpoliced, riddled with substance abuse, and project a terrible sense of hopelessness and despair. That doesn't need to be, but for reasons that seem clearly policy driven, we have pushed crime into the inner city to make the rest of the country safer with a terrible impact on the brave and resolute people who are often forced, by economic and racial factors, to live in America's worst urban areas.

Furthermore, our national approach to violence seems irrational to us. The young abused boy without professional help, without the benefits of a healthy environment, who begins showing his aggression before the age of five, becomes the violent offender at fourteen. It isn't a complex equation. Children who have been physically and emotionally damaged need the best help available, not the current level of help received in small, unprofessional doses offered through poorly staffed and trained and underfunded community mental health facilities and child protective service agencies. If you ask a preschool teacher to choose the children who will be violent, they will point them out to you without any difficulty. But when you ask them if they've been responded to when they report the possible child abuse and neglect of these same children to the appropriate agencies, they will tell you that seldom is anything done to help. And so, the cycle of violence continues and the troubled child of five who has a fighting chance of growing up with healthy and positive behaviors if help is provided, all too often is ignored by our helping institutions and becomes the child of twelve already fantasizing about the harm he will do to others.

To underscore the problems in our child protective services system, one of the authors met with a high level supervisor in a child protective service agency in a large Texas city (June, 2001) who told him that of 1,100 child-care workers under her supervision, only four held master's degrees in social work. Most of them, she said, were untrained, had negligible attitudes about their work, often took sick days when they weren't sick, or just didn't come to work because they weren't in the mood. Few had deep convictions about the work they did and most just thought of it as a job to pay bills. Of the 1,100 workers, few were bilingual even though many of the clients seen by this agency are Hispanic. The same problems have been reported by other child-care agencies. The Los Angeles child protective services agency has been in difficulty for many years after a series of disastrous foster home placements in which children were physically and sexually abused by foster parents. In Orange County, California, a ranking administrator of the child welfare agency advocated a policy that encouraged young pregnant Latina women under the age of eighteen (many were fourteen and fifteen) to marry the father of their child. Many of these men were abusive to the young women (Streeter, 2001). In this climate of disarray, increased numbers of abused and neglected children can expect a lack of care that has no rational excuse in a country with so many resources.

The political climate toward crime in America also fosters violence. It is an uncreative, punitive, and punishment-oriented climate that argues against violence treatment and prevention and instead supports longer prison sentences, tougher laws, and more jails. It is a system that is incarcerating more people for longer periods of time with no thought to the explosion of very violent people who will be leaving jail sometime soon and hitting America's streets with the full force of a good deal of pent-up anger. It is also a system so overextended by so many prisoners that many states have a revolving door with the same violent offenders cycling back and forth, into and out of jail, with no thought to treatment, rehabilitation, or planned change. When these violent people leave jail, their violence often escalates.

In Texas, which incarnates more people than any other state in America (one in five of the new prisoners in America are found in the Texas correctional system), the state's crime rate fell to half that of the average of the United States and the least of any of the five largest states in America (Gamboa, 2000).

An astonishing 5 percent of the adult population of Texas (706,000) are in prison, on parole or on probation. Of those prisoners in Texas, 89,400 of the 163,000 prisoners are incarcerated for nonviolent crimes. More Texans are in jail than in California, a state with twice the population of Texas. African Americans in Texas are incarcerated at seven times the rate of whites, while probation is given to black prisoners only 20 percent of the time as compared to the 45 percent of white prisoners (Gamboa, 2000). Putting people in jail does not reduce violence. When violent offenders are released from violent jails, they return to our communities without the benefit of treatment, with little real supervision, with few prospects of getting better, and with a sense that nothing will ever change in their lives. These conditions will surely lead to more crime and with it more violence.

To make matters worse, the mass media of America seems to care more about reporting violence than understanding its origins. And report violence it does, in ever increasingly lurid detail until it is the primary story on most local television news broadcasts. To reinforce this focus on reporting violence, the popular culture is obsessed with violence. Movies, computer games, television programs, and cartoons for children so transport children into the world of violence that they grow up with no real notion that when violence takes place, real people get hurt.

A recent report by the Federal Trade Commission, accompanied by much publicity, addresses the question of violence in the media (Pitofsky, 2000; Shiver Jr., 2000). Driven to some extent by concern over recent shootings and mass murders in schools, the 104-page FTC report (half of which contains citations to relevant literature) reviews self-regulation and industry practices in the motion picture, music recording, and electronic game industries with respect to their advertisement of products with violent content to youngsters (p. 1). Two specific questions were raised in President Clinton's mandate to the FTC: (1) Do the industries promote products they themselves acknowledge warrant parental caution in venues where children make up a substantial percentage of the audience, and (2) are these advertisements intended to attract children and teenagers? The answers to both questions for all three segments of the entertainment industry were plainly yes.

The report does not say that the media causes violence. It simply states the conclusions of scholars and others regarding the problem:

> Scholars and observers generally have agreed that exposure to violence in the entertainment media alone does not cause a child to commit a violent act and that it is not the sole, or even necessarily the most important, factor contributing to youth aggression, anti-social attitudes and violence. Nevertheless, there is widespread cause for concern. (Pitofsky, pp. i–ii)

With this thought in mind, the report continues to state that their literature search found a high correlation between exposure to media violence and aggressive, and at times, violent behavior (p. ii). The report notes that the rate for murders committed by youth in the United States is higher than other industrialized counties, in spite of recent declines, and many observers are concerned about the role of a violent media subculture in violent incidents such as the Columbine High School killings.

For the residents of the inner cities of the United States, the reported decrease in violent crime since 1993 must be of little comfort. These areas seethe with violence. Drive-by shootings, random violence, gang-related violence, the violence of everyday life are such definers of the daily experience of the inner city that violence often determines how people will live their lives. Schools are unsafe, killings take place outside of movie theaters, and the workplace is always unsafe because no one ever knows when a bank robbery, convenience store, or restaurant holdup will take place. Day or night, it doesn't seem to matter. If the United States has done anything to reduce the level of violence, it is to keep it largely confined to the inner-city areas of the largest cities and hope, often unsuccessfully, that it won't move into the safe havens where more affluent Americans live and believe that they will be free of violence. Too many poor Americans live in unsafe environments where violence is always nearby. It is tragic and it is mean-spirited to put our most vulnerable population at even more risk just to keep more affluent Americans safe. And on one thing we can agree with the FBI Crime Report: Violence continues to increase in our largest urban areas confined to the inner cities where violence rates show no tendency to decrease anytime in the near future.

The drug and alcohol epidemic that confronts America is a catalyst for a great deal of violence. The National Institute of Drug Abuse notes that "In 1999, about 14.8 million Americans were current users of illicit drugs . . . about 3.5 million were dependent on illicit drugs while 8.2 million were dependent on alcohol"

(NIDA, 1999). This suggests that about 5 percent of the U.S. population has a drug dependency problem. But rather than try to deal with the social and emotional origins of substance abuse, America tries to control it by legal means: drug czars, stiffer penalties for selling inebriated people more liquor, tougher drunk driving laws. None of these approaches work well. Drugs and alcohol are readily available to most Americans, even children, and all too many crimes of violence are committed when perpetrators are high on substances. The Justice Department reports that 54 percent of the perpetrators of all violent crimes leading to prison terms had used alcohol prior to the crime (Bureau of Justice Statistics, 1991).

Too little money for substantive research is being spent to develop effective treatment of violence. It is a field still in its infancy and judging by the limited data available on the effectiveness of treatment strategies, it will be in its infancy for a long time to come. If we thought of violence as a disease, we would consider it a full-blown epidemic. The fact is that other than a few findings related to the use of medication to lessen drug and alcohol abuse and to deal with the more seriously mentally ill perpetrators of violence, talking therapies for violence control and prevention have been largely underfunded and understudied. When something is found to work, all too frequently continued funding is eliminated or reduced because it isn't politically popular or because it looks as if felons are being coddled. There is still a sense among too many Americans that anything that doesn't cause physical and emotional pain to prisoners won't be an effective deterrent to violence. We believe that an increase in the study and funding of violence is absolutely essential to the well-being and to the sense of safety of Americans who feel constantly at risk because of their fear of violence.

The issues of drug abuse and the definitions of sanity continue to present vexing problems for Americans. Clearly, a great deal of violent crime is related to both substance abuse and behavior that skirts the edges of sanity. We are presenting two cases that look at the difficult decisions we will need to make in the future regarding drug use while committing violent crimes as well as the difficulty in accurately diagnosing mental illness. We should also keep in mind that increasing numbers of babies born in America have drug and alcohol addictions at birth because of the addictions of their mothers. The National Institute on Drug Abuse reports that of the 4 million women who gave birth in 1992 to 1993, 750,000 used alcohol during their pregnancies while 221,000 women used illegal drugs during their pregnancies (NIDA, 1997). The use of alcohol and illegal drugs, particularly in the last three months of pregnancy, greatly increases the risk of birth defects, fetal alcohol syndrome, and drug addictions in newly-born babies. Will the behavior of the children born addicted be taken into consideration as a mitigating factor in their violent behavior? It certainly should be, in our view.

Case Study: Early Detection of Mental Illness

Jason Conner is a seventeen-year-old African American adolescent who lives in a poor part of a suburb of Minneapolis. His parents are divorced but his father and mother both care about him and put a great deal of energy into his welfare. Jason is an angry young man who frequently gets into fights and has begun carrying a gun. He deals in drugs and needs a gun, he says, for his own protection. Jason hates drug addicts and frequently cheats them or takes advantage of their addictions by berating them. Sometimes he beats them if they don't have enough money to pay for the drugs they need in ever increasing quantities. Jason has been in and out of court-ordered counseling, but it doesn't appear to do any good. He is too angry to trust a therapist and frequently ridicules them. He has also spent several six-month sentences in a youth correctional facility where he was found to be highly intelligent, but very defiant. He hardly sees his parents, preferring to spend his time with friends or to use his drug earnings to stay in expensive hotels for weeks on end.

Jason has begun thinking about killing someone. He doesn't know why but the thought is almost sensuous to him. Sometimes he masturbates while thinking about killing someone. It gives him a great deal of pleasure to think about killing and he has made certain that his gun is always loaded and available.

One evening, his father found him on the streets selling drugs. The argument and confrontation they had led to Jason shooting his father. Luckily his father, while seriously injured, did not die from the gunshot wounds. As a result of the incident, Jason was sent to a psychiatric facility for the criminally and emotionally impaired where he will stay until he is twenty-one.

Discussion of the Case

It took Jason three months to reach a point where he could talk to his therapist. But this therapist, an African American M.S.W. with special training in work with violent perpetrators, used some very successful techniques with Jason. He listened, made no judgments, remained calm when Jason became angry, and helped Jason use his considerable intelligence to understand the origins of his anger.

Jason's father had been a drug addict when Jason was a very small child. Jason's early years were spent listening to arguments between his mother and father, arguments that often escalated into domestic violence. Jason was a frightened child with a number of psychosomatic problems including childhood asthma and frequent stomach aches. As he began to grow and to become much larger than most of the other children his age, Jason became a bully, discovering that his size gave him a sense of mastery and superiority and that it made the other children afraid of him. Being a bully also left him full of self-loathing. The angrier he became and the more he acted out his anger, the more he disliked himself. He even made a number of suicide attempts whose lack of success made him feel ever weaker and more self-deprecating.

The therapist took a great deal of time to let Jason talk about these early life issues in a supportive and accepting way. No one had ever done this with him before. When the time was right, the therapist augmented individual therapy with group therapy, carefully placing Jason with other youth whom Jason could relate to without the need to bully or dominate. The group served to reinforce the issues that were discussed in individual therapy. Within a year, Jason earned his GED and began taking college courses offered in prison by a local university. His grades are good and he's thinking of sociology as a major. He has begun seeing his parents in supervised visits with his therapist doing a type of family therapy meant to move Jason and his parents toward reconciliation. The progress has been rapid and the parents are feeling very hopeful.

Jason is eighteen at present with three more years to completion of his sentence. He will stay in the psychiatric facility where his progress is deemed excellent. Occasionally, old patterns return and Jason become belligerent and defiant but with much less danger to others. The therapist is hopeful that Jason will be able to resolve the remaining life issues that sometimes cause Jason to have angry responses to others. He has set an agenda for treatment that is very behaviorally oriented. Jason will continue his individual and group treatment and his educational work. At some point soon, he will be given a weekend pass to visit his parents where he will stay in a supervised halfway house to test his gains in treatment.

The therapist wrote a report for the juvenile authorities in which he said the following:

> Jason is an eighteen-year-old African American male of superior intelligence who was sent to our facility after shooting and seriously wounding his father. Jason is full of rage that has its origins in his father's use of drugs and the subsequent spousal abuse of his wife. Like many children who have witnessed domestic violence, Jason has classic signs of someone who has witnessed domestic violence: distrust of others, hyper-vigilance, problems with anger control and difficulty with intimate relationships. He has beaten other children and has seriously hurt several of the addicts who have purchased drugs from Jason. While his progress has been rapid, it would be premature to say that Jason's prognosis is anything other than guarded. His progress needs to be tested in the community. We are arranging visits where he will be supervised in an appropriate halfway house. Even with his rapid progress, Jason will need to live in supervised settings after his release from our facility. He will also need to continue in long-term counseling.
>
> Anyone who works with violent offenders realizes that rage is close to the surface and that progress made in a locked facility can be quickly negated once the client returns to the community. We live in hope and we hope for the best, but severe trauma early in life has a way of cycling back in adulthood. We are guarded but hopeful about Jason's recovery and eventual return to the community.

Case Study: Sanity and the Joint Issues of Treatment and Guilt

What happens in the legal system when the defendant is too mentally ill to understand and take part in his defense? John Rayborn is an example from California. John, a thirty-two-year-old Caucasian male, shot and killed his seventy-three-year-old mother and had intercourse with her as she was dying from the gunshot wounds. When the police answered neighbor's calls of a shooting, they found John curled up in the fetal position ranting incoherently about voices from a space ship telling him to commit the crime. John had a long history of mental illness and had been in and out of state and private facilities since he was sixteen. He has been diagnosed as paranoid schizophrenic with hallucinations and delusions. When he shot and raped his mother, he thought she was an ex-girlfriend who had jilted him.

Because John was deemed too mentally ill to conduct a defense, he was sent to a forensic hospital in California that treats offenders until they are ready to stand trial. The average length of treatment to reach trial, according to a survey by Roll (1997), is 1,010 days, or roughly three years. After intensive treatment using psychotropic medications and group and individual treatment, John was remanded from the hospital two years later to the State Department of Corrections where he was held in a county jail and bound over for trial.

At the time of the trial, he seemed lucid and aware of his surroundings. The establishment of guilt was made on forensic evidence including John's fingerprints on the gun and powder burns on his hand. The semen in his mother's body was consistent with John's DNA. There seemed no question of guilt. The trial, instead, hung on the issue of whether John was mentally ill when the crime was committed. John was interviewed and said he had no memory of the crime and felt deep feelings of remorse and repulsion that he could have done such a thing. It was also established that John had gone off his medications voluntarily. For a time, the trial focused on John's prior threats against his family during times when he was off medication.

The jury believed that John was mentally ill when he committed the crime but that his mental illness could have been under control had he used his medication. The act of not taking his medication caused the mental illness that lead to the death of his mother. John was found guilty of killing his mother but because he was also insane at the time and didn't know right from wrong, innocent by reason of insanity. They believed that without supervision, that John posed a threat to the community and recommended ongoing institutional treatment in a state facility for the mentally ill. The judge in the case, familiar with insanity pleas, voided the jury finding and found John both guilty of the crime and sane. He said that John's mental illness was self-induced and likened the condition he was in to similar states of behavior where people self-medicate themselves into mental illness by taking dangerous drugs. In those cases, he noted, the court always finds the offender guilty and the insanity defense is never accepted. John was bound over to a state facility for the treatment of the criminally insane. He was given an indeterminate sentence. Parole would be based on the judgment of the professional staff that John would no longer be a danger to the community with the concurrence of the parole board.

The judge told the court, "The mentally ill are sane when using their medication. To go off the medication is a voluntary act that cannot be condoned by the court. All people, unless they are intellectually unable to recognize the consequences of their behavior, must be held to a standard that assumes that they have free will. When behavior interferes with the laws of the state, they are obligated to pay the same penalties as any other citizen of the state."

The institution John has been sent to is a forensic institution and not a treatment facility. John's need for medication is recognized but the integrating and supportive work that needs to be done to help John deal with his mental illness is lacking and John's environment is a dangerous and violent one. The men in the prison are among the state's most violent and dangerous people. As with all too many violent but mentally ill people, John faces a very high probability of being hurt in prison. The rape of a mother, even in the midst of mental illness, is a heinous crime to the prisoners and John is marked for beatings, rapes, and perhaps even death. He would have done better in a treatment-oriented facility and his safety would have been less in question. The judge's argument that the mentally ill have great control over the schedules required in the use of anti-psychotic medication seems punitive and irrational and John's attorney has successfully voided the placement. John has been moved to a treatment facility, but not without harm done to John in his prior prison confinement where he was gang raped by a group of violent prisoners before the change in settings took place. John is on medication and receives treatment, but the stay in prison has left him more deeply psychotic than ever. He seems out of touch much of the time and is often unable to coherently involve himself in even the simplest interactions with others.

Discussion of the Case

The establishment of insanity is a difficult thing to do, particularly when insanity hinges on the knowledge of the difference between right and wrong. With offenders whose intellectual functioning is so low that such knowledge is easy to determine, that's one thing. But when mental illness is at play, how can we know with certainty that the offender was mentally ill when the crime was committed? When the offender is examined months and sometimes years later, prior to a trial, how can we know that a current mental illness is consistent with the state the offender was in when he or she committed the crime? And more to the point, mentally ill offenders often intellectually know the difference between right and wrong but feel strong impulses to act out violently that they may be unable to control. Moments of intense rage in normal people may be moments of insanity, but the offender may seem perfectly sane after the fact. We all know of ordinary people who have acted out of rage and done things, when provoked or when under great stress, that they might never have done otherwise.

That is why a plea of innocent by reason of insanity is difficult to use in trials involving violence. The more likely plea is guilty, but under the influence of mental illness. If violence is an act of rage and bad impulse control, aren't we all capable of violence? If that's the case, shouldn't our laws be more lenient for the first-time violent offender? Most murders, for example, are acts of violence against family members by a spouse or mate. Do these people pose the same danger to the community as someone with a long and dangerous history of random violence?

The state of insanity is difficult to prove because it strikes most juries as an excuse for violence. In the case of the judge finding the offender guilty because he should have continued on his medication, the reality is that many of us, sane or insane, go off medicine before we should. Kane and Glicken (1979) found that half the people on prescribed medications for a variety of illnesses fail to complete the treatment as prescribed. Mentally ill people are no different. When they feel better, they believe their improved condition no longer requires them to use medications that often have severe side effects. Psychotropic medications make people feel sluggish and fatigued. They slow down thinking and sometimes cause patients to have jerky gaits or jaws that become so rigid that normal speech is difficult. Isn't it understandable why mentally ill people would not want to be on psychotropic medications??

These are some of the issues that face the justice system in the future as psychotropic drugs are increasingly used by many citizens who are certainly not dangerous but are rather unhappy, depressed, or anxious. Do crimes committed by people who are on any mood-changing medication, but have decided to go off them, constitute either a reason for the crime or an example of bad judgment on the part of the offender? The future will find us asking some interesting questions regarding the issues of insanity and the impact of mood-altering medications.

Responding to Violence in the Future

We have discussed the potential problems facing us in the future. Violence, we believe, will increase. What should be done to limit or eliminate the increase in violence we predict for the future? In this next section, we provide suggestions with several case studies.

More Successful Treatment Approaches

The level of treatment of violence in America is shameful. Other than incarceration to keep violent people off the streets, there seems to be no consistent policy of providing help to violent people. When help is given, it often lacks research validation.

We think there is validity in using treatment for early signs of aggression in children. More research needs to be done to find out what works and specially trained workers need to be prepared for work with extreme early aggression in children and adolescence, but early intervention in the social and emotional lives of children with violent tendencies seems to be a sensible way to approach the most likely in our society to transition from aggressive social behavior to violent behavior.

Once people do become violent, there are all too few treatment approaches available to us with anything close to universal acceptance or with good research validity. Violence is a public health issue. It should be studied, evaluated, and treated as such. We fail to see any evidence that other than tougher laws and more prisons, that violence is being dealt with in an objective and coherent way. We also believe that the helping professions have been remiss by failing to train more professionals for work with violent perpetrators. In fact, many professionals are antagonistic toward the notion of help to violent perpetrators, believing instead that help to victims is always more essential and productive. We, of course, believe that victims come first but when violence continues to plague us and when years of tougher laws and more jails end in an increase of violence to women and children, we have to start believing that perpetrators need help and that society can ill-afford to permit violent people to go untreated.

A Sensible Policy Toward Violence in the Popular Culture

We are not advocating censorship. We do believe more restraint needs to take place in the way violence permeates the lives of our most vulnerable citizens: the children of the United States. From movies to television cartoons to video games, violence surrounds the lives of children. It is no longer logical to say that only children with predispositions toward violence or children who have emotional problems are affected by a violent popular culture. All too many otherwise normal children find themselves drawn to violence as an acceptable outlet for feelings of insecurity, unpopularity, social isolation, and rejection. A rash of killings in U.S. schools more than supports this.

We believe that parents should stop buying violent video games for their children. We think restraint should be used in the films children can see and in the television programs that make violence gratuitous and attractive. This is not a violation of the civil rights of the popular culture, but a campaign that should reduce the profitability of producing harmfully violent films, cartoons, and video games. We think the helping professions, the physicians, social workers, and psychologists of the United States, should enter this campaign against a violent popular culture. Perhaps together, the parents and the helping professionals can reduce the availability of violent material and make it somehow less than attractive.

Reducing the Emphasis on Violence in the News

We believe that the news media glorifies violence by the amount of violence it reports. On any given night, the evening news in most communities spends a great deal of its time reporting violent behavior. One of the reasons Americans continue to fear violence is that the media makes us so conscious of its presence that we automatically assume that it is everywhere. Violence is almost never reported in any depth. Why something happened or the larger reasons a crime took place are almost never discussed. Instead, the grisly details of the crime and some shots of crying and distraught family members seem to be the only way the media has of portraying violent behavior.

We think Americans should let the news media know that there are affirming and positive things that happen in our communities, and that it is all too difficult to get the media to report it. Getting a TV station to televise a few minutes of an affirming community activity or a conference on an issue of value to others in the community is often impossible and it serves to underscore our contention that violent events are preferred topics. We suggest a campaign against the predominance of violence in the local television broadcasts of the United States. Television has a responsibility to the community to not make people feel that their communities are dangerous when this may not be the case.

A Substance Abuse Policy That Stresses Treatment

The war on substance abuse has been lost. Drugs and alcohol are readily available to anyone. Much more needs to be done in developing treatment approaches that help addicted Americans withdraw from substance abuse. And much more creative thinking must go into developing strategies for early intervention in the lives of those most prone to substance abuse and addiction: the children of substance abusers, children who have been physically and sexually abused, children who have witnessed domestic violence in their homes, and the downsized, laid off, unemployed, and underemployed Americans with little to keep them active or optimistic about the future. We should not forget that a good deal of violent crime is committed in conjunction with alcohol and drug abuse. The U.S. jails and prisons should all have drug treatment programs for drug-addicted inmates. As one report indicates:

> Consider that by the end of the 1980s, about one-third of people in state prisons were there because of drug offenses . . . and 60 percent had a history of substance abuse. Yet despite this, in 1991, only 13.5 percent of state prisoners were enrolled in drug programs. (Substance Abuse and Crime, 2001)

The following is a case study used to point out the terrible problems we have with drugs and alcohol in this country and the impact substance abuse has on some potentially highly-troubled people.

Case Study: Drug Addiction and Violence

Jack is a twenty-seven-year-old unemployed Caucasian male who has been addicted to a number of drugs and to alcohol since he was thirteen. Jack's life is spent in a drug culture whose main purpose is to secure and maintain sufficient numbers of drugs to continue what he calls a party life. Jack joins other drug users at local parks or at someone's home and spends most of his day in a communal effort to get high. Almost all of his talking time is spent discussing drugs and the way they make him feel. Jack has been in drug rehabilitation twice for up to a month each time. He has always found ways of obtaining drugs while in rehabilitation and has never seriously thought of ending his addictions. He's had a number of minor scrapes with the law for vagrancy and petty theft but nothing serious, or so he likes to say.

High on a drug one evening, he entered what he thought was an empty house and started to rob the home when a young woman walked into the house and caught him. Jack raped, mutilated, and then killed the young woman. He has no memory of the act and is dismayed that he could do such a thing. When he was discovered later by the parents of the dead young woman, he had fallen asleep next to the dead girl's body and was covered in blood. Jack has no explanation for the crime. He feels detached from it saying that it must have been the drugs that did it, or that the drugs must have been bad. In the days preceding the killing, Jack had consumed over two quarts of alcohol each day for a week, sniffed glue, smoked crack cocaine for hours, and had used a street drug whose base was an amphetamine. The street drug also contained a combination of drugs that in some people cause violence (angel dust was one ingredient). Jack was robbing the home so that he could purchase more of the street drug. He denies any culpability and says instead, "What do you think drug addicts do? They act crazy. That's what drugs do to people. You should get the drugs off the street then people like me wouldn't become addicts."

Jack was found guilty of murder and is spending the rest of his life in a maximum-security prison. He is not contrite and misses his old life. Drugs are easy to get in prison, however, and Jack and his drug-using friends continue life as they had before, but now they don't have to worry about shelter or food. The state takes care of that. The small wage he receives to buy toiletries goes entirely to purchase drugs that are brought in by the prison staff and sold at reasonable prices most prisoners can afford. An association between several entrepreneurial prisoners and some of the guards runs an efficient and well-priced drug business. Jack likes to say that "There are some smart dudes in the joint. They can get you anything you want. It's a damn good life."

Discussion of the Case

If drugs are readily available in America's maximum-security prisons, and they are, how is it possible to stop drugs from reaching the streets? Jack has moved the locus of his addiction from the community to prison but he is still an addict and, in the long run, someone will get hurt again. It may be another prisoner or a guard, but Jack's addiction has been untreated for so long that it's unlikely prison will have any impact. In the ideal prison setting, Jack's addiction would be controlled and treated. In fact, had the treatment rehabilitation centers that originally treated Jack been more competent, Jack's imprisonment and the terrible crime he committed might not have happened. But treatment for addictions, like treatment for violence, is in its infancy and Jack is unlikely to get much in the way of help from his prison confinement.

A counselor who was assigned Jack's case in prison had this to say about Jack:

> Jack is a twenty-seven-year-old drug addict. He is impulsive, narcissistic, and morally aloof from the harm his behavior creates. His early life was spent in a home where both of his parents and most of the adults around him were alcoholics. Jack was introduced to alcohol at age eight and has been using it steadily since. It is likely that he was an alcoholic by puberty and a drug addict by sixteen.

He takes anything he thinks will make him high including drugs he steals from people's homes. He isn't concerned about what the drug will do and takes anything he can get his hands on. He hasn't worked at a paying job, has no time orientation, is unconcerned about personal hygiene, and has no regard for other people or their feelings.

Jack likes the addict's life and believes that it leaves him free to experience the wonders of drug-induced reality. As for treatment, there is little we can do since he is unmotivated to change. He believes that he lives a superior life to the rest of us and is unrepentant about the crime he committed. In his view, it was society's fault that he became an addict in the first place and it continues to be society's fault that the drug rehabilitation programs he was in were so badly run. Jack believes that he was the victim in the crime he committed and has no sympathy at all for the young woman he killed whom he says "came from a rich home and had it a lot better than I did. She was in the wrong place at the wrong time. That's life. If she wanted to live longer, she could have traded places with me when I was kid. Then she could have known what it was like to live in hell and she'd have been glad that she didn't have to stick around and live this miserable life I've been living. You want to feel sorry for somebody, feel sorry for the kids like me who had rotten parents who did everything bad a parent could do. Don't feel sorry for some rich kid who had a good life. One of her good years was better than any of mine."

More Understanding of Terrorism

When we developed the idea for this book, like most Americans, we felt confident that our problems with terrorism were either behind us or that law enforcement would take care of terrorist activities as they had repeatedly done over the prior several years. The events of September 11, 2001 with the hijacking and subsequent crashes of three large airplanes into the World Trade Center towers and the Pentagon, with almost 4,000 people killed to date, makes it clear that of all the violent activities we have written about, terrorism has geometrically increased the risk of random violence. As the sharp decline in air travel following the attacks suggests, terrorism can be an effective tool for the suppression of our feelings of safety and the increase of fear.

Before September 11, 2001, Americans believed that the best way to avoid violence was to stay away from high crime areas, but now any area at home or at work is a potential target for terrorist activity. And much as we had hoped that terrorists would play by some rules of decency, it is clear that they won't. Consequently, we can anticipate the use of chemical warfare, computer disruptions, and the violent crimes that will ensue as a result of technological advances in the hands of people who will abuse and create havoc through the very advances we consider the reasons for our recent economic growth. Life in the United States will be different, and as it becomes different, and as people stay closer to their homes without the usual vacations and trips to lessen frustrations and to renew their lives, violence rates related to more traditional reasons could increase. We sincerely hope not. We hope that the threat of terrorism will draw us closer as a nation and cause us to be much more concerned about creating an United States we can all be proud of. We hope that a renewed country will work to resolve many of the reasons we have noted for high rates of violence: substance abuse, child abuse, poverty, a violence-obsessed mass media, and far too many people who feel alienated from life in our country and are capable of a great deal of harm.

While the threat of international terrorism looms large in everyone's mind, the threat of radical U.S.-born terrorists should not fade from memory. The 168 lives lost in Oklahoma City must be a constant reminder that Americans are also capable of terrorist acts. And if these two groups somehow pool their resources, manpower, and finances, what then? We live in perilous times and for the first time in our memory, people are actually afraid of random violence, not from inner-city juvenile gang members or carjackers, but often from highly-educated, seemingly-benign, middle-class people capable of destruction that makes gang violence pale in comparison.

We would like to say something wise about the personality makeup and the emotional development of terrorists, but the fact is, we know all too little about the personalities, the early life experiences, the reasons, and the conditions that prompt otherwise normal men and women to become terrorists. Ted Kaczinsky, the Unibomber, had a doctorate in math from MIT and taught at UC Berkeley. Timothy McVeigh, responsible for car bombing the federal building in Oklahoma City, was a decorated soldier in the Gulf War. Many of the terrorists who planned and carried out the World Trade Center and Pentagon atrocities were middle-class men from healthy and normal families. How does one make these facts compute with any degree of logic? These people should not be terrorists, but they are. It should tell us that our ability to profile terrorists is very much in its infancy.

Even more worrisome are the potential terrorists, the Columbine generation of violent middle-class youth whose behavior, even now, is difficult for us to understand. Obviously, a deep feeling of alienation and anger drives these young people, but why? We aren't really sure. And what happens when they reach adulthood with new technical capabilities and the benefit of sophisticated educations? What manner of terrorism and on what scale will they be capable of?

And finally, what of the emotionally deteriorating but highly intelligent men like Ted Kaczinsky who, hidden from us and socially isolated, plot killing and destruction because they are increasingly troubled? Out of feelings of social isolation, lack of intimacy and loneliness, their pathology often takes the shape of retribution to a society that permitted them to become so unhappy. We do not see Ted Kaczinsky as mentally ill. Ted Kaczinsky was angry at his condition in life and his inability to develop relationships. He felt isolated, disliked, and misunderstood. He was an unhappy and brutally angry person who outwardly hid his anger. According to his neighbors in Montana, he was quiet and a little eccentric, but normal. That no one outside of his family could identify this sense of isolation and anger makes the perceived threat of similar people doing similar acts of random terror that much more troubling. With the increasing technical sophistication of people like Ted Kaczinsky, one can only guess that mail bombs will not exactly satisfy their need for retribution in the future.

Following the September 11, 2001 bombings, letters with the Anthrax virus were being sent to people around the country, an act that is all too reminiscent of Ted Kazinsky and his letter bombs. It appears that there is another Uniabomber in the country who has progressed from crude bombs to the use of chemical warfare.

The conditions that create international terrorism are too complex in nature for us to comment on. We know too little about the environment that produces suicide bombings and the hatred of America. But of U.S.-born terrorists, we can say a great deal. The one thing that seems obvious is that many of them have connections with hate groups that often take the form of bigotry against groups by race, color, ethnicity, religious orientation, and gender orientation. In 1999, there were 1,500 serious acts of anti-Semitism against Jewish Americans including the burning of three synagogues in California and the killing of two people and the wounding of six Jewish people in Chicago (ADL, 2000). The FBI in 1995 reported 8,000 hate crimes, most against Jewish Americans and African Americans (Bureau of Justice Statistics, 1997). One can anticipate an increase in hate crimes against Arab Americans related to anger over the September 11, 2001 tragedies. The fact that so many angry and bigoted people coexist among us, unnoticed, ignored or discounted, creates a disturbing and lethal situation for our country.

It seems to us that the violence we see in the United States is partially created by a sense of social isolation that has developed in the midst of great affluence. We are wealthy beyond our wildest dreams but unhappy in spite of it. Road rage, domestic violence, date rape, juvenile violence, and now acts of random terror exist in the midst of a country with great affluence and resources. We seem unwilling, however, to use those resources wisely to identify, treat, and prevent violent behavior. The young men at Columbine High School were dangerous. They were full of rage. To say that their behavior came from nowhere or that it was unanticipated is the same as saying that workplace violence isn't predicable or preventable. We often see very troubling behavior and we ignore it, hoping that it won't affect us. The seeds of violence are in the classrooms of U.S. schools where they are often ignored or untreated until harm has been done. This unwillingness to prevent violence should trouble us all as we move into a new era of random violence on an unimaginably large scale.

Case Study with Integrating Questions

Dr. Drago Litvas is a thirty-seven-year-old Caucasian medical doctor with a specialty in anesthesiology, practicing medicine in a small town in the mid-west. Upon finding out that his beautiful young wife had been unfaithful to him, he tied her to a chair one night, used medical instruments to cut open her body, and poured acid into her wounds, her eyes, and her vagina. The mutilation took place throughout the night but it wasn't until morning that the police arrived after complaints from neighbors about screams coming from the house. She was immediately taken to the hospital and sedated, but died shortly thereafter. The hospital staff at the trial said that they had never seen anyone in such pain or a body so mutilated.

Dr. Litvas is a Hungarian immigrant whose culture, so he told the jury, doesn't tolerate infidelity. While people in the community thought that he was remote and strange, small-town residents are used to doctors who reside temporarily in their community and are grateful that anyone will come at all. Professionally, he seemed competent enough and his credentials all checked out. None of his former employers noted evidence of mental illness, although it was determined later that he had been released from a series of jobs because of his strange behavior. One doctor remembered him hallucinating during an operation and another wrote a letter to the hospital administrator reporting behavior consistent with mental illness. None of this was reported to the small town hospital by any of his prior employers and he held a valid medical license to practice medicine.

During the trial, it became increasingly clear that Dr. Litvas was seriously mentally ill. His eyes darted around the courtroom and he seemed to be having auditory and visual hallucinations. His testimony, while establishing his guilt, was chaotic and difficult to follow. He ranted about the infidelity of U.S. women and blamed the drinking water for his crime. He said he had no recollection of the crime itself but was glad that his wife was dead. The more pain she suffered, the better, he told the jury.

Dr. Litvas was examined by two psychiatrists, one court-appointed and the other hired by the defense. They both concluded that Dr. Litvas was currently mentally ill and that he had probably been mentally ill before and during the crime. They also agreed that, using the McNaughten rule to determine mental illness on the basis of knowing right from wrong, that Dr. Litvas certainly knew that what he had done was wrong, but believed that it was justified by his wife's infidelity. "In my country," he told the court, "a woman pays with her life when she sleeps with another man." The court found him guilty of murder but also judged him to be mentally ill. He was sent to a special forensic facility for the criminally and mentally ill where he was incarcerated for fifteen years.

One of the authors met Dr. Litvas during his incarceration at the forensic mental health facility. His feeling was that Dr. Litvas was probably paranoid schizophrenic but not dangerous, at least in the facility. In fact, the facility was using Dr. Litvas to do autopsies. While incarcerated, Dr. Litvas was treated with psychotropic medications and underwent individual and group psychotherapy. His progress appeared to be satisfactory and after fifteen years of incarceration, with his mental illness seemingly in remission, he was paroled to a halfway house with required medication and counseling as part of the requirements for parole.

Dr. Litvas is not able to practice medicine and has been urged not to date women. He seems to have lost interest in relationships and now lives on a farm with a Hungarian family where he helps around the property. His behavior is odd and he still hears voices but the family reports that he is "just a lonely man who feels guilty about what he did and now wants to live a peaceful life." The family he lives with doesn't feel that he is mentally ill or dangerous and he enjoys being able to converse in Hungarian and to hear stories about his homeland. The state parole officer who interviews Dr. Litvas monthly has him see a psychiatrist every six months who checks his mental status periodically. It is not felt that he is actively mentally ill and that he is safe in his current placement.

Integrating Questions

1. Is it possible that Dr. Litvas faked mental illness to reduce his sentence and to spend time in a medical facility instead of jail?
2. Is it more humane to have mentally ill people who commit crimes do their time in prison where their terms are set in advance than to place them in institutions for the criminally mentally ill where they may stay indefinitely?
3. The issue of sanity aside, do you think the punishment for this heinous act should have been the death penalty?
4. It is worrisome to think that Dr. Litvas is out of prison. Regardless of his supposed rehabilitation, is this the type of crime that warrants life in prison because it could, conceivably, happen again?

While we believe that violence may increase in the coming years, we also believe that violent behavior can be managed and that the individual and social conditions that often produce violence can be effectively treated. The programs for juveniles cited in Chapter 11 suggest that some approaches can be used that may produce successes for juveniles. However, we also believe that far too little money, time, and resources are devoted to the treatment and prevention of violence. If we consider the amount of money spent to develop effective treatments of disease and illness and compare it to the money spent on violence research, it is an unconscionably small amount. Most of the money spent to deal with violence is spent on the building of prisons rather than funding research to prevent the terrible impact of violent behavior on the lives of far too many innocent Americans. With problems related to terrorism, a subject we currently know very little about, certainly more research needs to be done to identify, treat, and prevent those most likely to be involved in violent activities.

Programs for adults are more difficult to implement because these individuals are usually sent to prisons where few treatment programs for violent offenders can be found. In this sense, a case can be made for early intervention in the lives of young people before they become candidates for the adult criminal justice system. A safe environment for all Americans should be our goal in the coming years.

REFERENCES

Anti-Defamation League. 2000. *Bulletin. www.adl.org.*

Bureau of Justice Statistics. (1991). *Alcohol and crime.* Washington, DC: U.S. Department of Justice.

Bureau of Justice Statistics. (1997). *Hate crimes: National statistical report.* Washington, DC: U.S. Department of Justice.

Bureau of Justice Statistics. (2001, October 1). Washington, DC: U.S. Department of Justice. www.ojp.usdoj.gov/search97cgi/s97_cgi

Cowley, G. (2001, October 1). After the trauma. *Newsweek,* pp. 50–52.

Eisenhower Commission. (2000). National commission of the causes and prevention of violence. *www.aypf.org/forumbreifs/2000/fb102700.htm.*

FBI Press Office. (2001, May 30). *Preliminary crime statistics for 2000.* Washington, DC: FBI Press Office.

Gamboa, S. (2000, August 28). Texas incarcerates most, fastest in U.S. *San Antonio Express News,* p. 1A.

Kane. R., & Glicken, M. (1979, Winter). *Compliance and consumerism: Complimentary goals of social work practice.* National Association of Social Workers Symposium on Professional Practice. New York: NASW Publications.

Lennon, T. M. (2001). *Statistics on social work education: 1999.* Alexandria, VA: Council on Social Work Education.

National Institute of Drug Abuse. (1997). *Pregnancy and drug use trends.* National Institute of Health. Publication No. 13568.

National Institute of Drug Abuse. (1999). *Nationwide trends (in drug and alcohol use).* National Institute of Health. Publication No. 13567.

Newsweek. (2001, October 8). p. 55.

Pitofsky, R. (2000, September). *Marketing violent entertainment to children: A review of self-regulation and industry practices in the motion picture, music recording & electronic game industries.* Report to the Federal Trade Commission.

Roll, B. (1997). The impact of treatment on the date of trials for mentally-ill felons. Master's thesis, California State University, San Bernardino.

Satcher, D. (2001). Youth violence: A report of the surgeon general. Washington, DC: U.S. Department of Health and Human Services, Office of the U.S. Surgeon General. *http://surgeongeneral.gov/library/youthviolence/report.html.*

Shiver Jr., J. (2000, September 11). Hollywood sells kids on violence, FTC says. *L.A. Times,* p. A1.

Streeter, K. (2001, June 21). Couple charged with death in foster care. *L.A. Times,* p. B1.

Substance Abuse and Crime [Online]. Retrieved October 13, 2001 from the World Wide Web: *http://www1.jointogther.org/sa/issues/ hot_issues/crime/.*

INDEX